HOW TO CHEAT AT
Windows System Administration
USING COMMAND LINE SCRIPTS

Pawan K. Bhardwaj

KEY	SERIAL NUMBER
001	HJIRTCV764
002	PO9873D5FG
003	829KM8NJH2
004	94287PLK49
005	CVPLQ6WQ23
006	VBP965T5T5
007	HJJJ863WD3E
008	2987GVTWMK
009	629MP5SDJT
010	IMWQ295T6T

PUBLISHED BY
Syngress Publishing, Inc.
800 Hingham Street
Rockland, MA 02370

ISBN: 1-59749-105-5

Publisher: Andrew Williams   Page Layout and Art: Patricia Lupien
Acquisitions Editor: Gary Byrne   Copy Editor: Audrey Doyle
Technical Editor: Kimon Andreou   Indexer: Odessa&Cie
Cover Designer: Michael Kavish

Distributed by O'Reilly Media, Inc. in the United States and Canada.
For information on rights, translations, and bulk sales, contact Matt Pedersen, Director of Sales and Rights, at Syngress Publishing; email matt@syngress.com or fax to 781-681-3585.

Transferred to Digital Printing 2010

Lead Author

Pawan K. Bhardwaj (MCSE, MCT, Security+, Network+, I-Net+ and A+) is an independent technical trainer and author. He has been actively involved in Windows administration ever since Windows NT 3.51 was released. In the past 16 years he has worked at various system and network support levels for small and medium-sized companies. Some of his major projects included working for one of India's largest newspaper groups and a large e-commerce organization in the United States where he had an active involvement in design and implementation of large-scale LAN and WAN solutions based on Windows technologies.

Pawan was one of the first 100 in India to attain MCSE certification back in 1997. He teaches Windows administration and networking classes and also acts as a consultant to training institutions. He has authored or contributed to more than 12 certification books by Syngress/McGraw Hill. He also coauthored *MCSE 2003 Electives Exams in a Nutshell* (O'Reilly Media, Inc., 2006).

This book is dedicated to the loving memory of my father, Sudershan Bhardwaj, and my father-in-law, Ghanshyam Pandit, both of whom passed away during the writing of this book.

—*Pawan K. Bhardwaj*

Technical Editor and Reviewer

Kimon Andreou is IT Portfolio Manager at Royal Caribbean International in Miami, FL. His expertise is in software development, software quality assurance, data warehousing, and data security. Kimon's experience includes positions as CTO for Secure Discovery Solutions, an e-Discovery company; Manager of Support & QA at S-doc, a software security company; and as Chief Solution Architect for SPSS in the Enabling Technology Division. He also has led projects in Asia, Europe, North America, and South America. Kimon holds a Bachelor of Science in Business Administration from the American College of Greece and a Master of Science in Management Information Systems from Florida International University.

Kimon wrote Chapter 12.

Contributing Authors

Brian Barber (MCSE, MCP+I, MCNE, CNE-5, CNE-4, CNA-3, CNA-GW) is coauthor of Syngress Publishing's *Configuring Exchange 2000 Server* (ISBN: 1-928994-25-3), *Configuring and Troubleshooting Windows XP Professional* (ISBN: 1-928994-80-6), and two study guides for the MSCE on Windows Server 2003 track (exams 70-296 [ISBN: 1-932266-57-7] and 70-297 [ISBN: 1-932266-54-2]). He is a Senior Technology Consultant with Sierra Systems Consultants Inc. in Ottawa, Canada. He specializes in IT service management and technical and infrastructure architecture, focusing on systems management, multiplatform integration, directory services, and messaging. In the past he has held the positions of Senior Technical Analyst at MetLife Canada and Senior Technical Coordinator at the LGS Group Inc. (now a part of IBM Global Services).

Brian wrote Chapter 11.

Dave Kleiman (CAS, CCE, CIFI, CISM, CISSP, ISSAP, ISSMP, MCSE) has worked in the Information Technology Security sector since 1990. Currently, he is the owner of SecurityBreach Response.com. A former Florida Certified Law Enforcement Officer, he specializes in litigation support, computer forensic investigations, incident response, and intrusion analysis. He has developed a Windows Operating System lockdown tool, S-Lok (www.s-doc.com/products/slok.asp), which surpasses NSA, NIST, and Microsoft Common Criteria Guidelines.

Dave was a contributing author for *Microsoft Log Parser Toolkit* (Syngress Publishing, ISBN: 1-932266-52-6) and *Security Log Management: Identifying Patterns in the Chaos* (Syngress Publishing, ISBN: 1-59749-042-3). He was also technical editor for *Perfect Passwords: Selection, Protection, Authentication* (Syngress Publishing, ISBN: 1-59749-041-5) and *Winternals Defragmentation, Recovery, and Administration Field Guide* (Syngress Publishing, ISBN: 1597490792). He is frequently a speaker at many national security conferences and is a regular contributor to security-related newsletters, Web sites, and Internet forums. Dave is a member of many professional security organizations, including the International Association of Counter Terrorism and Security Professionals (IACSP), International Society of Forensic Computer Examiners® (ISFCE), Information Systems Audit and Control Association® (ISACA), High Technology Crime Investigation Association (HTCIA), Association of Certified Fraud Examiners (ACFE), Anti Terrorism Accreditation Board (ATAB), and ASIS International®. He is also the Sector Chief for Information Technology at the FBI's InfraGard® and Director of Education at the International Information Systems Forensics Association (IISFA).

Dave cowrote Chapter 13.

Mahesh Satyanarayana is a final-semester electronics and communications engineering student at the Visveswaraiah Technological University in Shimoga, India. He expects to graduate this summer and has currently accepted an offer to work for Caritor Inc., an SEI-CMM Level 5 global consulting and systems integration company, headquartered in San Ramon, CA. Caritor provides IT infrastructure and business solutions to clients in several sectors worldwide. Mahesh will be joining the Architecture and Design domain at Caritor's development center in Bangalore, India, where he will develop software systems for mobile devices. His areas of expertise include Windows security and related Microsoft programming technologies. He is also currently working toward administrator-level certification on the Red Hat Linux platform.

Mahesh wrote Appendix A.

Companion Web Site

Some examples of syntax or code for the command utilities discussed in this book are available for download from **www. syngress.com/solutions**. Look for the Syngress icon in the margins indicating which examples are available from the companion Web site.

Contents

Introduction

Welcome to *How to Cheat at Windows System Administration Using Command-Line Scripts*. This book is designed to help you learn the power of Windows command shell. There was a time in the history of computers when there was no graphical user interface (GUI), and every small and big task was performed using the commands and batch files. With every new version of Windows, Microsoft is trying to ease administrators' jobs by adding more and more layers of GUI or configuration wizards (dialog boxes). Although these "wizards" are interactive and make the administrator's job easier, they are not always the most convenient and efficient way to accomplish the everyday administration tasks. These wizards are time-consuming and, at times, may seem a bit confusing. There is certainly a way to avoid these wizards and still accomplish a given task using the command-line utilities included with the operating system.

Consider a situation where you wish to add a user to the Active Directory using the Windows wizards or the GUI, assign him/her appropriate permissions to access certain resources, and restrict access to others. It would take roughly one hour to complete the job. By using command line the same task could be done in about half the time. That not only saves you time but also increases your productivity as an administrator.

Although the importance of Windows GUIs should not be underrated, the command-line tools have their own importance and utility when it comes to increasing efficiency, boosting effectiveness, and saving time. Command-line tools are both problem solvers as well as time-savers. Not many administrators explore the usefulness of these tools. The purpose of this book is to let administrators know how to utilize these command-line tools to complete everyday administrative jobs, solve recurring network problems, and improve their efficiency.

This book contains a total of 13 chapters, divided into five different parts. The first part deals with the basics of Windows command shell, batch files, and scheduled tasks. The second part of the book deals with basic Windows system administration, which consists of managing files and hard disks. The third part of the book covers system services, event logs, performance, and printing services. In the fourth part of the book, we cover Active Directory services. The fifth part of the book deals with managing networking services in a Windows Server 2003 environment.

Your journey starts in Chapter 1 with the basics of the Windows command shell. You will learn how to access the command shell and how to customize its properties. You will learn that the command shell's properties can be modified in several different ways to suit your needs. Installing the support tools included with the Windows Server 2003 setup CD Windows is also covered in this chapter. You will also learn how to access the Windows A–Z Command Reference available in the Help and Support Center.

In Chapter 2 we explain how to work safely with the command line using a non-administrative account. While working with the command shell, you sometimes need to specify a path where commands or batch files are located. You will learn how to change or modify the command path by modifying the environment variable either from the command prompt or from the *System Properties* dialog box. This chapter also explains how to change command input and output from the standard keyboard and the command shell window, respectively, and how to handle errors generated by commands. Moving ahead, we will discuss the concept of creating simple batch files. You will learn about commonly used commands in batch files and how to use each command inside a batch file.

In Chapter 3, we discuss the task scheduler service, the Scheduled Tasks GUI, and the *schtasks* command-line utility. If the task scheduler service is not running, you will not be able to schedule any script or application to run automatically. The Scheduled Tasks wizard is a perfect tool for scheduling tasks to run at predetermined schedules, but you can also use the *schtasks* utility to perform the same tasks. This utility replaces the older *AT* command, which is still supported in Windows XP and Windows Server 2003. You will learn to use different subcommands of the *schtasks* utility to create, change, delete, query, run, or end a task. *schtasks* is considered to be one of the most complex command sets in Windows.

In Chapter 4, we discuss some of the very common commands used to manage and maintain files, folders, and floppy disks. Having in-depth knowledge of these commands, their syntax, and their use is a great help when you want to use them in batch files or scripts to simplify your administrative tasks. Traditional *Copy*, *Xcopy*, *Move*, and *Del (Erase)* commands are covered in this chapter, and examples of their usage are included. We continue with the discussion on the use of the *Diskcopy* command for duplicating disks and comparing disks using the *Diskcomp* command. Other commands related to file and folder management such as *Tree*, *MD (Mkdir)*, and *RD (Rmdir)* are also covered in this chapter.

Chapter 5 covers maintenance of file systems and hard disks. The most notable utilities covered in this chapter include *Fsutil*, *Chkdsk*, and *Defrag*. The *Fsutil* utility is new to the Windows XP and Windows Server 2003 families of operating systems. Although you might have experience with older utilities such as *Chkdsk* and *Defrag*, you will need to have thorough knowledge of the operating systems to use the *Fsutil* command and its subcommands when creating scripts. We will also discuss *Format*, *Convert*, and *Compact* commands in this chapter.

Chapter 6 is dedicated to the *Diskpart* command-line utility used to manage hard disk partitions and volumes. This utility is different from other command-line utilities in that it runs in the Windows command shell as a text-based command interpreter. This utility consists of several commands that run only after the *Diskpart* interpreter has started. You can use this utility to perform simple disk-related tasks, such as creating and deleting partitions and volumes, and complex tasks, such as creating, maintaining, and managing fault-tolerant volumes. Because *Diskpart* works in a more enhanced mode than its counterpart, the *Disk Management* snap-in, it has more control over the selected disk, partition, or volume. *Diskpart* supports scripting, and you can create scripts to automate repeated disk-related administrative tasks. *Diskpart* error codes make it easy for you to handle command execution more precisely.

In Chapter 7, we explain some of the key issues with maintaining the Windows operating system, including services, drivers, and most importantly, the Windows Registry. We discuss the *SC* and *Reg* command-line utilities, which offer sets of several subcommands that are helpful in configuring and maintaining the Windows operating system. You will rarely need to edit the Windows Registry directly, either from the GUI or from the command line, but it is good to understand how you can query, add, delete, save, and restore Registry entries.

In Chapter 8, we discuss some command-line utilities for monitoring and managing event logs, processes, and performance logs. Monitoring is an important aspect of system and network administration, and you cannot ignore it. The command-line utilities related to managing Windows event logs covered in this chapter include *Eventcreate*, *Eventtriggers*, and *Eventquery*. You will learn how to view system services and applications using the *TaskList* command and how to terminate nonresponsive processes using the *TaskKill* command. This chapter also includes some command-line utilities for monitoring and managing performance logs. These utilities include *TypePerf* for displaying performance data in the command shell window, *Lodctr* for registering new performance counters in the Windows Registry, and *Relog* for extracting and resampling stored performance data.

We move on to Chapter 9 to discuss the command-line utilities used to manage printers and print jobs. It is interesting to note that most of these commands have very simple, facile syntax. You will learn that you can use the *Prnmngr* command to install printers while the *Prncnfg* command is used to view and configure installed printers. Other commands discussed in this chapter include *Prndrvr*, *Prnport*, *Prnqctl*, and *Prnjobs* to manage printer drivers, create and configure TCP/IP ports, manage print queues, and manage print jobs, respectively.

In Chapter 10, we introduce you to the basic syntax of the Directory Services (DS) commands for managing Active Directory objects. You will learn that the object classes that you can use with DS commands include computers (desktops and member servers), contacts, users, groups, servers (domain controllers), OUs, sites, subnets, quotas, and directory partitions. You will learn how to use the *DSQuery* command with different types of objects to search for objects in Active Directory, the *DSGet* command to display properties of specified objects, and the *DSAdd* and *DSRm* commands to add objects to or remove objects from the directory database, respectively. We explain the usage of the *DSMod* command to modify certain properties of specified objects and the *DSMove* command to move objects from one container to another within the domain.

In Chapter 11, we take our discussion of Directory Service commands to the next level. This chapter includes several examples that will help you understand how simple it is to use the DS commands that otherwise look so complex.

Chapter 12 covers the procedures for performing basic network troubleshooting tasks and discusses the use of standard network tools available with Windows command-line utilities. We discuss the utilization of the *Net* command and its associated subcommands. We then examine a number of other network diagnostic tools, such as *Ping, IPConfig, Pathping, Finger,* and *ARP.* We examine the use of more powerful utilities, such as Netstat and *NBTStat,* and learn to interpret the results of these commands. We also cover the versatile DNS querying command-line tool, NSLookup, in this chapter. Finally, we look at how to communicate with remote UNIX computers and the services they use—services that are not commonly, if at all, found on Windows computers.

You finish your learning journey in Chapter 13 with the discussion of the *NETSH* commands. You learn how the *NETSH* commands can be used to view the settings and configure networking components in a Windows Server 2003 environment. *NETSH* runs as a separate command interpreter within the Windows command shell and has a bundle of subcommands associated with it. Although it is not possible to discuss each *NETSH* command or subcommand within the scope of this book, we try to explain the most commonly used commands in this chapter.

With Windows XP and Windows Server 2003, Microsoft made several changes to the command-line functionality. It added several new commands and made changes to the functionality of some other commands. But at the same time, several commands have been dropped from the list of supported commands. These are some of the commands you had been using ever since the MS-DOS operating system was introduced. The appendix in this book discusses the MS-DOS commands not supported in 32- and 64-bit editions of Windows XP and Windows Server 2003.

This book is an effort to introduce you to the powerful command-line utilities available in Windows XP and Windows Server 2003 operating systems. You will learn how to write batch files once you get a strong understanding of these utilities. Although this is not a scripting book, writing scripts or batch files is the next step after you get a grip of the basics. Most of the experienced system administrators depend on preconfigured batch files or scripts to manage networking services. A search on the Web can be very helpful for you to find ready-made scripts. But you must try these freely available scripts on a test server before using them on any production server.

Working on this book has been a great experience for all of us. We do hope that the results of the efforts put in by the team of authors, technical editors, and the editorial staff at Syngress Publishing will result in an informative, useful, and enjoyable experience for our readers. We are always open to your suggestions.

—*Pawan Bhardwaj*
MCSE, MCT, Security+, Network+, A+

Part I
Getting Started
with Command Line

Chapter 1

Basics of the Command Line

Topics in this chapter:

- Basics of the Windows Command Shell
- Starting the Windows Command Shell
- Internal Commands for the Command Shell
- Command History
- Accessing the Windows Command Reference
- Installing Windows Support Tools

Introduction

Most system administrators think that the primary way to manage Windows-based networks is through Windows graphical user interfaces (GUIs). This is true to some extent. If you are working in a small or medium-sized organization, you can complete most of your everyday administration tasks via Windows GUIs. But you may not realize that an even more powerful interface exists within the Windows operating system: the command line. Most administrators think the command line has something to do with programming. This is not true. The Windows command line is actually another type of administration utility that is much more powerful than wizards and other interfaces.

Basics of the Windows Command Shell

Each time Microsoft has shipped a new version of Windows, it has tried to simplify the task of managing the operating system by introducing new GUIs in the form of wizards. As a result, veteran administrators have already started to forget the command prompt, which at one time used to be the only means of managing operating systems and applications. Furthermore, many novice administrators have never even opened the command prompt window. When an easier method exists to perform a task, why muddle with commands and their switches and syntaxes?

The Windows command shell is becoming increasingly versatile with every new version of Windows Microsoft introduces. When the first version of Windows appeared in the early 1990s, support professionals started thinking that the era of MS-DOS commands would soon be over. Although Microsoft provided newer GUIs with each new version of the operating system, it never stopped supporting the command line. Instead, support for the command line increased, and new command-line tools accompanied every new Windows release.

The Windows command shell, which we will discuss in this chapter, is probably the most powerful administration tool that Microsoft has included with the operating system to date. We will begin our discussion with the MS-DOS command shell, and then move on to the Windows command shell. We will discuss different methods you can use to access the command shell and how you can configure its properties to customize its look and functionality. We also will look at the internal commands built into the command shell itself. The Windows command shell keeps a history of previously used commands in its command history buffer; we will discuss how to manage the command history buffer and different ways to access and reuse commands. Later in this chapter, we will discuss how you can refer to the command library or the command reference and install additional advanced sets of commands from the Windows Support Tools.

The MS-DOS Command Shell

The MS-DOS command shell was originally known as the DOS prompt. Administrators and users alike used to perform almost every operating system task they needed to perform from the DOS prompt—whether it was copying a file from one directory to another, creating a directory, or setting the attributes of a file. In addition, people used to write batch files directly from the DOS prompt, and then save them and execute them from there.

Today, people refer to the DOS prompt as the MS-DOS command shell, and it still exists in all versions of Windows. Although the MS-DOS command shell works in a 32-bit environment by default, it supports older, 16-bit commands in Windows XP and Windows Server 2003. However, support for some commands has been discontinued; for instance, several older MS-DOS external commands are not supported on 64-bit versions of Windows Server 2003.

You can access the MS-DOS command shell from the Run dialog box as follows:

1. Click **Start | Run** and type **command** in the **Open** field of the **Run** dialog box.

2. Click **OK** or press **Enter**.

This starts the MS-DOS command shell. You will notice the words *Microsoft Windows DOS* in the window. This is different from the Windows command shell (discussed next), where you'd see the words *Microsoft Windows*. Another difference is that you cannot close the MS-DOS window by just clicking the **cross (X)** button in the top right-hand corner. If you do this, the End Program error message will appear and you will have to click **End Process** to close the window. To properly close the MS-DOS command shell, you must type **Exit** and press **Enter**.

Starting the Windows Command Shell

The first step in learning to work with command-line utilities is to determine the different methods you can use to start the Windows command shell. The Windows command shell, in turn, starts the command interpreter.

The Windows command shell is actually an application built into the Windows operating system. CMD.exe is the command interpreter that accepts your commands and executes them in the way you want. You can access the Windows command shell in one of the following ways:

- Click **Start | Run** and type **cmd** in the **Open** field of the **Run** dialog box. Click **OK** or press **Enter**.

- Click **Start | Programs | Accessories** and click **Command Prompt**.

Either of the aforementioned actions will open the Windows command interpreter and provide you with a 32-bit environment for executing commands. You can also place a shortcut for the command prompt on your desktop if you will be using it often. Figure 1.1 shows the command shell.

Figure 1.1 The Windows Command Shell

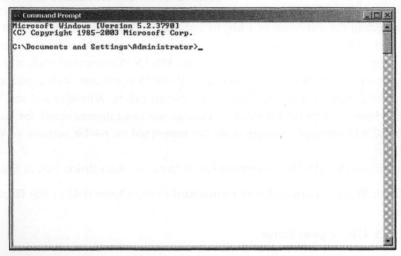

The command interpreter executable, CMD.exe, is placed in the %SystemRoot%\System 32 folder. In Windows XP, the command shell window title will read C:\Windows\System32\CMD.exe, and in Windows 2003, it will simply read Command Prompt. By default, the command shell starts in the user profile folder of the currently logged on user. That's why the current working directory is shown as C:\Documents and Settings\Administrator in Figure 1.1.

A blinking cursor following the command prompt indicates that it is in interactive mode. This mode allows you to enter commands directly at the prompt and press the **Enter** key to execute them. For example, if you type the command *Dir* at the command prompt and press the **Enter** key, the command will execute immediately and the results will appear in the window. You can also write a series of commands and save them as a *batch file*. When the batch file is executed, the command interpreter reads the commands, one line at a time, and executes them in order. You can also group multiple commands in a single command line and process them sequentially. We discuss these techniques, along with the basics of batch files, in Chapter 2.

Customizing the Command Shell Startup

As we discussed earlier, you can start the command shell either from the Run dialog box or from Accessories in the Programs menu. This starts the command interpreter in its default mode. You can customize the default behavior of the CMD.exe interpreter using a number of available parameters or switches. Changing the defaults affects the applications or other commands you run inside the command shell. For example, you can configure the command prompt to execute a string of commands and then exit interpreter mode by typing **Cmd /c** in the Run dialog box, or you can type **Cmd /q** to turn off echo, which is enabled by default.

The syntax for CMD.exe is:

```
Cmd [{/A | /U}] [/Q] [/D] [/E: {ON | OFF}] [[/S] [{/C | /K}] string] [/V:{ON |
/OFF}] [/T:FG]
```

Table 1.1 explains the switches for the *cmd.exe* command.

Table 1.1 CMD.exe Parameters for Setting the Command Shell Working Environment

Parameter	Description
/C string	Executes the command specified in the string and then exits the command shell.
/K string	Executes the command specified in the string and does not exit the command shell.
/S	Modifies the commands used as strings with the */C* and */K* parameters. Usually, you place quotes around command strings. The */S* parameter removes the opening and closing quotes before processing the command.
/A	Causes the output of internal commands to be sent to a file (this process is also called *piping*) in ANSI character format.
/U	Causes the output of internal commands to be sent to a file (this process is also called *piping*) in Unicode character format.
/Q	Turns off echo, which is on by default. Echo off mode is also known as quiet mode. When echo is on, each command is displayed as it is processed.
/D	Disables the *AutoRun* command from the Registry.
/E:ON	Enables command extensions if they were disabled. Command extensions are enabled by default.
/E:OFF	Disables command extensions.
/F:ON	Enables the completion of characters for files and directories, which help improve typing speed at the command prompt.
/F:OFF	Disables the completion of characters for files and directories.
/V:ON	Enables delayed environment variable expansion by using the exclamation point character (*!*) as the delimiter. This means that using *!ThisVar!* will expand the variable *ThisVar* at the time of execution.
/V:OFF	Disables delayed environment variable expansion.
/T:FG	Sets the foreground and background colors. The *F* and *G* represent color values. They must be used without spaces.

From Table 1.1, it is clear that you cannot use some variables together. For example, if you are using /A, you cannot use /U at the same time. Similarly, you can use either /E:ON or /E:OFF. Besides this, several parameters are set by default when you start the command shell.

Master Craftsman...

Commands and Caps Lock

The commands you use at the command prompt in Windows are not case sensitive. You do not have to worry about the Caps Lock key when you are typing commands. This means that *DelTree.exe, DELTREE.exe,* and *deltree.exe* have the same meaning. We have used upper- and lowercase in this book just to increase the clarity and readability of the commands. You might find this to be different from UNIX and Linux environments, where commands are case sensitive.

You also may have noticed in Table 1.1 the function of the /S parameter that modifies the strings when using the /C or /K parameter. The /S parameter removes the quotation marks from the beginning and end of the command. The quotation marks are preserved only if all of the following conditions are met:

- You are not using the /S switch.
- There is exactly one set of quotation marks.
- There are no special characters, such as &, <, >, (,), @, and ^, between two quotation marks.
- There are one or more spaces between the quotations marks.
- The string is the name of an executable file.

If any of these conditions are not met, the /S switch removes the opening and closing quotes.

You use the /T:FB switch to set the colors of the command shell. Table 1.2 provides the values of these colors.

Table 1.2 Color Values for the Command Shell

Color Value	Color
0	Black
1	Blue
2	Green
3	Aqua
4	Red
5	Purple
6	Yellow
7	White
8	Gray
9	Light blue
A	Light green
B	Light aqua
C	Light red
D	Light purple
E	Light yellow
F	Bright white

Customizing the Command Shell Window

The command prompt window shown in Figure 1.1 has several properties that you can con-figure to customize your working environment. For example, the window is 80 characters wide and is 25 lines long by default. The characters are displayed in white over a black back-ground. You can set the cursor size, fonts, colors, and number of commands in the command history, and whether the command shell should use a small window or the full screen.

To change the default settings of the command shell, right-click the **command icon** in the top-left corner of the window and select **Properties** from the menu. The following sec-tions explain the settings in each tab in this window.

The Options Tab

The Options tab allows you to set the cursor size, command history, display options, and editing options, as shown in Figure 1.2. You can choose from small, medium, or large cursor sizes. You use the Command History portion to set the number of commands that the com-mand interpreter can remember. The number of buffers indicates how many separate histo-ries are maintained. The larger the number of commands you keep in the history, the more memory you will need. By default, there are four buffers and each buffer stores 50 commands. You can set these numbers at anywhere from zero to 999. If you are not sure how many buffers you will need, you should not change this setting. You can choose to discard duplicate commands in the history to avoid unnecessarily filling up the buffer by repeating the same command.

Figure 1.2 The Options Tab in the Command Shell Properties Window

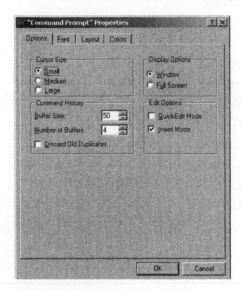

You can use Quick Edit Mode or Insert Mode when editing commands. Use Quick Edit Mode when you want to use the mouse to edit entries. Insert Mode works by inserting text without overwriting the existing text in a line. For example, if you want to copy a line from another application and paste it directly into the command line, you can use Insert Mode.

The Font Tab

The Font tab allows you to choose a font and its size, as shown in Figure 1.3. These options let you control the size of the text within the command shell. The default font is 12-point Lucida Console. With Raster fonts the size of the window automatically changes when you change the font size. You can also make the fonts appear in boldface.

Figure 1.3 The Font Tab in the Command Shell Properties Window

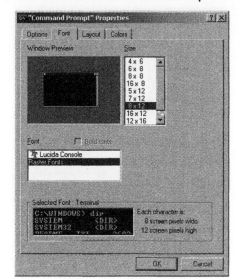

The Layout Tab

You can change the layout of the command shell window from the Layout tab, as shown in Figure 1.4. The screen buffer size affects the size of the window and is set at 80 x 300 by default. A smaller screen buffer size lets you scroll through the window so that you can check previously used commands and their outputs. Some scripts require a large screen buffer, but a buffer setting of 1,000 by 1,500 would suffice in most cases. The combination of screen buffer size and window height lets you view the executed commands easily and scroll up and down the command shell window. You can also set the window position to any corner of the screen, or let Windows manage the position automatically.

The Colors Tab

The Colors tab, shown in Figure 1.5, allows you to customize the colors of the command shell. You can set the background and the text foreground to the color of your choice. You can also set the background and text colors for pop-up windows. Usually, you select the colors from the color bar and the resulting window is displayed at the bottom so that you can see how the command shell window will look after the changes take effect. By changing the values of the red, green, and blue colors, you can fine-tune the selected color. These values range from zero to 255 for each color.

Figure 1.4 The Layout Tab in the Command Shell Properties Window

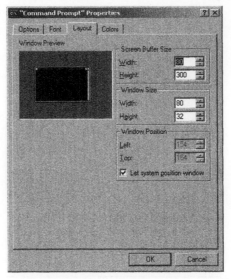

Figure 1.5 The Colors Tab in the Command Shell Properties Window

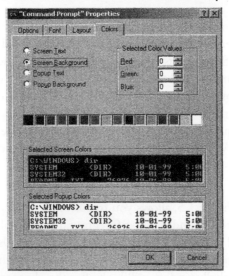

When you finish changing the properties of the command shell, click **OK**. A small **Apply Properties** dialog box will prompt you to select how the changes should take effect. This is shown in Figure 1.6. You can choose to apply the changes to the current window only, or save the settings for future windows with the same title. If you select the second option, the changes will apply to all command shell windows that you open in the future. If you have placed a shortcut for the command prompt on the desktop or in the Start menu, the second option changes to "Modify shortcut that started this window" and every time you start the command prompt from that shortcut, the changes will take effect.

Figure 1.6 Applying Changes to Command Shell Window Properties

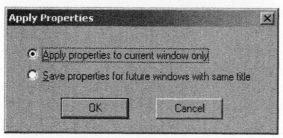

Internal Commands for the Command Shell

You can execute two types of commands from within the command shell. The first type is an *internal command*—these commands are built in the command shell itself and do not appear as executable files anywhere in the system. Most of these commands are very similar to MS-DOS commands. Examples of internal commands are *Dir* for generating a directory listing, *Cls* for clearing the screen, and *Del* for deleting a specific file.

The second type of command you can execute from within the command shell is an *external command*. External commands are separate executable files located in the %SystemRoot\System32 folder. Although these are called external, they still run from within the command shell. Examples of external commands are *XCOPY.exe* for copying the entire directory tree, *DISKPART.exe* for managing disk partitions, and *IPCONFIG.exe* for displaying the computer's Transmission Control Protocol/Internet Protocol (TCP/IP) configuration. External commands are more versatile and offer more advanced capabilities than internal commands. Most of this book is focused on using the external commands for everyday system administration. But in this section, we list some of the more common internal commands:

- **Assoc** Displays or modifies the current filename extension associations. When you use this command without any parameters, it displays a list of all filename extension associations. For example, if you type **assoc .doc** at the command prompt, the extension association will be displayed as *.doc=Word.Document.8*.

- **Call** Used to call another batch program file or a procedure from within a batch file. Control of the currently running batch file is then transferred to the called batch file. This command accepts labels as arguments. It has no effect if you use it outside a batch file.

- **CD (ChDir)** Displays the name of the current working directory or changes the current working directory. If you use it without any parameters, the current working directory is displayed. For example, to change the working directory to C:\Adminfiles\Support, assuming your current working drive is C:, type **cd \adminfiles\support** at the command prompt.

- **Color** Changes the foreground and background colors for the current session of the command shell. This command has the same effect as using the *cmd /t:FB* command discussed earlier. The parameters *F* and *B* are values of the colors, as shown in Table 1.2. For example, the command *color 17* will change the foreground color to blue and the background color to white.

- **Cls** Clears the screen of the current command shell and erases the screen buffer, resulting in a blank command prompt window.

- **Copy** Copies the specified file from one location to another. If the source and destination locations are the same, an error is returned that says *"File cannot be copied on to itself."*

- **Date** Displays or changes the current date on the computer.

- **Dir** Displays the contents of the current working directory, including names of the subdirectories. You can specify a different directory and use wildcards to limit the results. This command also displays the total number of files and subdirectories, their size, total space used, and space remaining on the drive.

- **Del (Erase)** Deletes the specified file, multiple files, or all files within a given directory. For example, the command *Del C:\Reports* will delete all files in the C:\Reports folder. You can use wildcards to specify certain types of files to delete; for example, *Del C:\Reports*.doc* will delete all files with a .doc extension in the C:\Reports folder.

- **Echo** Displays text strings used with the command line and sets the echo on or off. This command is similar to using the command *Cmd.exe /e:on | off*. You can also use this command to display a message.

- **Endlocal** Ends localization of the environment variables in a batch file and restores them to their values before the *Setlocal* command. This command works only in batch files and has no effect if you use it separately at the command prompt.

- **Exit** Used to exit from the command shell window.

- **For** Used to run a specified command for each file in a set of files. You can use it within a batch file or directly from the command prompt.

- **Ftype** Displays current file types or modifies the file types used in filename extension associations. If you use it without any parameters, it displays the file types that have open command strings defined. The open command string specifies the open command used to open the file type.

- **Goto** Used to direct the command interpreter to jump to a command specified with the label. You use it in batch files to direct the processing from the command identified by the label.

- **If** Used in batch files to perform conditional processing of commands. If the condition is satisfied, the command following the *If* command is processed. Otherwise, the interpreter processes the command that follows the *Else* command.

- **Md (Mkdir)** Creates a directory or a subdirectory. For example, *Md C:\Reports\MyFiles* or *Mkdir C:\Reports\MyFiles* will create a Myfiles subdirectory within the Reports directory on the C: drive.

- **Move** Moves one or more files from one directory to another. The source and target locations of the files are specified in the command. If the source is not specified, files are moved from the current working directory.

- **Path** Displays or changes the command path for searching the executable files. When you use this without any parameters, it displays the current command path the operating system uses to search for executables.

- **Pause** Suspends the processing of a batch file and prompts the user to press any key to continue processing. Using *pause* in a batch file is different from using the Ctrl + C key combination. This key combination stops the batch program from processing and asks the user whether she wants to terminate the procedure.

- **PopD** Changes the directory stored by the *PushD* command as the current working directory in a batch file. The *PushD* command creates a virtual directory, and repeated use of the *PushD* command creates a stack of multiple directories. The *PopD* command changes the current directory to the one most recently stored by *PushD*.

- **Prompt** Sets the display text for the command prompt. You use it to customize the command prompt to display any text, such as the current date and time. To reset the prompt to its default, use the *Prompt* command without any parameters.

- **PushD** Stores the name of the current directory for use by *PopD* before changing to another specified directory. The directories are stored in a stack with the last directory on top.

- **Rd (Rmdir)** Removes or deletes the directory or directories and subdirectories specified in the command. This command cannot delete a directory that has hidden or system files. You must empty the directory before using this command,

and you cannot delete the current working directory. You must first use the *Cd* command to change the current directory.

- **Rem** Used to insert comments or remarks in a batch file. The text after the *Rem* command is not processed.

- **Set** Displays, sets, or removes the environment variables. When you use this command without any parameters, it displays the current environment variables. The environment variables are used to control the behavior of batch files. You would commonly use this command in the Autoexec.nt file.

- **Setlocal** Starts localization of environment variables in a batch file. The localization ends when the command interpreter encounters the *Endlocal* command. This command is effective only in batch files.

- **Shift** Changes the position of a replaceable parameter in a batch file.

- **Start** Opens a second command prompt window to run a specified program or an executable. If no program or command is specified, the command just opens another command prompt window.

- **Time** Displays or changes the current time on the computer.

- **Title** Used to change the title of the command prompt window during the processing of a batch file. You can reset the title to its default by using the *Title* command again.

- **Type** Displays the contents of a text file. This command does not modify the text file.

- **Vol** Displays the volume number and serial number of a disk.

Swiss Army Knife...

Commands for Batch Files

Many of the commands discussed previously are frequently used in batch files and scripts. For example, the *Echo, Rem, For, If,* and *Goto* commands are some of the building blocks of batch files. It is simply not possible to write a batch file or script without using some of these commands. These commands help you to write scripts that can perform conditional processing of commands and as well as repetitive tasks within a file. We discuss them in more detail in Chapter 2.

Getting Help for Commands

In the preceding section, you learned about several internal commands available in the command shell. In addition to these internal commands, several external commands are available with Windows XP and Windows Server 2003. It is not possible to remember the syntax of every command available. Fortunately, you can get help on both internal and external commands in either of the following ways:

- Open the command prompt window and type **Help** at the command prompt. This will give you a list of available commands and a brief description. You can select the command you want to use.

- To get help on a specific command, type **Help [*command*]** and press **Enter**. The complete syntax and parameters of the command are displayed. You can also type the command followed by **/?** to view the syntax and parameters of the specified command. For example, you can type either **Help tasklist** or **Tasklist /?** to get help on the *Tasklist* command.

Command History

When you are working at the command prompt, you may need to keep track of the commands that you use during a session. In some cases, you may need to reuse some complex commands as is, or with a minor modification. Each session of the command shell keeps a history of recently used commands in the history buffer. The default size is 50 commands; you can change it to your preference. Earlier in this chapter, in the section Customizing the Command Shell Window, we discussed how you can configure the command history buffer and the number of buffers from the Options tab. Remember that each instance of the command shell keeps a separate command history buffer independent of the other command shell windows that might be running simultaneously.

If you want to change the command history buffer settings and apply the settings to all instances of the command shell window, follow these steps:

1. Open the **Command Shell Properties** dialog box from the title bar. The **Options** tab is displayed by default.

2. Change the **Command History Buffer** to **250**. Click **OK**.

3. You are prompted to choose whether you want to apply changes to the current command window only or save the properties for future windows with the same title. Select the second option and click **OK**.

The command history buffer makes it simple to reuse commands. This saves you time, as you do not have to retype the entire command. By just using the Up- and Down-arrow keys you can scroll through the previously used commands or list a command and edit it for reuse. You can also display, in a separate pop-up window, a list of all the commands you've used so far and choose one. The following sections explain how you can use all of these options.

Displaying Previous Commands with Arrow Keys

You can use the Up- and Down-arrow keys to display the previously used commands in the sequence they were used. When you find the command you are looking for, you can either press **Enter** to execute it or edit it before pressing the **Enter** key.

Viewing the Command History in a Pop-Up Window

If you press the **F7** key, a separate window pops up that displays all the commands stored in the command history buffer. Once again, you can scroll through the commands using the Up- and Down-arrow keys. To use a particular command, highlight it and press **Enter**. The command is pasted and executed at the command prompt. Press the **Esc** key to close the pop-up window.

Using Function Keys

The last command you type in the command shell window is stored in a special memory buffer known as the *template*. Function keys provide several options for using the commands in the command history buffer, as listed in Table 1.3.

Table 1.3 Using Function Keys to Search the Command History Buffer

Function Key	Description
F1	Copies one character from the same column in the template to the same column in the command prompt.
F2	Searches forward in the template for the next key you type after pressing the F2 key.
F3	Copies the remainder of the template to the command line.
F4	Deletes characters from the current insertion point up to a position you specify.
F5	Copies the command in the template (the previous command) to the command line.
F6	Places an end-of-file character (Ctrl + Z) at the current insertion point position.

Continued

Table 1.3 continued Using Function Keys to Search the Command History Buffer

Function Key	Description
F7	Displays a pop-up window that contains all commands stored in the command history buffer. Use the Up- and Down-arrow keys to select a command and press **Enter** to execute it.
F8	Displays all commands in the command history buffer that start with the characters you type in the command line.
F9	Prompts you to specify a number corresponding to a command stored in the command history buffer. The selected command is inserted into the command line.
Alt + F7	Clears all commands stored in the command history buffer.
Alt + F10	Deletes all macro definitions.

Many of the command history functions listed in Table 1.3 are also provided by the DOSKEY.exe utility. In addition, you can use DOSKEY.exe to create macros for use in applications. The DOSKEY.exe utility has several limitations, and very few applications use this utility. You can get help on DOSKEY syntax and parameters by typing **Doskey /?** at the command prompt.

Accessing the Windows Command Reference

You can find a complete, alphabetized list of commands available with Windows XP and Windows Server 2003 in the Help and Support Center. You can access this reference as follows:

1. Click **Start | Help And Support**.
2. Click **Administrative and Scripting Tools**.
3. Expand the **Command Line Reference** node.
4. Click **Command-Line Reference A-Z**.

The resulting details pane shows an alphabetical listing of all available commands. You can click on any command and get help on its syntax, parameters, and correct usage. This reference also contains examples with each command.

Figure 1.7 shows the command reference window for Windows Server 2003.

Figure 1.7 Command Reference Window for Windows Server 2003

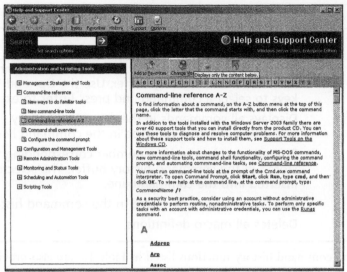

Installing Windows Support Tools

In addition to built-in command-line utilities, Windows Server 2003 includes several other tools to help you simplify your everyday administration jobs. They are called *Support Tools* and they are included on the Windows Server 2003 installation CD. You must install them before you can use them. When you install the Support Tools, the installation process modifies the Help and Support Center screen shown in Figure 1.7. You must close the Help and Support Center window before starting the installation.

To install the Support Tools, follow these steps:

1. Insert the **Windows Server 2003 CD**.

2. In the **Windows Welcome** screen, click **Perform Additional Tasks**.

3. Click **Browse This CD**.

4. Double-click the **Support** folder and double-click the **Tools** folder.

5. Double-click the **SUPTOOLS.msi** file. This starts the Windows Support Tools Installation Wizard. Click **Next**.

6. Click **I Agree** in the End User License Agreement dialog box and click **Next**.

7. Enter your **name and the name of the organization** in the **User Information** page and click **Next**.

8. Select an **installation folder**. By default, the support tools are installed in the %Program Files%\Support Tools folder.

9. Click **Install Now**. The installation starts.

10.   Click **Finish** in the **Completing the Windows Support Tools Wizard** page.

Once the support tools are installed, you can access them from the Start menu by pointing to **All Programs | Windows Support Tools** and selecting **Support Tools Help**. If you are using the classic Start menu, click **Start Programs | Windows Support Tools** and select **Support Tools Help**. This opens the Help and Support Center, which provides an alphabetical list of support tools as shown in Figure 1.8.

Figure 1.8 Windows Support Tools in Help and Support Center

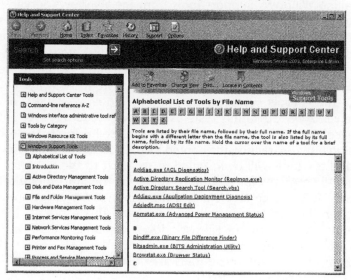

The Help and Support Center shows the support tools organized in categories in the left pane and arranged alphabetically on the right. If you know which tool you need help for, you can click the tool directly in the right pane where the help page for the selected tool will be displayed. The help page contains the syntax for the tool along with several examples to help you understand the tool's correct usage. An icon in the top right-hand corner allows you to open the command prompt window. Because most of these tools are for advanced system and network diagnostics, you should read the help documentation very carefully and test any tool you want to use before using it in a production environment or including it in your batch files.

Master Craftsman...

Windows Resource Kit Tools

Besides installing Windows Support Tools from the Windows Server 2003 installation CD-ROM, you can also download and install Windows Server 2003 Resource Kit Tools from the Microsoft download center. These tools are meant for advanced administrators who work in large and complex network environments. These tools are very helpful for managing and troubleshooting the Windows Server 2003 Active Directory, network, and system security and services. Interestingly, these tools work on both the Windows XP (SP1 or later) and Windows Server 2003 operating systems. You will need at least 30MB of free hard-disk space to download and install the Resource Kit Tools. The tools are contained in a single self-extracting file named RKTOOLS.exe. Double-click the downloaded file and the tools will be installed. A shortcut to the Resource Kit Tools is added to the All Programs (or Programs) folder of the Start menu after installation. Shortcuts to Resource Kit Help and the command prompt are also added. When you open the command shell window from this shortcut, the command prompt changes to C:\Program Files\Windows Resource Kits\Tools. Here is the direct link to the download page from the Microsoft Web site: www.microsoft.com/downloads/details.aspx?FamilyID=9d467a69-57ff-4ae7-96ee-b18c4790cffd&DisplayLang=en

After you install the Support Tools, another shortcut to the command shell window is placed in the program files folder under the Windows Support Tools header. When you open the command shell window from this shortcut, the command prompt changes to C:\Program Files\Support Tools. In the next chapter, you will learn how you can change the default command paths.

Summary

In this chapter, we discussed the basics of the Windows command shell. We learned how we can access the command shell and how to modify its startup. We also learned how to customize the properties of the command shell window to get a larger command history buffer, and how to access previously used commands in the history buffer. After discussing the Windows Command Reference available in the Help and Support Center, we installed the Support Tools included with the Windows Server 2003 setup CD.

In the next chapter, we will look at the basics of batch files. But before we dive in, we will discuss some additional techniques for working with the command shell. You will learn how to work safely with the command shell and how you can take commands from different sources or directories by modifying the command path. You will also learn about redirecting the input and output of commands and how to use groups of commands in a single command line.

Chapter 2

Using Batch Files

Topics in this chapter:

- Working Safely with the Command Line

- Configuring the Command Path

- Using Command Redirection

- Using Groups of Commands

- Creating Batch Files

- Batch File Commands

- Batch File Parameters

Introduction

This chapter introduces you to *batch files*. A batch file uses a combination of different commands to perform one or more specific tasks. The purpose of batch files is to simplify administration as well as to save time performing repetitive administrative tasks. In this chapter, we will discuss the basics of creating batch files and batch file commands.

But before we do that, we will discuss how to work safely in the command shell with nonadministrative credentials using the *RunAs* command. We will discuss how to change command path variables and how command redirection works. *Command redirection* refers to taking input for one command from another command and sending the output of one command to another command, file, or device. We also will discuss how you can group commands in a single command line to be processed sequentially by the command interpreter.

Working Safely with the Command Line

The *RunAs* command allows you to work with the command shell using any user account that has sufficient permissions to perform a task from the command line. It is particularly useful when you are working on a user's computer and the user is currently logged on to the system. You don't want the user to log off because you want to run some commands with your credentials. You can simply run them using the *RunAs* command; the user does not need to log off and log on to the system when you are done.

Another benefit of using the *RunAs* command is safety. You would not want to use your administrative credentials to perform a simple task that you could complete without having administrative rights. A simple rule of thumb is that you should use your administrative user account only when it is *extremely* necessary. This is because the administrative account is powerful. It has control over the entire system—or even the entire domain if it is a domain admin account. A small mistake at the command prompt can result in big trouble if you use any command incorrectly. In large organizations, administrators usually create a secondary account for everyday administrative functions instead of using their domain admin accounts. Most importantly, when you are working on a user's computer, you do not want the user to notice your administrator username and password while you are typing them. A better practice to secure an administrator account is to use the *RunAs* utility.

The *RunAs* utility also allows a user or an administrator to use multiple accounts at the command prompt. If you are writing batch files or scripts and want to test them using multiple accounts, you can use the *RunAs* utility to see whether the application runs well with every account.

Swiss Army Knife...

Secondary Logon Service

The *RunAs* utility requires that the Secondary Logon service be running on the computer where it is used. This service starts by default on Windows XP and Windows Server 2003 computers. If you are not able to use this utility or if you get an error message, make sure that the Secondary Logon service is up and running and that the user account has sufficient rights to run the file.

The *RunAs* command syntax is:

```
Runas [{/profile | /noprofile}] [/env] [/netonly] [/savedcreds]
[/smartcard] [/trustlevel] [/showtrustlevels] /user:UserAccountName program
```

Here are the different parameters for the *RunAs* command:

- **/profile** Loads the user profile for the user specified in the */user* parameter. User profiles are used in Windows environments to store user-specific settings, such as those for the desktop, home directory, logon scripts, and Internet Explorer. Loading a user profile causes a delay in processing the command. This is enabled by default.

- **/noprofile** Specifies that no user profile is to be loaded. The command may execute a little faster but some applications may not function properly if the user profile is not loaded.

- **/env** Specifies that the current environment, rather than the network environment, should be used.

- **/netonly** Indicates that user access specified in the */user* parameter is for remote access only.

- **/savecreds** Uses the credentials (username and domain name) the user has saved instead of loading a new copy.

- **/smartcard** Indicates that the smart card is to be used for supplying user credentials.

- **/trustlevel** Indicates the level of authorization at which the user can run the application. You can use the */showtrustlevels* parameter to display a list of available trust levels.

- **/showtrustlevels** Displays a list of options for the */trustlevel* parameter.

- **/user:***UserAccountName* Specifies the name of the user account to be used to run the program. The user account name following the *RunAs* command must be specified in the *username@domain* or *domain\username* format.

- **program** Specifies the command, program, or application to be run under the credentials of the user specified in the */UserAccountName* parameter.

Even when you are logged on to a system with administrative credentials, it is better to use an account with lesser privileges for performing administrative tasks that do not require full administrative privileges. To open a file named newfile.txt in Notepad, for example, use the following *RunAs* command:

```
RunAs /user:mike@syngress.com "notepad newfile.txt"
```

You will then be prompted to supply the password for the given user account name.

Another way to run programs and administrative utilities in Windows Server 2003 is to use the **Run As** option from the **Start** menu. This option is available when you highlight the program and select **Run As** from the context menu. A dialog box appears that prompts you to use either the current administrative credentials or different credentials, as shown in Figure 2.1.

Figure 2.1 Using the Run As Option from the Start Menu

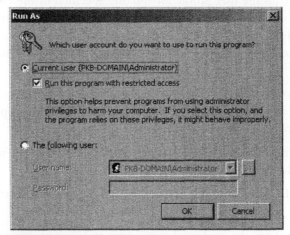

Configuring the Command Path

The command path in Windows specifies where Windows looks for commands and other executables when you do not specify a path in the command. *Path* is an environment variable that allows you to execute files even when they are not in the command shell's current working directory. By default, the command shell executes commands from the \Windows\System32 and \Windows directories. If you do not specify a path with the executable, Windows will search for the executable in the default directory. In order to configure multiple path names in the command shell, you must use one of the following methods:

- Use the *Path* command.
- Use the *Setx* command.
- Change the environment variables in System Properties.

We will discuss each method in the following sections.

Using the Path Command

You use the *Path* command to display or change the current command paths in the command shell. The changes you make affect only the current session of the command shell. When you type the command *Path* at the command line, the currently configured paths are displayed as follows:

```
Path=C:\Program Files\Support Tools;C:\Program Files\Windows Resource
Kits\Tools;C:\Windows\System32;C:\Windows;C:\Windows\System32\Wbem
```

The preceding command path includes paths to support tools and resource kit tools. These paths are added to the command shell when you install Windows Support Tools and Resource Kit Tools. The order in which paths appears in the path command output is also important. When you run a file without specifying its location, the command shell tries to locate the file in the configured paths in the order they appear. If the file is located in the last configured path, it will take a little longer to execute. There are two ways to add new paths to the command shell environment. The first method is to use the *Path* command at the command prompt. Here is the syntax for adding a new path in the command shell:

```
Path [%path%];[drive:]path
```

For example, if you have stored your batch files or scripts in the Myfiles directory on the C: drive, the *Path* command would look like this:

```
Path %path%;C:\Myfiles
```

The *%path%* variable retains the old paths and adds the new path, C:\Myfiles, to the current list of available paths. The paths are separated by a semicolon (;). You can add multiple paths to the *path* variable, each separated by a semicolon. However, you must be careful about the search order discussed earlier. For example, if you have saved all your batch files and scripts in the C:\Myfiles folder and you want the command shell to search this folder first, use the following command:

```
Path C:\Myfiles;%path%
```

When you execute a file from the command prompt, Windows will search the C:\Myfiles folder first to locate the file and, if it is not found, will continue to try to locate the file in other folders in the search order.

Master Craftsman...

The Path Command

You must be very careful when using the *Path* command. First, the order in which the paths appear in the output of the command is important. Second, if you use the *Path* command with just one semicolon, you will delete all the existing paths. It is always better to make a backup of the existing paths before adding or altering the currently configured paths. Open a new file in Notepad and note the existing paths as follows:

> C:\Program Files\Support Tools;
>
> C:\Program Files\Windows Resource Kits\Tools;
>
> C:\Windows\System32;
>
> C:\Windows;
>
> C:\Windows\System32\Wbem

If you accidentally delete the existing paths, you can always refer to this file for reconfiguring them in the command shell. Do not forget to add the %path% parameter when you reconfigure the paths. Remember that the *Path* command displays or changes command paths only for the current command shell session. You must either use the *Setx* command or edit the environment variables in System Properties to permanently change command paths.

Using the Set and Setx Commands

You can use the *Set* and *Setx* commands to change the *path* variable in the command shell. You also can use these commands to change several other environment variables for the command shell, but we will discuss only the *Path* variable in this section. You use the *Set* command to change the *Path* for the current session of the command shell, and you use the *Setx* command to change system variables permanently. You can use the *Setx* command to change the *Path* variable so that the command paths you configure are available in any session of the command shell.

Using the Set Command

The syntax for using the *Set* command to change the *path* variable for the current command shell session is:

```
Set Path=%path%;C:\Myfiles
```

This command appends the C:\Myfiles path to the current command path. When you open a new command shell window, this path will not be available. You must use the *Setx* command to permanently append the C:\Myfiles path to the command path environment variable. This is explained in the next section.

Using the Setx Command

The syntax for using the *Setx* command to change a command path is:

```
Setx Path "%PATH%;C:\Myfiles"
```

This command will permanently append the C:\Myfiles path to the currently configured command paths. This command does not include an equals sign (=), but the *path* variables are enclosed in quotation marks.

Also, note that the command path is enclosed in quotation marks as well, and that each path is separated by a semicolon. Although we have only discussed the use of the *Set* command for changing the command path in this section, you can use the *Set* and *Setx* commands to change several environment variables in Windows. In Windows Server 2003, the *Setx* command is available by default. If you are working on a Windows XP Professional computer, you will need to install the Windows XP Resource Kit Tools to use this command.

Changing Environment Variables in System Properties

As noted earlier, you can permanently configure the command path for all sessions of the command shell by changing the environment variables in System Properties. You can do this from either the Control Panel or the My Computer icon on the desktop, depending on whether you are using the new Start menu or the classic Start menu. Here are the steps involved in changing environment variables in Windows Server 2003:

1. Right-click the **My Computer** icon on the desktop and click **Properties**. (If you are using the classic Start menu, click **Start | Settings | Control Panel** and double-click the **System** icon.)

2. Click the **Advanced** tab.

3. Click the **Environment Variables** button at the bottom of the screen. This opens the **Environment Variables** page.

4. Locate the *Path* **variable** in the **System Variables** box in the lower half of the page, as shown in Figure 2.2.

Figure 2.2 Adding a Path in Environment Variables of System Properties

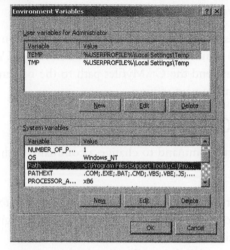

5. Highlight the *Path* **variable** and click **Edit**.

6. Add the new path in the dialog box that appears and click **OK**.

7. Click **OK** to close the **Environment Variables** page.

8. Click **OK** to close the **System Properties** page.

The *Setx* command and the Environment Variables in System Properties change the command paths in the Windows Registry permanently so that every time you use the command shell, the same configured paths are available. When you use the *Path* command within a command shell, the paths you configure remain available for the current session only. Also, each window of the command shell maintains its own command path.

Master Craftsman...

Environment Variables

The word *environment* when discussing Windows operating systems refers to different system-specific and user-specific settings that the operating system uses to configure its working environment.

Continued

Environment variables control the behavior of various programs and applications that run on the system. *System* environment variables include variables that are used when the system is installed, such as the %SystemRoot% folder, the Windows folder, program files, and the location of temporary directories. In the Active Directory network, system variables also include the domain where the computer is a member. Application-specific variables are native to the applications that use them.

Environment variables are used in batch files with percent (%) signs, such as *%Homedrive%*, *%Path%*, and *%Windir%*.

Using Command Redirection

By default, commands executed in the command shell take input from the command, execute the file from its default location, and display the output on the screen. This output includes errors that the command shell generates if the command does not run successfully due to a syntax error, a missing operator, or an incorrect variable value. You can change these default input and output locations using redirection techniques. In some cases, you may want to use input from another command or file and send the output to a location other than the onscreen display. This output location may be another file or a device such as a printer.

Command Redirection Operators

Table 2.1 lists command redirection operators and provides a brief description of each.

Table 2.1 Command Redirection Operators

Redirection Operator	Description
>	Sends command output to a specified file or device (such as a printer) instead of displaying it on the screen. If the file does not exist, it creates a new file, and if a file with the same name already exists, it overwrites it.
<	Takes input for the command from the specified file rather than the keyboard.
>>	Appends command output in the specified file instead of overwriting the file when the file already exists. If the file does not exist, it creates a file with the specified name.
>&	Sends the output of one command to the input of another.
<&	Reads the input of one command and sends it to the output of another.
|	Reads the output of one command and sends it to the input of another. This is also known as *command piping*.

The following sections explain how to use these redirection operators.

Input Redirection

Input redirection refers to receiving input for a command from a file. By default, the command shell takes input from the keyboard when you type a command. It does this by using the input redirection operator (<). This parameter causes the command line to receive input from a file rather than the keyboard. For example, the following command sorts the contents of a text file named Userlist.txt and displays the results in the command shell window, in alphabetical order:

```
Sort<Userlist.txt
```

One condition for using this operator is that the Userlist.txt file must already exist. If you just want to list the contents of the file in the command shell, use the following command:

```
<Userlist.txt
```

Since we did not use the *Sort* command in this example, the output is displayed in the command shell window in an unsorted form.

Output Redirection

Output redirection refers to sending command output to a file or a printer instead of displaying the results on the screen. By default, the command shell displays output of all commands on the screen. It does this by using the output redirection operator (>). This operator sends the output of the command to a specified file or to the printer. For example, the following command sends the output to a text file named Test.log:

```
Ipconfig>Test.log
```

If the Test.log file does not exist, the command will create a new file with this name and will write the output to the file. If there is another file with the same name, the command will overwrite the existing contents of the file with the new information. To avoid overwriting existing information in a file, you can use the (>>) operator instead. This will append the output of the command to the file. The following example illustrates the use of this operator:

```
Ipconfig>>Test.log
```

This will append the output of the command to the existing information in the file named Test.log.

Redirecting Output to Other Commands

As noted earlier, you can send the output of most commands to other commands by using a technique called *command piping*. To do this, you use the piping redirection operator (|). You also can use the piping operator if you do not want to send the output to the display or to a file or device, but you do want to use the output as input for the next command. You can use the piping operator multiple times. Here is the syntax for command piping:

```
Command1 | Command2
```

In this example, the output of *Command1* is sent as input to *Command2*. The following example shows how you can use the output of the *Dir* command as input for the *Sort* command:

```
Dir | sort
```

In this example, the *Sort* command waits for output from the *Dir* command and then sorts the directory listing alphabetically. Consider the next example, where two different redirection operators have been used:

```
Dir | sort>FileList.txt
```

In this example, the output of the *Dir* command is sent as input to the *Sort* command. The *Sort* command sorts the directory alphabetically. The output of the *Sort* command is then sent to the file named FileList.txt. Here is another example where multiple operators are used:

```
Dir | find ".txt" | more
```

In this example, we used three commands with the piping operator. The *Find* command uses the output of the *Dir* command to find all files with a .txt extension. The results of the *Find* command are then displayed in the command shell window. The *More* command causes the output of a command to be displayed one page at a time.

Swiss Army Knife...

Find More Pipes

What do we mean by "Find More Pipes"? *Find* and *More* are the two most common commands used with the piping redirection operator. You use the *Find* command to locate files from a directory or folder with a specified extension. It can also search a file for a given character. The *More* command comes in handy when the output is large and cannot fit on a single page or on a single screen.

Continued

When you use the *More* command, only one page is displayed on the screen. When you finish reading the page you can press any key to display the next page, and so on. These two commands, along with the *Sort* command, are collectively known as *filter* commands.

Error Handling with Redirection Operators

In command-line vocabulary, the location of the input or output stream is known as a *handle*. When you execute a command or a group of commands and you receive an error, the error is displayed in the command shell window by default. In some situations, you may not want this to happen. For example, if a batch file is scheduled to run during off-hours, nobody will be in the office to notice the errors generated by one or more commands. You may not even know whether the batch file executed properly and may end up checking the errors when you return to work the next day. A solution to this problem is to send the errors to a file instead of displaying them on the screen.

Redirection techniques allow you to send the errors generated by commands to a named file. You use handles to specify the filenames for sending error messages. The following example illustrates how to use handles to redirect output:

```
Netstat >Report.txt > 2>&1
```

In this example, the output of the *Netstat* command, along with the errors, is sent to a text file named Report.txt. The numbers *2* and *1* are known as *handle numbers*. We actually redirected handle 2 (STDERR) into handle 1 (STDOUT). The syntax for redirecting handles is:

```
2>&1
```

Table 2.2 lists the standard handles used in command redirection.

Table 2.2 Standard Handles for Command Redirection

Handle Name	Value	Description
STDIN	0	Standard input is sent from the keyboard.
STDOUT window.	1	Standard output is sent to the command shell
STDERR	2	Standard error output is sent to the command shell window.
UNDEFINED	3 through 9	Application-specific handles.

Using Groups of Commands

Now that you are familiar with different input and output command redirection techniques, let's discuss how you can group commands to create a single command line. When you group two or more commands using symbols such as &, &&, and ||, the command interpreter processes the commands either in a sequence or based on certain conditions, depending on which symbol you used. You can also group sets of commands using parentheses. When you use commands with special symbols, the process is known as a *chaining of commands*. The following sections explain how to use these symbols.

Using & for Sequential Processing

You can process two commands in a single command line when you separate them with an ampersand (&) symbol. Here is the syntax for using this symbol:

Command1 & Command2

The command interpreter first processes *Command1* and then processes *Command2*. The following is an example of using & to process the *Md* and *Cd* commands:

Md C:\Reports\Final & Cd C:\Reports\Final

This command first creates a directory named Final in the C:\Reports directory and then changes the current working directory to C:\Reports\Final.

Using && and || for Conditional Processing

When you use *&&* between two commands in a single command line, the command interpreter processes the first command and, if successful, processes the second command. On the other hand, if you use || between two commands, the command interpreter processes the second command only if processing of the first command failed. The syntax for using these two symbols is:

Command1 && Command2
Command1 || Command2

With *&&*, the command interpreter processes the second command only if it is successful in processing the first command. But with ||, the command interpreter processes the second command only if processing of the first command failed. Check the following examples:

Cd C:\Reports\Mar98 && Copy Rep5.txt D:\Reports
Cd C:\Reports\Mar98 || Md C:\Reports\Mar98

In the first example, the file Rep5.txt is copied to the D:\Reports directory only if the first command is able to change the current working directory to C:\Reports\Mar98. In the second example, if the directory Mar98 does not exist, the second command is processed to create this directory.

Grouping Sets of Commands with Parentheses

You can use sets of chained commands with parentheses to form groups of command sets. The syntax is:

```
(Command1 & Command2) && Command3
```

The command interpreter processes *Command3* only if both *Command1* and *Command2* are executed successfully. You can reverse this condition using || as follows:

```
Command1 || (Command2 & Command3)
```

In this case, the command interpreter processes *Command2* and *Command3* only if *Command1* does not complete successfully.

Creating Batch Files

Batch files are simply collections of multiple commands in a single file. They are also called *script files*. They are useful for everyday administrative tasks for which you do not want to remember commands or their syntax. You can create batch files using a text editor such as Notepad; you save batch files with a .bat or .cmd extension. When a batch file is run from the command prompt or called from within another batch file, the commands in the file are executed one by one in the order in which they appear in the batch file. Batch files are very useful in the following situations:

- When you need to perform similar administrative tasks on a regular basis on a single computer

- When you need to perform a series of administrative tasks on a number of computers in the network

- When you want to run specific administrative tasks on remote computers and it is not possible to go to the computer and work on a GUI

- When you want to organize the output of commands run on a computer

- When you need to repeat exactly the same administrative tasks on a number of computers

You do not need to be a programmer to create batch files. Batch files are simple collections of commands combined with some operators and parameters. Just open Notepad and write a few simple commands as follows:

```
Rem * This file is my first batch file *
Echo My First Batch File
Echo Off
Dir
Echo You Just Saw Directory Listing
Echo Bye For Now
```

When you are done writing these lines, save the file as Mybatch.bat. Open the command prompt, type **Mybatch**, and press **Enter**. You will see the output of the batch file displayed in the command shell window, as shown in Figure 2.3.

Figure 2.3 Output of a Batch File

You might have noticed that all commands used in the batch file are also displayed as they are processed. Every time a command is processed, the command prompt is displayed along with the command itself. To get around this problem, you can use the *Echo Off* command. This stops commands from being displayed when they are processed. You use the *Rem* statement in the beginning of the file to insert comments into the file. The text after the *Rem* command is not processed. You use the *Echo* command to display a message. You will learn about batch file commands in the next section.

NOTE

Batch files are considered executable files. You do not need to add the .bat extension from the command line when running batch files. This means that it does not make any difference whether you type Mybatch.bat or Mybatch at the command prompt.

Batch File Commands

As we discussed earlier, batch files are simply text files that contain a number of commands. When a batch file is run, these commands are processed one line at a time in the order they appear in the file. Table 2.3 lists some of the commands that are commonly used in batch files.

www.syngress.com

Table 2.3 Commands Commonly Used in Batch Files

Command	Description
Call	Used to call one batch file from within another batch file without stopping the processing of the original batch file.
Choice	Pauses batch file processing and displays a prompt to the user to choose one of the given options using a specified key.
Echo	Turns the echo on or off. Also used to display a message.
Endlocal	Ends the localization of environment variables changed by the *Setlocal* command. The variables are set back to their original values.
For	Repeats the processing of a command for each file in a group of files.
Goto	Directs the batch processing to a specified line identified by a label. After jumping to the specified command line, the processing continues with the next command.
If	Used to perform conditional processing of commands in a batch file.
Pause	Suspends the processing of the batch file and prompts the user to press any key in order to continue processing it.
Rem	Used to add comments in batch files. The text after the *Rem* command is not processed.
Setlocal	Starts the localization of environment variables in a batch file until a matching *Setlocal* command is found.
Shift	Used to change the position of batch parameters in a batch file.

In the following sections, we explain each batch file command.

Call

You use the *Call* command to call another batch file or to direct the file to another location within the same file identified by a label. You can use this command only in batch files; it does not have any effect when you use it at the command prompt. For example, if you have two batch files named Mybatch1.bat and Mybatch2.bat in the C:\Myfiles folder and you want to call Mybatch2.bat from within Mybatch1.bat, you can use the following command in the Mybatch1.bat file:

```
Call C:\Myfiles\Mybatch2.bat
```

Besides using other files as the target of the call, the *Call* command also accepts a label within the same file as the target of the call. A *label* is an argument within the same file. Consider the following example:

```
Call: Label1
```

In this example, the *Call* command is used to call a label that is specified as *Label1*.

> **NOTE**
>
> You can also use the *Goto* parameter to call another subroutine in a batch file. The difference between the *Call* and *Goto* parameters is that you use *Goto* to call a subroutine within the same file, and you use *Call* either to jump to a subroutine within the same file or to transfer control to a different batch file.

Choice

You use the *Choice* command to suspend processing of a batch file and prompt the user to make a choice from the given options. You can add a message before the available choices so that the user understands what input she is required to provide for further processing, and why. This makes batch file processing a little more interactive and ensures that the user is making the correct choice. The command interpreter pauses until the user presses a key corresponding to her choice. You can have the command interpreter wait for user input for a specified time in seconds. A simple example of this command's usage is:

```
Do you want to delete this file [Y/N]?
```

The syntax of this command is:

```
Choice [/c [keys]] [/n] [/cs] [/t Timeout /d KeyChoice] [/m Text]
```

Here is an explanation of the syntax used in the preceding command:

/c keys Displays the keys from which the user can make a choice, followed by a question mark (*?*). If you do not specify any keys with the */c* parameter, *Y* (yes) and *N* (no) are displayed by default and are followed by a question mark. The keys are enclosed in brackets [ ] and are separated by commas.

/n Used to hide the display of key options. For example, if you use the */c:YN* and */n* parameters, the command interpreter will not display *[Y,N]?* at the command prompt, but the options will still be available.

/cs Used if you want the key choices to be case sensitive. By default, the keys you specify in the */c keys* parameter are not case sensitive.

/t Timeout /d KeyChoice Specifies the number of seconds the *Choice* command will wait for the user to press a key. If the user does not press any key, the command takes the default key choice specified in the */d* parameter. The value of */t* can be anything from 0 to 9999 seconds. A value of 0 will cause the *Choice* command to take the default key choice from the */d* parameter without waiting for the user input. For example, */t 10 /d Y* it will cause the *Choice* command to wait 10 seconds for user input. Use the *Y* (yes) option if the user does not press any key.

/m *Text* Used to display a text message just before the key choices. For example, you can display "Do you want to continue?" by using the */m* parameter.

The following is an example of using the *Choice* command:

```
Choice /c YNC /t 10 /d C /m "Press Y for Yes, N for No, or C to Cancel"
```

When you run this command from the command prompt, the following message will appear:

```
Press Y for Yes, N for No, or C to Cancel
```

The command prompt will wait 10 seconds for the user to press a key and then use C (cancel) as the default choice. Note that the message must be enclosed in quotation marks; otherwise, the command prompt will display an error message.

Echo

You use the *Echo* command to turn command echoing on or off, or to display a message. When you use the *Echo* command without the *On* or *Off* parameter, the current echo setting is displayed. The following is the syntax for the *Echo* command:

```
Echo [ON | OFF]
Echo Message
```

Echo is enabled (on) by default. The command interpreter displays every command in a batch file as it is processed. You can turn this off by using the *Echo off* command at the beginning of the file. It is interesting to note that when the *Echo off* command is processed, it is also displayed. To get around this problem you can use the at sign (@) just before the *Echo off* command, as follows:

```
@Echo off
```

NOTE

You can use @ to suppress display of any command, but it is commonly used with the *Echo* command.

You can use the *Echo* command to display a message when echo is turned off in a batch file. You can also use the *Echo* command multiple times to display a long message spread over several lines. The following example illustrates how you can display a message using the *Echo* command:

```
Echo off
Echo This is my first batch file.
Echo I am testing some commands.
Echo I will use these commands in batch file.
Echo on
```

When you run these commands at the command prompt, the messages are displayed in three lines, as follows:

```
This is my first batch file.
I am testing some commands.
I will use these commands in batch file.
```

You should leave echo on when you are testing a batch file so that you can see how each command is processed. When you turn echo off, you will not be able to see the commands or the command prompt, and this may cause trouble when you are testing a batch file.

Endlocal

The *Endlocal* command ends the localization of environment variables set by the *Setlocal* command and restores the variables to the values they held before the *Setlocal* command was used. If you use the *Setlocal* command but forget to add the *Endlocal* command, the command interpreter automatically restores the environment variables to the values they held before the *Setlocal* command was used. This command is not effective when used outside a batch file. Please refer to the example given with the *Setlocal* command later in this section.

For

You use the *For* command to run a specified command for each file for a given set of files. This is called *iteration*. You can use this command both at the command prompt and in batch files or scripts. The command has the following syntax:

```
For %%variable IN (set) do Command [Command-options]
```

Here is an explanation of each parameter of the *For* command:

%% variable A required parameter that is replaced by its actual value and controls the execution of the command. This variable is case sensitive. The %% variable is also called the *iterator*. If you want to run the *For* command from the command prompt, you would use the % variable instead. Note that from the command prompt only one % is used with the variable.

(Set) Defines a set of files, a set of directories, a range of values, or a set of text strings. These are the values that you want to process with the command. The values or text strings must be enclosed within parentheses.

Command Specifies the command that you want to process for each file, directory, value, or text string defined in the *(Set)* argument.

Command parameters Parameters for the command that you want to process for the variables.

As discussed earlier, the *For* command can work for a group of files, a group of directories, a range of values, and a collection of text strings. When the *For* command is executed, the type of variable takes its values from the specified set, one by one, and processes the command for each file, directory, or value. The following sections explain different forms of variables used in the *For* command.

Group of Files

The syntax of the *For* command when working with a group of files is as follows:

```
For %% variable in (FileSet) do Command [Command Parameter]
```

You can specify a single file or a group of files in the *FileSet* parameter. When using a group of files, you can use a wildcard such as *.txt* or *.doc*. It is also possible to use files with different extensions, each separated by a space, such as *.txt* *.doc* *.exe*, *feb*.txt* *april2*.doc*, and so on. The command is processed for each file specified in *FileSet*. For example, if you want to list all files in a directory named C:\Myfiles that have an extension of .doc, you can use the following command:

```
For %%A in (C:\Myfiles\*.doc) do (echo %%A)
```

The command is initialized by the *%%A* variable. The value of the *%%A* variable is replaced in each file with a .doc extension found in the C:\Myfiles directory and the *Echo* command is processed for each of these files. The final output echoes or displays a list of all files.

Directories

The syntax of the *For* command when working with directories is:

```
For /D %% variable in (DirSet) do Command [Command Parameter]
```

You can specify a single directory or a group of directories in the *DirSet* parameter. This command syntax is similar to the command syntax for files, except that you specify directory paths rather than file paths. When you are working with a directory with multiple subdirectories, the command takes the following syntax:

```
For /R [[Drive:[path]] %% variable in (DirSet) do Command [Command
Parameter]
```

In this case, the command is executed for each directory in the directory tree. Note that the */D* parameter is replaced with the */R* parameter when working with the directory tree.

If you do not specify any drive letter or path with the /R parameter, the current directory is assumed by default.

Range of Values

The syntax of the *For* command when working with a range of values is as follows:

```
For /L %% variable in (Start#,Step#,End#) do Command [Command Parameter]
```

In this case, you specify a start number to set the starting value of the variable, a number to set the step value, and an end value to specify the stop number. When the command is executed, the values of the start and end numbers are compared. The end number must be larger than the start number for the command to execute successfully. When the value of the variable becomes larger than the value of the end number, execution of the *For* loop is stopped. The following example illustrates the use of this form of the *For* command:

```
For /L %%A in (0,4,20) do echo %%A
```

In this command, we specified a start value of 0, a step value of 4, and an end value of 20. When this command is executed, the *%%A* variable takes the values of 0, 4, 8, 12, 16, and 20, and the *Echo* command is executed for each of these values. The final output is:

```
0
4
8
12
16
20
```

It is also possible to use negative step values. You can use the following example with a negative step value. The command will appear as:

```
For /L %%A in (20,-4,0) do echo %%A
```

The output will be:

```
20
16
12
8
4
0
```

Parsing Text Strings

Parsing file contents and text strings involves somewhat complex iterations with the *For* command. You can use the parsing techniques with names of files and directories and other text strings. These commands work well for output of commands as well as for the contents of specified files. You use the variables to define the string you want to parse or examine. You use *parsing keywords* to further modify the parsing. The three different forms of the syntax are:

```
For /F ["Parsing Keywords"] %% variable in (FileNameSet) do Command [Command
Parameter]
For /F ["Parsing Keywords"] %% variable in ("LiteralString") do Command [Command
Parameter]
For /F ["Parsing Keywords"] %% variable in ('Command') do Command [Command
Parameter]
```

Table 2.4 lists parsing keywords, along with an explanation and examples for each.

Table 2.4 Parsing Keywords Used with the For Command

Parsing Keyword	Description	Example
eol=c	Specifies the end-of-line character. You can use only one character. Anything after the end-of-line character is considered a string.	*"eol=;"*
skip=N	Specifies the number of lines that should be skipped at the beginning of the file.	*"skip=5"*
delims=xxx	Sets delimiters to use for fields that replace the default space and tab delimiters.	*"delims=,.:"*
Tokens=X,Y,M-N	Specifies the tokens that you should use from each source line for each iteration of the *For* command. You can specify a maximum of 26. The *M-N* specifies a range of tokens.	*"tokens=1,3,5"* *"tokens=1-6"* *"tokens=*"*
usebackq	Specifies that you can use quotation marks to enclose filenames in *FileNameSet*. A back-quoted string is executed as a command and a single-quoted string is treated as a literal string.	---

Let's consider an example from the stock file of an electronics store. This file is a text file named Stock.txt that contains the name of the items, their part number, the number currently in stock, their reorder level, and the total number sold. The first line of this file reads as follows:

```
Calculators    CA5600125    75    15    45
```

You can parse the file using the *For* command as follows:

```
For /F "tokens=1-5" %%A in (stock.txt) do )@echo Item: %%A Part Number:
%%B In Stock: %%C Reorder: %%D Sold: %%E)
```

The command specifies that the first five fields are to be processed identified by the *"token=1-5"* parameter. The fields are separated by spaces or tab characters. They will be identified by variables from *%%A* to *%%E*. The *Echo* command will be executed for each field or variable. When this command is executed, the output is displayed as:

```
Item: Calculators Part Number: CA5600125 In Stock: 75 Reorder: 15 Sold:
45
```

If you do not want to use all of the fields from the file, you can specify the token value to get only the fields you need. For example, if you want to extract only the item name and balance in the previous example, you can replace *"token=1-5"* with *"token=1,3"*.

Swiss Army Knife...

One or Two Percent Signs?

You should use a single % with the variable parameter when you want to use the *For* command directly at the command prompt. Within batch files, you must use %%. For example, the command *For %%A in (C:\Myfiles*.doc) do (echo %%A)* in a batch file would read as For %A in (C:\Myfiles*.doc) do (echo %%A) at the command prompt.

Goto

You use the *Goto* command in a batch file to transfer control of the command interpreter to another section of the file identified with a specified label. This is different from the *Call* command, which can transfer control to a section within the batch file or can call another batch file. The *Goto* command works only within the batch file that is currently being processed. A *label* is a text string within the batch file that identifies another section of the file. The *Goto* command is commonly used with the *If* command for conditional processing of commands. The following is a simple example of the *Goto* command:

```
@Echo off
Echo Please insert a disk in drive A
Pause
Chkdsk A: /f
If not errorlevel 1 goto End
Echo An error occurred while performing disk check.
:End
```

In this example, *:End* is a text string known as a *label*. The batch file first prompts the user to insert a floppy disk in drive A:. The user would insert the disk and press the Enter key. If the *Chkdsk* command runs successfully, the *Goto* command transfers control to the line identified by the *:End* label and the program ends. Otherwise, an error message is displayed.

If

You use the *If* command for conditional processing of commands in a batch file. Large and complex batch files usually perform multiple tasks, and you can program tasks to run if certain conditions are satisfied. In some cases, you might want to verify that a previous command has completed without generating any errors *before* processing the next command. In other cases, you might want to process a certain command if the condition is satisfied, but process a different one if the condition is not satisfied. The following is the syntax for the *If* command:

```
If [not] errorlevel Number Command [else Expression]
If [not] String1==String2 Command [else Expression]
If [not] exist FileName Command [else Expression]
```

You might have noticed the use of the *not* operator in each command syntax. This is an optional operator that is often used to perform a reverse condition check. This operator specifies that the following command should be processed only if the given condition is *not* satisfied. The *else* clause is used to tell the command interpreter to execute the command that follows the *else* clause whether the command is satisfied or not (if the *not* operator is used). The *else* clause must be on the same line as the *If* command.

The first command syntax uses a *not* operator with the error level. Different commands have different error levels that start with zero. Error levels may also vary depending on the type: a user's error, a command-execution error, or an application error. In most cases, error level zero represents no error, meaning that the command or the task was executed successfully. The error levels are also sometimes known as *exit codes* for applications. The exit code is actually a number that indicates whether the application processed successfully.

Table 2.5 lists exit codes for the *Format* command.

Table 2.5 Exit Codes for the Format Command

Exit Code	Description
0	The format process completed successfully, without errors.
1	Incorrect parameters were supplied with the *Format* command.
4	A fatal error occurred during the format process. This may be any error other than errors 1, 4, and 5.
5	The user pressed the N key to stop the format process when prompted with "Proceed with Format (Y/N)?"

In the second command syntax shown in the preceding code snippet, two strings are compared. If the value of the first string is equal to the value of the second string, the following command is executed. Otherwise, the command following the *else* clause is executed. You may use this command syntax to compare user input with a preconfigured string and decide on the next command to be processed based on the input.

The third command checks whether the specified filename exists. If it does exist, the following command is executed; if it doesn't exist, the command following the *else* clause is executed. You may use this *If* command syntax when working with files.

The following example illustrates use of the *If* command with *errorlevel* and *else* clauses:

```
@Echo off
:Begin
Format A: /s
If errorlevel 1 goto End
Echo An error occurred during the formatting process.
:End
```

This file has two labels named *:Begin* and *:End*. If the *Format* command encounters an error during formatting, it displays an error message and control is transferred to the section labeled *:End*. Let's look at another example:

```
@Echo off

:Begin
If exist C:\Myfile.txt goto Copyfile
Echo Cannot copy the file because it does not exist.
Goto End

:Copyfile
Copy C:\Myfile.txt C:\Myfile2.txt
Goto End

:End
```

This file checks whether the file named Myfile.txt exists in the C: drive. If the file exists, control is transferred to the section labeled *Copyfile*. Otherwise, the file displays the message "Cannot copy the file because it does not exist." and then jumps to the section labeled as *:End*. The *Copyfile* section (or procedure) copies the file to another file named Myfile2.txt and then transfers control to the section labeled *:End*.

Pause

The *Pause* command suspends processing of the batch file and prompts the user to press any key to continue processing. This command is most commonly used when you want the user to insert a floppy disk or a CD-ROM and then press any key to continue. For example, if you want the user to insert the Windows Server 2003 installation CD-ROM in the CD drive E:, you can use the following:

```
@Echo Off
:Begin
Copy E:\Suptools\*.*
Echo Please insert Windows Server 2003 CD-ROM in the CD drive
PAUSE
Goto End

:End
```

When the command interpreter encounters the *Pause* command, it suspends processing until the user presses any key. The user now has time to insert the CD-ROM and can then press a key so that the batch file can continue processing. You may have noticed the *@Echo Off* command at the beginning of this example, and you might be aware that the *Echo Off* command turns off echo but the command itself appears when it is processed. The function of the *@* before the *Echo Off* command is to hide the command itself. When you run these commands in a batch file the command interpreter copies all files in the E:\Suptools folder. But prior to that it pauses and displays the following output in the command shell window:

```
Please insert Windows Server 2003 CD-ROM in the CD drive
Press any key to continue...
```

:Begin and *:End* in this example are the labels. When you insert the CD-ROM and press a key, the processing continues and the command interpreter reaches the *Goto* command, which sends control back to the start of the file that has the *:Begin* label.

Terminating a Batch Job

When you use the *Pause* command in a batch file and the previous message appears, you also have the option to terminate batch processing by using the **Ctrl + C** key combination. When you do this the following message is displayed:

```
Terminate batch job: (Y/N)?
```

If you want to stop or terminate further processing of the batch file, press **Y** (yes) and the command interpreter will return to the command shell window. In fact, you can terminate the processing of any batch file using this key combination at any time during the execution of the file.

Swiss Army Knife...

Suspend or Terminate?

The *Pause* command has two functions: It can either suspend the program or terminate it. You can pause the batch file and wait for a key press while you insert a floppy disk or a CD-ROM, or change media. If you are unsure about what will happen next, you can just press the **Ctrl + C** key combination to terminate the processing of the batch file. While this may facilitate the author who has written the batch file, it may also give another user the option to terminate the batch file before it completes processing. As you may not want this to happen, you should be very careful when using the *Pause* command.

Rem

The *Rem* command allows you to insert comments into a batch file. You use this command to organize different parts of the batch file. This command is useful in understanding a batch file when you did not create it, or when you are troubleshooting a file that causes errors when it is processed. The command interpreter does not process or display the text written after the *Rem* command. This is different from the *Echo* command, where the text after the command is displayed on the screen. The following example illustrates use of the *Rem* command:

```
@Echo off
Rem *File Name: CDCopy.bat*
Rem *This batch file copies the contents of a CD-ROM drive E
Rem * To a folder C:\test on the hard drive*
Rem *Author-Gary B.*
Rem
Echo Insert the CD-Rom in CD drive
Pause
Xcopy E:\*.* C:\test
```

The text after the *Rem* command cannot include quotation marks or pipes.

Master Craftsman...

A Neatly Written Batch File

You use the *Rem* (remarks) command to insert comments in a batch file. You should make it a habit to use this command as often as possible to neatly organize different sections of your batch file. When working with several batch files on a regular basis, you will obviously be dealing with a large number of files every day. It is quite possible that after a while you will start forgetting their purpose. Inserting comments in the beginning of a file helps you immediately recognize its purpose. If it is a large file containing several sections, these comments not only help you organize different file sections (or subroutines), but they also help with troubleshooting. And if someone else is working on a file you created, your comments will make it easy for him to understand how the file is supposed to work. The *Rem* command helps keep your work neatly organized for yourself and others.

Setlocal

The *Setlocal* command starts the localization of environment variables in a batch file. This localization continues until a matching *Endlocal* command is found. You should use the *Setlocal* and *Endlocal* commands only inside a batch file. Outside a batch file or a script file, these commands have no effect. The following is an example of this command:

```
@Echo off
Rem This command sets local variables
Rem Localization ends when
Rem Processing of Mybatch2.bat file is complete
Setlocal
Path=%path%;C:\Myfiles;D:\Myscripts
Call Mybatch2.bat
Endlocal
```

It is also possible to place one *Setlocal* command within another. This is called *command nesting*. If you do not use the *Endlocal* command, the command interpreter restores the environment variables to the values they were at before the *Setlocal* command was used.

Shift

The *Shift* command changes the position of the parameters in a batch file from %0 through %9. Each parameter is copied into the previous parameter. If you are using parameters from %0 through %4, the *Shift* command would shift the value of *%5* to *%4*, *%4* to *%3*, and so on. Since you can use only *%0* through *%9* parameters, use the *Shift* command when you need to work with more than 10 parameters.

It is important to note that the *Shift* command works in one way only. If you use it to accommodate an eleventh parameter (because you can use only 10 parameters at a time), the values of the parameters will start shifting and the value of the *%0* parameter will be lost. Once the shift has been completed, you cannot recover the value of the *%0* parameter.

Batch File Parameters

You use parameters in batch files to get information about environment settings. These parameters are denoted by the expansion variables *%0* through *%9*. The *%0* variable is replaced with the name of the batch file currently being processed. You can specify other variables from *%1* to *%9* inside the batch file using argument types at the command prompt. For example, if you have two folders named Folder1 and Folder2, and you want to copy all the files and subfolders in C:\Folder1 to D:\Folder2, you would use the following command at the command prompt:

```
Xcopy C:\Folder1\*.* D:\Folder2
```

Using batch file parameters, you would create a batch file named Mybatch.bat and include the following command:

```
Xcopy %1\*.* %2
```

Save the file and run the following command from the command prompt:

```
Mybatch1.bat C:\Folder1 D:\Folder2
```

In this command, the variable *%1* refers to C:\Folder1 and the variable *%2* refers to D:\Folder2. When the command is run, all the files and folders from C:\Folder1 will be copied to D:\Folder2.

Using Variable Modifiers

You can replace the parameter variables we discussed in the previous section with modifiers. Modifiers use the current drive and directory information to expand batch parameters to make them directory names. A tilde (~) is placed between the % and the modifier. The syntax for using the modifiers always remains as follows:

```
%~modifier
```

Table 2.6 provides a list of available modifiers.

Table 2.6 Batch File Modifiers to Expand Parameters

Modifier	Description
%~1	Expands the variable specified by %1 and removes the surrounding quotation marks.
%~f1	Expands %1 to a fully qualified path name.
%~d1	Expands %1 to only a drive letter.
%~p1	Expands %1 to a path.
%~n1	Expands %1 to only a filename.
%~x1	Expands %1 to a file extension.
%~s1	Expands the path variable to a full name and then changes it to the short names.
%~a1	Expands %1 to file attributes.
%~t1	Expands %1 to the date and time of the file.
%~z1	Expands %1 to the size of the file.
%~f1	Searches the directories specified in the *Path* variable for the file specified by the %1 parameter. Expands the first file that it finds to its fully qualified name. If no matching file is found, an empty string is returned.

Using a Combination of Modifiers

Along with using modifiers individually in command parameters, you can use a combination of them to obtain the desired output. The following examples show how you can combine two or more modifiers to obtain the desired output:

- **%~dp1** Modifiers *d* and *p* are used together to obtain the drive letter and path of the %1 variable.

- **%~fs1** Modifiers *f* and *s* are used together to obtain file information using the short names.

- **%~nx1** Modifiers *n* and *x* are used together to obtain a filename and its extension.

- **%~ftza1** Modifiers *f*, *t*, *z*, and *a* are used together to produce a complete listing similar to the output of a *dir* command.

- **%~dp$PATH:1** Modifiers *d* and *p* are used together to obtain the drive letter and path for a file from the path specified by the *Path* parameter. The output only contains information about the first file found.

Summary

In this chapter, we discussed how to work safely with the command line using a nonadministrative account that has just enough privileges to run the command. While working with the command shell, we sometimes need to specify a path where commands or batch files are located. We can change or modify the command path by modifying the environment variable either from the command prompt or from System Properties.

We also discussed how we can change command input and output from the standard keyboard and the command shell window, respectively, and how to handle errors generated by commands. Then we discussed the concept of batch files and how to create simple batch files. We learned about commonly used commands in batch files and how to use each command inside a batch file.

You can run batch files directly from the command prompt or schedule them to run at a specified time. In the next chapter, we will focus our attention on scheduling batch files to run at specified times. Running batch files at preconfigured schedules requires configuration of the Task Scheduler service. In the next chapter, we will discuss how tasks such as batch file processing can be scheduled and managed from GUI wizards, as well as from the command line.

Chapter 3

Managing Scheduled Tasks

Topics in this chapter:

- Scheduling Tasks
- The Task Scheduler Service
- Managing Tasks Using the Task Scheduler
- The schtasks Command-Line Utility
- Creating New Tasks with schtasks
- Managing Tasks with schtasks

Introduction

Although administrators can perform most of their everyday administrative functions during office hours, they must carry out certain tasks during off-hours or on the weekend. System and data backups are good examples of such tasks. Backups consume a significant amount of network bandwidth; when performed during office hours, backups could consume the bandwidth employees need to get their jobs done. Furthermore, administrators cannot be expected to be in the office at all times.

This is why administrators rely on batch files and scripts that run automatically at predefined times. Using such programs, administrators can perform certain tasks, such as system and data backups, at any time of the day or night. Windows operating systems depend on a built-in service known as the *Task Scheduler* to run these tasks automatically. In this chapter, we will learn about the Task Scheduler, the components on which it depends, and how to configure tasks using the Task Scheduler Wizard as well as from the command line.

Scheduling Tasks

The Task Scheduler service in Windows is an automation utility that helps administrators run commands, batch files, scripts, utilities, and other applications on preconfigured schedules. The configured task runs automatically in the background—without requiring any interaction from the administrator. It is not necessary to schedule all administrative tasks to start or finish during off-hours. The service allows you to configure any task to start and stop at any time, and repeat it every hour, every day, every week, or every month. You may also schedule the task to run just once. To automatically run tasks at predetermined schedules, you can use either the Task Scheduler or the command-line utility, *schtasks*. Both provide more or less similar functionality and depend on the task scheduler service, which must be running when the tasks are scheduled to run.

The Task Scheduler

The Task Scheduler is a graphical user interface (GUI) utility that you can use to schedule applications or batch files using configuration wizards. These easy-to-use wizards help you create tasks, view and modify scheduled tasks, and check whether the scheduled tasks are running. You can also enable or disable a scheduled task, or delete a task completely if it is not required to run anymore.

schtasks

Choosing to use a command-line utility depends on how comfortable you feel working with the Windows command prompt. *schtasks* is a little more advanced than its GUI counterpart, and it is a more powerful version of the older *AT* command-line utility in Windows. Windows still supports the *AT* command but we will discuss only *schtasks* in this chapter.

You can use both the Task Scheduler GUI and *schtasks* to create and manage scheduled tasks on either local or remote computers. You do not have to be at the console of the remote computer in order to run a task on it. Task scheduling makes it easy to run batch files, scripts, programs, or other applications automatically, anywhere in the network. You can also combine these two utilities to perform a complex task if you feel that using only one will not be enough. Since you can use these utilities together, this chapter will discuss both of them. Each scheduled task on a Windows system runs only one script or program at a time. For multiple tasks, you will need to schedule each task independently.

Swiss Army Knife...

The AT Utility

The *AT* utility has been used for a long time on Windows computers. You may still use it for performing simple jobs. All batch jobs created using the *AT* utility run as a background process. The output is never displayed on the screen but you can redirect the output to a file using the redirection operator (>). Like *schtasks*, *AT* also uses the task scheduler service. Jobs created by *AT* appear in the Scheduled Tasks window. Starting and stopping the task scheduler service does not remove any jobs from the Scheduled Tasks window. *AT* has several limitations compared with *schtasks*, and you may soon find that you are better off with the latter for automating your routine administrative jobs.

The Task Scheduler Service

As discussed earlier, scheduling tasks to run automatically at predetermined times requires the task scheduler service. It does not matter whether you create tasks using the GUI wizard or the *schtasks* utility; both require the task scheduler service to be running. The Task Scheduler service is enabled by default on Windows XP and Windows Server 2003 computers and runs automatically on startup as a background service. In some situations, you may need to start the service manually or restart a stopped service, or even enable it if some of your previous administrators have disabled it. You can start, stop, pause, restart, and enable/disable this service from the Services snap-in located in the Computer Management Console.

Accessing the Task Scheduler Service

You can access the Task Scheduler service (see Figure 3.1) either from the My Computer icon on the local computer, or by creating a custom Microsoft Management Console (MMC). The Services node in the Computer Management console contains Task Scheduler. To access the Computer Management Console from the My Computer icon on the local computer, follow these steps:

1. Right-click the **My Computer** icon on the desktop and select **Manage**. This opens the Computer Management Console.

2. Click the **+ sign** next to the **Services and Applications** node to expand it.

3. Click **Services** to view the services running on the computer.

4. Locate the Task Scheduler service.

Figure 3.1 Task Scheduler Service Running Automatically on Computer Startup

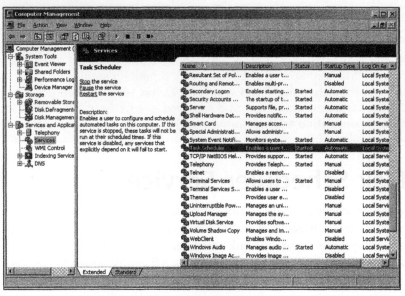

You also can access the Services snap-in in one of the following ways:

■   From Administrative Tools in the Start menu

■   From the Control Panel

■   By running the SERVICES.mmc from the Run dialog box in the Start menu

It does not matter what method you use to access this snap-in; the same Services window opens.

Creating a Custom MMC for Services

Another way to open the Services snap-in and access the task scheduler service is to create a custom MMC. A custom MMC for the Services snap-in will allow you to manage the Task Scheduler and other services on local computers as well as any remote computer on the network. To use the MMC, follow these steps:

1. Click **Start | Run**.

2. Type **MMC** in the **Run** dialog box and click **OK** or press the **Enter** key.

3. In the empty **Microsoft Management Console**, click **File** and select **Add/Remove Snap-in**.

4. In the **Add/Remove Snap-in window**, click **Add**.

5. Select **Services** from the **Add Stand Alone Snap-ins** window. Click **Add**.

6. The next dialog box allows you to add the snap-in for the local computer or another computer on the network. Click **Local Computer** if you want to manage services on the local computer or type the **name of a remote computer** in the **Another computer** box (see Figure 3.2).

Figure 3.2 Adding the Services Snap-in for a Local or Remote Computer

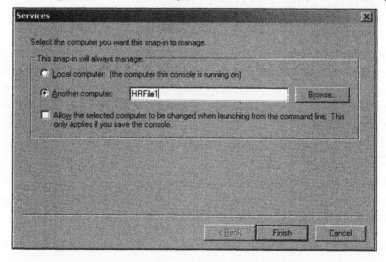

7. Click the **Browse** button if you do not know the name of the remote computer. When you click **Browse**, a **Select Computer** dialog box appears where you can specify the computer name or any other attributes of the remote computer to find it in the Active Directory database.

8. Click **Finish** to add the Services snap-in to the MMC.

As shown in Figure 3.1, the task scheduler service runs using the Local System account by default. You can change to another account if you are concerned about the security of the current account. Also, notice that the status of the service is in *Started* state and its startup type is shown as *Automatic*.

When you right-click the service, you can select one of the following options:

- **Start** If the service is stopped or if the startup type of the service is configured as Manual.

- **Stop** If the service is running.

- **Pause** To temporarily pause the service.

- **Resume** To resume a service that is currently paused.

- **Restart** To stop and restart the service automatically.

- **Properties** To open detailed property pages of the task scheduler service.

These options are enabled or disabled depending upon the state of the service. For example, if the service is started, you cannot start or resume it. If the service is stopped, you can only start it—all other options are disabled.

Configuring the Properties of the Task Scheduler Service

You configure and manage the properties of the Task Scheduler service from its properties pages. To open the task scheduler service properties, either right-click the **Task Scheduler service** and select **properties** or just double-click the **Task Scheduler service**. Four different tabs on the properties pages allow you to configure the service, as explained in the following sections.

The General Tab

The General tab allows you to configure the startup service type. You can start, stop, pause, and resume the task scheduler service from this tab. You can configure the startup type in one of the following ways:

- **Automatic** The service starts automatically when the system starts. It remains in the started state until it is manually stopped or it fails.

- **Manual** The service is not started when the system starts. It starts when some application calls for it or when an administrator starts it from the Services snap-in or from the command prompt.

- **Disabled** The service remains in a disabled state on system startup. If some applications or scripts are configured to run on the system, they do not run until the service is re-enabled.

The Log On Tab

The Log On tab allows you to change the user account that the service uses to run. By default, the task scheduler service uses the Local system account. If you feel that this account should not be used for security reasons, you can specify a more secure user account from this tab. If multiple hardware profiles are configured on a computer, you can enable or disable the service for a particular profile.

The Recovery Tab

The Recovery tab allows you to configure how the system behaves when the service fails. In its default configuration, the service restarts on first and second failures. You can configure the first, second, and subsequent failures of the service in one of the following ways:

- **Take No Action** The system does not take any action when the service fails. You will have to restart the service manually from the Services snap-in or from the command prompt.

- **Restart the Service** The system attempts to restart the service when it fails.

- **Run a Program** You can specify an application or a script to run when the service fails. For example, you can run a script that sends you an e-mail that informs you that the service has failed.

- **Restart Computer** The computer restarts when the service fails. You should choose this option only if other attempts to restart the service have failed.

The Recovery tab also allows you to reset the fail count (the number of times the service has failed) as well as specify the number of days when the fail count should be reset to zero. You can also specify the number of minutes the system should wait before restarting the service when it has failed.

Swiss Army Knife...

Service Recovery

In its default configuration, a Windows Server 2003 computer will restart the service when it fails for the first and second times. The wait time to restart the service is also set to zero, meaning that the system will immediately attempt to restart the service. The system will not take any action when the service fails more than twice a day. It is interesting to note that the fail count is also reset every day. This means that the system will attempt to restart the service twice a day and

Continued

take no action if it fails again. Another method is to create a script that will inform you about the service failure when it fails for the first time. This configuration is very important on mission-critical servers where you might have scheduled a task to run automatically every day and you find that the task did not even start.

The Dependencies Tab

The Dependencies tab displays the services that are required for the task scheduler service to run. You can also view the services that depend on this service. The task scheduler service depends on the Remote Procedure Call (RPC) service to run. If for some reason, the RPC service has failed, the task scheduler service will also fail. If you find that the task scheduler service has failed and you are not able to restart it, you should check the RPC service.

Managing Tasks Using the Task Scheduler

Scheduled Tasks is a type of GUI you can use to create and manage scheduled tasks. The Scheduled Tasks GUI is located in the System Tools folder under the Accessories category in Program Files. If you use this utility very frequently, you should create a shortcut to it on your desktop.

If you are using the Classic version of the Start menu, you can open the Scheduled Tasks window as follows:

1. Click **Start | Control Panel** to open the **Control Panel** window.

2. Double-click the **Scheduled Tasks** icon in the **Control Panel** window.

To open Scheduled Tasks on a network computer, follow these steps:

1. Right-click the **My Computer** icon on the desktop and click **Explore**.

2. Click the **+ sign** next to **My Network Places**.

3. Click the **+ sign** next to **Microsoft Windows Network**.

4. Click the **+ sign** next to the Windows domain where the remote computer is located.

5. Continue expanding the tree until you locate the computer.

6. Click the **computer name** and the **Scheduled Tasks** icon will appear in the right-hand-side details pane.

Figure 3.3 shows the Scheduled Tasks window with two scheduled jobs.

Figure 3.3 Scheduled Tasks Window with Tasks Scheduled on the System

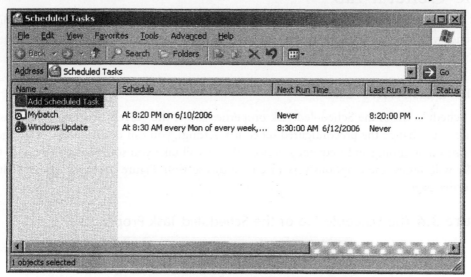

It does not matter whether you have scheduled tasks by using the Scheduled Task Wizard or by using the *schtasks* utility; the tasks will always show in the Scheduled Tasks window. You can access the Scheduled Tasks window for any computer on the network and manage the scheduled tasks. You can use the Scheduled Tasks window to change the properties of scheduled tasks, rename them, or even delete them—and you can do this for any computer where you have permission to perform these actions.

In Figure 3.3, two tasks have been scheduled to run automatically. The first task, Windows Update, is configured to run on a weekly basis: every Monday at 8.30 A.M. The second task, the Mybatch.bat file, was scheduled to run only once, at 8.20 P.M. on June 10, 2006. The window also shows the Next Run Time, the Last Run Time, and the status of both of the scheduled tasks, telling you immediately the last time the task ran and the next time it will run. You can manage these properties—as well as several properties of the scheduled task—from this window.

Managing the Properties of Scheduled Tasks

You can right-click any task in the Task Scheduler window to access its properties. From these properties pages you can modify scheduled tasks as you wish. You can change when the task should run, change the account under which the task should run, and delete the task that is scheduled to run only once after it has been completed. You can also set security permissions for scheduled tasks so that an unauthorized user cannot accidentally or deliberately delete them or modify their properties. We explain the different tabs of the Scheduled Task properties in the following sections.

The General Tab

The General tab of the Scheduled Task properties allows you to enable or disable a scheduled task and even change the program application of a script that is to be run. You can change the user account used to run the task and set a new password for the account, as well.

The Schedule Tab

The Schedule tab of the Scheduled Task properties shows the current schedule of the task. If you need to change the preconfigured schedules' settings, you can do that here. This page offers so many timing and frequency options that it will take you some time to explore them all. We will discuss these options very briefly in this section. Figure 3.4 shows the Schedule properties page.

Figure 3.4 The Schedule Tab of the Scheduled Task Properties

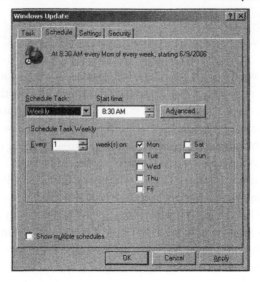

The Schedule Task drop-down menu gives you the following options to run a task at desired times and frequencies:

- **Daily** Used when you want the task to run daily at specified timings. You can also set the frequency as daily, every other day, or every three days.

- **Weekly** Used when you want the task to run weekly at specified times and days. You can choose any day from Monday through Sunday, or choose multiple days when the task should run automatically. You can also choose every week or alternate weeks.

- **Monthly** Used when you want the task to run on either a certain day of the month or a certain date. Additionally, you can choose the months (January to December) from the Select Months window by clicking the **Months** button.

- **Once** Used when you want the task to run only once. This option is good for when you want to install an application on the local or remote system. The Run On box opens the calendar (where you can select the month and day of the month when the task should run).

- **At System Startup** Used when you want the task to run every time the system is started. This option also allows you to specify the number of minutes to wait before starting the task (after the system starts up). The task will continue to run in the background until it is completed or terminated, or when the system is shut down.

- **At Logon** Used when you want the task to run when someone logs on to the system. Once the task starts running, it will continue to run in the background until it is completed or the user terminates it, provided she has permission. The task can run with or without user intervention. If the task has been configured with a user account and some other user logs on, it will run using the originally configured user account. The task will not stop, even when the user logs off.

- **When Idle** Used to configure certain tasks that require that the system be idle for a certain amount of time before it can be started. The When Idle tab allows you to configure such tasks by setting the amount of idle time in minutes. For example, you can configure a batch job or application to run when the system idles continuously for 10 minutes. Once the task starts, it continues to run, even if someone starts working on the system and it is no longer idle.

In all of these schedules, the Advanced button opens up another dialog box where you can set the Start Date and End Date for the scheduled task. This is useful when you want a task to run for a few days, weeks, or months. You can also configure the task to repeat itself at predetermined times during the day. The times are set in minutes.

The Settings Tab

The Settings tab allows you to configure the following properties for a scheduled task:

- Delete the task that is scheduled to run only once when it has completed.

- Stop the task if it continuously runs for a specified number of hours. This option is enabled by default and is set to 72 hours.

- Run the task only if the system is idle for a specified amount of time in minutes. By default, this option is not enabled.

- Stop the task when it has already started if the system is no longer idle. By default, this option is not enabled.

- For portable computers, the task should not be started if the computer is running on batteries, and a running task should be stopped if the computer switches to battery mode. These two options are enabled by default.

The Security Tab

The Security tab of the Scheduled Task properties allows you to set permissions for the scheduled task. When you create a task that is configured to run under a user account, you need to give appropriate permissions so that the task can be run with the account. For tasks that are critical to network function (services such as performing backups or collecting security event logs), you should be very careful about who gets access. A small mistake in configuring access control for scheduled tasks can ruin the entire task—as well as create trouble for you as the administrator.

Monitoring Tasks in the Scheduled Tasks Window

All scheduled tasks appear in the Scheduled Tasks window of Windows Server 2003 and Windows XP systems. This is the best place to monitor and manage scheduled tasks on either a local or a remote computer. It does not matter whether the task was created using the *schtasks* command-line utility or the Scheduled Task Wizard; it appears in the Scheduled Tasks window. By default, the window shows the following information for every task, in a single line:

- A list of scheduled tasks

- A schedule for the task

- The next run time

- The last run time

- The task's status

- The last result of the task

- The user who created the task

- Whether the task is disabled

If a task is disabled, it will show as Disabled in the Scheduled and Next Run Time columns.

Viewing the Scheduled Task Logs

The task scheduler service writes information about scheduled tasks in a log file. This log file is named SchedLgU.txt and is stored in the %SystemRoot% folder of the local computer. You can open the file either using Notepad or in the Scheduled Tasks window. This file contains detailed information about the task scheduler service, as well as tasks that have completed. If an error occurred when running a scheduled task, it is also written in this file.

To open the log file from the Scheduled Tasks window, click **Advanced** in the menu bar and select **View Log**. Figure 3.5 shows a sample file.

Figure 3.5 Scheduled Tasks Log

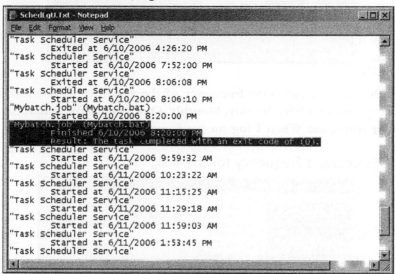

Creating New Tasks

The Scheduled Task Wizard makes creating a new task pretty straightforward. Once you have decided which task you want to run and its schedule, the rest of the job is fairly simple. The following steps will help you understand the procedure:

1. Open the **Scheduled Tasks** window using any of the methods discussed earlier in this section.

2. Double-click the **Add Scheduled Task** icon to start the Scheduled Task Wizard.

3. Select the **application** from the list and click **Next** (as shown in Figure 3.6). Alternatively, you can click the **Browse** button to locate a file, script, or application.

Figure 3.6 Selecting an Application in the Scheduled Task Wizard

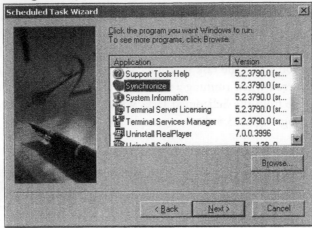

4. On the next page, select the **frequency of the task** from the available options. The options are **Daily, Weekly, Monthly, One time only, When my computer starts**, and **When I log on** (see Figure 3.7). Click **Next**.

Figure 3.7 Selecting a Frequency for the Task

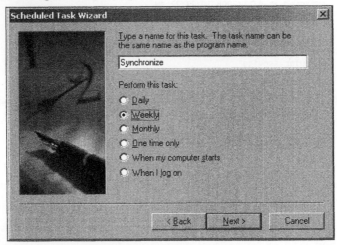

5. If you selected the **Daily** schedule, you'll see the page shown in Figure 3.8.

6. In this page, you can set the time, frequency, and start date for the task. In the **Perform this task** section, select whether the task should run **Every Day** (seven days a week), **Weekdays** (Monday through Friday), or **Every N days**, where N is any number.

Figure 3.8 Setting the Daily Schedule for the Task

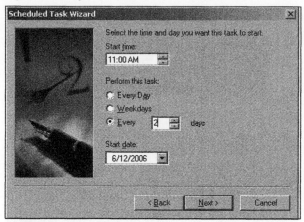

7. If you selected the **Weekly** schedule in step 4, as shown in Figure 3.7, you'll see the page that appears in Figure 3.9.

Figure 3.9 Setting the Weekly Schedule for the Task

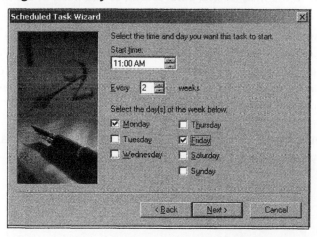

8. On this page you can set the start time, weekly frequency, and days of the week when the task should run. In the **Select the day(s) of the week** section, you can choose the days you want the task to run.

9. If you selected the **Monthly** schedule in step 4, you'll see the page shown in Figure 3.10.

Figure 3.10 Setting the Monthly Schedule for the Task

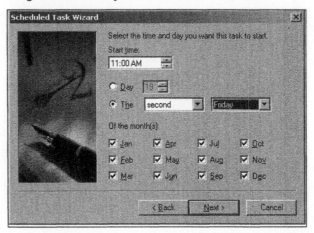

10. On this page, you can select the start time, day, and month from a wide range of options. You can choose a particular day from the selected months or select a particular day of the week. You can also specify whether the task should run on a particular day in the first, second, third, fourth, or last week of the month. This option does not allow you to choose a particular day of the week.

11. When you have made your selections, click **Next**. The next page prompts you to set the username and password that the task will use to run. Every scheduled task on a Windows computer needs a user account. Select the **user account** in the **Enter the user name** box. Specify the username in the *Domain\User* format. Type and confirm the password as shown in Figure 3.11.

Figure 3.11 Setting the User Account and Password for the Task

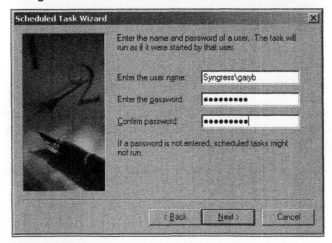

12. Click **Next** to go to the final page of the wizard.

13. Click **Finish** to create the task. It will appear in the Scheduled Tasks window.

Another way to create a new task is to click the **File** menu option, select **New**, and select **Scheduled Task**. A task named *New Task* that starts on the following day and is scheduled to run every day at 9:00 A.M. is created. You can edit the properties of this task to customize it to fit your requirements.

Master Craftsman...

Misconfigured Tasks

When you are creating a task using the Scheduled Task Wizard, you may enter incorrect information—either because you don't realize the information is incorrect or because you mistyped something. The best way to deal with this is to click the **Back** button and check all the information on each page before clicking the **Finish** button on the final page. If you type an incorrect username or password, the wizard will display an error message. Interestingly, the task will still be created. Once the task is created, you can always edit its properties and change any incorrect information. If you let the task run with incorrect parameters, it will fail and an error entry will be created in the Scheduled Tasks log file. If you later find that the scheduled task did not run on schedule, you can check the SchedLgU.txt log file. You can open this file by selecting **View Log** from the **Advanced** menu in the **Scheduled Tasks** window.

Deleting a Scheduled Task

Deleting a scheduled task from the Scheduled Tasks window is fairly simple but you must have the appropriate permission to do so. Right-click the **task** and select **Delete** from the context menu. This will delete the scheduled task. Remember that deleting a task from the Scheduled Tasks list does not affect the actual program or file that the task was scheduled to run.

Running a Scheduled Task Immediately

You can run a scheduled task immediately from the Scheduled Tasks window. Running a task does not affect its actual schedule. The task will still start at its scheduled time even if it has been run off-schedule. To run a task, right-click the **task** and select **Run** from the context menu.

Once the task has completed, you can view the scheduled tasks menu to check whether it completed successfully. This feature is good for testing scheduled tasks to make sure their configurations are correct. If you configure a complex task, you must perform a test run to verify that the configuration is correct. The most common configuration mistake made is incorrect specification of the username and password used to run the task. By running a task immediately after creating it, you verify that these parameters are correctly configured.

Enabling or Disabling a Scheduled Task

In some situations, you may feel that a configured task needs to be disabled for a while so that you can carry out certain changes in its configuration. This is particularly important when the task is scheduled to run very frequently. For example, you may need to disable a task that is scheduled to run every hour because you want to make changes to the script the task is running. It may take a few hours to carry out and test the changes. If the task is enabled, it will generate errors, as the task scheduler service won't be able to run the script file.

You can disable scheduled tasks from the Task Properties page. When you open it, the Task tab is displayed by default. At the bottom of this page is a check box (enabled by default) indicating that the task is enabled. Clear this check box to disable the task. The task will then be shown as Disabled in the Scheduled Tasks window. You can re-enable a disabled task by clicking the check box again.

Ending a Running Task

Stopping or ending a running task is as easy as running it from the Scheduled Tasks window. Right-click the **task** and click **End Task** in the context menu. This will immediately stop the task from running. Ending a scheduled task in this manner does not affect the task's regular schedule. The task will again start at its scheduled date and time.

Event-Based Tasks

Tasks that are scheduled to run when some system event happens are known as *event-based tasks*. These tasks are scheduled to run automatically when one of the following conditions is met:

- When the system is started
- When a user logs on to the system
- When the system is idle
- When an application triggers the task

These tasks start as soon as the event takes place and continue to run until finished. Any user who has appropriate permission can terminate them. You can configure these tasks using the Scheduled Task Wizard or the *schtasks* command-line utility.

Swiss Army Knife...

Accessing Remote Systems

If you are working in the Scheduled Task Wizard or using the *schtasks* utility to configure tasks on remote computers, you need to be aware that these utilities require that the File and Printer Sharing for Microsoft Networks service is running on all the systems where the tasks will be running. Scheduled tasks frequently require access to resources located on local or remote systems and you cannot access these resources if the File and Printer Sharing for Microsoft Networks service is not running. In Windows XP and Windows Server 2003 computers this service is installed and configured to run automatically when networking is installed. When you are troubleshooting a failed scheduled task, you should also make sure that this service is not the cause of the problem.

The schtasks Command-Line Utility

schtasks is a command-line utility that provides all the functions of the Scheduled Tasks GUI utility. It helps with creating new tasks and running them at scheduled times. You can also start and stop tasks, display the settings of a particular task, and modify tasks if required. You can query a scheduled task and delete it if it is no longer required or has completed. *schtasks* has replaced the *AT* utility, which provided similar but limited functions for scheduling tasks in older versions of the Windows operating system.

schtasks has several parameters and arguments that are required to perform a specific function using this command. These parameters are as follows:

- **schtasks /Create** Used to create new scheduled tasks.
- **schtasks /Query** Used to display the settings of an existing scheduled task.
- **schtasks /Change** Used to change or modify existing tasks.
- **schtasks /Run** Used to run tasks that have been scheduled.
- **schtasks /End** Used to stop a running scheduled task.
- **schtasks /Delete** Used to delete a scheduled task.

We discuss these commands in the following sections. If you run the *schtasks* command without any parameters on the local computer, it performs a query and returns the results shown in Figure 3.12.

Figure 3.12 Output of schtasks When Run without Parameters

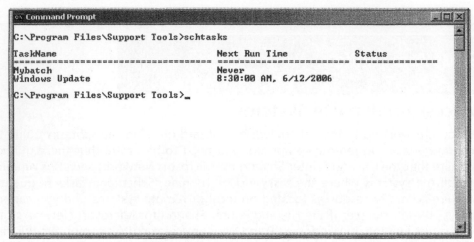

Creating and Running Tasks Using schtasks /Create

You use the *schtasks* command with the */Create* parameter to create new scheduled tasks from the command line. The task you create can be run on any computer and you can specify the username and password that the task will use to run. You also can specify a start time and end time with a predetermined interval, and schedule the task to run every minute, hour, day, week, or month as specified in the optional modifier argument */mo* used with the */sc* parameter. The syntax of this command is as follows:

```
schtasks /create /sc ScheduleType /tn TaskName /tr TaskRun [/s Computer
[/u [Domain\]User [/p Password]]] [/ru {[Domain\]User | System}] [/rp Password]
[/mo Modifier] [/d Day[,Day...] | *] [/m Month[,Month...]] [/i IdleTime] [/st
StartTime] [/ri Interval] [{/et EndTime | /du Duration} [/k]] [/sd StartDate]
[/ed EndDate]
```

We describe each parameter in the following sections.

/sc

The */sc* parameter specifies the schedule type and its frequency. The schedule types are *Minute, Hourly, Daily, Weekly, Monthly, OnIdle, Once, OnStart*, and *OnLogon*. You use this parameter with the */mo, /m*, and */d* optional parameters, known as *modifiers*, to specify the exact schedule and interval when the task should run. Table 3.1 defines different types of schedules and modifiers that you can configure.

Table 3.1 Schedule Types and Their Modifiers

Schedule Type	Description	Modifier /mo
Minute	The task runs once a minute by default. You can specify an interval in minutes.	You can set the interval as once every one to 1,439 minutes. The default interval is one minute.
Hourly	The task runs every hour by default. You can specify an interval in hours.	You can set the interval from one to 23 hours.
Daily	The task runs every day by default. You can specify an interval in days.	You can set the interval from one to 365 days.
Weekly	The task runs every week by default on the specified days. You can specify the interval in weeks.	You can set the interval from one to 52 weeks. Optionally, you can use the /d modifier to specify one or more days of week, such as Mon, Tue, Wed, Thu, Fri, Sat, and Sun. By default, the task runs every Monday (MON).
Monthly	The task runs every month by default on the specified days.	You can set the interval in months from one to 12. You use the /mo LASTDAY modifier to run the task on the last day of the specified month. Optionally, you can use the /m and /d modifiers along with the /mo modifier to specify the months and days of the month. You can set the /m modifier as JAN, FEB, and so on, and the /d modifier from one to 31 days.
Onidle	The task runs when the system is idle for a specified number of minutes. You can specify a date for the task, or the task will run automatically the next time the system is idle.	You can set the time the system should be idle before the task starts. You can set the /I modifier from one to 999 minutes. The default is 10 minutes.
Once	The task runs only once on the specified date and time.	--
Onstart	The task runs every time the system is started. You can specify a start date, or the task will run the next time the system is started.	--

Continued

Table 3.1 continued Schedule Types and Their Modifiers

Schedule Type	Description	Modifier /mo
Onlogon	The task runs whenever some user logs on to the system. You can specify a start date, or the task will run the next time any user logs on to the system.	--

/tn

The */tn* parameter specifies the name of the scheduled task. You must specify the task name for every task. It cannot be more than 238 characters in length. If the name includes blank spaces, you must enclose it in quotation marks, (e.g., *"System Backup"*).

/tr

The */tr* parameter specifies the name of the command, script, or application that is to be run on the specified schedule. You must include the complete path of the command, script, or application. The name cannot have more than 262 characters. If you do not specify the complete path, it is assumed that the command, script, or application is located in the default path—that is, %SystemRoot%\System32 folder.

/s Computer

The */s Computer* parameter specifies the name or Internet Protocol (IP) address of the remote computer on which the task is scheduled to run. (It is run on the local computer by default.) Optionally, you can use the */u* and */p* parameters for the username and password of the account that will be used to run the task on the remote computer.

/u [Domain\]User /p Password

The */u* and */p* parameters specify the username and password, respectively, for the user account that runs the scheduled task on a local or remote computer. When working in a domain, you will need to specify the domain name as well. If the password is omitted, the system will prompt you for a password when the task is run.

/ru {[Domain\]User | System}

The */ru* parameter runs the task with the permission of the specified user account. By default, the task takes the permission granted to the current user of the local computer or the user specified by the */u* parameter. Alternatively, you can use the SYSTEM account to utilize the local system account that is normally employed to run services on the computer.

/rp Password

The */rp* parameter specifies the password for the user account specified by the */ru* parameter. If you do not provide a password, the system will prompt you for one. If you are using the *SYSTEM* option with the */ru* parameter, you should not use the */rp* parameter.

/mo Modifier

The */mo* parameter specifies a modifier for the schedule type parameter, */sc*. Modifiers give you granular control over the frequency of scheduled tasks. Refer to Table 3.1 for an explanation of the different types of modifiers.

/m Month

The */m* parameter specifies the frequency of the tasks as months of the year. Valid values for *Month* are *JAN, FEB, MAR, APR, MAY, JUN, JUL, AUG, SEP, OCT, NOV*, and *DEC*. This parameter is required only if you are using the *LASTDAY* parameter.

/i IdleTime

You use the */i* parameter when you want to schedule the task to run when the system is idle for a specified number of minutes. The number of minutes can vary from one to 999. You can also set a start date. Otherwise, the task starts running the next time it finds the system idle.

/st StartTime

The */st* parameter specifies the time when the task should start on the chosen month, date, or day. You can use it with the *ONCE, MINUTE, HOURLY, DAILY, WEEKLY*, or *MONTHLY* schedule. It is required for the *ONCE* schedule.

/ri Interval

The */ri* parameter defines the repetition interval for the task. You cannot use it when you are using the *ONCE, MINUTE, HOURLY, DAILY, WEEKLY*, or *MONTHLY* schedule.

/et EndTime | /du Duration

You use the */et* and */du* parameters only with the *MINUTE* and *HOURLY* schedules; they specify the time when the task should end. By default, *EndTime* is not specified. Optionally, you can specify the duration of the task. *EndTime* and *Duration* both use the 24-hour format, *HH:MM:SS*.

/sd StartDate

/sd is an optional parameter that specifies the date when the task should start. It uses the current date on the local computer by default. The format for the */sd* parameter is *MM/DD/YYYY*. Check with your regional options to specify the correct date format.

/ed EndDate

The */ed* parameter is optional; it specifies the date when the task should end. You cannot use it with the *ONCE, ONLOGON, ONSTART,* and *ONIDLE* schedule types.

Examples of Using schtasks /Create Effectively

schtasks is one of the most complex command sets available in the Windows Server 2003 operating system. It takes a little while to get used to its different parameters. If at any point in time, you need to review the command parameters or need help using the command properly, you can type **Schtasks /?** or **Help Schtasks** at the command prompt. In this section, we have tried to provide you with some examples of how to effectively use the *schtasks /Create* command.

Scheduling a Task That Runs Only Once

The following command creates a task named *"Run Once"* and runs the batch file, Mybatch.bat, located in the C:\MyFiles folder on the local computer. The task runs only once, on June 6, 2006 at 6:00 P.M. Note that the task name has a space in it and is enclosed in quotation marks:

```
Schtasks /create /tn "Run Once" /tr C:\MyFiles\Mybatch.bat /sc once /sd 06/01/06
/st 18:00
```

If you want the *schtasks* utility to delete the task when it has completed, you can use the */z* parameter. This command is supported only in Windows Server 2003 and not on the Windows XP operating system.

Scheduling a Task That Runs When a User Logs On

The following command creates a task named *LogonTask* and runs it whenever a user logs on to the system. The task runs the file named Dskchek.bat from the C:\Utilities folder on the local computer. Note that the */sc* logon is used as the schedule type option.

```
Sctasks /create /tn LogonTask /tr C:\Utilities\Dskchek.bat /sc logon
```

Scheduling a Task That Runs When the System Starts

The following command creates a task named *"Startup Task"* and runs it every time the system starts or is restarted. The task runs a file named Dskchek.bat in the C:\Utilities folder on a remote computer named HRSvr02. Note that the */s Computer* parameter is used to specify a remote computer and that the schedule type option is used as */sc onstart*.

```
Schtasks /create /tn "Startup Task" /tr C:\Utilities\Dskchek.bat /sc onstart /s
HRSvr02
```

Scheduling a Task That Runs When the System Is Idle for 15 Minutes

The following command creates a task named *"Idle Task"* and runs a file named Mybatch.bat located in the C:\MyFiles folder on the local computer. Note that the schedule type option is specified as */sc onidle* and the */i 15* parameter specifies that the system should be idle for at least 15 minutes before the task starts.

```
Schtasks /create /tn "Idle Task" /tr C:\MyFiles\Mybatch.bat /sc onidle /i 15
```

Master Craftsman...

Specifying Names with schtasks

You should enclose all names specified with the *schtasks* command-line utility in quotation marks (" ") when there is a space in the name. This includes path names for files and folders. It is not unusual these days to have a file, folder, or computer name with two, three, or more words because most of the newer versions of Windows operating systems support long names. You may omit the quotation marks if the name is spelled as one word. For example, you do not need quotes when writing Myfile or HRServer. But when you use names such as My File or HR Server, you should enclose them in quotation marks: i.e., "My File" and "HR Server". It is good practice to always use quotes with names, regardless of whether the name contains a space. If for some reason, you forget to enclose the filename or path, the *schtasks* utility will generate an error when the task is run and will write an entry in the log file.

Scheduling a Task That Runs Every 10 Minutes

The following command creates a task named *MinTask* and runs it every 10 minutes on the local computer. The task runs a batch file named Mybatch.bat from the C:\MyFiles folder on the local computer. Note that the schedule type option is specified as */sc minute* and the interval is set at 10 minutes using the */mo 10* modifier.

```
Schtasks /create /tn MinTask /tr C:\MyFiles\Mybatch.bat /sc minute /mo 10
```

Now, check the following command, which creates a task to run every 30 minutes starting at 8:00 every night and ending the next day at 7:00 A.M. This command is useful for scheduling a task that should start after office hours and stop before the office reopens. The /st and /se parameters have been used for start and end time, respectively. In addition to this, you can set the /k parameter to stop the task at 7:00 A.M. if it is still running.

```
Schtasks /create /tn MinTask /tr C:\MyFiles\Mybatch.bat /sc minute /mo 30 /st
30:00 /et 07:00
```

Scheduling a Task That Runs Every Four Hours

The following command creates a task named *MinTask* and runs it every four hours on the local computer. The task runs a batch file named Mybatch.bat from the C:\MyFiles folder on the local computer. Note that the schedule type option is specified as /sc hourly and the interval is set at four hours using the /mo 4 modifier.

```
Schtasks /create /tn MinTask /tr C:\MyFiles\Mybatch.bat /sc hourly /mo 4
```

Scheduling a Task That Runs Every Day

The following command creates a task named *"Daily Task"* and runs it every day on the local computer. The task runs a batch file named Mybatch.bat from the C:\MyFiles folder on the local computer. Note that the schedule type option is specified as /sc daily and /sd and /ed parameters are used to specify the start and end dates, respectively. Since we are not using the /mo modifier in this command, the task will run every day with a default value of 1.

```
Schtasks /create /tn "Daily Task" /tr C:\MyFiles\Mybatch.bat /sc daily /sd
03/01/2006 /ed 09/30/2006
```

Scheduling a Task That Runs Every 10 Days

The following command creates a task named *10DayTask* and runs it every 10 days on the local computer. The task runs a batch file named Mybatch.bat from the C:\MyFiles folder on the local computer. Note that the schedule type option is specified as /sc daily with the modifier /mo 10, which means every 10 days. The /sd and /ed parameters are used to specify the start and end dates, respectively. The /st parameter specifies the time when the job should start.

```
Schtasks /create /tn 10DayTask /tr C:\MyFiles\Mybatch.bat /sc daily /mo 10 /sd
03/01/2006 /st 12:00 /ed 09/30/2006
```

Scheduling a Task That Runs Every Week on Wednesday

The following command creates a task named *WedTask* and runs it every week on Wednesday on the local computer. The task runs a batch file named Mybatch.bat from the

C:\MyFiles folder on the local computer. Note that the schedule type option is specified as /sc weekly with the modifier /d wed, which means every Wednesday.

```
Schtasks /create /tn WedTask /tr C:\MyFiles\Mybatch.bat /sc daily /d wed
```

Scheduling a Task That Runs Every Alternate Week on Monday and Friday

The following command creates a task named *2Week Task* and runs it every alternate week on Monday and Friday on the local computer. The task runs a batch file named Mybatch.bat from the C:\MyFiles folder on the local computer. Note that the schedule type option is specified as /sc weekly with the modifier /d mon,fri, which means every Wednesday and Friday. The /mo 2 modifier sets the interval at every two weeks.

```
Schtasks /create /tn 2WeekTask /tr C:\MyFiles\Mybatch.bat /sc weekly /mo 2 /d
mon,fri
```

Scheduling a Task That Runs on the First Day of Every Month

The following command creates a task named *"First of Month"* and runs it on the first day of every month on the local computer. The task runs a batch file named Mybatch.bat from the C:\MyFiles folder on the local computer. Note that the schedule type option is specified as /sc monthly. Since the /mo modifier is not used, the task defaults to the first day of every month.

```
Schtasks /create /tn "First of Month" /tr C:\MyFiles\Mybatch.bat /sc monthly
```

Scheduling a Task That Runs on the Fifteenth of Every Month

The following command creates a task named *"Day 15 Every Month"* and runs it on the fifteenth of every month on the local computer. The task runs a batch file named Mybatch.bat from the C:\MyFiles folder on the local computer. Note that the schedule type option is specified as /sc monthly. Since the /mo modifier is not used, the default interval of one month is used. The modifier /d 15 sets the task to run on the fifteenth of every month.

```
Schtasks /create /tn "Day 15 Every Month" /tr C:\MyFiles\Mybatch.bat /sc monthly
/d 15
```

Scheduling a Task That Runs on the Last Day of Every Month

The following command creates a task named *"Last Day of Month"* and runs it on the last day of every month on the local computer. The task runs a batch file named Mybatch.bat from the C:\MyFiles folder on the local computer. Note that the schedule type option is specified as */sc monthly*. The */mo lastday* modifier sets the interval to the last day of every month.

```
Schtasks /create /tn "Last Day of Month" /tr C:\MyFiles\Mybatch.bat /sc monthly
/mo lastday
```

Scheduling a Task That Runs on the Second and Fourth Friday of Every Month

The following command creates a task named *"Two Fridays"* and runs it on the second and fourth Friday of every month on the local computer. The task runs a batch file named Mybatch.bat from the C:\MyFiles folder on the local computer. Note that the schedule type option is specified as */sc monthly*. The */mo second,fourth* modifier sets the interval to the second and fourth and the */d fri* parameter sets the day to Friday.

```
Schtasks /create /tn "Two Fridays" /tr C:\MyFiles\Mybatch.bat /sc monthly /mo
second,fourth /d fri
```

In the preceding command, the weeks of the month have been specified as second and fourth with the */mo* parameter. Valid options for this modifier are *first, second, third, fourth,* and *last*.

Scheduling a Task That Runs on the Second Friday in March, June, September, and December

The following command creates a task named *"Selected Days and Months"* and runs it on the second Friday of the months of March, June, September, and December on the local computer. The task runs a batch file named Mybatch.bat from the C:\MyFiles folder on the local computer. Note that the schedule type option is specified as */sc monthly*. The */mo second* modifier sets the interval to the second and the */d fri* parameter sets the day to Friday. The */m mar,jun,sep,dec* parameter sets the months to March, June, September, and December, respectively.

```
Schtasks /create /tn "Selected Days and Months" /tr C:\MyFiles\Mybatch.bat /sc
monthly /mo second /d fri /m mar,jun,sep,dec
```

Scheduling a Task That Runs on a Remote Computer with a User Account

The following command creates a task named *"Remote Task"* to run every 30 minutes on a remote computer named HR File Server01. The task is run with the username *garyb* from the *Syngress* domain. The task starts at 8:00 every night and ends the next day at 7:00 A.M. This command is useful for scheduling a task that should start after office hours and stop before the office reopens. The */st* and */se* parameters have been used for start and end time, respectively. You can also use the */k* parameter to stop the task at 7:00 A.M. if it is still running.

```
Schtasks /create /tn "Remote Task" /s "HR File Server01" /u Syngress\Garyb /tr
C:\MyFiles\Mybatch.bat /sc minute /mo 30 /st 30:00 /et 07:00
```

In this example, we have not specified a password for the user account. The system will prompt for a password when the task starts. You can add the password using the */p* parameter but this is not recommended unless you have created a special user account for the task. You should not use the administrator account or any other account with high privileges to run a scheduled task.

TIP

Different date formats are used in different parts of the world. If you are working for a large multinational organization and are scheduling one or more tasks to run on remote computers located in different parts of the world, you need to be very careful about date formats. Microsoft Windows has three different formats for dates. They are configured according to the Locale settings in the Regional and Language Options in the Control Panel. Windows supports the following three types of date formats:

- **MM/DD/YYYY** Used for countries that use the name of the month first, then the date, followed by the year.
- **DD/MM/YYYY** Used for countries that use the date first, followed by the name of the month and then the year.
- **YYYY/MM/DD** Used for countries that use the year first, followed by the name of the month and then the date.

Before you finalize a script or schedule a task to run your script, you must make sure that the dates in the file conform to the date format used by the remote computer.

Different Forms of the /d Parameter

You might have noticed in the examples given in the preceding section that the */d* parameter is used to specify the day. The */d* parameter is used only when you use the schedule type */sc* as *weekly* or *monthly*. It is not a valid parameter for other schedule types such as *onlogon*, *once*, or *startup*. In some examples, we used *First*, *Second*, and so on, with the */d* parameter, and in other examples we used numbers such as one, two, and 15. This is because the value of the */d* parameter changes with the modifier (*/mo*). Table 3.2 lists valid values for the */d* parameter.

Table 3.2 Valid Values for the /d Parameter

Schedule Type	Modifier	Value of Day	Description
Weekly	1 to 52	MON, TUE, WED, THU, FRI, SAT, SUN	This is an optional param eter. If you include an asterisk (*), the task will be performed every day. The default value is MON.
Monthly	FIRST, SECOND, THIRD, FOURTH, LAST	MON, TUE, WED, THU, FRI, SAT, SUN	This value is required if you want the task to run on specific days.
MONTHLY	1 to 12	1 to 31	This is an optional param- eter. Use it if you are not using the /mo parameter or are using the /mo param- eter with the 1 to 12 value. The default value is 1, which means the first day of every month.

Managing Tasks with schtasks

So far, you have learned how to create new tasks from the *schtasks* command-line utility. But creating tasks is just one part of the job. It is equally important to monitor and manage these tasks. Once you have created a number of tasks for your everyday administrative functions, you will need to take time to check that the scheduled tasks are running as they should. You may also need to modify the tasks, as and when required, to meet the changing needs of your organization. In some cases, you might have to use the *schtasks* utility to immediately run a batch file or script from the command prompt. Or you may be called upon to end a running task or delete an unwanted task that is consuming resources on a particular system. In this section, we will discuss how you can perform all of these functions from the com- mand line using the *schtasks* utility.

Using schtasks /Query to Query a Scheduled Task

You use the *schtasks /Query* command to display detailed information about the scheduled tasks on a local or remote computer. It also displays any tasks that have already been com- pleted. This command helps in troubleshooting if you find that any scheduled task com- mands have not completed successfully. The syntax for the command is:

```
Schtasks [/query] [/fo {TABLE | LIST | CSV}] [/nh] [/v] [/s Computer [/u
[Domain\]User [/p Password]]]
```

The */s Computer*, */u [Domain\]User*, and */p Password* parameters are similar to the ones discussed earlier in this chapter. You can use the */u* and */p* parameters only when you use the */s* parameter. You can use either the computer name or the IP address with the */s* parameter. You use other parameters to view the advanced properties of the scheduled task. These parameters are explained in the following paragraphs.

/fo {TABLE | LIST |CSV}

You use the */fo* parameter to specify the output format. By default, the output is displayed in a TABLE format. You can also display the output in LIST or Comma Separated Value (CSV) format.

/nh

You use the */nh* parameter to hide the column headings with the output. It is valid only with the TABLE and CSV output formats.

/v

You use the */v* parameter to display the advanced properties of the scheduled task. It is valid only with the LIST and CSV formats.

Displaying the schtasks /Query Results Onscreen

When you use the *schtasks /Query* command without any parameters, it just displays a list of tasks scheduled on the computer. For example, the following output is derived from using the *schtasks /Query* command without any additional parameters:

```
Task Name                     Next Run Time              Status
------------------------      ----------------           --------
Mybatch                       Never
Windows Update                8:30:00 AM, 6/19/2006
```

When you use the same command with the */fo list* and */v* parameters, the output looks like this:

```
HostName:                     PKB-DC
TaskName:                     Mybatch
Next Run Time:                Never
Status:
Logon Mode:                   Interactive/Background
Last Run Time:                8:20:00 PM, 6/10/2006
Last Result:                  0
Creator:                      Administrator
Schedule:                     At 8:20 PM on 6/10/2006
Task To Run:                  D:\Pawan K. Bhardwaj\Command\Mybatch.bat
```

```
Start In:                             D:\Pawan K. Bhardwaj\Command
Comment:                              N/A
Scheduled Task State:                 Enabled
Scheduled Type:                       One Time Only
Start Time:                           8:20:00 PM
Start Date:                           6/10/2006
End Date:                             N/A
Days:                                 N/A
Months:                               N/A
Run As User:                          PKB-DOMAIN\Administrator
Delete Task If Not Rescheduled:       Disabled
Stop Task If Runs X Hours and X Mins: 72:0
Repeat: Every:                        Disabled
Repeat: Until: Time:                  Disabled
Repeat: Until: Duration:              Disabled
Repeat: Stop If Still Running:        Disabled
Idle Time:                            Disabled
Power Management:                     No Start On Batteries,
                                      Stop On Battery Mode
```

As you can see, the *LIST* and */v* options are very useful for collecting detailed information about scheduled tasks on a computer. In the next section, we will discuss how to save the query results in a log file.

Using Log Files for schtasks Queries

Sometimes it is not possible to view the results of an *schtasks* query onscreen. When this happens, you can run the *schtasks /Query* command and collect the results in a log file using the CSV format. In the following example, the *schtasks /Query* command collects the query results and saves them in a file named C:\MyFiles\TaskLogs\SchQuery.csv on the local computer. The */nh* parameter is used to suppress column headings from the query results and the *redirection* parameter (**>>**) sends the output to a file rather than to the command prompt window.

```
Schtasks /query /fo /nh CSV >> C:\MyFiles\TaskLogs\SchQuery.csv
```

The following example illustrates how you can use this command to collect information about the scheduled tasks on a remote computer named HRFileSvr01and save the results in a log file named C:\MyFiles\TaskLogs\SchQuery1.csv on a local computer named MyComp1. In this example, you have to specify the complete computer name and the path of the log file on the local computer because the command will run on the remote computer. If you do not specify the full path, the command will send the output to the remote computer where it is run.

```
Schtasks /query /s HRFileSrv01 /fo /nh CSV >>
\\MyComp1\C:\MyFiles\TaskLogs\SchQuery1.csv
```

Modifying a Scheduled Task with schtasks /Change

You use the *schtasks /Change* command to change one or more properties of a scheduled task. After you have scheduled one or more tasks on a local or remote computer, you may need to change some of its properties—such as the command it uses to run, its start and stop date or time, or the user account used to run the task. The *schtasks /Change* command can change one or more properties in a single command. However, you cannot change the name of the task. The command syntax is:

```
Schtasks /change /tn TaskName [/s Computer [/u [Domain\]User [/p
Password]]] [/ru {[Domain\]User | System}] [/rp Password] [/tr TaskRun] [/st
StartTime] [/ri Interval] [{/et EndTime | /du Duration} [/k]] [/sd StartDate]
[/ed EndDate] [/{ENABLE | DISABLE}] [/it] [/z]
```

You might have noticed that most of the parameters are similar to those discussed earlier with the *schtasks* command. We'll now look at some new parameters:

- **/tn Taskname** The name of the task that you want to change. If you do not know the exact name, you can use the *schtasks /Query* command to note the correct name and other properties of the task. Remember that you cannot change the name of the task. The parameter identifies only the task that you need to change.

- **/s Computer** The name or IP address of the computer where the task is scheduled to run.

- **/u [Domain\]User** The domain name and user account name used to create the task. The domain name is optional if you are working in a single domain network. You can use this parameter only with the */s* parameter.

- **/pPassword** The password of the user account specified in the */u User* parameter. You can use this parameter only with the */s* parameter.

- **/ru {[Domain\]User | System}** The name of the domain and user account that should be used to run the task. If you are using the SYSTEM account, you will not need to specify a password. You can use this parameter only with the */s* parameter.

- **/rp Password** The password of the username specified in the */ru User* parameter. The password is not required if you are using the SYSTEM user account. You can use this parameter only with the */s* parameter.

- **/tr Taskrun** The name of the command, script, batch file, or application that the task is supposed to run.

- **[/{ENABLE | DISABLE}]** Used to enable or disable the scheduled task.

- **/it** Used to configure the scheduled task so that it runs only when the user, whose account is specified in the /u or /ru parameter, is logged on to the computer. This parameter has no effect when the SYSTEM user account is used to run the task.

- **/k** Used to stop the scheduled task if it is still running when it is not supposed to be. If a task starts at 7:58 A.M. because its intervals are specified this way, and the end time is 8:00 A.M., this command will stop the task. This command is not available in Windows XP.

- **/z** Used to delete a scheduled task that has completed. You can use it for tasks that are supposed to run only once. Alternatively, you can use the *schtasks /Delete* command with the /tn parameter to identify and delete the task. This command is not available in Windows XP.

The following examples illustrate the correct syntax and usage of the *schtasks /Change* command. The first command changes the task named *"File Check"* to run a file named C:\MyFiles\FileCheck.bat on the local computer:

```
Schtasks /change /tn "File Check" /tr C:\MyFiles\FileCheck.bat
```

When the command is run, the following message is displayed:

```
SUCCESS: The parameters of the scheduled task "File Check" have been changed.
```

In the following example, we will use the same command to change the user account parameter to use the SYSTEM account, instead of the previously configured user account name using the /ru parameter:

```
Schtasks /change /tn "File Check" /ru "SYSTEM"
```

When this command is run, the following message is displayed on the screen:

```
INFO: The run as user name for the scheduled task "File Check" will be changed to
"NT AUTHORITY\SYSTEM"

SUCCESS: The parameters of the scheduled task "File Check" have been changed.
```

Master Craftsman...

Local System Account

There are three ways to specify the Local system account using the *schtasks* utility. The following three parameters have the same meaning as the */u* and */ru* parameters:

- */ru "NT AUTHORITY\SYSTEM"*
- */ru "SYSTEM"*
- */ru ""*

When you use this account, you do not have to specify a password because this highly privileged account works without one.

With any of the preceding values for the */u* or */ru* parameter, the following two messages will appear in the command shell window when the command is run:

- *INFO: The run as user name for the scheduled task "TaskName" will be changed to "NT AUTHORITY\SYSTEM"*
- *SUCCESS: The parameters of the scheduled task "TaskName" have been changed.*

Running a Scheduled Task with schtasks /Run

You can use *schtasks* to run any task, application, batch file, or script immediately from the command prompt. You use the *schtasks* command with the */Run* subcommand to run a task immediately on a local or remote computer. The syntax for this command is:

```
Schtasks /run /tn TaskName [/s Computer [/u [Domain\]User [/p
Password]]]
```

We'll now discuss the different parameters used in the command syntax:

- **/tn Taskname** Used to specify the name of the task that you want to run. If the name has spaces in it, you must enclose it in quotation marks (" "). The name identifies the task you want to run if multiple tasks are configured on the computer.

- **/s Computer** Used to identify the computer on which you want to run the task. If you do not specify a computer, the task is run on the local computer where you are using the *schtasks /Run* command. You can specify the computer with a computer name or an IP address.

- **/u[Domain\]User** Used to specify the name of the user account that runs the task. You can choose to specify the name of the domain where the computer is a member. If you do not specify a user account, the current one on the local computer is used.

- **/p Password** Specifies the password for the user account you have specified with the */u* parameter. If you do not specify a password, the system prompts you for one when you run the command.

Using the *schtasks /Run* command to run a task immediately does not affect the normal schedule of any task—if the task has been scheduled to run at regular intervals. The following examples illustrate the use of this command:

```
Schtasks /run /tn "Disk Check"
Schtasks /run /tn "Disk Check" /s "HR File Server02"
Schtasks /run /tn "Disk Check" /s 192.168.0.25 /u Syngress\garyb
```

When you run a task using the *schtasks /Run* command, it does not verify whether the task was run successfully. It only displays a message that an attempt was made. However, if there was an error running the task, an error message is displayed. To verify that the task ran successfully, you can check the log file named SchedLgU.txt in the %\SystemRoot% folder.

NOTE

It is always a good idea to test all the scripts or batch files that you create for your regular administrative jobs *before* you schedule them on the network. This is where the *schtasks /Run* command is best utilized. If the file has some errors or bugs in it, you can find and fix them immediately.

Ending Running Tasks with schtasks /End

You can stop any scheduled tasks currently running on a local computer or on a remote computer using the *schtasks /End* command. The command syntax is:

```
Schtasks /end /tn TaskName [/s Computer [/u [Domain\]User [/p
Password]]]
```

All the parameters for the *schtasks /End* command are similar to those for the *schtasks /Run* command. For example, if a task named *"Disk Check"* is running, you can stop it using the following command:

```
Schtasks /end /tn "Disk Check" /s 192.168.0.25 /u Syngress\garyb
```

When the command is run, the following message is displayed:

```
SUCCESS: The scheduled task "Disk Check" has been terminated
successfully.
```

Deleting Scheduled Tasks with schtasks /Delete

When a scheduled task has completed and is no longer needed, you can delete it using the *schtasks /Delete* command. The command only deletes the scheduled task—it does not affect the actual file that it is running. The command syntax is as follows:

schtasks /delete /tn {TaskName | *} [**/f**] [**/s** Computer [**/u** [Domain\]User [**/p** Password]]]

Most of the parameters in this command are similar to the earlier commands. You can use this command on a local computer as well as on a remote one. For example, the following command deletes the task named *"Disk Check"* from a computer with the IP address 192.168.0.25 using the *garyb* account in the *Syngress* domain:

```
Schtasks /delete /tn "Disk Check" /s 192.168.0.25 /u Syngress\garyb
```

When this command is issued at the command prompt, the following warning message appears:

```
WARNING: Are you sure you want to delete the task "Disk Check" (Y/N)?
```

When you press the **Y** key, the task is deleted and the following message is displayed:

```
SUCCESS: The scheduled task "Disk Check" was successfully deleted.
```

You can use the */f* parameter to force the command to delete the scheduled task without displaying the warning message. If you want to delete all scheduled tasks from the computer, you can use the * key, as in the following example:

```
Schtasks /delete /tn * /s 192.168.0.25 /u Syngress\garyb
```

This will delete all scheduled tasks from a computer with the IP address 192.168.0.25 (after you press **Y** in response to the warning message).

Master Craftsman...

The Warning Prompt

In both of the examples given here, we have not provided the password for the user account garyb. Exercise caution when using the schtasks /End, schtasks /Change, and schtasks /Delete commands. If you provide the password along with the command and use the /f option, you will not get a chance to review your action, and the scheduled task will be deleted without prompting you for a password or displaying the warning message.

Summary

In this chapter, we discussed the task scheduler service, the Scheduled Tasks GUI, and the *schtasks* command-line utility. All scheduled tasks in Windows computers depend on the task scheduler service. If this service is not running, you will not be able to schedule any script or application to run automatically. The Scheduled Task Wizard is a perfect tool for scheduling tasks to run at predetermined schedules (such as hourly, daily, weekly, or monthly). The Scheduled Tasks window shows all tasks scheduled on a computer, regardless of the tool they were created with. You can enable/disable a task, run it immediately, end a running task, or edit the properties of a task to make changes in its schedule or the program it runs. *schtasks* is a command-line counterpart of the Scheduled Tasks GUI. *schtasks* replaces the older *AT* command, which is still supported in Windows XP and Windows Server 2003. You can use both the Scheduled Tasks GUI and *schtasks* interchangeably. *schtasks* has a set of subcommands to create, change, delete, query, run, or end a task. *schtasks* is considered to be one of the most complex command sets in Windows. But once you understand the syntax of this command, it becomes one of the easiest ones to use.

Part II
Basic Windows
Administration

Chapter 4

Managing Files and Directories

Topics in this chapter:

- **Using Wildcards in Commands**
- **File and Folder Attributes**
- **Basic File and Folder Operations**
- **Duplicating and Comparing Disks**
- **Directory-Specific Commands**

☑ **Summary**

☑ **Solutions Fast Track**

☑ **Frequently Asked Questions**

Introduction

As an administrator, you cannot escape from regular network file and folder maintenance tasks, even though these tasks are easy enough for normal users or help desk employees to perform. You may be required to maintain files and folders on servers and other critical computers on the network, including yours, that nobody else can handle. Many of the tasks related to file and folder maintenance are very easy, and although you can handle them using graphical user interfaces (GUIs) such as Windows Explorer, you may find that using GUIs is very time-consuming and that using the command line is a better option. Moreover, when you want to streamline your administrative jobs by using batch files, you will definitely need to know how to create files and folders using simple commands and how you can use these commands in your batch files or scripts.

This chapter discusses the commands you can use for everyday file and folder maintenance tasks. You might already be familiar with several of them, but you might not be aware of their complete functionality. This chapter begins with a discussion on using wildcards in filenames, and explains file and folder attributes as well as some of the common commands used to copy, move, and delete files. You can use certain commands, such as *Xcopy*, with both files and directories. We will also discuss some commands for expanding and comparing files. If you work with floppy disks or CD-ROMs, you will find the section relating to duplicating and comparing disks useful. Finally, we will discuss some commands that you can use with directories only.

NOTE

Throughout this book, we use the words *folder* and *directory* interchangeably. In fact, they have the same meaning. Both refer to the section on a hard drive, or any removable media such as a floppy drive or a CD-ROM, where files can be stored in an organized fashion. When working with older DOS systems, the words *directory* and *subdirectory* are commonly used. In the Windows environment, the words *folder* and *subfolder* are used, though they have the same meaning. So a directory refers to a folder, whereas a subdirectory refers to a subfolder. These terms are used interchangeably in the entire book.

Using Wildcards in Commands

We cannot start a discussion on managing files and directories (folders) without first introducing wildcards. It is very difficult to work with files and directories without using wildcards, especially when working on the command line. A *wildcard* or a *wildcard character* is a keyboard character that helps you determine the complete name of a file, folder, printer, or other resource on the local or remote computer. This is useful when you either do not want to type the entire name of a file or you know only a few characters of the file or folder name. Wildcards are also useful when you want to work with a group of files and directories.

Windows supports two types of wildcard characters: asterisks (*) and question marks (?). You use the asterisk to replace one or more characters (or even no characters) in the name of the file or folder. You use the question mark to replace only a single character in the name. The following examples illustrate the use of both types of wildcards with the *Dir* command.

```
Dir My*
Dir My*.*
```

Either of the preceding commands will list all files that start with the characters "My" and have extensions, such as Myreport.txt, Myaccount.doc, and Myfile.bat. This is useful when you know only the first few characters of the filename.

```
Dir My*.txt
```

This command will narrow down the directory listing to only those files that start with the characters "My", with .txt as the extension. This is useful when you know that the file you are looking for is definitely one with a .txt extension.

```
Dir Myfile?.*
```

This command will replace only the last missing character of the filename. The directory listing will contain files such as Myfiles.doc, Myfile1.txt, and Myfile5.zip. Since the command contains only six characters in the filename and a question mark as the wildcard, it will add only one more character to the file search. The directory will not list Myfilephotos.doc, since its name has more than seven characters. Now, look at another example:

```
Dir Myfil??.*
```

This command will look for two more characters after the characters "Myfil" to replace the two question marks. The directory listing will include all files with any type of extension where the first five characters are "Myfil."

Wildcards are commonly used in scripts and batch files to ease file searching or to apply a single command to multiple files. Wildcards are handy tools that simplify use of the command line.

File and Folder Attributes

Each file has a defined set of properties that describe several elements, including the owner of the file or directory, security settings, assigned permissions, the date of creation, and the last modification date. A file or directory may be archived or it may be stored in a compressed or encrypted state. Although some of the attributes are available on File Allocation

Table (FAT), FAT32, and New Technology File System (NTFS) file systems, other attributes such as file compression and encryption are available *only* on NTFS. The attributes of a file or directory are a part of its larger set of properties. If a file is marked as read-only, this is known as one of its attributes. Other attributes of the file might include its being defined as a hidden or a system file. You manage file attributes from the command line using the *Attrib* command, which allows you to view, add, change, and remove file attributes. The syntax of this command is:

```
attrib [[Drive:][Path] FileName] [{+r | -r}] [{+h | -h}] [{+s | -s}]
[{+a | -a}] [/s[/d]]
```

You use the *[[Drive:][Path] FileName]* parameters to specify the correct path of the file. If the file is located in the current working directory, you may omit the path. As discussed earlier, you can also use wildcards such as * and ? with filenames. Table 4.1 explains other parameters you can use with the *Attrib* command.

Table 4.1 Parameters for Use with the Attrib Command

Parameters	Description
+r or −r	Sets the read-only attribute of the file or folder. You cannot modify a file or folder with a read-only attribute without first removing the attribute. The +r parameter sets the attribute and the −r parameter removes it.
+h or −h	Sets the hidden attribute of the file or folder. A hidden file or folder is not visible in Windows Explorer unless the **Show hidden files** option is selected in the folder options. The +h parameter sets the attribute and the −h parameter removes it.
+s or −s	Sets the system attribute of the file. The +s parameter sets the attribute as read-only and the −s parameter removes it.
+a or −a	Sets the archive attribute of the file. Backup applications use this attribute to check whether the file has changed since the last backup. The +a parameter sets the attribute and the −a parameter removes it.
/s	Applies attributes to all files and subdirectories in the current directory.
/d	Applies attributes to all directories.

Viewing Attributes

You can view the attributes of a file or directory using the *Attrib* command without any parameters. In the following example, the attributes of a file named Mybatch.bat located in the C:\MyFiles folder are displayed using the *Attrib* command:

```
Attrib C:\MyFiles\Mybatch.bat
```

If you do not specify a filename, the *Attrib* command will display the attributes of all files in the current directory. You can also use wildcards to view the attributes of multiple files. For example, the following command shows the attributes of all files with a .txt extension in the C:\Reports folder:

```
Attrib C:\Reports\*.txt
```

Changing Attributes

You can use the *Attrib* command with files as well as with directories. It is a simpler way to change the attributes of multiple files instead of performing the same task using Windows Explorer (where you have to navigate to each file or folder to change its attributes). Simply use the *Attrib* command with an appropriate parameter and a correct **+** or **−** sign and you are done. For example, the following command changes the read-only attribute of the HRReport.doc file in the D:\HRFiles folder to make it read-only:

```
Attrib +r D:\HRFiles\HRReport.doc
```

The following command will change the attributes of all files with .log extensions in the C:\Logs folder to hidden:

```
Attrib +h C:\Logs\*.log
```

The following command will clear the read-only attribute of all files and subdirectories in C:\MyFiles\Scripts. Note the use of the */s* parameter:

```
Attrib -r C:\MyFiles\Scripts\*.* /s
```

Basic File and Folder Operations

Copying files and folders are probably the most common operations you perform on a regular basis. While you can use commands with their simple syntax, a thorough knowledge of the complete syntax of any command makes life on the command line even easier. You can use certain commands with files only, and you can use some for both files and folders. This section discusses both types. You can copy files using either the *Copy* command or the *Xcopy* command. You can use the *Xcopy* command for copying both files and directories. It is important to know the correct syntax and use of these and other commands in order to make the most of the Windows command line.

In the following sections, we have included examples to explain the proper use of commands so that you can use them in your batch files and scripts. Commands such as *Xcopy* and *Diskcomp* have their own set of exit codes that indicate the commands' success or problem status. They are normally used in batch files with the *Errorlevel* parameter for conditional processing using the *if* and *goto* statements. We have included these exit codes for quick reference wherever applicable.

Copying Files with the Copy Command

You use the *Copy* command to copy one or more files from one location. You can use it to copy files from one directory to another on the local computer or on the mapped network drive of another computer. You can also use this command to copy files to devices such as LPT1 or COM1 in binary format. The syntax of this command is:

```
Copy [/d] [/v] [/n] [{/y | /-y}] [/z] [{/a | /b}] Source [{/a | /b}] [+
Source [{/a | /b}] [+ ...]] [Destination [{/a | /b}]]
```

Table 4.2 explains these parameters.

Table 4.2 Parameters for Use with the Copy Command

Parameter	Description
/d	Used if the source file is encrypted. The command will copy the file and save it at the destination as a decrypted file.
/v	Used to verify that the files are copied and written to the destination correctly. Then the destination file is compared to the source file to verify that both files are identical. This parameter slows down the copy operation for large files because each part of the destination file must be compared to its corresponding source.
/n	Used to copy the file with a shorter name, as per the 8.3 filename format. If the source filename is longer than eight characters or the extension is longer than three characters, a shorter name is used for the destination file.
/y or /-y	You use the /y parameter to suppress the warning message when the file being copied will overwrite an existing file with the same name at the destination. By default, the message is displayed. You use the /-y parameter to display the warning message if it has been suppressed earlier in a batch file by the /y parameter.
/z	Used to copy files from a network destination in a resume mode. If the connection is lost during the file copy operation, it is resumed when the connection is available again.
/a or /b	You use the /a parameter to copy the specified file in ASCII text format. The /b parameter indicates that the file will be copied in binary format. Most files fall into the binary category.
+	Used when you want to combine more than one file into a single file at the destination.
Source	The location of the file that you want to copy. You specify the source as a drive letter (or a networked drive letter), a colon, a directory, and the filename. You can use wildcards with filenames.
Destination	The destination where you want to copy the file. You specify the source as a drive letter (or a networked drive letter), a colon, a directory, and the filename.

Copying a Single File

You can copy a file from the source location to the destination location by using the *Copy* command, as shown in the following examples.

```
Copy Report1.txt C:\Reports
```

The preceding command will copy the file named Report1.txt to the C:\Reports folder. The name of the destination file will be the same as the source file.

```
Copy C:\Reports\Report1.txt D:\OldReps
```

This command will copy the file named Report1.txt from the C:\Reports folder to the D:\OldReps folder. The name of the destination file will be the same as the source file.

```
Copy Report1.txt Report2.txt
```

This command will make a copy of the file named Report1.txt and save it as Report2.txt in the same drive and folder.

From these examples, it is clear that the source and destination locations are specified as a drive letter, a colon, a directory, and the filename. If no source location is specified, the current working drive and directory are assumed as the source. Similarly, if no destination location is specified, the current drive and directory are assumed as the destination. If you have specified a destination directory that does not exist, the *Copy* command will create a new directory with the specified name.

Now, see what happens when you use the following command:

```
Copy C:\Reports\Report1.txt
```

You will get the following error message:

```
The file cannot be copied onto itself.
0 File(s) copied.
```

The message is displayed because you did not specify a different destination location and the command interpreter is smart enough to know that you are trying to copy the file onto itself, which is impossible.

You can also use a mapped network drive as the source or destination. When you use a mapped drive, you should also include the /z option if you are copying files over an unreliable wide area network (WAN) link.

NOTE

The *Copy* command cannot copy any file that has zero bytes or no data in it. This type of file is known as an *empty file*. Use the *Xcopy* command to copy empty files.

Choosing the ASCII (/a) or Binary (/b) Format

You can use the ASCII or binary format to copy files by using the /a and /b parameters, respectively, with the *Copy* command. By default, all files are copied using the binary format. In other words, the command uses the /b parameter, regardless of whether you specify it. You use the /a parameter with ASCII files that contain an end-of-file character (**Ctrl + Z**) to indicate the end of the file. If you use the /a parameter before a filename, the following source files are treated as ASCII text until the /b parameter is found in the command. The effect of the /a and /b parameters in the *Copy* command depends on their position in the command, as explained in the following list:

- If you use the /a parameter before a filename or a list of filenames, all files following this parameter are treated as ASCII text until the command interpreter finds a /b parameter in the command. The /b parameter applies only to the file preceding it.

- If the /a parameter follows a filename or a list of filenames, all files are treated as ASCII text until the command interpreter finds a /b parameter in the command. The /b parameter applies only to the file preceding it.

- When you use /a in the destination, the command interpreter adds an end-of-file character (**Ctrl + Z**) to the destination file.

- When you use /b in the destination, the command interpreter does not add an end-of-file character (**Ctrl + Z**) to the destination file.

As discussed earlier, if you do not use the /a parameter, the command interpreter will treat all files as binary text. The ASCII text format works faster but it causes loss of file formats.

Appending Multiple Files to a Single File

The *Copy* command allows you to add data from multiple files and write it to a single file at the destination. You can separate several source files with a plus sign (**+**); all the files will be combined to make one file at the destination. In the following example, files named Report1.txt, Report2.txt, and Report3.txt are used as source files separated with a +. These files will be combined using the *Copy* command and written to a single file named ComboRep.txt at the destination specified as the D:\FinalRep folder.

```
Copy Report1.txt + Report2.txt + Report3.txt D:\FinalRep\ComboRep.txt
```

When you do not specify the destination location, the destination file is written to the current folder. When you do not specify the destination filename, the destination filename is taken as the name of the first file you specify in the *Copy* command. In the following example, three files named Report.txt, Report1.txt, and Report2.txt are combined to make one destination file named Report.txt, which is the name of the first file in the list because the destination filename is not specified:

```
Copy Report.txt + Report2.txt + Report3.txt D:\FinalRep
```

You can also use wildcards to combine several source files into one. The following two examples show how to do this. The first command combines all files with a .txt extension and writes them to a destination file named ComboRep.txt in the D:\FinalRep folder. The second command combines all files whose first six characters are "Report" and whose extension is .txt to make one file at the destination:

```
Copy *.txt D:\FinalRep\ComboRep.txt
Copy Report?.txt D:\FinalRep\ComboRep.txt
```

Copying Files to and from Devices

You can specify the source and destination in the *Copy* command as devices such as COM1 and LPT1, instead of as files or folders. In this case, the command either takes the input from a device or writes to it. When copying to and from a device, you must use the **Ctrl + Z** character to mark the end of the file. This character is shown in the command-line window as ^Z but is not sent to the destination device. The following sections discuss the supported devices you can use with the *Copy* command.

CON

CON stands for console and refers to the keyboard and the monitor. You can input any file by typing it on the keyboard while the monitor displays the output. When you finish typing, just press **Ctrl + Z** to indicate the end of the file.

PRN

PRN stands for printer and you can use it only as a destination with the *Copy* command. You specify the destination of a file as a printer connected to any of the computer's ports. If the computer is using a network printer, the port can be local or networked. When copying a file to the printer, you can insert a **Ctrl + L** character to print only a part of the file.

LPT

LPT refers to devices that are connected to the system's parallel ports (typically printers), connected to the computer's LPT1 through LPT4 ports. You can specify these devices only as destinations with the *Copy* command. As with PRN, the port can be either local or networked.

COM

COM refers to devices connected to the computer's communications ports (serial ports), from COM1 through COM4. The devices can be modems, keyboards, a mouse, or even a printer. Unlike with the PRN and LPT ports, you can specify the COM port as both source (input) and destination (output) with the *Copy* command.

NUL

A NUL device refers to a NULL device. When you use the NUL device as a destination with the *Copy* command, the command interpreter does not copy the output to any destination. NUL is actually a nonexisting device for the *Copy* command.

When you use a device as the destination for the *Copy* command, you should use the */b* parameter so that all data is sent to the device in binary mode. All special characters including **Ctrl + Z**, **Ctrl + C**, and **Ctrl + S** are copied to the device. If you omit the */b* parameter, the *Copy* command sends the data in ASCII text mode. In ASCII mode, the *Copy* command may combine all files at the destination. To avoid this situation, it is best to use the */b* parameter with devices (unless you have a reason to use the default ASCII mode).

Swiss Army Knife...

Windows Explorer versus the Command Line

People generally use Windows Explorer to copy, move, rename, or delete files on the computer. But using the command line certainly has its own advantages. For example, you can use the *Copy* command to copy files to devices such as LPT1 and COM1 in binary format. When you are copying files from a mapped network drive and the connection is lost, you can use the */z* parameter to resume the copy operation from the point at which the connection was lost. This is a functionality you do not get with Windows Explorer. The flexibility of the command line makes it extremely useful in batch files.

Copying Files and Directories with the Xcopy Command

While the *Copy* command is good for copying a single file—and even multiple files—using wildcards, the *Xcopy* command is more versatile and has several parameters that provide flexibility in copying files, subdirectories, and directories in bulk. This command has built-in exit codes that you can use in batch files to handle errors during the file copy process. The *Xcopy* command's flexibility makes it very popular among administrators who love writing batch files or scripts. The syntax of this command is:

```
Xcopy Source [Destination] [/p] [/c] [/w] [/v] [/q] [/f] [/l] [/g]
[/d[:MM-DD-YYYY]] [/u] [/i] [/s [/e]] [/t] [/k] [/r] [/h] [/o] [/n] [/x] [{/a |
/m}] [/exclude:FileName1[+[FileName2]][+[FileName3]]
```

Table 4.3 explains the different parameters of the *Xcopy* command.

Table 4.3 Parameters for Use with the Xcopy Command

Parameter	Description
/p	Used to prompt a confirmation message before creating each file at the destination.
/c	Used to continue copying even when the command encounters errors while the files are being copied. By default, the command interpreter will stop the *Xcopy* command when errors are encountered.
/w	Displays the following message before starting the copy process: *Press any key to begin copying file(s)*
	You can use this parameter to allow a user to insert or change a floppy disk before the command starts copying files. This command is useful when copying a large number of files to floppy disks.
/v	Used to verify that the file is copied and written to the destination correctly. The destination file is compared to the source file to verify that both are identical. This parameter slows down the copying of large files because each part of the destination file must be compared to its corresponding source file part after writing to the destination file.
/q	Used to suppress the display of *Xcopy* command messages. The messages usually contain filenames that are being copied.
/f	Used to display the names of source and destination files while copying files, including their full paths. By default, the command displays only the filenames.
/l	Used when a list of files that are to be copied is displayed, but the files are not actually copied.
/g	Used to store files in a decrypted state at the destination. It is a useful option when the destination does not support encryption.
/d:[MM-DD-YYYY]	Used to copy only those files that have changed since the specified date in MM-DD-YYYY format. Files older than the specified date are not copied. If you do not specify the date but use only the /d parameter, the command copies only those files that are newer than the existing files at the destination. This option is good for updating existing files at the destination.
/u	Used to copy only those files from the source that already exist at the destination.

Continued

Table 4.3 continued Parameters for Use with the Xcopy Command

Parameter	Description
/I	Used to let *Xcopy* know that the destination name is a directory when the source is a directory and the destination directory does not exist. *Xcopy* then creates a directory and copies all files into it. If you do not use this parameter, the *Xcopy* command will prompt you as to whether the destination is a directory. If used in a batch file, this will cause the file to pause and wait for user input.
/s	Used to copy the directory and all subdirectories. Empty directories are not copied. Without this parameter, the *Xcopy* command assumes that the destination is a single directory.
/e	Used to copy all subdirectories, including empty ones. The /e parameter is used with the /s and /t parameters.
/t	Used to copy only the subdirectory structure (known as the *Tree*) but does not actually copy any files. You can use the /e parameter to copy empty directories.
/k	Used to retain the read-only attributes of files and directories after copying them to the destination. By default, the *Xcopy* command removes the read-only attributes.
/r	Used to copy files to the destination, even when the destination has files marked with read-only attributes. By default, the *Xcopy* command does not copy files onto the destination if the destination files have read-only attributes.
/h	Used to copy files to the destination, even when the source files are marked with hidden attributes. By default, the *Xcopy* command treats files with hidden attributes as system or confidential data and does not copy them.
/o	Used to copy the ownership and discretionary access control list (DACL) information with the files. You use a DACL to set security permissions for files and directories. Without this parameter, the files will inherit the access control settings of the destination directory.
/n	Used when you are copying files from an NTFS volume to a FAT file system volume. NTFS uses long filenames; the /n parameter converts them to the short filename format or the 8.3 format while copying to the FAT file system volume. This parameter also works if the destination is an NTFS volume.
/x	Used to copy the system access control list (SACL) and audit settings of the source files.

Continued

Table 4.3 continued Parameters for Use with the Xcopy Command

Parameter	Description
/a or /m	The /a parameter copies only those files that have their archive bits set. It does not change them. The /m parameter, on the other hand, copies the files which have their archive bits set but removes the archive bits after copying them to the destination. You can use only one of these parameters in a single command.
Exclude: FileName1 [+ [FileName2] [+FileName3]...	Specifies a file or a list of files to be excluded from copying. This parameter can be a file or a string.

Besides the parameters given in Table 4.3, you can use also the following ones (which are similar to the *Copy* command):

- You use the /y parameter to suppress a prompt that confirms whether you want to overwrite an existing file.

- You use the /z parameter to start the *Xcopy* command in resume mode. If you are copying files over an unreliable network link, you should use this option. If the link is broken while the files are being copied, copying can resume when the connection is reestablished.

- As with the *Copy* command, you can use the plus sign (+) to combine multiple files into one file at the destination. You can also use wildcards to combine multiple files.

Specifying Source and Destination

You specify the source drive and directory in the regular *[Drive: [FileName]]* format. You can use wildcards to specify source files. It is important to remember the following:

- If you do not specify a source drive and directory, the current drive and directory are assumed as the source location.

- If you do not specify a destination drive and directory, the current directory is assumed as the destination.

- If the specified destination does not contain an existing directory and a backslash sign (\) is not included with the specified destination, the following message displays:

```
Does destination specify a file name or directory name on the target
(F=file, D=Directory)?
```

If you want the files to be copied to a file, press the **F** key. Press the **D** key if you want to copy the files to a directory. You can suppress this message using the */i* option, at which point the *Xcopy* command assumes that the destination is a directory when the source contains multiple files and directories.

Excluding Files from the Copy Process

You can exclude certain files from the source drive and directory by using the */exclude* parameter. This is particularly useful when you are using the *Xcopy* command and you want to give some files to a user but do not want certain confidential files to be copied. Or you may want to exclude certain larger files that will not fit onto one floppy disk. To exclude just one or two files, use a + to separate the filenames.

You can specify as a string the file or list of files to be excluded from the copying process. For example, if you specify the string as *\Reports*, all files in the Reports directory will be excluded. On the other hand, if you specify the string as *.doc* using the */exclude* parameter, all files with a .doc extension will be excluded.

Examples of Using the Xcopy Command

The following examples explain the correct use of the *Xcopy* command.

```
Xcopy a: b: /s /e /h
```

The preceding command copies all files and subdirectories, including hidden files, from the A: drive to the B: drive. The */e* parameter will force the command to copy empty subdirectories, and the */h* parameter will enable the copying of hidden files.

```
Xcopy C:\Reports\NewReps D:\Reports /d:06-30-2006
```

This command will copy all files from the C:\Reports\NewReps source directory to the destination specified as D:\Reports. You use the */d* parameter to specify that only the files that have changed since June 30, 2006 should be copied.

```
Xcopy C:\Reports\NewReps D:\Reports /d:06-30-2006 /l >CopyList.txt
```

In this example, we added the */l* parameter to get a list of files, but we are not copying them. The output of the file has been redirected to a file named CopyList.txt.

```
Xcopy C:\Reports\NewReps N:\AllReps /s /e /k /p
```

This command will copy all files and subdirectories from the C:\Reports\NewReps directory to a networked destination drive N: in the directory named AllReps. The */s* and */e* parameters copy all files and subdirectories, including empty ones. The */k* parameter retains the read-only attribute of the files after copying and the */p* parameter forces the *Xcopy* command to prompt the user before creating each file and directory at the destination.

Xcopy Exit Codes

The *Xcopy* command is very flexible and versatile. It works with a combination of several parameters, giving you full control of the file and directory copy process. When you use the *Xcopy* command in a batch file or script, the script may produce some errors if it is not formatted using correct syntax or because of some incorrect parameter. The command has a set of exit codes that you can use in your batch files using the *Errorlevel* parameter. This will help you to handle errors appropriately when the file is executed. Table 4.4 lists these exit codes.

Table 4.4 Exit Codes for Use with the Xcopy Command

Exit Code	Description
0	No error was encountered during the file copy process.
1	The command did not find any files to copy.
2	The user pressed the **Ctrl + C** key combination to terminate the file copy process.
4	An initialization error occurred. Incorrect command syntax, invalid source or destination drives, and insufficient memory or insufficient disk space all result in an initialization error.
5	There was an error writing to the disk. For example, the disk may be write protected.

Example Batch File with Xcopy Exit Codes

The following is an example of a batch file named Copyall.bat that can be used to copy all files and subdirectories from the source drive to the destination drive. The variables *%1* and

%2 are used to input source and destination drives, respectively. The *Xcopy* command in the file uses the */s* and */e* parameters. Depending on the exit codes for the *Xcopy* command, the file has three different sections or subroutines to handle the situation appropriately using the *Errorlevel* parameters. The *if* and *goto* parameters are used as decision-making statements depending on the type of exit code the batch file encounters when it is executed. Each of the three different labels (*Lowspace, Abort,* and *End*) identifies the three subroutines in the file.

```
@Echo off
Rem This file is named COPYALL.bat
Rem It copies all files in all subdirectories of the
Rem Source drive or directory (%1) to the
Rem Destination drive or directory (%2).
Rem It copies only those files that exist on destination.

Xcopy %1 %2 /s /e

If errorlevel 0 goto End
If errorlevel 2 goto Abort
If errorlevel 4 goto Lowspace

:Lowspace
Echo Insufficient space on the destination drive,
Echo Invalid destination drive or
Echo Incorrect command-line syntax.
Goto End

:Abort
Echo You have opted to abort the copy process by pressing CTRL+C keys.
Goto End

:End
```

You can run this file from the command prompt by running the file named Copyall.bat as follows:

```
Copyall.bat C:\TstFiles B:
```

You do not always have to use the .bat extension when running batch files because batch files are considered executables. When file execution starts it replaces the *%1* variable with a value of *C:\TstFiles* and the *%2* variable with a value of *B:*. If there is no error, the *Xcopy* command will use the */s* and */e* parameters to copy all files and subdirectories from the source to the destination, which is the B: drive. If it encounters an error, it will read the *Errorlevel* values and jump to an appropriate subroutine in the file identified by the label specified in the *goto* statement.

Renaming Files with the Rename (Ren) Command

You can rename files and directories using the *Rename* or *Ren* command. You can give a different name to an existing file and use the free name for another document. Renaming files becomes necessary when you want to reuse existing filenames for your new documents. The syntax of this command is:

```
Rename [Drive:][Path] FileName1 FileName2
Ren [Drive:][Path] FileName1 FileName2
```

FileName1 is the existing name of the file and *FileName2* is the new name that you want to assign to the file. If you do not specify a drive letter and path, the current drive and directory are assumed. The following example illustrates the use of this command:

```
Rename MyDoc.txt MyDoc1.txt
Ren D:\Tests\OldTest.doc OldTest.txt
```

In the first line, the file named MyDoc.txt is renamed to MyDoc1.txt. Since the drive letter and path are not specified, the command interpreter assumes that the file is stored in the current working directory. In the second line, we are using the *Ren* command to rename a file from OldTest.doc to OldTest.txt in the D:\Tests directory. Now, consider the following example:

```
Rename C:\Reports\*.doc *.txt
```

This command changes the extension of all files in the C:\Reports folder from .doc to .txt. If the new name you specify for the file already exists in the directory, the command will not work and will return the following error message:

```
Duplicate file name or file not found.
```

Remember that you cannot specify different drives and directories for the *FileName1* and *FileName2* parameters. This means that both files should be located in the same drive and directory. You cannot use the *Rename* command to copy or move files and then rename them. If you rename an encrypted file, the renamed file retains the encryption status of the file.

Moving Files Using the Move Command

You can move one or more files from one directory to another using the *Move* command. The source and destination are specified with the command. When a file is moved from the source location, it is copied to the destination before being deleted from the source location. This is different from the *Copy* and *Xcopy* commands, where the original files(s) at the source are retained as is. The syntax of this command is:

```
Move [{/y | /-y}] [Source] [Destination]
```

The *Source* and *Destination* parameters define the drive and directory for the source files and destination files, respectively. You use the */y* parameter to suppress the warning message that appears if a duplicate file is found at the destination. You use the */-y* parameter if you want to make sure that any existing files at the destination are not accidentally overwritten. You can use either */y* or */-y*, but not both in a single command.

If you are trying to move encrypted files from the source to another location that does not support encryption, the command displays an error message. This usually happens when you try to move encrypted files to a non-NTFS volume or to a floppy drive that does not support encryption. The resulting file will be decrypted. To work around this problem, you must decrypt the files before moving them.

As with other commands, you can use wildcards with the *Move* command. The following examples illustrate the use of the *Move* command:

```
Move C:\Tests\Mar*.* D:\Final
Move C:\Reports\*.doc \OldReps\
```

In the first line, all files whose names start with Mar in the C:\Tests directory are moved to the D:\Final directory. The command in the second line will move all files with a .doc extension to another directory named \OldReps on the same drive (since we did not specify the drive name in the destination).

Master Craftsman...

Copying and Moving Encrypted Files

Copying and moving encrypted files to different directories or different volumes on the computer has different effects on the destination file, depending on several factors. The destination file may or may not remain encrypted. When you are copying or moving encrypted files, the following points are important to remember:

- When you copy or move encrypted files to a volume that does not support encryption (such as a FAT file system volume or other non-NTFS volume), the encryption is lost.

- Copying or moving files from an encrypted folder to a folder that is not encrypted does not decrypt them. The files retain their encrypted status unless the destination folder is located in a FAT file system volume or other non-NTFS volume.

- When you copy or move files to an encrypted folder, the files get encrypted using the encryption properties of the destination folder.

Deleting Files with the Del (Erase) Command

You can delete unwanted files from a system by using the *Del* or *Erase* command. In Windows XP and Windows Server 2003, the syntax and functionality of both commands are similar. You cannot recover files you've deleted with the *Del* or *Erase* command. The syntax of these commands is:

```
Del [Drive:][Path] FileName [ ...] [/p] [/f] [/s] [/q] [/a[:Attributes]]
Erase [Drive:][Path] FileName [ ...] [/p] [/f] [/s] [/q] [/a[:Attributes]]
```

As with other commands, you use the *[Drive:][Path] FileName* parameter to specify the full path of the file or files to be deleted. Table 4.5 explains other parameters of the *Del* and *Erase* commands.

Table 4.5 Parameters for Use with the Del and Erase Commands

Parameter	Description
/p	Used to display a confirmation prompt before deleting the file (or each file when multiple files are specified).
/f	Used to force deletion of files marked with read-only attributes. By default, if a file is marked read-only, the user is prompted to confirm whether the file should be deleted.
/s	Used to delete all files from the current directory and all subdirectories. The name of each file is displayed as it is deleted.
/q	Used to let the command work in quiet mode. The user is not prompted for confirmation.
/a[:Attributes]	Used to delete all files with a specified attribute. The file attribute may be set as *Read-only*, *Archive*, *Hidden*, or *System*.

If you want to delete multiple files, you can use either wildcards or the */a* parameter that deletes all files that have the specified attribute. Please refer to the "File and Folder Attributes" section earlier in this chapter for more information. The following example shows how you can use wildcards to delete multiple files:

```
Del C:\Reports\Mar*.* /p
```

When this command is run, all files that have filenames whose first three characters are "Mar" are selected for deletion, regardless of their extension, because a wildcard is being used for the extension as well. The */p* parameter forces the command to display a confirmation prompt before deleting the file. The name of each file is displayed and you will need to press the **Y** or **N** key to specify whether you want to delete the file. This feature is very helpful for deleting selective files. The confirmation prompt reads:

```
FileName, Delete (Y/N)?
```

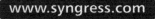

If you want to delete all files in a directory, just specify the drive and directory name with the command (*without* specifying any filenames). This will delete all files in the specified folder. For example, the following command deletes all files in the D:\Reports folder. The /q parameter is used to suppress confirmation prompts:

```
Del D:\Reports /q
```

Since you cannot recover files deleted with the *Del* or *Erase* command, it is better to either display a list of the files using the *Dir* command, or use the /p parameter so that you can at least give a second thought to the files before permanently deleting them.

WARNING

Remember that unlike with Windows Explorer, where the deleted files are first moved to the Recycle Bin, you cannot recover files deleted with any of these commands. Files in the Recycle Bin are deleted when you manually empty it. Until then, you can restore the deleted files to their original locations. If you have multiple partitions in your hard disk, each partition maintains its own Recycle Bin. If you want to permanently delete the file from within Windows Explorer, hold down the **Shift** key and drag the file to the Recycle Bin. The Recycle Bin is one of the safety features of the Windows operating system that allows you to recover files if you delete them by mistake. Unfortunately, this functionality is not available with the command line. So be careful when using the *Del* and *Erase* commands.

Comparing Files with the Comp Command

When you need to check two files—regardless of whether they are identical—you can use the *Comp* command. This command performs a byte-by-byte comparison of the specified files. The two files can be located on the same drive or on different drives and directories. They can have different names and can be different sizes. You can also perform a sequential comparison of multiple files within a single file by using wildcards.

With this command, you can even compare two files that have the same filename, provided they are stored in different directories. This command is very useful when you are working on two different versions of the same file. For example, you can check to see whether the file you have on your computer is the same as the one with the same name on the file server. The syntax of this command is:

```
Comp [Data1] [Data2] [/d] [/a] [/l] [/n=Number] [/c]
```

Data1 and *Data2* specify the names of the two files you want to compare. These parameters can contain the drive and directory where the files are located. The following information is important in regard to the *Data1* and *Data2* parameters:

■ When you run the *Comp* command without any parameters, the command prompts you to specify the files that you want to compare.

■ If you do not specify a name for the *Data2* parameter, the filename specified in the *Data1* parameter is assumed as the filename for *Data2*.

■ If you specify a drive and directory name with the *Data1* parameter, all files in the directory are compared to the file specified in the *Data2* parameter.

■ You can also use wildcards (* or ?) for filenames with the *Data1* and *Data2* parameters.

■ If any other required information in *Data1* and *Data2* is missing, the command interpreter prompts you for it.

Table 4.6 explains other parameters for the *Comp* command.

Table 4.6 Parameters for Use with the Comp Command

Parameter	Description
/d	Forces the command to display the differences in two files in a decimal format. By default, the differences are displayed in a hexadecimal format.
/a	Used to display the differences in two files as characters.
/l	Used to display the number of the line where the command finds a difference.
/n=Number	Used to specify the number of lines to compare in two specified files. For example, if one file has 50 lines and the second file has 100 lines, specify the number as 30 to compare only the first 30 lines in each file.
/c	Forces the command to perform a comparison of two files that are not case-sensitive.

The following examples illustrate the correct use of the *Comp* command for comparing two files:

```
Comp C:\Reports\Report1.doc Report11.doc
```

This command compares a file named Report1.doc in the C:\Reports directory with another file named Report11.doc in the same directory. If the files contain identical data, the results are displayed in the command shell window. If the files do not have identical data, the mismatching results are displayed in a hexadecimal format. The command stops the compare process when it encounters 10 mismatches, and displays the following message:

www.syngress.com

```
10 Mismatches - ending compare.
```

Now, consider another example:

```
Comp C:\Reports\  D:\OldReps\
```

This command compares the files in the C:\Reports directory with the files in the D:\OldReps directory. Note that the directory names are followed by the backslash sign (\).

```
Comp \Tests\*.txt D:\TestBack\*.txt /n=25 /d
```

This command compares the contents of all files with a *.txt extension in the current directory with all files in the D:\TestBack directory that have a *.txt extension. The /n=25 parameter makes the command compare only the first 25 lines in each file. The /d parameter is used to display the differences in the files in a decimal format. The differences are displayed in a hexadecimal format by default. In this command, we have specified wildcards with the filename parameter (*Data1*). This means that more than one file is to be compared using the *Comp* command. When wildcards are used the files are compared in a sequence. The *Comp* command finds the first file matching the filename in the *Data1* parameter with a file in the *Data2* parameter. It then compares them and displays the results. Then it moves to the next file, where the process continues. When the process is complete, the following message is displayed:

```
Compare more files (Y/N)?
```

If the two specified files are of different sizes, you must use the /n parameter. Otherwise, the command will not compare the files. The following message is displayed:

```
Files are different sizes.
Compare more files (Y/N)?
```

You may press the **Y** key to start comparing specified files of unequal sizes. Press the **N** key if you want to stop comparing files.

Comparing Files with the FC Command

FC is an advanced file comparison utility that you can use at the command line to compare files in binary or ASCII mode. This command performs a low-level comparison of the specified files and displays results depending on the parameters used with the command. The command has the following syntax:

```
FC [/a] [/b] [/c] [/l] [/lbN] [/n] [/t] [/u] [/w] [/NNNN]
[Drive1:] [Path1]FileName1 [Drive2:] [Path2]FileName2
```

As with other commands, the *Drive1:[Path1]FileName1* and *Drive2:[Path2]FileName2* parameters are used to specify the first and second files, respectively, that you wish to compare. Since you want to compare two files, both *FileName1* and *FileName2* are required parameters. You can use wildcards with the *FileName1* and *FileName2* parameters. When a wildcard (*) is used for the *FileName1* parameter, the *FC* command compares all matching files with the file specified in the *FileName2* parameter. But if the wildcard is used for *FileName2*, a corresponding value from *FileName1* is used for comparison.

Table 4.7 explains other parameters of the *FC* command.

Table 4.7 Parameters for Use with the FC command

Parameter	Description
/a	Used to display only the first and last line of each set of differences between two files. By default, the *FC* command displays all lines in each set of differences in two files. This may make the output too messy to read.
/b	Used to compare the files in binary mode. Files are compared in ASCII mode by default. ASCII mode is used by default for files with .exe, .com, .obj, .sys, .lib, and .bin extensions. In binary mode, the files are compared byte by byte.
/c	Used to ignore case sensitivity in the comparison.
/l	Used to compare two files in ASCII mode. The specified files are compared line by line. Attempts are made to resynchronize after a mismatch is found.
/lbN	Used to set the internal line buffer to *N* number of lines. The internal line buffer refers to the maximum number of lines that can mismatch. The default value of *N* is 100. This means that the *FC* command stops comparing files when it finds 100 mismatched lines.
/n	Used to display the line number when files are being compared in ASCII mode.
/t	Used to force the *FC* command to stop converting tabs to spaces. By default, the *FC* command treats tabs as spaces.
/u	Used to compare files in a Unicode text format. The Unicode format has additional characters for languages other than English. It also contains characters for mathematical and scientific purposes.
/w	Used to compress spaces and tabs during comparison. When tabs and spaces are widely used for formatting the text in a file, use this option to treat all tabs and spaces as a single space.
/NNNN	Used to specify the number of lines that must match after a mismatch before the *FC* command starts resynchronizing files. The default value of this parameter is 2.

The following examples will help you understand the correct syntax and use of the *FC* command.

```
FC C:\Reports\MarRep.txt AprRep.txt
FC C:\Reports\*.txt FinRep.txt
```

```
FC C:\Reports\MarRep.txt D:\LastRep\*.txt
```

In the first line, the two files named MarRep.txt are compared to AprRep.txt. These files are located in the C:\Reports folder. In the second line, we are trying to compare all files with a .txt extension in the C:\Reports directory with a file named FinRep.txt in the same directory. In the third line, the file named MarRep.txt in the C:\Reports directory is compared with a file with a similar name and a .txt extension in the D:\LastRep directory.

The results of the comparison look like this:

```
FC: No differences encountered.
```

If the two files are unequal, the following result is displayed:

```
FC: C:\Reports\MarRep.txt is shorter than AprRep.txt
```

Performing ASCII File Comparisons

You can force the *FC* command to compare the specified files in ASCII format. By default, all files except those with a .exe, .com, .obj, .sys, .lib, or .bin extension are compared in ASCII format, line by line, and when the first mismatch is found, the command tries to resynchronize the files. The following example shows how you can use the */l* parameter for an ASCII comparison of two files:

```
FC /l /a C:\Reports\MarRep.txt AprRep.txt
```

When the command is run it compares the file named MarRep.txt in the C:\Reports directory with the file named AprRep.txt in the same folder. The */l* parameter forces an ASCII comparison. You use the */a* parameter to display abbreviated differences in the two files. The differences in the two files are displayed and include the following information:

- The name of the first file specified in the *FileName1* parameter
- The lines from *FileName1* that differ
- The first line that matches in both files
- The name of the second file specified in the *FileName2* parameter
- Lines from *FileName2* that differ
- The first line that matches

By default, all files are compared in ASCII mode.

Performing Binary File Comparisons

The *FC* command compares all files in binary mode that have a .exe, .com, .obj, .sys, .lib, or .bin extension. You can force the command to compare other files in binary mode by using the */b* parameter. Using binary mode, the *FC* command performs a byte-by-byte comparison of files. The following example shows how you can do this:

```
FC /b C:\Reports\March1.txt April.txt
```

The *b* switch will force the *FC* command to perform a binary mode comparison. You can add the */a* parameter to display the comparison results in an abbreviated format:

```
FC /a /b C:\Reports\March1.txt April.txt
```

When you use the */a* parameter the displayed results show only the first and last lines for each set of differences in the files.

Sorting Files with the Sort Command

You use the *Sort* command to take input from a file, sort the contents, and send the output to either the command shell window or to another file. Either you can specify a file as input for this command, or the input can come from the results of another command. There is no limit on the size of the file you specify as the input file. Besides this, the command does not consider what case the characters are in when sorting. The characters in the file or command input can be lowercase or uppercase. The syntax of this command is:

```
Sort [/r] [/+N] [/m Kilobytes] [/l Locale] [/rec Characters]
[[Drive1:][Path1]FileName1] [/t [Drive2:][Path2]] [/o [Drive3:][Path3]FileName3]
```

In this command syntax, the *Sort* command is taking input from a file. Here is a list of the parameters of this command:

- **/r** Used to reverse the sort order. When you use the *Sort* command with this parameter the contents are sorted from Z to A and then from 9 to 0. The default sort order is from A to Z and then from 0 to 9.

- **/+N** Specifies the position number of the character at which the sort process begins. For example, if you specify the value of *+N* as *5*, the comparison starts from the fifth character in each line. The comparison begins from the first character in each line by default.

- **/m Kilobytes** Specifies the amount of physical memory (RAM) to be used to process the command. The minimum memory you can specify is 160 KB and the maximum cannot exceed 90 percent of available memory. If you omit this parameter, the command interpreter uses 45 percent of available memory as the maximum. In most cases, sorting performs best at the default settings.

- **/l Locale** Used to override the default sorting order of characters defined in the system default locale. You configure the system default locale in the Regional and Language options. The only available option for this parameter is the C locale. It performs the fastest sorting by using binary encoding of characters.

- **/rec Characters** Used to specify the maximum number of characters in a record, in an input, or in the input command. By default, 4,096 characters are used; you can specify a maximum of 65,535 characters.

- **[Drive1:][Path1]FileName1** Used to specify the complete path and filename of the file that is to be sorted. The sort process works faster when a filename is specified.

- **/t [Drive2:][Path2]** Used to temporarily store data when there is not enough memory in the computer. By default, the contents are stored in the temporary directory used by the operating system.

- **/o [Drive3:][Path3]FileName3** Specifies the file where the sorted input is to be stored. If this parameter is not specified, the output of the command is displayed on the screen.

Using the Sort Command to Sort File Input

The *Sort* command can take as input a file or the output of another command. The following examples show the correct syntax and use of this command.

```
Sort /r C:\Reports\June05.txt
```

This command sorts the file named June05.txt in reverse order and displays the results on the screen. You can send the output to another file using the */o* parameter, as shown in the following command:

```
Sort /r C:\Reports\June05.txt /o D:\Final\June06R.txt
```

This command sorts the file named June05.txt located in the C:\Reports folder in reverse order and stores the output in the file named June06R.txt located in the D:\Final folder.

Using the Sort Command to Sort Command Output

The *Sort* command can also take input from the keyboard or from the output of another command. For example, imagine that you have a large text file named REPS05.txt and you want to find all the names in this file that start with "McD." Once you have found the names, you want to sort them in alphabetical order and send the output to a file named MCList.txt. We will use the *Find* command and the standard piping character (|) for this example. The following is the correct syntax of this example command:

```
Find "McD" REPS05.txt | Sort /o D:\Reports05\MCList.txt
```

In this example, the *Find* command searches for all names starting with "McD"—such as McDonald, McDavid, and McDaniels—and the output is redirected to the *Sort* command. The *Sort* command sorts the names alphabetically and sends the output to another file named MCList.txt located in the D:\Reports folder.

It is important to remember that redirecting input or output data for the *Sort* command is not the best use of the command. Instead, you should try to specify filenames as given in the command syntax earlier in this section. Using redirection slows down the sorting process.

> **NOTE**
>
> If the system does not have enough memory to process the *Sort* command, it will try to sort the input in two passes rather than one. The output of the first pass is stored in a temporary file until the second pass is complete. The final output file is created when the sorting is complete. If the sort process is not complete after two passes, an error message is displayed.

Recovering Files with the Recover Command

If you find that there are some bad sectors in your hard disk and you cannot open certain files because of them, you can try to recover these files with the *Recover* command. This utility attempts to read the hard-disk sectors and, if possible, recover the lost files. File recovery depends on the condition of the hard disk and there is no guarantee that *any* files will be recovered. This command is normally used as a last resort. The syntax of the command is:

```
Recover [Drive:][Path] FileName
```

You use the *Drive* and *Path* parameters to specify the location of the file in the directory tree. *FileName* is the name of the file that you are not able to open and want to recover with the command. If a file is recovered, it may still be missing some information. You can restore this missing information by manually editing the file. The *Recover* command can recover only the readable information in the specified file from the hard disk. Other information in the file is lost.

Since the *Recover* command tries to read sectors on the hard disk to recover a particular file, you cannot use wildcards with the filenames. You must recover each lost file individually. The following example shows how to use this command:

```
Recover C:\Tests\March06.doc
```

When you run this command at the command prompt, the command interpreter uses low-level utilities to read the information on the hard disk sector by sector. Depending on the condition of the hard disk, it may take a significant amount of time before the file is recovered. It is very important to use the *Chkdsk* utility to locate and fix bad sectors in the hard disk regularly. Chapter 5 explains the *Chkdsk* utility.

Decompressing Files with the Expand Command

You use the *Expand* utility to extract files from a compressed Windows CAB file and store them in the specified directory on the hard disk. This utility is most commonly used to extract compressed files from Windows CD-ROMs. Microsoft usually compresses files and distributes them using the CAB file format. The syntax of this command is:

```
Expand [-r] Source Destination

Expand -r Source [Destination]

Expand -d Source.cab [-f:Files]

Expand Source.cab -f:Files Destination
```

The *Source* and *Destination* parameters specify the location of the compressed source file and the destination where you want to store the uncompressed files, respectively. You can use wildcards with source filenames. Table 4.8 explains additional parameters of the *Expand* command.

Table 4.8 Parameters for Use with the Expand Command

Parameter	Description
-r	Expands the file from the source location and renames each file as it uncompresses it to the specified destination directory. The names of the uncompressed files are based on the names of the files in the compressed source file. For example, if a compressed file is named READ.EX_, the uncompressed file will be named READ.EXE.
-d	Used to display the list of files contained in the compressed source files. It does not actually uncompress the files.
-f:Files	Used to specify the files in the compressed cabinet (.cab) files that you want to expand. You can expand only the selected files with this parameter. The use of wildcards is also allowed.

If the source consists of multiple compressed files without the −*r* parameter, you must specify a directory name with the destination.

The *Expand* utility is most commonly used with software distribution disks. You can use this command in your batch files to expand selected files to one or more computers in the network.

> **NOTE**
>
> Although several Windows-based utilities are available to compress and uncompress files (including WinZip and WinRar), you need a working Windows operating system to use them. Using the *Expand* command line enables you to work with batch files and scripts without having the Windows operating system installed on your computer.

Duplicating and Comparing Disks

It's easy to duplicate floppy disks using the *Diskcopy* command; then you can compare the copied disk to the original disk using the *Diskcomp* command (covered shortly). *Diskcopy* is particularly useful when you want to make copies of a particular disk for distribution. The disks can be made bootable for starting up new computers that do not have any operating systems installed. The commands work even if you have only a single floppy disk drive in your computer. They are explained in the following sections.

Duplicating Disks with the Diskcopy Command

You can use the *Diskcopy* command to copy files and folders from one disk to another. This command works only with removable disks (such as floppy disks). You cannot specify any hard disk as the source or destination drive. The syntax of this command is:

Diskcopy [Drive1: [Drive2]] [/v]

Drive1 is the source drive and *Drive2* is the destination drive. These drives are usually assigned the letter A or B. The destination disk may be formatted or unformatted. If you do not use the destination drive parameter, the source drive is used as the destination drive as well. In this case, you will be prompted to insert a different floppy disk, which will be treated as the destination drive. You use the */v* parameter to verify the file copy operation by comparing files as they are copied. Use of this parameter slows down the file copy process.

Using Two Drives for Source and Destination

When you use the *Diskcopy* command to specify the source and destination drives, the command interpreter prompts you to insert both of the disks. The following example shows how you can use the command to copy a disk in drive A: to drive B:

```
Copy A: B:
```

You are prompted to insert the source disk first, as follows:

```
Insert SOURCE disk in drive A:
and press ENTER when ready...
```

When you insert the disks in the specified drives, the data is copied from the source disk to the destination disk track by track. When the copy operation is completed, you are asked whether you want to copy another disk:

```
Copy another diskette (Y/N)?
```

If you want to copy more disks, press the **Y** key. Otherwise, press the **N** key to stop the copy operation.

Using a Single Drive as Source and Destination

If you have only one floppy disk drive on your computer, you can omit the source and destination drive letters with the *Diskcopy* command. However, your current working drive should be one of the hard-disk drives, such as the C: drive. You can use this option with most of the newer computers that come with just one floppy drive. In this case, the command interpreter treats the same drive as the source and the destination. You will need to switch to the C: drive and then use the following syntax for the *Diskcopy* command:

```
Diskcopy A: A:
```

The command will prompt you for the source disk and then the destination disk in the same disk drive. If your computer does not have sufficient physical memory (RAM), the computer will first copy a portion of the source disk to the destination disk, and then prompt you for the source disk to complete the copy process.

Using Unformatted Disks as Destinations

When you insert an unformatted disk in the destination drive, the *Diskcopy* command formats the disk in exactly the same format as the source disk. The following message is displayed on the screen:

```
Formatting while copying
```

When the copy process is complete, you are asked whether you want to copy another disk.

Diskcopy Exit Codes

The *Diskcopy* command has its own set of exit codes, which you can use in batch files with the *if* and *goto* commands set with the *Errorlevel* parameter to perform conditional processing of the file. Table 4.9 lists the exit codes for this command.

Table 4.9 Exit Codes for Use with the Diskcopy Command

Exit Code	Description
0	The command completed successfully. No error was encountered.
1	The command encountered a nonfatal read/write error.
3	The command encountered a fatal hardware error.
4	The command encountered an initialization error.

TIP

When you have two floppy disks with different formats and you want to copy the files and directories from one floppy to the other, you should use the *Xcopy* command rather than the *Diskcopy* command. This is because the *Diskcopy* command copies data from one disk to another by reading each track from the source disk and copying it to the destination disk. If the two disks are not identically formatted, the use of the *Diskcopy* command may result in errors. *Xcopy* does not have any such requirement. Use *Diskcopy* when you need to copy images from one disk onto other identically formatted disks. Another limitation of the *Diskcopy* command is that if the source disk is fragmented, the fragmentation gets copied to the destination disk. But the *Xcopy* command has a limitation as well: You cannot use it to make bootable disks.

Comparing Two Disks with the Diskcomp Command

You can compare data in two floppy disks using the *Diskcomp* command. This command works specifically with floppy disks. You cannot use this command to compare the contents of two hard disks or two hard-disk partitions. It does not matter whether you have a single floppy disk drive or two drives; the command works the same way. You will be prompted to insert the appropriate floppy disks when you use the command. The syntax of the command is:

```
Diskcomp [Drive1: [Drive2:]]
```

The *Drive1* and *Drive2* parameters specify the two disks you want to compare. You can use either a single disk drive or two separate drives for comparison. If you are using a single disk drive, the command interpreter prompts you for the first and second disks, one by one. You use the following command syntax for computers with a single drive:

```
Diskcomp A: A:
```

If your computer does not have enough physical memory (RAM) available, you may be prompted for the disks more than once (depending on the amount of available memory). This is because the computer copies the contents of one disk into memory and then compares it with the contents of the second disk. When working with a single disk drive, you can omit the *Drive2* parameter or both *Drive1* and *Drive2* parameters. You will be prompted to insert disks as required. The following two commands have the same functionality when working with single drives:

```
Diskcomp A:
Diskcomp
```

When you compare two identical disks by using either the same disk drive (A:) or two different drives (A: and B:), the following message is displayed:

```
Compare Ok.
Compare another diskette (Y/N)?
```

You can insert another disk to compare with the first, or press the **N** key to exit. If the two disks do not have identical contents, a message similar to the following is displayed:

```
Compare error.
Side 2, track 3
```

Now, let's see what happens when you try to compare the contents of a removable disk with those of a fixed disk. In the following example, we will try to compare floppy disk A: with the contents of drive D:, where the D: drive is a hard–disk partition:

```
Diskcomp A: D:
```

You will get the following error message:

```
Invalid Drive Specification.
Specified drive does not exist or is non-removable.
```

Exit Codes for the Diskcomp Command

Like other commands, *Diskcomp* has a set of exit codes which you can use in batch or script files for performing conditional processing. You use the exit codes with *Errorlevel* statements for decision making, along with the *if* and *goto* parameters. Table 4.10 lists the exit codes for the *Diskcomp* command.

Table 4.10 Exit Codes for Use with the Diskcomp Command

Exit Code	Description
0	Compared disks are the same and have identical data.
1	The command found differences in two disks.
3	The command encountered some hardware-related error.
4	There was some initialization error.

NOTE

When comparing two floppy disks, the *Diskcomp* command can compare only identical ones. This means that you cannot compare the contents of a single-sided disk with a double-sided disk. If you try to perform the comparison, the command interpreter displays the following error message:

Drive types or diskette types not compatible.
The same message will be displayed if you compare a double-density disk with a high-density disk.

Directory-Specific Commands

In this section, we will discuss some of the common directory-specific commands. Unlike commands that work with both files and directories, the commands discussed in this section work only with directories. Some of these commands have been used since the introduction of the earliest MS-DOS operating system. With the passage of time, we got lost in the jungle of Windows GUIs and forgot the utilization and usefulness of these commands. This is true with every command-line utility. In this section, we will focus on some very useful directory-specific commands that you can use in your batch files and scripts.

Displaying the Directory Structure (Tree)

You use the *Tree* command to get a graphical display of the directory structure in the specified drive and directory. This is something that you cannot get with Windows Explorer. It allows you to get an actual snapshot of the different directories and subdirectories in a specific drive. The command works for removable drives as well. One great use of this command is that you can print its output, look for obsolete or unwanted files, and delete them to make space on your hard disk. This command has the following syntax:

`Tree [Drive:] [Path] [/f] [/a]`

You use the *Drive* and *Path* parameters to specify the exact disk and directory location for which you want to view the directory tree. If you do not specify either of these parameters, the directory tree is shown for the current drive and directory. Other parameters include:

- **/f** Used to display the names of the files in each directory, along with the names of their parent directories.

- **/a** Used to force the *Tree* command to use ASCII text characters rather than graphic characters to display the directory.

Figure 4.1 shows the result I got when I tried running this command on my computer.

Figure 4.1 Graphical Output of the Tree Command

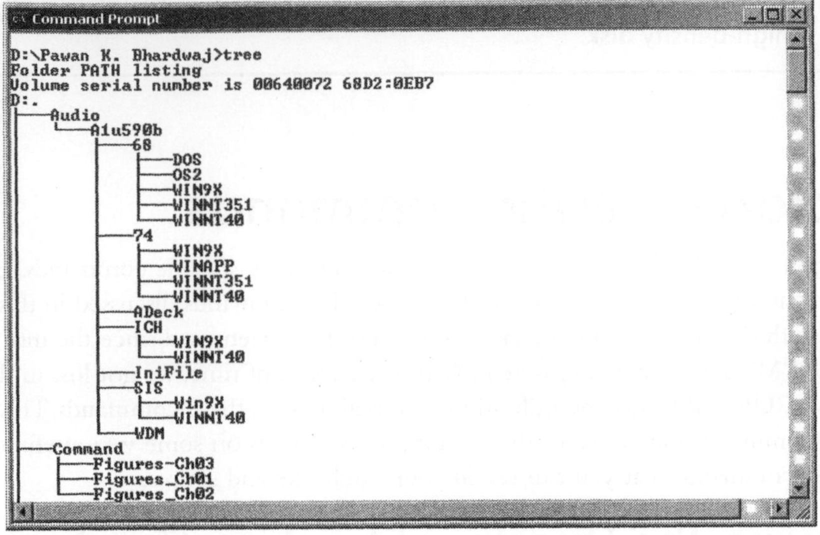

```
Command Prompt                                                    _ □ X
D:\Pawan K. Bhardwaj>tree
Folder PATH listing
Volume serial number is 00640072 68D2:0EB7
D:.
├───Audio
│   └───A1u590b
│           ├───68
│           │   ├───DOS
│           │   ├───OS2
│           │   ├───WIN9X
│           │   ├───WINNT351
│           │   └───WINNT40
│           ├───74
│           │   ├───WIN9X
│           │   ├───WINAPP
│           │   ├───WINNT351
│           │   └───WINNT40
│           ├───ADeck
│           ├───ICH
│           │   ├───WIN9X
│           │   └───WINNT40
│           ├───IniFile
│           ├───SIS
│           │   ├───Win9X
│           │   └───WINNT40
│           └───WDM
├───Command
│       ├───Figures-Ch03
│       ├───Figures_Ch01
│       ├───Figures_Ch02
```

You might have noticed in Figure 4.1 that the output of the command is too big to fit on one page. To get around this problem, you can use the | *more* parameter to display the output one page at a time. For example, try running the following command:

```
Tree C:\Windows /f | more
```

You can redirect the output of the command to a printer connected to the computer and get a hard copy of the directory structure. This is useful when you want to examine a hard drive's contents and mark files for later deletion. The following command will send the output of the directory tree structure to the printer:

```
Tree C:\Reports >prn
```

This command will print a hard copy of the output (provided that the printer is connected to the LPT port).

Creating a New Directory with MD or Mkdir

When you need to create new directories, you can use the *MD* command or the *Mkdir* command. Their functionalities are the same. You can create and use the new directories from within the batch or script files. Directories created from the command line are displayed in Windows Explorer as normal directories. It does not matter whether you create a directory from the command line or from Windows Explorer; Windows treats both directories in a similar way. In fact, you can create a complete directory tree from within batch files. The syntax of this command is:

MD [Drive:][Path]
Mkdir [Drive:][Path]

To extend the utilization of this command within batch files, you can create the entire directory structure using a single command. Consider the following example:

```
Mkdir C:\Annual\Tests\March
```

This command creates the March directory located in the Tests directory that is further located in the Annual directory on the C: drive. Using this command is the same as using the following individual commands:

```
Mkdir C:\Annual
Cd Annual
Mkdir Tests
Cd Tests
Mkdir March
```

So you see how the command line can simplify your work. It would take you much longer to create these directories from Windows Explorer.

Removing a Directory with RD or Rmdir

You can remove unwanted directories by using the *RD* or the *Rmdir* command. You cannot recover directories that you have removed (deleted) using any of these commands. They are permanently removed from the system—not temporarily moved to the Recycle Bin, as with Windows Explorer. The syntax of this command is:

```
Rmdir [Drive:]Path [/s] [/q]
RD [Drive:]Path [/s] [/q]
```

Unlike other commands, *Path* is a required parameter with the *RD* and *Rmdir* commands. You can omit the *Drive* parameter, in which case the current drive letter is assumed to be the drive letter for the command. Just as you cannot cut the branch of a tree on which you are sitting, you cannot delete the current directory in which you are working. If you try to delete the current directory, the following error message is displayed:

```
The process cannot access the file because it is being used by another process.
```

To get around this problem, you must first change to another directory and then delete the directory. Other parameters for this command are:

- **/s** Used to delete the specified directory and all subdirectories located within it. You must use the */s* parameter if you want to delete the entire directory tree or directory structure.

- **/q** Used to delete all directories and subdirectories (if the */s* parameter is used) in quiet mode. The command interpreter will not prompt you for confirmation before deleting any directory.

The following examples illustrate the use of this command:

```
Rmdir D:\Final\Reports
RD /s D:\Final
```

Deleting Subdirectories of the Root Directory

When working with the command prompt, you will most likely be working in the default path that is in the computer's root drive. This root drive is normally the C: drive. But this may be another drive, depending on the disk and drive in which the operating system is installed. When you do not specify a drive letter for any command, including the *Rmdir* command, the current drive letter is assumed. If you want to delete a directory tree from the root drive, you can use a command similar to the one shown here:

```
Rmdir /s /a \Reports\Dec98
```

When this command is executed, the command interpreter assumes the root drive as the drive letter. The first backslash character (\ ) indicates that the \Reports\Dec98 folder is located in the root drive. If the directories are located in another drive, you will need to specify the drive letter as follows:

```
Rmdir /s /a D:\Reports\Dec98
```

Master Craftsman...

Directories with Hidden and System Files

You cannot delete directories containing hidden or system files. Before you use the *RD* or *Rmdir* command, you should use the *Attrib* command (as discussed earlier in this chapter) to view the attributes of files and subdirectories. The command interpreter will display the following message when a directory contains hidden or system files:

```
The directory is not empty.
```

If you find any files or directories with *Hidden* or *System* attributes, think twice before deleting them. They might contain some files critical to the functioning of the operating system. If you are unsure of your actions, consult a senior administrator before proceeding. If you still want to delete the directory, all subdirectories, and files, you will need to change the attributes using the *Attrib* command.

Removing a Directory Tree with the Deltree Command

The *Deltree* command provides the same functionality as *Rmdir*. You use it to delete the entire directory structure in one shot. The command first removes all files in all subdirectories of the specified directory and then deletes the directory. You cannot recover the directories, subdirectories, or files deleted with this command. The syntax of this command is:

```
Deltree [/y] [Drive:]Path […]]
```

You use the *Drive* and *Path* parameters to specify the exact location of the directory that you want to delete. The command allows you to specify multiple paths. You use the */y* parameter to force the command to delete the directory, all subdirectories, and files—without prompting for confirmation.

> **NOTE**
>
> The Windows XP and Windows Server 2003 family of operating systems do not support the *Deltree* command. It has been replaced by *Rmdir*. You can use the *Rmdir* command with the */s* parameter to delete a directory, including all subdirectories and files.

Summary

In this chapter, we discussed some of the very common commands used to manage and maintain files, folders, and floppy disks. Having in-depth knowledge of these commands, their syntax, and their use is of great help when you want to use them in batch files or scripts to simplify your administration tasks. We also discussed the traditional *Copy*, *Xcopy*, *Move*, and *Del (Erase)* commands and provided some examples of their use, and we discussed how you can compare files using the simple *Comp* command, and then using the advanced file comparison command, *FC*. We followed this with a discussion on duplicating disks using *Diskcopy* and comparing disks using *Diskcomp*. Some commands come with built-in exit codes that you can use for the conditional processing of batch files. *Xcopy* is an example of one such command. You can use commands such as *Tree*, *MD (Mkdir)*, and *RD (Rmdir)* only with directories for viewing directory structure, and for creating and removing directories, respectively. In the next chapter, we will discuss the common administrative task of maintaining disk drives.

Chapter 5

Maintaining Hard Disks

Topics in this chapter:

- Physical and Logical Disks
- Understanding Basic and Dynamic Disks
- Supported File Systems
- Converting File Systems
- Maintaining Disks and File Systems

Introduction

Computers store information on hard disks, as well as in random access memory (RAM). However, RAM storage has limitations, in that information stored in RAM is lost when the computer is restarted, RAM is much more expensive per megabyte (MB) than hard-disk space, and the total storage capacity of RAM is very limited. Hard disks, on the other hand, provide large storage capacity and efficiency in read-write operations. As an administrator, you will often be required to configure and maintain hard disks on computers in a network. In this chapter, we will introduce the general concepts of basic and dynamic hard disks, the file systems used with hard disks, and conversion from one file system to another. We will then discuss how you can maintain hard disks using command-line utilities.

Physical and Logical Disks

It is important to understand the Windows operating system terminology associated with hard disks. Hard disks are referred to as *physical* or *logical* disks when used in Windows systems. The following sections provide a brief explanation of physical and logical disks.

Physical Disks

A physical disk is the actual piece of hardware, or the hard disk itself. A physical disk is of no use to Windows or any other operating system unless it is formatted and converted into a logical disk. When we monitor disk performance, the physical disk is treated as a performance object.

Logical Disks

You organize the available storage space on physical disks by creating logical drives. You can create multiple logical drives on a single physical disk; you also can create a single logical disk that spans multiple physical disks. You create logical volumes on logical disks, with each volume representing a single, discrete storage unit. Like a physical disk, the logical disk is also treated as a performance object when monitoring disk performance.

Understanding Basic and Dynamic Disks

Before Microsoft introduced the Windows 2000 operating system, all hard disks were treated as *basic* disks. The concept of *dynamic* disks was introduced with the Windows 2000 operating system. Even with newer operating systems such as Windows XP and Windows Server 2003, hard disks are first initialized as basic disks. You can convert from a basic to a dynamic disk using the disk management utility that runs as a graphical user interface (GUI), or from the command line using the *Diskpart* utility. We discuss *Diskpart* in Chapter 6.

Basic Disks

Basic disks are what we have always been using. They are the traditional storage type in computers with all kinds of operating systems. Even with Windows 2000, Windows XP, and Windows Server 2003 operating systems that support *dynamic* disks, all hard disks are initialized as basic unless they are converted to dynamic. Basic disks are divided into *partitions,* and *logical volumes* are created in those partitions. Each physical disk must have at least one partition. Partitions help you organize the disk space so that you can store different types of data or different operating systems in different partitions. All versions of Windows operating systems support basic disks.

Partitions and Logical Drives

Basic disks can be divided into three different types of partitions:

- **Primary partition** You can create up to four primary partitions on a basic disk. Each hard disk must have at least one primary partition where you can create a logical volume. You can set only one partition as an active partition. Primary partitions are assigned drive letters.

- **Extended partition** A primary partition can also have an extended partition. When you want to have more partitions on a basic disk, you can create an extended partition to meet your extra disk partition requirements. You can create logical drives in the extended partition to organize your data files.

- **Logical drives** You use logical drives to organize your data files when there aren't enough primary partitions to meet your storage requirements. Unlike primary and extended partitions, logical drives are not assigned any drive letters. You can create any number of logical drives within the extended partitions.

Master Craftsman...

Active Partition

In every operating system, the hard disk must have at least one partition marked as an active partition. The computer's basic input/output system (BIOS) uses the active partition to load the operating system. In your batch files, you will refer to this partition as *SystemRoot* or *SysVol.* In most desktops and servers, this partition is normally the hard disk's C: drive. This is the partition where the operating system stores the boot information and hardware-specific files that are used during the startup process.

Tasks Associated with Basic Disks

Here is a list of some of the tasks you can perform only on basic disks:

- Create and delete primary and extended partitions.
- Create and delete logical drives.
- Format a partition and mark it as active.
- Convert a basic disk to a dynamic disk without losing data.
- Delete volumes, striped sets, mirror sets, or striped sets with parity. You cannot create them on basic disks.

In order to use fault-tolerant features such as mirrored or Redundant Array of Inexpensive Disks (RAID) 5 volumes, you must convert the disks into dynamic disks.

Dynamic Disks

The Windows 2000, Windows XP, and Windows Server 2003 operating systems support dynamic disks. They support features that you don't get with basic disks and give you more flexibility in structuring the available storage space. You can convert basic disks to dynamic disks using either the Disk Management console or the *Diskpart* command-line utility. The logical storage units created on dynamic disks are known as *volumes*. When you have only one dynamic disk on a computer you can create a *simple* volume. With more than one dynamic disk, you have the option of creating *spanned*, *striped*, *mirrored*, or *RAID 5* volumes. Mirrored and RAID 5 volumes provide disk fault tolerance. These volumes use space on more than one dynamic disk.

Dynamic disks are not supported on removable media or on most portable computers. The basic idea behind creating dynamic disks is to provide enhanced hard-disk features such as the ability to create spanned volumes using multiple disks, and creating disk fault tolerance.

Tasks Associated with Dynamic Disks

Here is a list of some of the tasks you can perform only on dynamic disks:

- Create and delete simple, spanned, striped, mirrored, or RAID 5 volumes.
- Extend a simple or spanned volume.
- Remove the mirror from a mirrored volume.
- Break the mirrored volume into two separate volumes.
- Repair mirrored or RAID 5 volumes.
- Reactivate a missing or offline disk.

- Convert a dynamic disk to a basic disk. This action destroys all data on the dynamic disk.

NOTE

Converting a basic disk to a dynamic disk is a one-way process, if you want to retain existing data. When you convert a dynamic disk back to a basic disk, all data on the disk is lost. As a precaution, you must back up all your data before taking this step.

Volume Types on Dynamic Disks

Dynamic disks provide us with several ways to organize available space on a computer's hard disk. A single disk can have up to 2,000 logical volumes, but Microsoft recommends that you limit the number to 32. When you convert a basic disk to a dynamic disk, you can create the following types of dynamic volumes:

- **Simple volume** A simple volume uses the free or unallocated space on a single dynamic disk. If you have only one disk, you can create only simple volumes. When you add unallocated space from other disks to a simple volume, it becomes a spanned volume. Simple volumes do not provide any fault tolerance.

- **Spanned volume** You create a spanned volume using unallocated space from more than one hard disk. When data is written to a spanned volume, it is written to the first disk in the volume; when that disk is full, the next disk is used, and so on. You can use space from up to 32 dynamic disks to create a single spanned volume. Spanned volumes do not provide fault tolerance. If one of the disks in a spanned volume fails, the entire volume fails and all data is lost. You cannot create striped volumes or mirrored volumes using spanned volumes. It is also not possible to extend a spanned volume without first deleting the entire volume. The advantage of using spanned volumes is that you can create large disk volumes.

- **Striped volume** You create a striped volume using unallocated space from two to 32 disks. Data is written to the striped volume in chunks of 64 KB. Although you can add space from dynamic disks of unequal capacity, it's best in terms of space utilization if all disks have the same capacity. This is because the striped volume uses equal space from all participating dynamic disks. Like spanned volumes, striped volumes are not fault tolerant and cannot be extended. If one of the disks in a striped volume fails, the entire volume fails and all data is lost. The advantage of using striped volumes is enhanced read/write performance.

- **Mirrored volume** You create a mirrored volume using two identical dynamic disks. Mirrored volumes provide fault tolerance by keeping a duplicate copy of the data stored in the volume, on each participating disk. If one of the disks in the mirrored volume fails, you can recover the data from the other disk. You cannot extend mirrored volumes to increase storage capacity. On the other hand, only 50 percent of the total storage capacity in the computer can be utilized.

- **RAID 5 volume** A RAID 5 volume is also known as a striped volume with parity. These volumes consist of three to 32 dynamic disks. RAID 5 volumes provide fault tolerance as well as enhanced disk performance. As with striped volumes, data is written to the participating disks in chunks (blocks) of 64 KB. In addition to this, parity information is written to each disk, and this parity information is used to rebuild data in case one of the disks in the volume fails. One limitation of RAID 5 volumes is that you cannot use them for system and boot partitions, unless you are using a hardware-based RAID solution.

Tasks Common to Basic and Dynamic Disks

The following tasks are common to both basic and dynamic disks:

- Check the properties of a disk, partition, and volume. These properties include capacity, available free space, assigned drive letter, label type, file system in use, and volume status.

- Establish drive letters.

- Configure file and folder sharing and assign security permissions.

- Upgrade a disk from basic to dynamic, or revert from dynamic to basic.

- Copy and move files and folders.

- Encrypt files and folders to secure them.

- Compress and decompress files and folders to manage disk space.

- Configure disk quotas for users to manage use of disk space.

- Configure auditing of files and folders.

Some of the tasks we refer to in this section depend on the file system used for the disk partitions or volumes. We discuss file systems in the next section.

Supported File Systems

Windows XP and Windows Server 2003 support the following types of file systems:

- **FAT file system** The File Allocation Table (FAT) file system is the original file system used by MS-DOS and other Windows operating systems. It is a data structure Windows creates when a volume is formatted. This structure stores information about each file and directory so that it can be located later. The maximum disk partition size is 4 GB. On floppy disks, this is limited by the capacity of the disk. The maximum supported file size on hard disks is 2 GB.

- **FAT32 file system** FAT32 stands for File Allocation Table32, an advanced version of the FAT file system. The FAT32 file system supports smaller cluster sizes and larger volumes than the FAT file system, which results in more efficient space allocation. FAT32 file systems support a maximum partition size of 32 GB for Windows XP and Windows Server 2003. The maximum size file size is 4 GB.

- **NTFS** NTFS, which stands for New Technology File System, is an advanced file system that provides performance, security, reliability, and advanced features not found in FAT and FAT32 file systems. Some of the features of NTFS include guaranteed volume consistency by means of transaction logging and recovery techniques. NTFS uses log file and checkpoint information to restore the consistency of the file system. Other advanced features of NTFS include file and folder permissions, compression, encryption, and disk quotas. You cannot use NTFS on floppy disks due to its limited capacity (Sysinternals has a utility for using NTFS on floppy disks. For more information check out Syngress Publishing's *Winternals Defragmentation, Recovery, and Administration Field Guide*, ISBN 1-59749-079-2). The maximum supported partition size ranges from 2 TB to 16 TB. The maximum file size can be up to 16 TB minus 16 KB. The minimum and maximum partition sizes vary by the partition style chosen when the operating system was installed.

Formatting a Disk or Partition with the Format Command

A hard disk or a partition is of no use to any operating system unless it is formatted. You use the *Format* command to format raw disks or disk partitions with a selected file system. You can use the FAT, FAT32, or NTFS file system when formatting a disk with Windows XP and Windows Server 2003 operating systems. When a disk is formatted, all data on the disk is lost, but the *Format* command displays a warning message before it starts. After the disk is formatted, a new root directory and the specified file system are created on the disk. The syntax of this command is:

```
Format Volume [/fs:FileSystem] [/v:Label] [/q] [/a:UnitSize] [/c] [/x]
Format Volume [/v:Label] [/q] [/f:Size]
Format Volume [/v:Label] [/q] [/t:Tracks /n:Sectors]
Format Volume [/v:Label] [/q]
Format Volume [/q]
```

Table 5.1 explains the parameters of this command.

Table 5.1 Parameters of the Format Command

Parameter	Description
Volume:	Specifies the drive, volume, or mounted volume that you wish to format. The drive letter is followed by a colon (:).
/fs:FileSystem	Specifies the file system to use for formatting. This parameter supports the FAT, FAT32, and NTFS file systems. When you are using this command for floppy disks, you can use only the FAT file system.
/v:Label	Used to assign a label to the formatted volume. If you do not use it, or if you use it without specifying the label, the Format command prompts you to specify a label once the formatting is complete.
/q	Used to perform a quick format of a previously formatted volume. It causes the command to delete the existing root directory and file table and cuts the time required to format a disk when you are sure that it does not have any bad sectors.
/a:UnitSize	Used to specify the allocation unit size for disk clusters.
/c	Used only with NTFS file systems. It automatically compresses all files created on the new volume.
/x	Used to dismount the mounted volume (if required) during the formatting process.
/f:Size	Used for floppy disks to specify their size. Accepted parameters include 1,440, 1,440 k, 1,440 KB, 1.44, 1.44 M, and 1.44 MB. It is preferred over the */t:Tracks* and */n:Sectors* parameters.
/t:Tracks /n:Sectors	Used together to specify the number of tracks (*/t:Tracks*) and sectors per track (*/n:Sectors*) on the disk. Microsoft recommends that you use the */f:Size* parameter instead of using these two parameters together. When you use */f:Size* to define the size of the disk, you cannot use the */t:Tracks* or */n:Sectors* parameter.

Allocation Unit Size

You can specify the size of the allocation unit with the *Format* command by using the */a:UnitSize* parameter. Each hard disk is made up of small units known as *sectors* or *clusters*. The allocation unit size defines the number of bytes per cluster on the formatted disk. The following is a list of the supported allocation unit sizes for the FAT, FAT32, and NTFS file systems:

- **512** Sets the unit size to 512 bytes per cluster.
- **1024** Sets the unit size to 1,024 bytes per cluster.

- **2048** Sets the unit size to 2,048 bytes per cluster.

- **4096** Sets the unit size to 4,096 bytes per cluster.

- **8192** Sets the unit size to 8,192 bytes per cluster.

- **16K** Sets the unit size to 16 kilobytes (16 KB) per cluster.

- **32K** Sets the unit size to 32 kilobytes (32 KB) per cluster.

- **64K** Sets the unit size to 64 kilobytes (64 KB) per cluster.

When you do not use the */a:UnitSize* parameter with the *Format* command, the system chooses an appropriate unit size based on the size of the volume.

Master Craftsman...

Cluster Size and Number of Clusters

The advantage of using smaller sizes for disk clusters when formatting a disk or a partition is the creation of small placeholders for files on the disk. Smaller cluster sizes are very useful in situations where you need to store a large number of small files on a disk with limited storage capacity. This helps reduce wasted space on small disks when you are creating clusters of sizes as large as 64 KB. Another limitation of large cluster size on NTFS partitions is that you cannot use NTFS compression if the cluster size is larger than 4,096 bytes (or 4 KB).

The number of clusters is also limited in FAT and FAT32 volumes. With FAT volumes you can have a maximum of 65,526 clusters and with FAT32 volumes you can have between 65,527 and 4,177,917 clusters.

WARNING

The following section contains some examples of the *Format* command. Do not use this command on any production computer because it will delete all data on the disk or partition you specify. Even when you are trying this command on a test computer, make sure that you back up all data first.

Examples of the Format Command

The following are some examples of the *Format* command:

```
Format A:
Format A: /v:Backup
```

The first command formats the floppy disk in the computer's A: drive with all default settings. The second command formats the floppy disk and assigns it the *Backup* label. When you do not use the */v:label* parameter or do not specify a volume label with the */v* parameter, the following message is displayed after the floppy disk is formatted:

```
Volume label (11 Characters, ENTER for none)?
```

You can enter a label for the floppy disk or press the **Enter** key if you do not want to use one. Since a floppy drive is formatted in the given example, and floppy disks support only the FAT file system, the number of characters you can include in the label is limited to 11. Here are two more examples:

```
Format E: /fs:NTFS /q
Format F: /fs:FAT32 /a:512
```

The first command performs a quick format of the E: drive with the NTFS file system. The second command formats the F: drive with the FAT32 file system and an allocation unit size of 512 bytes. Before the command starts formatting a partition on the hard disk, it displays the following warning message:

```
WARNING, ALL DATA ON nonremovable DISK
DRIVE E: WILL BE LOST!
Proceed with Format (Y/N)?
```

This is your chance to cancel the *Format* command, if you have used it by mistake or selected a wrong partition to format. Press the **Y** key if you want to proceed with the format or press the **N** key to abort the command. During the format process, the command displays its progress as a percentage of the total disk space formatted. When formatting is complete the *Format* command displays the total disk space and the available disk space in kilobytes (KB).

If you want the newly formatted volume to compress all files stored in it, you can use the */c* parameter. This feature is available on NTFS volumes only. Here is an example:

```
Format E: /fs:NTFS /c
```

After the volume is formatted, all files created on the E: volume will be automatically compressed.

NOTE

You cannot use the *Format* command over the network to format a disk on a remote computer. Even on a local computer you must have administrative rights to use the *Format* command.

Exit Codes for the Format Command

The *Format* command comes with its own set of exit codes that indicate the success or failure of the command, and the reason for failure. When you use the *Format* command in a batch file, you can control the process by using the exit codes it generates. Exit codes are normally used as arguments with the *Errorlevel* parameter in *if* and *goto* statements for conditional processing of batch file commands. Table 5.2 lists the exit codes for the *Format* command.

Table 5.2 Exit Codes for the Format Command

Exit Code	Description
0	The format process completed successfully without errors.
1	Incorrect parameters were supplied with the *Format* command.
4	A fatal error occurred during the format process. This may be any error other than errors 1, 4, and 5.
5	The user pressed the **N** key to stop the format process when prompted with the question, "Proceed with Format (Y/N)?"

Converting File Systems

For most new Windows systems, the volumes you create during installation are automatically formatted using NTFS, unless you choose to use the FAT file system for specific reasons (such as dual-booting the system with Windows 98, which does not support NTFS). In systems that come with preinstalled operating systems, the drives are normally formatted with NTFS. Formatting the volume during installation gives the best NTFS drive performance.

Swiss Army Knife...

NTFS Performance

When you create a new volume and format with NTFS, the system places the Master File Table (MFT) as close as possible to the beginning of the drive. This helps you to easily locate and read the file, resulting in improved performance. When you convert systems from the FAT or FAT32 file system to NTFS using the Disk Management or command line, the performance of the converted partition or volume may not be as good as NTFS volumes created from scratch. This is because the volume already has some data stored in it and the MFT is created in a different location than the newly created NTFS volumes. With the passage of time, the MFT may also become fragmented, causing performance degradation. To get the best performance benefits, consider re-creating the volume instead of converting it. You can solve this problem in Windows XP and Windows Server 2003 operating systems by using the /cvtarea parameter with the Convert command, which allows you to use a file as a placeholder for NTFS, MFT, and metadata files.

You cannot convert existing FAT and FAT32 volumes to NTFS using the Disk Management snap-in and the *Convert* command-line utility. The data in the volume remains intact after the conversion. Before you start the conversion process for one or more FAT or FAT32 volumes, consider the following important points:

- At least 25 percent of the volume's space must be free for use. For example, if the total space on the volume you wish to convert is 60 GB, you must have at least 15 GB of free space to successfully convert it to NTFS. The conversion process will terminate automatically if sufficient free space is not found.

- If the volume you want to convert is an active system or boot partition, the conversion will not take place immediately. You will be prompted to restart the system, or reschedule the conversion to take place at the next restart.

- When the boot volume is converted, the *Convert* utility applies the same default security that is applied during Windows operating system installation.

- No utility is available to convert an NTFS system back to a FAT or FAT32 file system. You should not perform this conversion, but if you must, the only way to do it is to delete the volume, re-create it, and format it with a FAT or FAT32 file system.

Converting a File System with the Convert Command

You use the *Convert* command to convert a partition formatted with the FAT or FAT32 file system to NTFS. The data on the disk partition or volume remains intact after the conversion, but the converted volume may not retain its original security settings. The syntax of this command is:

```
convert [Volume] /FS:ntfs [/v] [/x] [/nosecurity] [/cvtarea:FileName]
```

The *Volume* parameter specifies the volume, drive, or mount volume that is to be converted to NTFS. When a drive letter is used, it should be followed by a colon (:). For example, if you want to convert the E: drive to NTFS, it should be noted as *E:*. Other parameters of this command are:

- **/FS:ntfs** A required parameter that implies that the volume, drive, or mount point is to be converted to NTFS.

- **/v** Used to display all messages and prompts before, during, and after the conversion.

- **/x** Used to dismount a volume, if required, before the conversion process starts.

- **/nosecurity** Used to remove all security settings for the directories in the specified drive or volume, making the volume accessible to everyone.

- **/cvtarea:FileName** Used by advanced users to specify a contiguous file located in the root directory to become a placeholder for the NTFS system files, which are usually the MFT and metadata files. Using this parameter prevents fragmentation of the volume after conversion.

The following examples illustrate the correct use of the *Convert* command.

```
Convert D: /FS:ntfs /v
```

In the preceding line of code, the D: drive is converted to the NTFS file system. All messages before, during, and after the conversion process are displayed on the screen. That */FS:ntfs* was written using upper- and lowercase letters does not matter. The command interpreter treats */FS:ntfs*, */fs:NTFS*, and */FS:NTFS* the same. You can add the */nosecurity* parameter to this command in order to remove any previously assigned directory permissions, as shown here:

```
Convert D: /FS:ntfs /v /nosecurity
```

This command will remove all the security settings of the original volume. When the conversion is complete, you can apply NTFS security permissions as required.

Specifying a File with the /cvtarea Parameter

As discussed earlier, you can use the */cvtarea:FileName* parameter with the *Convert* command to specify a contiguous file for MFT and NTFS metadata files. This helps improve the performance of the converted NTFS volume. The filename you specify with the */cvtarea* parameter must be created in the root directory of the file system that you wish to convert. You use the *Fsutil* command to create this file; we discuss *Fsutil* later in this chapter.

The size of the file you create for use with the */cvtarea* parameter should preferably be equal to 1 KB multiplied by the number of files and directories in the file system. Although this is not a requirement and the *Convert* command will accept any file size, it is best to calculate the size of the file for best results. For example, if you have 800 files and directories in the volume, this number is to be multiplied by 1 KB (1,024 bytes) so that the resulting file size is 819,200 bytes.

The following example shows how you can use the *Fsutil* command to create a temporary file named Temp.txt to be used for the *Convert* command:

```
Fsutil File Createnew Temp.txt 819200
```

After this file is created, you are ready to use the file with the *Convert* command using the */cvtarea* parameter, as shown in the following example:

```
Convert D: /FS:ntfs /v /cvtarea:Temp.txt
```

For more information on the *Fsutil* command, please refer to the section "Using the Fsutil Utility for Advanced Disk Management," later in this chapter.

> **NOTE**
>
> Although a file size of 1 KB multiplied by the number of files and directories is recommended for best performance of the converted volume, it is not a requirement. The *Convert* command will accept files of any size for the conversion process.

Examining Volume Serial Numbers with the Vol Command

The *Vol* command is perhaps one of the simplest commands in Windows XP and Windows Server 2003. You can use it to gather information about a drive or a volume. The syntax of this command is:

```
Vol [Drive:]
```

The only parameter used with this command is *Drive:*, which specifies the drive letter about which you need to get information. If you do not use this parameter, the volume information for the current drive is displayed. The output of this command is shown in the following example:

```
Volume in drive D is Mydrive
Volume Serial Number is 68D2-0EB7
```

You can use this command to view the volume label and its serial number. Then, if required, you can change the volume label using the *Label* command, as discussed in the next section.

Managing Volume Labels with the Label Command

You use the *Label* command to create a new label and change or delete the existing label for a drive or a volume. You also can use this command with mounted volumes. When you use the *Label* command without any parameters, it deletes the existing label of the specified drive or volume. The syntax of this command is:

```
Label [Drive:] [Label]
Label [/MP] [Volume] [Label]
```

The parameters of this command are:

- **Drive** Specifies the drive letter whose label you want to create, change, or delete. The drive letter should be followed by a colon (:).

- **Label** Specifies the new volume label for the drive or the volume. The existing label is changed to the new label. Specifying the *Label* parameter defines a new label for the volume and deletes the existing label. You can also leave the *Label* parameter blank to delete the existing label.

- **/MP** Specifies a mounted volume. If you use the drive name, you do not need to use the */MP* parameter.

- **Volume** Specifies the name of the volume whose label is to be changed.

The volume label is displayed along with the directory listing when you use the *Dir* command or when you use Windows Explorer. The following sections provide some example uses of the *Label* command.

Changing the Existing Label

This example shows how you can change the label of the D: drive to "Rep2006":

```
Label D: Rep2006
```

When you run this command, the command interpreter changes the label to the specified name without displaying a message. If you need to, you can use the *Dir* command to view the existing label of the drive or volume before you change it.

Viewing and Deleting the Existing Label

When you use the *Label* command without specifying a new label, the command interpreter displays the existing volume label and serial number and then prompts you to specify a new label. The following example shows what is displayed when you use the *Label* command without the *Label* parameter:

```
Volume in drive D: is Mydrive
Volume Serial Number is 68D2-0EB7
Volume label (32 characters, ENTER for none)?
```

You can type a new label or you can press the **Enter** key to delete the existing label. If you choose to delete the label, the following message is displayed:

```
Delete current volume label (Y/N)?
```

Press the **Y** key to delete the existing label or the **N** key to keep it. You can also press the **Ctrl + C** key combination to abort the operation.

> **NOTE**
>
> When specifying labels you must remember that FAT volumes support only 11 characters and NTFS volumes support up to 32 characters. You cannot include the following characters in the label for a FAT volume: * , ? / \ | . , ; : + = [ ] < > ".
>
> Also, the system stores and displays the labels in uppercase regardless of how you typed them. And in NTFS volumes, the labels are displayed as they were created. So, for instance, if you create a label such as *MyRepVol*, it will be displayed as MYREPVOL on a FAT volume, but on an NTFS volume the case is retained and the label will be displayed as *MyRepVol*.

Maintaining Disks and File Systems

Most of the command-line utilities discussed in this chapter relate to hard-disk and file system management. You are probably familiar with many of these utilities; they have been around for a long time. But Microsoft continuously adds more functionality to its old command-line utilities to support advancements in the field of information technology (including both hardware and software). In Windows XP and Windows Server 2003 operating systems, Microsoft added several new commands to maintain hard disks and file systems while supporting the older ones. This section describes some of the command-line utilities that can be very helpful in maintaining disks and volumes in your network.

Using the Fsutil Utility for Advanced Disk Management

Fsutil is an advanced utility meant for advanced users of Windows XP and Windows Server 2003. It consists of several subcommands that effectively manage FAT and NTFS volumes. These subcommands are discussed in the following sections.

Behavior

The *Behavior* subcommands include *Fsutil Behavior Query* and *Fsutil Behavior Set*. You can use this set of subcommands to enable, disable, and view current settings for generating 8.3 format filenames. You can also change how often entries are written to the NTFS disk quota log files, change the internal cache settings of NTFS paged pool and nonpaged pool memory, and change the amount of reserved disk space for the MFT zone. The syntax is:

```
Fsutil Behavior Query {disable8dot3 | allowextchar | disablelastaccess |
quotanotify | memoryusage | mftzone}
```

```
Fsutil Behavior Set [{disable8dot3 {1 | 0} | allowextchar {1 | 0} |
disablelastaccess {1 | 0} | quotanotify Frequency | memoryusage Value |
mftzone Value}]
```

Dirty

The *Dirty* subcommands include *Fsutil Dirty Query* and *Fsutil Dirty Set*, and you use them to check and set the dirty bit on volumes, respectively. A *dirty bit* set on a volume indicates that there are problems with the file system on the volume. When the dirty bit is set on volumes, the *Autochk* command runs automatically to check for errors on the system. The syntax is:

```
Fsutil Dirty {Query | Set} VolumePathname
```

File

You use the *File* subcommand set to create a new file, find a file by specifying a username when disk quotas are enabled, query an allocated range of files, set a short name for a file, and set zero data for a file. The syntax is:

```
Fsutil File [Createnew] FileName Length
Fsutil File [Findbysid] UserName Directory
Fsutil File [Queryallocranges] offset=Offset length=Length FileName
Fsutil File [Setshortname] FileName ShortName
Fsutil File [Setvaliddata] FileName DataLength
Fsutil File [Setzerodata] offset=Offset length=Length FileName
```

Fsinfo

You use the *Fsinfo* subcommand set to query types of drives, information on volumes, file system statistics, and NTFS-specific volume information. The syntax is:

```
Fsutil Fsinfo [Drives]
Fsutil Fsinfo [Drivetype] VolumePathname
Fsutil Fsinfo [Ntfsinfo] RootPathname:
Fsutil Fsinfo [Statistics] VolumePathname
Fsutil Fsinfo [Volumeinfo] RootPathname:
```

Hardlink

You use the *Hardlink* subcommand set to create a *hard link entry* for a file. Every file has a directory entry that is referred to as its hard link. You can create hard links for a file on NTFS volumes so that the file can appear in multiple directories, or in a single directory with multiple names. The file is deleted when all of its links are deleted. The syntax is:

```
Fsutil Hardlink Create NewFileName ExistingFileName
```

ObjectID

You use the *ObjectID* subcommand set to manage Object Identifiers (OIDs). Services use OIDs such as the File Replication Service (FRS) and Distributed Link Tracking (DLT) Client Service to track other objects such as files, directories, and links. The syntax is:

```
Fsutil ObjectID [Create] FileName
Fsutil ObjectID [Delete] FileName
Fsutil ObjectID [Query] FileName
Fsutil ObjectID [Set] ObjectID BirthVolumeID BirthObjectID DomainID
FileName
```

Quota

You use the *Quota* subcommand set to manage disk quotas on NTFS volumes in order to provide more precise control of network-based storage. You can enforce, modify, disable, query, or track quota usage by specifying the volume path. The syntax is:

```
Fsutil Quota [Disable] VolumePathname
Fsutil Quota [Enforce] VolumePathname
Fsutil Quota [Modify] VolumePathname Threshold Limit [UserName]
Fsutil Quota [Query] VolumePathname
Fsutil Quota [Track] VolumePathname
Fsutil Quota [Violations]
```

Reparsepoint

You use the *Reparsepoint* subcommand set to query or delete reparse points. *Reparse points* are NTFS file system objects that have a definable attribute containing user-controlled data. You use them to extend functionality in the input/output (I/O) subsystem—i.e., for directory junction points and volume mount points. The syntax is:

```
Fsutil Reparsepoint [Query] FileName
Fsutil Reparsepoint [Delete] FileName
```

Sparse

You use the *Sparse* subcommand set to manage sparse files. A *sparse file* is a file containing one or more regions of unallocated data. Sparse file support allows data to be deallocated from anywhere in the file. The syntax is:

```
Fsutil Sparse [Queryflag] FileName
Fsutil Sparse [Queryrange] FileName
Fsutil Sparse [Setflag] FileName
Fsutil Sparse [Setrange] FileName BeginningOffset Length
```

USN

You use the USN subcommand set to manage the Update Sequence Number (USN) change journal. The *USN change journal* provides a persistent log of all changes made to files on the volume and to the volume when files and directories are added, deleted, or changed. The Indexing Service, FRS, Remote Installation Service (RIS), and Remote Storage use the journal. The syntax is:

```
Fsutil USN [Createjournal] m=MaximumSize a=AllocationDelta VolumePathname
Fsutil USN [Deletejournal] {/D | /N} VolumePathname
Fsutil USN [Enumdata] FileRef LowUsn HighUsn VolumePathname
Fsutil USN [Queryjournal] VolumePathname
Fsutil USN [Readdata] FileName
```

Volume

You use the *Volume* subcommand set to dismount a volume or check how much free space is available on a disk. The syntax is:

```
Fsutil Volume [Diskfree] VolumePathname
Fsutil Volume [Dismount] VolumePathname
```

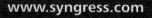

Examples of Using the Fsutil Command Set

The following sections explain how you can use the *Fsutil* command set for some common administrative tasks. Because these commands are meant for advanced administrators, you must exercise caution when using them. If you are just learning these commands, we recommend that you use them on a test computer. Do not use these commands on any production desktop or server.

Getting File Information

The following command obtains information on all types of drives on the system:

```
Fsutil Fsinfo Drives
```

The output of this command is:

```
Drives A:\ C:\ D:\ E:\ F:\
```

Getting Detailed Information on a Volume

The following command obtains and displays detailed information about the D: volume:

```
Fsutil Fsinfo Volumeinfo D:
```

The output is:

```
Volume Name : Mydrive
Volume Serial Number : 0x68d20eb7
Max Component Length : 255
File System Name : NTFS
Supports Case-sensitive filenames
Preserves Case of filenames
Supports Unicode in filenames
Preserves & Enforces ACL's
Supports file-based Compression
Supports Disk Quotas
Supports Sparse files
Supports Reparse Points
Supports Object Identifiers
Supports Encrypted File System
Supports Named Streams
```

Getting Detailed NTFS-Specific Information

The following command obtains and displays detailed NTFS-specific information about the C: volume:

```
Fsutil Fsinfo NTFSinfo C:
```

The output shows detailed information about the NTFS C: drive, including the number of sectors, clusters, bytes per cluster, free clusters, and start and end zones for the MFT. The results of this command are:

```
NTFS Volume Serial Number  :        0x5ae4e12ee4e10d57
Version :                           3.1
Number Sectors :                    0x000000000129d5fe
Total Clusters :                    0x0000000000253abf
Free Clusters   :                   0x00000000000b69d5
Total Reserved :                    0x0000000000001d00
Bytes Per Sector   :                512
Bytes Per Cluster :                 4096
Bytes Per FileRecord Segment    : 1024
Clusters Per FileRecord Segment : 0
Mft Valid Data Length :             0x0000000001ce7800
Mft Start Lcn   :                   0x00000000000c0000
Mft2 Start Lcn :                    0x0000000000129d5f
Mft Zone Start :                    0x00000000000c1cc0
Mft Zone End    :                   0x000000000010a760
```

Finding Files Owned by a User

The following command locates all files owned by a user named *Garyb* in the D:\Reports directory:

```
Fsutil File FindbySID Garyb D:\Reports
```

Specifying a Short Name for a File

The following command sets the short name MyFinRep.txt for a file named My Final Report.txt:

```
Fsutil File SetShortName D:\Reports\My Final Report.txt D:\Reports\MyFinRep.txt
```

Getting Information on Free Disk Space

The following command obtains information on the free disk space available on the C: drive:

```
Fsutil Volume Diskfree C:
```

The output of this command is:

```
Total # of free bytes       : 3032899584
Total # of bytes            : 9993711616
Total # of avail free bytes : 3032899584
```

The free disk space is shown in bytes. In this example, the free space is 3032899584 (a little less than 3 GB).

NOTE

Use of the *Fsutil* command should be left to advanced and senior-level administrators with sufficient Windows systems management experience. You can get help on Fsutil and the *Fsutil* command, and any of its subcommands, by typing the command set at the command prompt.

Checking Available Disk Space with the Freedisk Command

You use the *Freedisk* command to check whether the specified amount of free disk space is available on a specified drive. This command is available only in Windows Server 2003, not in Windows XP. When used in the command shell window, it checks the disk space and displays the results as *success* or *info*. When used in batch files or scripts, it returns a value of *1* for success and *0* for failure. You can use the command on any computer on the network using the appropriate user credentials. The syntax of this command is:

```
Freedisk [/s Computer [/u [Domain\]User [/p [Password]]]] [/d Drive]
[Value]
```

The parameters of this command are:

- **/s Computer** Used to specify the computer on which you want to check free disk space. You can use either the name of the computer or its Internet Protocol (IP) address.

- **/u [Domain\]User** Used to specify the domain name and username. You can use this parameter only if you use the */s* parameter.

- **/p [Password]** Used to specify the password for the username specified in the */u* parameter. As with the */u* parameter, you can use this parameter only if you use the */s* parameter.

- **/d Drive** Used to specify the drive on the computer for which you want to determine free disk space availability.

- **Value** Specifies the amount of disk space in bytes (B), kilobytes (KB), megabytes (MB), gigabytes (GB), or terabytes (TB).

The *Freedisk* command is very useful for remote installations using batch files when you are not sure about the remote computer's available free disk space. If the specified amount of disk space is available, the *Freedisk* command returns a value of *1*. If not, it returns a value of *0*. You can use these two values in batch files for conditional processing.

The following example shows how you can use the *Freedisk* command from the command prompt to check whether 20 GB of free disk space is available:

```
Freedisk /d D: 20GB
```

The results of this command are displayed as follows:

```
INFO: The specified amount of free space is not available on "D:\" volume.
```

The following command checks for 500 MB of free disk space on the D: drive on a remote computer named HRDesk1 with the username *Garyb* and a password:

```
Freedisk /s HRDesk1 /u Garyb /p ******* /d D: 500MB
```

The results of this command are displayed as follows:

```
SUCCESS: The specified 524,288,000 byte(s) of free space are available on current
volume.
```

Saving Disk Space with the Compact Command

One of the tasks associated with hard-disk administration is managing the available and used space on different volumes. Sometimes it becomes necessary to delete unwanted files to clear space on the disk. In other situations, it may not be possible to delete files or folders because they may be needed later. When normal, uncompressed files are eating up disk space on the computer and you do not want to delete them, you can use the *Compact* utility on NTFS volumes to compress files and directories. This helps you store more information in the same amount of disk space. You can use the *Compact* utility to set the compression on a directory so that any files added to the directory are automatically compressed.

Unlike its name suggests, you can use this command to uncompress files and directories as well, by changing their compression attributes. So if a file or directory is compressed, you can uncompress it with the *Compact* command, and vice versa. When you use this command without any parameters, the current compression attributes of the specified file or directory are displayed. The syntax of this command is:

```
Compact [{/c | /u}] [/a] [/i] [/f] [/q] [FileName[...]] [/s[:Dir]]
```

You can use either the */c* parameter (to compress) or the */u* parameter (to uncompress) with a single *Compact* command. Table 5.3 explains the parameters of this command.

Table 5.3 Parameters of the Compact Command

Parameter	Description
/c	Used to compress the specified files or the directory.
/u	Used to uncompress the specified files or the directory.
/a	Used to display hidden or system files in the directory.
/i	Used to ignore errors during the process. This parameter is of particular use in batch files because a batch file will stop processing once it encounters an error. By default, the *Compact* command will stop the compaction process when an error occurs.
/f	Used to force the compression of all specified files, including those that were previously partially compressed. When a file is partially compressed, the *Compact* command will not compress it again, unless the /f parameter is used. The partial compression might have been caused by a system crash during the compression process.
/q	Used to display just the summary information during the compression or uncompression process.
FileName[...]	Specifies the filename to be compressed or uncompressed. You can use wildcards with filenames.
/s[:Dir]	Used to compress or uncompress the subdirectories within the specified directory.

When used without any parameters, the *Compact* command shows the current compression state of the file or files in the specified directory. The following listing shows the output of this command when used in a computer's C:\Program Files\Support Tools folder. In this listing, all the files with a .exe extension were compressed using the *Compact* command with a *.exe wildcard.

```
Listing C:\Program Files\Support Tools\
New files added to this directory will not be compressed.


    87552 :     61440 = 1.4 to 1 C acldiag.exe
   216091 :    126976 = 1.7 to 1 C addiag.exe
   759808 :    759808 = 1.0 to 1   adprop.dll
   333824 :    333824 = 1.0 to 1   adsiedit.dll
    42986 :     42986 = 1.0 to 1   adsiedit.msc
     8704 :      8192 = 1.1 to 1 C apmstat.exe
    18432 :     16384 = 1.1 to 1 C bindiff.exe
    50176 :     28672 = 1.8 to 1 C Bitsadmin.exe
    41472 :     28672 = 1.4 to 1 C browstat.exe
    65024 :     53248 = 1.2 to 1 C cabarc.exe
    81676 :     81676 = 1.0 to 1   clone.vbs
```

```
33262 :     33262 = 1.0 to 1    clonegg.vbs
33418 :     33418 = 1.0 to 1    cloneggu.vbs
33315 :     33315 = 1.0 to 1    clonelg.vbs
91648 :     91648 = 1.0 to 1    clonepr.dll
97280 :     97280 = 1.0 to 1    clonepr.doc
32855 :     32855 = 1.0 to 1    clonepr.vbs
 8293 :      8293 = 1.0 to 1    connstat.cmd
----------

----------

Of 90 files within 1 directories
54 are compressed and 36 are not compressed.
24,082,972 total bytes of data are stored in 21,887,438 bytes.
The compression ratio is 1.1 to 1.
```

The following examples illustrate the use of the *Compact* command.

```
Compact /c MyFile.doc
Compact /c /i /s:\Reports *.txt
```

The first of the two preceding commands will compress the file named MyFile.doc in the current working directory. The second will compress all files with a .txt extension in the \Reports directory and all its subdirectories. The /i parameter forces the command to continue even if an error occurs during compression. Here are two more examples:

```
Compact /c /s *.*
Compact /c /s:\
```

The first command compresses all files in the current directory, all subdirectories within the current directory, and the files inside all subfolders. However, it does not change the current directory's compression state. The second command changes the compression state of the root directory, all directories on the volume, and all files on the volume.

> **NOTE**
>
> There are a few important things to note in this section. First, the *Compact* command works only on NTFS volumes. Compression is a feature of the NTFS file system; it does not work on FAT and FAT32 volumes. Second, you cannot use the command to read, write, or mount volumes that have already been compressed using the *DriveSpace* or *DoubleSpace* utility. You must uncompress those files first in order to use the *Compact* utility. Third, when you set the compression state of a directory, all new files added to it are automatically compressed.

Managing Mounted Volumes with the Mountvol Command

You learned earlier in this chapter that mounted volumes provide a way to increase space on a volume without having to add a separate drive letter. The *volume mount point* refers to the actual logical drive that is mounted to an existing empty folder. This can be quite helpful when you are running out of drive letters. You can use the *Mountvol* command to create, delete, and list mounted volumes from the command line. The syntax of this command is:

```
Mountvol [Drive:] Path VolumeName
Mountvol [Drive:] Path /d
Mountvol [Drive:] Path /l
Mountvol [Drive:] Path /p
Mountvol /r
Mountvol /n
Mountvol /e
Mountvol Drive: /s
```

Table 5.4 explains the parameters of this command.

Table 5.4 Parameters of the Mountvol Command

Parameter	Description
Drive: Path	Specifies the existing folder on an NTFS drive where the volume is to be mounted.
VolumeName	Specifies the volume name that is the target of the volume mount point.
/d	Used to remove the volume mount point from the specified NTFS folder.
/l	Used to list the name of the mounted volume for the specified folder.
/p	Used to remove a volume mount point from the specified directory. The basic volume is dismounted and is taken offline so that it becomes unmountable. Any open handles on the volume are closed before the volume is dismounted. When you dismount volumes using the /p parameter, they are listed in the volumes list as "NOT MOUNTABLE UNTIL A VOLUME MOUNT POINT IS CREATED." If the volume has additional mount points, you must dismount them first using the /p parameter, before using the /p parameter to dismount the volume. You can create the basic volume again by assigning it a volume mount point.

Continued

Table 5.4 continued Parameters of the Mountvol Command

Parameter	Description
/r	Used to remove the volume mount point directories and Registry settings that no longer exist on the system. This prevents the system from automatically mounting new volumes using the previously assigned mount points when the removed mount points are added to the system.
/n	Disables the automatic mounting of new basic volumes.
/e	Used to re-enable the automatic mounting of new basic volumes (if you have previously disabled this feature using the /n parameter).
/s	Can be used only on Itanium-based computers. It is used to mount the Extensible Firmware Interface (EFI) system partition to the specified drive.

NOTE

The following parameters of the *Mountvol* command are supported only on Windows Server 2003 computers; you cannot use them on Windows XP computers:

Mountvol *[Drive:]Path* **/p**
Mountvol */r*
Mountvol */n*
Mountvol */e*
Mountvol *Drive:* */s*

You can also manage mounted volumes using the *Diskpart* command-line utility, which we'll discuss in Chapter 6.

Checking and Fixing Bad Sectors with the Chkdsk Command

Chkdsk is one of the oldest command-line utilities supported on Microsoft operating systems. It checks for bad sectors and file system errors on the specified disk and attempts to fix the problems. It also checks and attempts to recover lost clusters on the disk. *Chkdsk* runs on FAT, FAT32, and NTFS volumes, but certain advanced parameters are available only on NTFS volumes. You must be a member of the administrators group to run the *Chkdsk* command. The syntax of this command is:

```
Chkdsk [Volume:][[Path] FileName] [/f] [/v] [/r] [/x] [/i] [/c]
[/l[:Size]]
```

Table 5.5 explains the parameters of this command.

Table 5.5 Parameters of the Chkdsk Command

Parameter	Description
Volume:	Specifies the drive letter and volume name of a mounted volume on which you want to check disk errors. The drive letter must be followed by a colon (:).
[Path] FileName	Used to specify the name of a file and path for FAT and FAT32 volumes only.
/f	Must be used if you want the *Chkdsk* command to fix errors. The drive where the command is run must be locked to successfully perform the disk check. If the disk is not locked (files are open), the command prompts you to run *Chkdsk* when the computer is restarted.
/v	Displays the name of each file in every directory as the check is performed.
/r	Used to locate bad sectors and recover readable information, in addition to fixing regular errors. The disk must be locked for this purpose.
/x	Used for mounted volumes. This parameter dismounts the mounted volume first, if required. If you use this parameter, you do not need to use the /f parameter. Dismounting a volume closes all open handles for all running processes. This ensures that the *Chkdsk* command can perform the checks and fix errors without any interruption from applications.
/i	Used to perform a less vigorous check of index entries in the drive. While this parameter does not take much time to complete, it does not perform a comprehensive check. If you are using the *Chkdsk* command for performance-related problems, do not use this parameter. You can use this parameter with NTFS volumes only.
/c	Used to skip the cyclic check of directories to reduce the amount of time required to complete the *Chkdsk*. As with the /i parameter, this parameter also does not let *Chkdsk* perform a comprehensive check on the drive. You can use this parameter with NTFS volumes only.
/l:Size	Used to change the size of the log files used by the *Chkdsk* command. When used without the size argument, the current size of the log file is displayed. You can use this parameter with NTFS volumes only.

One of the primary conditions for running the *Chkdsk* utility successfully is that the disk or volume must be locked. This is required if you want to check errors as well as fix them. If any applications are running on the disk, or if any remote applications are accessing the volume, you must close all applications and disconnect all remote users before starting. If *Chkdsk* finds any open files or applications when it starts, it displays the following message:

```
Chkdsk cannot run because the volume is in use by another process. Would you like
to schedule this volume to be checked the next time the system starts? (Y/N)
```

If you press the **Y** key, the *Chkdsk* command schedules the disk check when the system restarts. If the specified drive is a boot or system partition, the *Chkdsk* command automatically restarts the computer once the drive check is complete.

Checking the Disk without Fixing Errors

You also can use the *Chkdsk* command to analyze the specified disk without having to fix its errors. The syntax of this command is:

```
Chkdsk D:
```

When this command is run, it checks only the D: drive for disk and file system errors. It does not attempt to repair any errors that it finds. The following is the result of this command:

```
The type of the file system is NTFS.
The volume is in use by another process. Chkdsk
might report errors when no corruption is present
Volume label is Mydrive.

WARNING!  F parameter not specified.
Running CHKDSK in read-only mode.

CHKDSK is verifying files (stage 1 of 3)...
File verification completed.
CHKDSK is verifying indexes (stage 2 of 3)...
Index verification completed.
CHKDSK is verifying security descriptors (stag
Security descriptor verification completed.

  10233373 KB total disk space.
   1006748 KB in 4579 files.
      1056 KB in 276 indexes.
         4 KB in bad sectors.
     59181 KB in use by the system.
     53216 KB occupied by the log file.
   9166384 KB available on disk.
```

```
    4096 bytes in each allocation unit.
 2558343 total allocation units on disk.
 2291596 allocation units available on disk.
```

As you can see from this output, the *Chkdsk* command has performed a detailed analysis of the D: drive, but it has made no attempt to repair the 4 KB of bad sectors it found during analysis.

Checking Drives and Fixing Errors

The following example shows how you can use the *Chkdsk* command with the */f* parameter to repair the errors it finds during analysis:

```
Chkdsk D: /f
```

It is important to note that *Chkdsk* will not be able to repair any errors on a volume that has any open files. The disk must be locked in order to fix errors.

```
Chkdsk D: /f /v
```

In the preceding example, we added the */v* parameter along with */f* in order to view a detailed report.

Running Chkdsk on Mounted Volumes

If you have mounted volumes on the specified drive, you must dismount them by using the */x* parameter with the *Chkdsk* command:

```
Chkdsk D: /x /f
```

If you do not use this parameter, the following message is displayed:

```
The type of the file system is NTFS.
Cannot lock current drive.

Chkdsk cannot run because the volume is in use by a
process.  Chkdsk may run if this volume is dismount
ALL OPENED HANDLES TO THIS VOLUME WOULD THEN BE INV
Would you like to force a dismount on this volume? (Y/N)
```

You can press the **Y** key to dismount the volume and proceed with the disk check.

Exit Codes for the Chkdsk Command

The *Chkdsk* utility has built-in exit codes that you can use in batch files for conditional processing. These exit codes are used as arguments for the *Errorlevel* statements. Table 5.6 lists the exit codes for this command.

Table 5.6 Exit Codes for the Chkdsk Command

Exit Code Value	Description
0	The command did not encounter any errors on the disk.
1	Errors were found on the disk and were fixed.
2	Disk cleanup was performed (or not performed, if the /f parameter was not used).
3	The command could not check the disk, errors could not be fixed, or errors were not fixed because the /f parameter was not used.

Defragmenting Disks with the Defrag Command

Computer hard disks become fragmented with continuous usage. When you install an application, or when a large number of files are copied, moved, or deleted, the chances of data becoming fragmented increase. A file on a fragmented disk may not be stored on a contiguous space; it must be spread over several clusters in smaller parts. This degrades hard-disk read/write performance, as the heads have to move back and forth to locate data. You should regularly analyze and defragment hard disks to maintain their performance. You can perform disk analysis and defragmentation by using the Disk Defragmenter snap-in in the Computer Management console or by using the *Defrag* command-line utility. You can even use the *Defrag* command in your batch files to automate the analysis and defragmentation process. The syntax of this command is:

```
Defrag Volume
Defrag Volume [/a]
Defrag Volume [/a] [/v]
Defrag Volume [/v]
Defrag Volume [/f]
```

Table 5.7 explains the parameters of the *Defrag* command.

Table 5.7 Parameters of the Defrag Command

Parameter	Description
Volume:	Specifies the volume or drive that you need to analyze or defragment. You can also specify a volume mount point. This should be followed by a colon (:).

Continued

Table 5.7 continued Parameters of the Defrag Command

Parameter	Description
/a	Used only when you want to analyze the volume. Specifying it does not defragment the specified volume. A summary of the analysis is displayed, indicating what percentage of the hard-disk space is fragmented. You can decide whether to perform the defragmentation depending on how much of the disk is fragmented. This parameter is normally not used in batch files.
/v	Used to display a detailed report of the analysis and defragmentation process of the specified volume. You can use both the /v and /a parameters so that only the detailed analysis report is displayed.
/f	Used when the available free space on the disk or volume is low. (The *Defrag* command requires at least 15 percent free space.)

TIP

Interestingly, when you check the Windows XP or Windows Server 2003 command-line reference, you will find that the parameters are listed as /a, /v, and /f. When you check the command-line help by typing **DEFRAG /?** at the command prompt, these parameters are listed as –a, –f, and –v. In fact, the *Defrag* utility accepts both types of signs (/ and –) with these parameters.

You can run the *Defrag* command by specifying the drive letter or the volume, followed by a colon (:). The utility analyzes the disk and tells you what percentage of the disk is fragmented. It also suggests whether the disk requires defragmentation. The following example shows the results of the *Defrag* command when used to analyze a hard disk:

```
C:\Program Files\Support Tools>defrag D: /a
Windows Disk Defragmenter
Copyright (c) 2003 Microsoft Corp. and Executive Software International, Inc.

Analysis Report
    9.76 GB Total,  8.73 GB (89%) Free,  3% Fragmented (6% file fragmentation)

You do not need to defragment this volume.
```

As indicated by this report, the computer's D: drive is only 3 percent fragmented and the rate of file fragmentation is only 6 percent. The report also suggests that you need not defragment this volume. But this does not mean the disk will not become fragmented. You need to analyze your hard disks periodically to maintain their performance.

When defragmentation is complete, the summary report is displayed as follows:

```
C:\Program Files\Support Tools>defrag D:
Windows Disk Defragmenter
Copyright (c) 2003 Microsoft Corp. and Executive Software International, Inc.

Analysis Report
    9.76 GB Total,  8.73 GB (89%) Free,  2% Fragmented (5% file fragmentation)


Defragmentation Report
    9.76 GB Total,  8.73 GB (89%) Free,  0% Fragmented (0% file fragmentation)
```

In order to successfully defragment a disk, you need at least 15 percent of free disk space. If the available space is less than this, the *Defrag* utility will be able to perform only a partial defragmentation. This 15 percent of free disk space is used for temporary storage during the defragmentation process. You can use the */f* parameter to force the *Defrag* utility to defragment a hard disk even if the amount of free hard-disk space is less than 15 percent, as shown in the following example:

```
Defrag D: /f /v
```

In the preceding code, the */v* parameter is used to display a detailed analysis and defragmentation report. If you do not want to display the analysis and defragmentation report immediately, you can redirect the report to a text file, as shown in the following example:

```
Defrag D: /v >DefragRep.txt
```

You can open the DefragRep.txt file in Notepad at a later time to view the report.

Defragmenting Dirty Volumes

The system may mark some volumes as *dirty*. A dirty volume indicates possible volume corruption or file system errors. You can use the *Fsutil Dirty Query* command to check whether a volume has been marked as dirty. The following is an example of querying a volume using the *Fsutil* command:

```
Fsutil Dirty Query D:
```

One of the following results is displayed:

```
Volume -D is NOT Dirty.
Volume -D is Dirty.
```

If you find that a volume is marked as dirty, use the *Chkdsk* utility before running the *Defrag* command. The *Chkdsk* utility will attempt to fix file system errors.

NOTE

The Disk Defragmenter in the Computer Management console and the *Defrag* utility are mutually exclusive. You cannot run the *Defrag* command-line utility when the Disk Defragmenter is analyzing or defragmenting a disk. The *Defrag* command will fail. By the same token, if you are using the *Defrag* command on a volume and start the Disk Defragmenter on the same volume, the Disk Defragmenter will not work.

Checking Autocheck Status with the Chkntfs Command

In Windows XP and Windows Server 2003 operating systems, the installed disk drives are checked when the system is started. An internal program named Autochk.exe initiates the disk checks. If any errors are found, the system attempts to repair them. Since the operating system uses the *Autochk* utility to start the disk check automatically on system startup, you cannot use it directly from the command line. However, you can use the *Chkntfs* command-line utility to control *Autochk*. You can use the *Chkntfs* utility to see whether *Autochk* is scheduled to run automatically on system startup and exclude a volume from checking. This command works on FAT, FAT32, and NTFS volumes. The syntax of this command is:

```
Chkntfs Volume: [...]
Chkntfs [/d]
Chkntfs [/t[:Time]]
Chkntfs [/x Volume: [...]]
Chkntfs [/c Volume: [...]]
```

Table 5.8 explains the parameters of this command.

Table 5.8 Parameters of the Chkntfs Command

Parameter	Description
Volume:	Specifies the volume name, drive letter, or a volume mount point. It must be followed by a colon (:).
/d	Used to restore all default settings for *Chkntfs* (except the countdown for automatic file checking).
/t: Time	Displays or sets the countdown time in seconds for *Autochk* on system restart. If you do not specify the *Time* value, the default time is displayed.

Continued

Table 5.8 continued Parameters of the Chkntfs Command

Parameter	Description
/x Volume:	Used to exclude the specified volume from automatic checking even if the volume is marked as dirty.
/c Volume:	Used to schedule automatic checking of the specified volume on system startup.

The following examples illustrate the use of the *Chkntfs* command.

```
Chkntfs C: D:
```

The preceding command displays the status of the C: and D: drives. If the drives are marked as dirty, they will be scheduled for an automatic check on the next system startup. If the drives are not dirty, the following message is displayed:

```
The type of the file system is NTFS.
C: is not dirty.
The type of the file system is NTFS.
D: is not dirty.
```

All drives are checked automatically during system startup. You can exclude one or more drives or mount volumes using the following example command:

```
Chkntfs /x D: E: F:
```

The following example shows how you can use the /t parameter to display the count-down time:

```
Chkntfs /t
```

The output of the preceding command shows that the default countdown time is 10 seconds:

```
The AUTOCHK initiation countdown time is set to 10 second(s).
```

You can change the countdown time to 60 seconds (one minute) as follows:

```
Chkntfs /t:60
```

The following command shows how to schedule automatic checking of the C: and D: drives on system startup:

```
Chkntfs /c C: D:
```

When the system starts, the C: and D: drives will be automatically checked to determine whether they are dirty.

Summary

In this chapter, we discussed some of the command-line utilities used to maintain file systems and hard disks. The most notable utilities include *Fsutil*, *Chkdsk*, and *Defrag*. *Fsutil* is new to the Windows XP and Windows Server 2003 families of operating systems. While you might have experience with older utilities such as *Chkdsk* and *Defrag*, you need to have thorough knowledge of the operating systems to use the *Fsutil* command and its subcommands. This chapter provided only basic examples of how you can use this utility. We also discussed other commands in this chapter, including *Format*, *Convert*, and *Compact*. You need sufficient experience before using *Fsutil* or any other command in batch files or scripts. It is always best to try the commands on a test computer before starting to write a script. In the next chapter, we will discuss how to use the *Diskpart* utility to manage volumes on basic and dynamic disks.

Chapter 6

Managing Hard Disks with the Diskpart Utility

Topics in this chapter:

- The Diskpart Utility

- Diskpart Commands

- Scripting with Diskpart

- Diskpart Exit Codes

- Obtaining Volume Information

- Managing Dynamic Volumes

- Managing Fault-Tolerant Volumes

Introduction

You can perform most command-line-based disk management tasks in Windows XP and Windows Server 2003 using the *Diskpart* utility. *Diskpart* is a text-based command interpreter that runs on its own under the Windows command shell. You can use this utility either on a local computer or on a remote computer on the network. Whether you want to create a partition, assign it a drive letter, or perform a complex and advanced task such as managing fault-tolerant volumes, *Diskpart* is the utility of choice if you love to work at the command line. It does not matter whether you work with individual commands or create scripts to manage repeated tasks, the *Diskpart* utility allows you to work in whatever way you feel comfortable. This chapter introduces the *Diskpart* utility and discusses how you can use it to perform everyday disk management tasks.

The Diskpart Utility

You can use the *Diskpart* utility to convert basic disks to dynamic disks and vice versa. You can create, delete, and manage disks, partitions, and volumes as well as fault-tolerant volumes such as mirrored and Redundant Array of Inexpensive Disks (RAID) 5 volumes. You also can perform certain tasks that you cannot perform using the Disk Management snap-in, such as tasks that might result in accidental loss of data. Since the *Diskpart* command-line utility gets exclusive access to the object in focus, you should use it very cautiously.

Although you can perform most hard–disk–related tasks using the *Diskpart* utility on local and remote computers, it does have a few limitations. For instance, you cannot use it to format hard disks, nor can you use it to manage removable disks such as CDs, DVDs, tape drives, and Universal Serial Bus (USB) drives. To format hard disks, you would use the *Format* command, as discussed in Chapter 5.

The Object in Focus

The *Diskpart* command interpreter works with *focus* on a particular object. This object may be a disk, a partition, or a volume. You can choose only one object to be in focus at a time. The object remains in focus until you shift focus by choosing another object. In some cases, the *Diskpart* utility automatically shifts focus from one object to another. For example, when you create a new partition, focus automatically changes to the newly created partition so that you can assign it a drive letter.

Before you can use the *Diskpart* command, you must list and select an object to give it focus. To bring an object into focus, start the *Diskpart* interpreter by typing **Diskpart** at the command prompt. When you press the **Enter** key, the prompt changes as follows:

```
DISKPART>
```

To give focus to a particular object on a computer, such as a disk, a volume, or a partition, you would usually obtain a list of all the disks, volumes, or partitions on that computer by using one of the following three *List* commands:

- **List Disk** Used to display a list of hard disks in the system.

- **List Partition** Used to display partitions of the disk in focus.

- **List Volume** Used to display all volumes on the system, including partitions of the hard disks and logical drives.

For example, when you use the *List Disk* command, a list of disks is displayed along with other information such as status, size, available free space, and whether the disk is dynamic. Here is some sample output of the *List Disk* command:

```
Disk ###  Status       Size     Free     Dyn  Gpt
--------  ----------   -------  -------   ---  ---
Disk 0    Online        19 GB   8033 KB
Disk 1    Online        38 GB   21010 KB
Disk 2    Online        76 GB   54200 KB
```

You give focus to an object using one of the following three *Select* commands:

- **Select Disk** Used to select the specified disk to bring it into focus. You specify which disk by its number; for instance, *Disk 0* or *Disk 1*.

- **Select Partition** Used to select a partition to bring it into focus. You specify which partition by its number; for instance, *Partition 1* or *Partition 2*. Note that partition numbers start from 1 rather than 0.

- **Select Volume** Used to select a volume to bring it into focus. You can specify the volume by the volume number, a drive letter, or a mount path.

For example, if you type **Select Partition 2** at the *Diskpart* prompt, the focus shifts to partition number 2 and the following message appears:

```
Partition 2 is now the selected partition.
```

If you use the *List Partition* command, the list of partitions is displayed. The selected partition is indicated by an asterisk (*), as shown in the following example:

```
  Partition ###  Type              Size     Offset
  -------------  ----------------  -------  -------
  Partition 1    Extended           10 GB   8033 KB
* Partition 2    Logical            10 GB   8064 KB
  Partition 3    Primary             9 GB    10 GB
```

In this example, *Partition 2* is in focus. You can now use other disk commands on this partition. The focus will remain on this object until you change the focus to another disk, partition, or volume. We explain *List, Select,* and other *Diskpart* commands in more detail in the next section.

Master Craftsman...

Focus

Since volumes are created on physical hard disks and their partitions, when a partition has focus, the related volume (if any) also has focus. Similarly, when a volume has focus, the related disk and the partition also have focus when the volume is created on a single specific partition. Most of the *Diskpart* commands require that you give focus to a particular object. The *Diskpart* commands that do not require focus include *List, Rem, Help,* and *Exit.*

Diskpart Commands

The *Diskpart* command interpreter consists of several commands, which you can use to manage disks, partitions, and volumes on the computer. The only thing *Diskpart* cannot do is format a disk; for that, you need to use the *Format* command. The following sections discuss the commands you can use with the *Diskpart* utility. Remember that you can always get help on any command by typing the command, followed by **/?**. For example, if you want to create a partition or a volume but you are not sure how to use the *Create* command, you can type **Create /?** to get a list of available *Create* commands. More help is available if you type **Create Partition /?** or **Create Volume /?**.

Active

You use the *Diskpart Active* command to mark a partition that is in focus as *active.* This tells the basic input/output system (BIOS) or the Extensible Firmware Interface (EFI) that the marked partition is a valid system volume and that you can use it to boot the system. When you mark a partition as active, *Diskpart* does not check whether the marked partition actually contains the boot and system files. It only checks that the partition can be marked active. If you mark a partition active by mistake, the system may fail to boot. The syntax of this command is:

```
Active
```

Remember that you can mark only partitions as active.

Add Disk

You use the *Add Disk* command to add the specified disk to an existing *simple volume* that is in focus, to create a mirrored set. The syntax of this command is:

```
Add Disk=n [Noerr]
```

In the preceding command, *n* is the disk number that you want to add to make a mirror volume. This disk must have unallocated space that is at least equal to the simple volume in focus. You can add the *Noerr* parameter to tell the *Diskpart* command to continue processing a script even if an error is encountered. If you omit the *Noerr* parameter, the script will stop with an error code.

Assign

You use the *Assign* command to assign a drive letter or mount point to the volume in focus. You can also change the drive letter of a removable drive. The syntax of this command is:

```
Assign [{Letter=D | Mount=Path}] [Noerr]
```

Here is a description of the *Assign* command's parameters:

- **Letter=D** *Letter* is the drive letter you want to assign to the volume. If the letter is already in use, an error is returned. If you do not specify a letter, the next available letter is used.

- **Mount=Path** Specifies the path of the mount point that you want to assign to the volume.

- **Noerr** Can be added to tell the *Diskpart* command to continue processing a script even if an error is encountered.

NOTE

You cannot use the *Assign* command to assign drive letters to any system or boot volume, or to volumes that contain a paging file. You also cannot assign drive letters to GUID Partition Table (GPT) partitions that are not basic data partitions, or to partitions created by Original Equipment Manufacturers (OEMs).

Automount

Automount is enabled by default. Windows uses this to automatically mount basic volumes and assign drive letters to them when they are added to the system. The syntax of this command is:

```
Automount [Enable] [Disable] [Scrub] [Noerr]
```

Here is a description of the *Automount* command's parameters:

- **Enable** Used to automatically mount basic volumes and assign them drive letters when they are added to the system. This is enabled by default.

- **Disable** Used to disable the *Automount* feature. When *Automount* is disabled, Windows does not automatically mount and assign drive letters to basic volumes.

- **Scrub** Used to remove volume mount point directories and Registry settings for volumes that were previously configured but no longer exist in the system.

- **Noerr** Can be added to tell the *Diskpart* command to continue processing a script even if an error is encountered.

Break Disk

You use the *Break Disk* command to break the mirrored volume in focus into two simple volumes. This command works only with dynamic volumes. When the mirror is broken, one of the volumes retains the drive letter and the other becomes the focus of the *Diskpart* command so that you can assign it a drive letter. The syntax of this command is:

```
Break Disk=N [Nokeep] [Noerr]
```

Here is a description of the *Break Disk* command's parameters:

- **N** Specifies the disk number that is used to create the mirrored volume. This disk becomes the focus after the mirror is broken. You can assign it a drive letter after breaking the mirror.

- **Nokeep** Used when you want only one of the disks to be retained as a simple volume. The disk specified by *N* in the code is deleted and converted to free or unallocated space. None of the disks remains in focus.

- **Noerr** Can be added to tell the *Diskpart* command to continue processing a script even if an error is encountered.

NOTE

Windows will retain both volumes after you use the *Break Disk* command, and each volume will retain its contents. The volume specified by the *N* parameter will be in focus so that you can assign it a drive letter. If you use the *Nokeep* parameter, the volume specified by the *N* parameter is deleted and none of the disks remains in focus.

Clean

You use the *Clean* command to remove all volume and partition formatting from the disk in focus. All data is deleted. On Master Boot Record (MBR) partitions, the partition information and hidden sector information are overwritten, and on GPT disks, the GPT partition information and protected MBR are overwritten. The GPT partitions do not have any hidden sector information. The syntax of this command is:

```
Clean [All]
```

The only parameter of this command is *All*, which specifies that each sector on the disk be written with a *0*. This implies that the data on the disk will be deleted completely.

Convert

The *Convert* command is further classified into four commands for converting basic and dynamic disks as well as converting MBR and GPT partitions. You can use these commands with the *Noerr* parameter in scripts so that the *Diskpart* utility continues to run a script even if there is an error.

Convert Basic

The *Convert Basic* command converts an empty dynamic disk to a basic disk. You must back up all data and delete all partitions before using this command. The syntax of this command is:

```
Convert Basic [Noerr]
```

WARNING

Converting a dynamic disk by using the *Convert Basic* command or by using the Disk Management console requires that the disk be empty and contain no partitions. Before you use this command, make sure that you back up all data before deleting the partitions. Then delete all the partitions and use the command to convert the disk to basic. The same rules apply when you use the *Convert GPT* and *Convert MBR* commands to convert partition styles, discussed shortly.

Convert Dynamic

The *Convert Dynamic* command converts a basic disk into a dynamic disk. The partitions of the disk become simple volumes and all the data on the disk is retained. The syntax of this command is:

```
Convert Dynamic [Noerr]
```

Convert GPT

The *Convert GPT* command works only with Itanium-based computers. It converts an empty basic disk with an MBR partition style to a basic disk with a GPT partition style. The syntax of this command is:

`Convert GPT [Noerr]`

Convert MBR

The *Convert MBR* command works only with Itanium-based computers. It converts an empty basic disk with a GPT partition style to a basic disk with an MBR partition style. The syntax of this command is:

`Convert MBR [Noerr]`

Create

You use the *Create* commands to create disk partitions and volumes, as well as to create simple, striped, and RAID volumes. You can use the *Create* commands with the *Noerr* parameter in scripts so that the *Diskpart* utility continues to run a script even if there is an error. The following sections describe the different *Create* commands.

Create Partition Primary

You use the *Create Partition Primary* command to create a basic partition on the current disk. When the partition is created the focus is automatically shifted to the newly created partition. The syntax of this command is:

`Create Partition Primary [Size=N] [Offset=N] [ID={Byte | GUID}] [Noerr]`

Here is a description of the *Create Partition Primary* command's parameters:

- **Size=N** Specifies the size of the partition in megabytes (MB). If no size is specified, all of the available space on the disk is used. The specified size is snapped to the cylinder size. For example, if you specify a partition size of 500 MB, the partition size would be 504 MB.

- **Offset=N** The byte offset to start from the first available bit of free space on the disk. As with the *Size* parameter, this parameter also snaps the specified size to the closest cylinder boundary. For example, if you specify the *Offset* parameter as 26 MB and the cylinder size is 8 MB, the offset would be treated as 24 MB.

- **ID={Byte | GUID}** This parameter is used by OEMs only. Do not use this parameter if you do not know how it works. Improper use may render a system unable to start.

Create Partition Extended

You use the *Create Partition Extended* command to create an extended partition on the current disk. When the partition is created, the focus is automatically shifted to the newly created partition. The syntax of this command is:

```
Create Partition Extended [Size=N] [Offset=N] [Noerr]
```

For a description of this command's parameters, see the preceding section. You can use the *Offset* parameter in this command with MBR partitions only.

Master Craftsman…

Extended Partitions

You can create only one extended partition on a disk. The *Diskpart* utility will return an error if you try to create an extended partition within an existing extended partition. If you want to create logical drives, you must first create an extended partition on the disk.

Create Partition Logical

You use the *Create Partition Logical* command to create a logical drive on a disk that already has an extended partition on it. After the drive is created, the focus is automatically shifted to the new drive. The syntax of this command is:

```
Create Partition Logical [Size=N] [Offset=N] [Noerr]
```

Here is a description of the *Create Partition Logical* command's parameters:

- **Size=N** Specifies the size of the logical drive in megabytes (MB). If no size is specified, all of the available space on the disk is used. The specified size is snapped to the cylinder size. For example, if you specify a partition size of 500 MB, the size of the logical drive would be 504 MB. Remember that the specified size must be smaller than the size of the extended partition.

- **Offset=N** Used on MBR-style partitions only. This is the byte offset from which the logical drive is created. If you do not specify the *Offset* parameter, the partition is started from the first available disk offset.

Create Partition EFI

You use the *Create Partition EFI* command on Itanium-based computers to create an EFI system partition on a GPT disk. When the partition is created the focus is automatically shifted to the new partition. The syntax of this command is:

`Create Partition EFI [Size=N] [Offset=N] [Noerr]`

Here is a description of the *Create Partition EFI* command's parameters:

- **Size=N** Specifies the size of the partition in megabytes (MB). If you omit this parameter, all available space on the disk is utilized.

- **Offset=N** Specifies the byte offset at which the partition is to be created. If you omit this parameter, the partition is placed at the first available part of the disk that is large enough to hold it.

Create Partition MSR

You use the *Create Partition MSR* command on Itanium-based computers to create a Microsoft Reserved Partition (MSR) on a GPT disk. When the partition is created the focus is automatically shifted to the new partition. The syntax of this command is:

`Create Partition MSR [Size=N] [Offset=N] [Noerr]`

Here is a description of the *Create Partition MSR* command's parameters:

- **Size=N** Specifies the size of the partition in megabytes (MB). If you omit this parameter, all available space on the disk is utilized.

- **Offset=N** Specifies the byte offset at which the partition is to be started. The offset number you specify is rounded to fill the nearest sector of the partition. If you omit this parameter, the partition is placed at the first available disk extent of the partition that is large enough to hold it.

WARNING

You must be very careful when dealing with GPT partitions, which are usually created on 64-bit Itanium-based computers for 64-bit versions of Windows XP and Windows Server 2003. Any incorrect parameter can easily render your computer unable to start. On Windows XP 64-bit edition systems, the GPT partition used to boot the system has the EFI system partition as the first partition on the disk, followed by the MSR partition. The GPT disks that are used only for data storage do not use the EFI system partition, and hence, the MSR partition is the first partition on these disks.

Create Volume Simple

You use the *Create Volume Simple* command to create a simple volume on a dynamic disk. When the volume is created, the focus is automatically shifted to the newly created volume. The syntax of this command is:

```
Create Volume Simple [Size=N] [Disk=N] [Noerr]
```

Here is a description of the *Create Volume Simple* command's parameters:

- **Size=N** Specifies the size of the volume in megabytes (MB). If you do not specify a size, all available free space on the disk is utilized.

- **Disk=N** Specifies the dynamic disk on which the new volume is to be created. If you omit this parameter, the current disk is used.

Create Volume Stripe

You use the *Create Volume Stripe* command to create a striped volume using two or more dynamic disks. When the volume is created, the focus is automatically shifted to the newly created volume. The syntax of this command is:

```
Create Volume Stripe [Size=N] [Disk=N,N] [,N...] [Noerr]
```

Here is a description of the *Create Volume Stripe* command's parameters:

- **Size=N** Specifies the size of the volume in megabytes (MB) that the volume should use on each specified disk. If you do not specify a size, the command will take the available free space on the smallest disk and an equal amount of disk space from all other specified disks.

- **Disk=N,N[,N...]** Specifies the dynamic disks on which the new striped volume is to be created. You will need at least two disks to create a striped volume. You can use a maximum of 32 disks.

Create Volume RAID

You use the *Create Volume RAID* command to create a RAID 5 volume (a striped volume with parity) using three or more dynamic disks. When the volume is created, the focus is automatically shifted to the newly created volume. The syntax of this command is:

```
Create Volume RAID [Size=N] [Disk=N,N,N] [,N...] [Noerr]
```

Here is a description of the *Create Volume RAID* command's parameters:

- **Size=N** Specifies the size of the RAID 5 volume in megabytes (MB) that the volume should use on each specified disk. If you do not specify a size, the command will take the available free space on the smallest disk and an equal amount of disk space from all other specified disks. The actual size of the RAID 5 volume is less than the combined size of all the participating disks because some disk space is used for parity. If a size were specified in the *Size=N* parameter, the same amount of space would be used for parity.

■ **Disk= N,N,N[,N...]** Specifies the dynamic disks on which the new striped volume is to be created. You will need at least three disks to create a RAID 5 volume. You can use a maximum of 32 disks.

Delete

You use the *Delete* command to delete disks, partitions, or volumes, depending on the sub-command you use. The following sections detail the three subcommands of this *Diskpart* command.

Delete Disk

You use the *Delete Disk* command to delete a missing disk from a disk list. You would use this command when a disk becomes unusable due to a hardware problem. The syntax of this command is:

```
Delete Disk [Noerr] [Override]
```

You use the *Override* parameter when you want the *Diskpart* utility to delete all simple volumes on the disk. If the disk contains half of the mirrored volume, the half of the mirror on the disk is deleted.

> **NOTE**
>
> You cannot use the *Delete Disk* command with the *Override* parameter on a disk that is part of a RAID 5 volume. The command will fail if it detects that the disk is participating in a RAID 5 volume.

Delete Partition

You use the *Delete Partition* command to delete partitions on basic and dynamic disks. When you use it to delete a partition on a basic disk, it deletes the partition in focus. You cannot delete the system partition, boot partition, or a partition that hosts the paging file or memory dump. When you use it with a dynamic volume, it deletes all the data on the dynamic volume. The syntax of this command is:

```
Delete Partition [Noerr] [Override]
```

When you use the *Override* parameter, the *Diskpart* utility deletes any partition regardless of its type. Usually, if a partition is unknown, the *Delete Partition* command will not work.

> **WARNING**
>
> You should use the *Delete Volume* command to delete dynamic disks. If you use the *Delete Partition* command to delete a dynamic disk, it will delete all the volumes residing on that disk and all data stored on this volume will be lost.

Delete Volume

You use the *Delete Volume* command to delete volumes on dynamic disks. You cannot delete the system volume, boot volume, or any volume that hosts the paging file or the system memory dump. The syntax of this command is:

```
Delete Volume [Noerr]
```

Swiss Army Knife...

Why You Cannot Delete System or Boot Partition/Volumes

You might be wondering why you cannot use the *Diskpart Delete* commands to delete system or boot partitions and volumes. The reason is simple. You are using the *Diskpart* command from within a working Windows system and these partitions or volumes are currently in use. As mentioned earlier in this book, that would be like cutting the branch off a tree on which you are sitting!

Detail

You use the *Detail* command to display the properties of a disk, partition, or volume, whichever is in focus. We discuss the syntax for the three commands for these functions in the following sections. You will see from the syntax of these commands that none of them supports use of the *Noerr* parameter that you can use in scripts.

Detail Disk

You use the *Detail Disk* command to display the properties of the disk in focus and the volumes that reside on the disk. The syntax is:

Detail Disk

The following sample listing shows the output of this command:

```
HTS421280H9AT00
Disk ID: A315A315
Type   : IDE
Bus    : 0
Target : 0
LUN ID : 0
```

Volume ###	Ltr	Label	Fs	Type	Size	Status	Info
Volume 1	C		NTFS	Partition	29 GB	Healthy	System
* Volume 2	E	New Volume	NTFS	Partition	45 GB	Healthy	

Detail Partition

You use the *Detail Partition* command to display the properties of the partition in focus. The syntax is:

Detail Partition

The following sample listing shows the output of this command:

```
Partition 2
Type   : 07
Hidden: No
Active: No
```

Volume ###	Ltr	Label	Fs	Type	Size	Status	Info
* Volume 2	E	New Volume	NTFS	Partition	45 GB	Healthy	

Detail Volume

You use the *Detail Volume* command to display the disks on which the current volume was created. The syntax is:

Detail Volume

Exit

You use the *Exit* command to exit the *Diskpart* command interpreter and return to the Windows command shell. The *Exit* command does not support the *Noerr* parameter, for obvious reasons. The syntax is:

`Exit`

Extend

You can use the *Extend* command with a basic or a dynamic volume that is in focus to extend it to the contiguous unallocated space. When you want to extend a basic volume, the unallocated space you choose must be contiguous space on the same disk as the partition in focus. When extending dynamic volumes, the unallocated space can be taken from any dynamic disk. Note that you cannot extend system and boot partitions. The command works only on partitions formatted with the New Technology File System (NTFS). The syntax of this command is:

`Extend [Size=N] [Disk=N] [Noerr]`

Here is a description of the *Extend* command's parameters:

- **Size=N** Specifies the amount of unallocated space in megabytes (MB) to add to the current partition. If you omit this parameter, all contiguous unallocated space is used.

- **Disk=N** Used for dynamic disks only to specify the disk number on which the dynamic volume is to be extended by the size specified in the *Size=N* parameter. If you omit this parameter, the volume is extended to the unallocated space on the current disk.

GPT Attributes

You use the *GPT Attributes* command to assign GPT attributes to a basic GPT partition in focus. This helps in specifying additional attributes to the GPT partition. Only advanced professionals and OEMs should use this utility. The syntax of this command is:

`GPT Attributes=N`

In the preceding command, *N* specifies the GPT attribute. The GPT attribute field is a 64-bit-long field with two subfields. The higher subfield applies only to the partition identifier in context and the lower subfield applies to all partition identifiers. Currently, the following two subfields are supported:

- **0x0000000000000001** Applies to all partitions and marks that the partition is a required partition. This attributes indicates that Disk Management utilities will not delete the partition.

- **0x8000000000000000** Used for basic partitions and prevents automatic assignment of a drive letter to the partition. By default, when a partition is moved to a new system, it is automatically assigned a drive letter. The user can assign a drive letter manually to the partition.

NOTE

GPT Attributes is an advanced _Diskpart_ utility and you should not use it unless you have thorough knowledge of how GPT partitions work. Inappropriately changing GPT attributes can result in volumes that you will not be able to mount or to which you will not be able to assign a drive letter.

Help

As with any other Windows command, you can use the _Help_ command to display a list of available commands with the _Diskpart_ utility. The syntax is:

```
Help
```

Import

You use the _Import_ command to import a foreign disk group into the computer's local disk group. This command imports every disk that is in the same group that is in focus. The syntax of this command is:

```
Import [Noerr]
```

Inactive

You use the _Inactive_ command on MBR partitions to mark a system or boot partition as active. When the partition is marked inactive, the system BIOS looks for the next configured drive, such as a CD-ROM drive, to boot the system when it is restarted. The syntax of this command is:

```
Inactive
```

WARNING

Do not use the *Inactive* command on any system or boot partition if you do not have good knowledge of the Windows XP or Windows Server 2003 operating systems, as this may make your computer unable to start. A computer cannot start without an active partition. Systems administrators can use this command to boot a computer from the network using PXE-compliant network adapters for Remote Installation Service (RIS).

     If you make a system or boot partition inactive by mistake, you can use the Windows Setup CD-ROM to start the system using the *Recovery Console*. Once you are in the Recovery Console, you can use the *Fixmbr* and *Fixboot* commands to repair the inactive partition.

List

The *List* command displays information about disks, partitions, and volumes, depending on which subcommand you use with it. The following sections describe the three *List* commands.

List Disk

The *List Disk* command displays a list of disks in the system, along with information about each disk. This information includes the size of the disk, the amount of free space available, and whether the disk is a basic disk or a dynamic disk. It also indicates whether the disk uses the MBR or GPT partition style. The disk indicated with an * next to it is currently in focus. The syntax of this command is:

`List Disk`

List Partition

The *List Partition* command displays the information on all partitions in the currently selected disk. The information includes partition number, size, type, and offset from the beginning of the disk. The syntax of this command is:

`List Partition`

    List Partition may not represent the actual volumes on dynamic disks.

List Volume

The *List Volume* command lists the basic and dynamic volumes on all disks in the system. The information included contains the volume number, label, size, file system used by the volume, volume type, and status of the volume. The syntax of this command is:

`List Volume`

> **NOTE**
>
> When you use the *List Volume* command, the displayed list contains all volumes on the computer, including removable volumes such as CD-ROM, DVD-ROM, and USB storage devices. However, you cannot use the *Diskpart* command to manage these devices.

Online

You use the *Online* command to bring an offline disk or volume back online. For mirrored or RAID 5 volumes, this command resynchronizes the volume that is in focus. The syntax of this command is:

`Online [Noerr]`

Rem

You use the *Rem* command to add comments to a batch file. The *Diskpart* command interpreter does not process the arguments after the *Rem* statement. The syntax is:

`Rem`

Remove

You use the *Remove* command to remove a drive letter or a mount point from the volume in focus. You also can use this command to change drive letters for removable drives. It does not work for system or boot volumes or for volumes that host the paging file. The syntax of this command is:

`Remove [{Letter=D | Mount=Path | All}] [Dismount] [Noerr]`

Here is a description of the *Remove* command's parameters:

- **Letter=D** Specifies the drive letter that you want to remove.
- **Mount=Path** Specifies the mount point path that is to be removed.

- **All** Removes all currently assigned drive letters and mount points.

- **Dismount** Dismounts the basic volume when all drive letters and mount points have been removed from the basic volume. The basic volume is then taken offline and cannot be mounted again. A dismounted volume becomes unavailable. If drive letters remain on the basic volume, the *Dismount* command will fail. You can mount a dismounted volume by assigning it a drive letter or by creating a mount point path to the volume.

Swiss Army Knife...

Remove Options

Out of the given parameters for the *Remove* command, you can use one of the following three options: *Letter=D*, *Mount=Path*, or *All*. When you do not specify any parameter, the command will remove the first drive letter or the mount point it encounters. The *Dismount* parameter is optional and you can use it with any of these parameters. Microsoft recommends that you use the *Remove All Dismount* command when writing scripts.

Repair Disk

You use the *Repair Disk* command to repair a RAID 5 volume by replacing the failed disk with a specified disk. The new disk must be a dynamic disk and its free space should be equal to or greater than that of the failed disk. The syntax of this command is:

```
Repair Disk=N [Noerr]
```

In the preceding command, *N* is the number of the disk that will replace the failed disk in the RAID 5 volume.

Rescan

You use the *Rescan* command to rescan the computer hardware to locate any hard disk that may have been added to the computer. The syntax of this command is:

```
Rescan
```

Retain

You use the *Retain* command to prepare an existing dynamic simple volume to be used as the system or boot volume. When used on X86-based computers, *Retain* creates a partition entry in the MBR of the simple volume in focus. On Itanium-based computers, it creates a partition entry in the GPT of the simple volume in focus. The syntax of this command is:

```
Retain
```

This is an advanced-level command and only OEM professionals and advanced administrators should use it.

Select

The *Select* command selects the specified disk, partition, or volume. The selected object becomes the focus of the *Diskpart* command interpreter. You can use the commands in the following sections to select a disk, partition, or volume.

Select Disk

You use the *Select Disk* command to select the specified disk so that the focus is shifted to the specified disk. The syntax is:

```
Select Disk=[N]
```

In the preceding command, *N* is the number of the disk onto which you want to shift focus. If you do not use this parameter, the current disk receives the focus. You can get a list of disk numbers using the *List Disk* command.

Select Partition

You use the *Select Partition* command to select the specified partition to give it focus. The partition is specified by a partition number. The syntax is:

```
Select Partition=[N]
```

In the preceding command, *N* is the partition number of the partition that is to receive focus. If you do not specify a partition number, the partition currently in focus is listed. You can get a list of partition numbers by using the *List Partition* command.

Select Volume

You use the *Select Volume* command to select the specified volume and give it focus. The volume is specified by number, drive letter, or mount point path. When you use this command with a basic volume, the partition corresponding to the selected volume also gets focus. The syntax is:

```
Select Volume=[{N | D}]
```

In the preceding command, *N* is the volume number of the volume that is to receive focus. You can use the *D* parameter to specify the drive letter or a mount point path. If you do not use the *N* or *D* parameter, the volume currently in focus is listed. You can get a list of all volumes and their numbers on the system using the *List Volume* command.

Scripting with Diskpart

You can use the *Diskpart* command interpreter to automate disk management tasks by using scripts or batch files. Scripts are very helpful in automating tasks such as creating partitions and volumes, as well as assigning drive letters and converting disks from basic to dynamic. Scripting is particularly useful when installing Windows operating systems in a large number of computers in unattended modem using utilities such as the System Preparation tool and RIS.

Diskpart scripts run differently from other scripts. The *Diskpart* command interpreter works in text mode; therefore, all *Diskpart* scripts are given a .txt extension. Here is the syntax for running a *Diskpart* script:

```
Diskpart /s ScriptName.txt
```

In the preceding code, ScriptName.txt is the name of the script file. If you want to redirect the output of the *Diskpart* script to another file, you can use the > redirection operator. For example, if you want the output of a script file to be sent to a log file, you can use the following command syntax:

```
Diskpart /s ScriptName.txt > LogFile.log
```

In the preceding code, LogFile.log is the name of the file to which you want to send the output of the script. Here is an example of a *Diskpart* script file:

```
Rem *Diskpart Script to Select a Disk
Rem *Create a Primary and Extended Partitions and
Rem *Create Logical Drives in Extended Partition
Rem *Assign Drive Letters to Primary Partition and Logical Drives

Rem *Select Disk Number 2
Select Disk 2

Rem *Create a Primary Partition
Create Partition Primary Size=8192
Assign Letter=E

Rem *Create Extended Partition and 2 Logical Drives
Create Partition Extended size=8192
Create Partition Logical Size=4096
Assign Letter=F
```

```
Create Partition Extended Size=4095
Assign Letter=G
```

After creating this file in Notepad, or the text editor of your choice, you should name it using the .txt extension. When you run this script using the *Diskpart /s ScriptName.txt* syntax, the following actions take place:

- A primary partition with a size of 8,192 MB is created and the focus is shifted to this partition. The *Assign* command assigns the drive letter E: to this partition.

- An extended partition with a size of 8,192 MB is created and the focus is shifted to this extended partition.

- A logical drive with a size of 4,096 MB is created and the focus is shifted to this drive. The *Assign* command assigns the drive letter F: to this logical drive.

- Another logical drive with a size of 4,096 MB is created and the focus is shifted to this logical drive. The *Assign* command assigns the drive letter G: to this logical drive.

As shown in this example, the scripts you write for *Diskpart* should normally complete all related tasks in a single script. For example, when you create volumes using a script, the same script should assign them drive letters, too.

NOTE

Microsoft recommends that you create a single script to complete all tasks related to a *Diskpart* process and avoid using multiple *Diskpart* scripts simultaneously. You can, however, create multiple scripts that run one after another, but there should be a gap of 15 seconds between consecutive scripts. This is because the *Diskpart* utility must apply the changes specified in the script to the system and close all operations before running the next script. When creating a script, you can pause between consecutive scripts by using the *Timeout /t15* command.

Diskpart Error Codes

The *Diskpart* utility has its own set of error codes (also known as exit codes) that you can use in batch files or scripts to automate disk management tasks. *Diskpart* supports the use of the *Noerr* parameter with some of its commands. Usually the *Diskpart* command would stop execution of a command when it encounters an error in a batch file. A *Diskpart* script always returns the error code when it encounters syntax errors, regardless of whether you are using the *Noerr* parameter. You can use these error codes with *Noerr* parameters to gain more precise control over the execution of a batch file. Table 6.1 lists *Diskpart* error codes.

Table 6.1 Error Codes for the Diskpart Command

Error Code	Description
0	Is returned when the *Diskpart* script runs successfully without encountering any errors.
1	Indicates that a fatal exception has occurred and there may be a serious problem.
2	Is returned when you specify an incorrect parameter with a *Diskpart* command.
3	Indicates that the utility is not able to open the specified script file or an output file.
4	Is returned when one of the services that *Diskpart* uses fails due to some problem, or returns an error.
5	Is returned when there is a syntax error in the *Diskpart* script or batch file. This usually indicates that you selected an invalid object (disk, partition, or volume) with the *Diskpart* command.

Using the Noerr Parameter

When you are creating *Diskpart* scripts, always keep in mind the commands that support the use of the *Noerr* parameter. Certain commands use the *Noerr* parameter and will exit with an error code. Other commands do not use the *Noerr* parameter but will still exit with an error code. So, it does not matter which command uses the *Noerr* parameter; if there is a problem running the *Diskpart* script, the script will always exit with an error code. You should use the *Noerr* parameter, wherever possible, to control the execution of your *Diskpart* scripts.

The following commands support use of the *Noerr* parameter:

- *Add*
- *Assign*
- *Automount*
- *Break*
- *Convert*
- *Create*
- *Delete*
- *Extend*
- *Import*

- *Online*
- *Remove*
- *Repair*

In this case, the script will still exit with an error code. An error code of *0* indicates that the script executed successfully.

The following commands do not support use of the *Noerr* parameter:

- *Active*
- *Clean*
- *Detail*
- *Exit*
- *GPT*
- *Help*
- *Inactive*
- *List*
- *Rescan*
- *Retain*
- *Select*

In this case, the script will still exit with an error code. An error code of *0* indicates that the script executed successfully.

Obtaining Volume Information

When you need to get information on the volumes on a computer, you can use the *List Volume* command. The output of this command is as follows:

```
Volume ###   Ltr   Label        Fs      Type        Size      Status      Info
----------   ---   -----------  -----   ----------  -------   ---------   --------
Volume 0     E                          CD-ROM         0 B    Healthy
Volume 1     F                          CD-ROM         0 B    Healthy
*Volume 2    D     Mydrive      NTFS    Partition    10 GB    Healthy
Volume 3     C                  NTFS    Partition     9 GB    Healthy     System
Volume 4     G     OldDrive     FAT32   Partition   6144 MB   Healthy
Volume 5     H     MyMirror     NTFS    Mirror      2048 MB   Healthy
```

You may notice that the output contains the following information about all volumes on the computer:

- **Volume Number (###)** The number of the volume. Volume numbers start from zero. When you want to work with a specific volume, you will need this number (N) with the *Select Volume N* command to give focus to the volume.

- **Volume Letter (Ltr)** The drive letter currently assigned to the volume.

- **Volume Label** The currently configured label of the volume.

- **File System (Fs)** The file system in use by the volume. It may be a File Allocation Table (FAT) or FAT32 file system, or NTFS.

- **Type** The type of volume. Volume types include partition, mount point, CD-ROM, DVD-ROM, simple, spanned, striped, RAID 0, RAID 1, and RAID 5.

- **Size** The total storage capacity or size of the volume.

- **Status** The current status of the volume. Working volumes are usually indicated as *Healthy*.

- **Info** Additional information about the volume, such as *System* or *Boot*.

An * indicates that the volume is currently in focus. You can also get information about a particular volume by giving it focus and using the *Detail Volume* command. The output would include information about only the selected volume.

> **NOTE**
>
> You can use the *List Disk* and *List Partition* commands to get information on all disks and all partitions in the computer, respectively. Likewise, you can use the *Detail Disk* or *Detail Partition* command to obtain information about the disk or partition, respectively, that is currently in focus.

Understanding Volume Status

As we discussed in the previous section, you can get information on all volumes of a computer by using the *List Volume* command, and on the volume in focus by using the *Detail Volume* command. The output of these commands includes the volume's status information: for instance, *Healthy*, *Failed*, *Unknown*, and so on. It is important to understand the volume status and its meaning when working with *Diskpart* or any other disk management utility. This will help you to find an appropriate solution if there is a problem with a disk or volume. Table 6.2 details different status types and their meaning.

Table 6.2 Volume Status and Descriptions

Status	Description
Healthy	The volume is working normally and there are no problems.
Formatting	A temporary status shown when you are formatting a volume. The percentage of volume formatted is indicated.
Data Incomplete	Displayed in the foreign disk volumes, and occurs when data spans multiple disks, but not all of the disks were moved. Usually, the data on this volume is destroyed unless you move the remaining disks that contain this volume, and then import all of the disks together.
Data Not Redundant	Displayed in the foreign disk volumes, and occurs when you import all but one of the disks in a mirrored or RAID 5 volume. To resolve this problem, you must connect all disks from the foreign volume at the same time and then import the disks together.
Stale Data	Displayed in the foreign disk volumes, and occurs when the mirrored or RAID 5 volume has stale mirror information, stale RAID 5 information, or parity-related input/output errors. When you rescan or restart the computer, the status may change to *Failed Redundancy*.
Regenerating	Displayed temporarily when a missing disk in a RAID 5 volume or a mirrored volume is being reactivated. After reactivation, the status returns to *Healthy*. In RAID 5 volumes, the volume is still accessible when the status is shown as regenerating.
Resynching	Temporarily displayed when a disk in a mirrored volume is replaced and the mirrored volume is resynchronized. After the resynchronization is complete, the volume status returns to *Healthy*. You can access data on the mirrored volume during this status.
Failed	Normally indicates some problem with the disk, or that the disk is damaged. To get around this problem, make sure the underlying disk status is *Online*. You may also try to rescan the volume and bring it *Online*.
Failed Redundancy	Indicates that one of the disks in a mirrored or RAID 5 volume is not *Online*. This means the volume is no longer fault tolerant.
Unknown	Occurs when the boot sector on a volume is corrupted and the data on the volume is not accessible anymore. You may try to get around this problem by initializing the underlying disk.

Managing Dynamic Volumes

Dynamic volumes include simple, spanned, and striped volumes. These volumes are not fault tolerant. To create dynamic volumes you should convert the underlying disk to a dynamic disk. The following sections discuss how you can use the *Diskpart* utility to create dynamic volumes. Wherever possible, we have included examples to illustrate proper use of the necessary commands.

Simple Volumes

The *Diskpart* utility allows you to create and expand simple volumes on dynamic disks. The following sections show how you can use this utility.

Creating a Simple Volume

A simple volume contains unallocated space from a single dynamic disk. You can get information on dynamic disks and available unallocated or free space by using the *List Disk* command and selecting a disk to give it focus. Here is an example:

```
Create Volume Simple Size=4096 Disk=2
```

In this example, the dynamic disk number *2* is used to create a simple volume of 4,096 MB in size. Once the volume is created, the *Diskpart* utility will automatically bring it into focus.

Expanding a Simple Volume

You can extend simple volumes by using unallocated space from the same dynamic disk or from other dynamic disks by using the *Extend* command. You must first give focus to the simple volume that you want to extend. Here is an example:

```
Extend Size=2048 Disk=2
```

In this example, the simple volume in focus will be extended to dynamic disk *2* using 2,048 MB of unallocated space from the disk. An extended simple volume becomes a *spanned volume*.

NOTE

You cannot extend simple volumes that contain the system volume or the boot volume. A simple volume or a spanned volume does not provide any fault tolerance. If any of the disks in a spanned volume fail, the entire volume fails and all data is lost. Spanned volumes are basically created to increase the storage capacity of dynamic volumes.

Striped Volumes

You can create a striped volume using unallocated space from two or more dynamic disks. Striped volumes are also known as RAID 0 volumes. Striped volumes are not fault tolerant. The only advantage of creating striped volumes is that they give better read/write performance than simple volumes. Here is an example:

```
Create Volume Stripe Size=4096 Disk=1,2,3
```

In this example, dynamic disks *1*, *2*, and *3* are used to create a striped volume. Unallocated space equal to 4,096 MB (4 GB) is taken from each disk. If any of the disks has more than 4,096 MB (4 GB) of free space, the rest of the space will remain unallocated. When the striped volume is created, the focus is automatically shifted to the newly created volume.

You can use unallocated space from up to 32 dynamic disks to create a striped volume. If you omit the *Size=N* parameter in this command, a space equal to the smallest available unallocated size in the smallest capacity disk would be used from each specified disk. Here is an example:

```
Create Volume Stripe Disk=0,1,2
```

The *Diskpart* command interpreter will check for available unallocated space in disks *0*, *1*, and *2* to determine the minimum unallocated space. For instance, if the smallest available space is 1,024 MB (1 GB), the command will take 1,024 MB (1 GB) from the other disks to create a 3,072 MB (3 GB) striped volume.

> **NOTE**
>
> You cannot include system or boot volumes in a striped volume, nor can you extend or mirror striped volumes. They do not provide any fault tolerance. If one of the disks in the striped volume fails, the entire volume fails and all data is lost.

Managing Fault-Tolerant Volumes

Fault-tolerant volumes in Windows include mirrored volumes and RAID 5 volumes. None of the Windows XP versions supports fault-tolerant volumes. However, you can use a Windows XP computer to create RAID volumes on remote Windows Server 2003 computers. The following sections discuss how you can use the *Diskpart* utility to manage mirrored and RAID 5 volumes.

Mirrored Volumes

Mirrored volumes (also known as RAID 1 volumes) contain exactly two identical disks. Unlike simple, spanned, or striped volumes, a mirrored volume can contain system and boot volumes. But you cannot extend a mirrored volume. To improve fault tolerance, you can connect each dynamic disk to a separate disk controller, a process known as *disk duplexing*. This ensures that failure of a single disk controller does not result in failure of the mirrored volume.

To create a mirrored volume with the *Diskpart* utility, you must first make sure that both of the disks are dynamic disks. Select the first dynamic disk to give it focus. Then use the *Add Disk* command to add the second dynamic disk to create a mirrored volume. Here is an example:

```
DISKPART>Select Disk=0
```

The output of the preceding command is as follows:

```
Disk 0 is now the selected disk.
```

Type the following command to create a mirrored volume:

```
DISKPART>Add Disk=1
```

This command creates a mirrored volume using disks *0* and *1*. Once the mirrored volume is created, the focus is shifted to the newly created volume. If you look at the Disk Management console, the status of the new volume is shown as *Resynching,* as discussed earlier in this book.

Resolving Mirrored Volume Problems

When a mirrored volume fails, its status is shown as one of the following:

- Offline
- Missing
- Online (Errors)

If the volume is offline or missing, try to resolve the problem using the *Rescan* command from the *Diskpart* utility. If the volume is detected, use the *Online* command to start the resynchronization process. If this succeeds, the volume status should change to *Healthy*. But if none of these commands works, the underlying disk may have failed. You can use the *Break Disk* command as follows to break the mirror.

```
DISKPART>Break Disk=1
```

Once the mirrored volume is broken, replace the failed disk with a new disk of equal or larger capacity, convert it to a dynamic disk, and use the *Add Disk* command to re-create the mirrored volume.

RAID 5 Volumes

RAID 5 volumes contain equal space from a minimum of three dynamic disks. A RAID 5 volume is also known as a *striped volume with parity*. Before you can create a RAID 5 volume, you must make sure that all the disks that you want to add in the RAID 5 volume are dynamic disks. Select the first dynamic disk to give it focus. Then use the *Create Volume RAID* command to create a RAID 5 volume. Here is an example:

```
DISKPART>Select Disk=0
```

The output of this command is as follows:

```
Disk 0 is now the selected disk.
```

Type the following command to create a RAID 5 volume:

```
DISKPART>Create Volume RAID Size=8192 Disk=0,1,2
```

This command creates a RAID 5 volume, taking 8,192 MB (8 GB) of unallocated space from each of the disks *0*, *1*, and *2*. You can specify up to 32 disks in the *Disk=N,N,N,...* parameter. If you omit the *Size=N* parameter in this command, a space equal to the smallest available unallocated size in the smallest capacity disk would be used from each specified disk. Here is an example:

```
DISKPART>Create Volume RAID Disk=0,1,2
```

This command creates a RAID 5 volume, taking unallocated space from disks *0*, *1*, and *2*. The total size of the RAID 5 volume will depend on the size of the smallest disk in the RAID volume. Once the RAID 5 volume is created, the focus is automatically shifted to the newly created volume.

Repairing a Failed RAID 5 Volume

If you find out that one of the disks in a RAID 5 volume has failed, replace it with a new disk of equal or larger capacity and convert it to a dynamic disk. Then start the *Diskpart* command interpreter and bring the new disk to focus. For example, if disk *2* has been replaced, use the following command to repair the RAID 5 volume:

```
DISKPART>Repair Disk=2
```

In the preceding code, *Disk=2* is the replaced disk. The new disk will be added to the RAID 5 volume, and the status of the RAID 5 volume will be shown as *Regenerating* in the Disk Management console. Once the process is complete the status will show as *Healthy*.

Summary

We dedicated this chapter to the *Diskpart* command-line utility. You learned that this utility is different from other command-line utilities in the sense that it runs on its own in the Windows command shell as a text-based command interpreter. This utility consists of several commands that run only after the *Diskpart* interpreter has started. You can use this utility to perform simple disk-related tasks, such as creating and deleting partitions and volumes, as well as to manage, create, and maintain fault-tolerant volumes. You also can convert partition styles, and convert disk types from basic to dynamic and vice versa. *Diskpart* works only with fixed disks and cannot be used to manage removable drives. Since *Diskpart* works in a more enhanced mode than its counterpart, the Disk Management snap-in, it has more control over the selected disk, partition, or volume. *Diskpart* supports scripting and you can create scripts to automate repeated disk-related administrative tasks. *Diskpart* error codes make it easy for you to handle command execution more precisely.

Part III
Managing
Windows Systems
and Printers

Part III
Managing Windows Systems and Printers

Chapter 7

System Services, Drivers, and the Registry

Topics in this chapter

- Obtaining System Information
- Shutting Down and Restarting the System
- Configuring the System Startup
- Managing System Services
- Obtaining Driver Information
- Managing the Windows Registry

Introduction

With this chapter, we are stepping into the next round of command-line tasks that we can use to maintain a system. We will discuss how to obtain system configuration information, query and configure system services, obtain information about device drivers, shut down and restart local and remote systems, and work with the Registry from the command line. The main commands we will cover in this chapter include the *Systeminfo* command, for obtaining system configuration information; the *Driverquery* command, for getting information about device drivers; the *SC* (*Service Control*) command set, for querying and configuring system services and device drivers; and the *Reg* command, for managing the Windows Registry. The *SC* and the *Reg* commands are composed of several subcommands and, as we will learn in this chapter, are very useful for troubleshooting as well as configuring local and remote computers. The *Shutdown* command allows you to shut down and restart a local or remote computer without having to be present at the console.

Obtaining System Information

When you want to work with a system's components or configure any of its services and device drivers, it is helpful to get detailed information about the system's current configuration first. This information includes the system services, installed device drivers, their configurations, and hardware components such as processors and memory. At a minimum, you must have knowledge of the operating system version and installed service packs. Sometimes you may need to determine the specific files on the system, and other times you may need to know whether the protected files are intact and are not infected by viruses or other malicious software. This section focuses on command-line utilities that will help you obtain this information.

Determining the Operating System Version

When you sit down at a system for the first time to perform a specific task or to resolve a problem, you might need to know which operating system version it is running and what service packs are installed on it. You can get this information quickly using the *Ver* command. The syntax for this command is fairly simple, as it does not have any associated parameters. Here is the syntax:

```
Ver
```

That's about it. The command prompt displays the version of the installed operating system. You can obtain the same information by using the *Winver* command. But this command displays the information as graphical output, as shown in Figure 7.1.

Figure 7.1 Output of the Winver Command

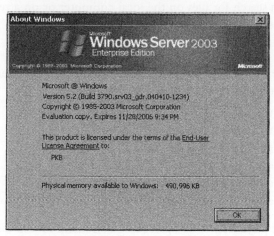

The *Winver* command actually opens the About Windows page that shows the currently installed operating system, any service packs, and the name of the person to whom the license is granted. You will also see the amount of memory currently available. Later in this chapter, we will learn how to obtain complete system configuration information using the *Systeminfo* command.

Locating Files with the Where Command

If you need to locate certain files on a computer that match a given parameter or a pattern, you can use the *Where* command, which can help you locate the files very quickly. This command is equivalent to using the *Search* option in the Start menu. The syntax for this command is:

```
Where [/r Dir] [/q] [/f] [/t] Pattern ...
```

Table 7.1 explains the parameters of this command.

Table 7.1 Parameters of the Where Command

Parameter	Description
/r Dir	Indicates that the search is recursive and starts with the specified directory.
/q	Used to return only an exit code, but the filenames are not displayed. An exit code of 0 stands for success and 1 stands for failure.
/f	Used to enclose filenames in quotation marks.
/t	Used to display the file's size and the date and time it was created.
Pattern ...	Specifies a search pattern. You can use wildcards with filenames.

The *Where* command conducts a recursive search and can take environment variables in place of a path. You can search for files on the local computer or on a remote computer. The following examples illustrate use of this command.

```
Where My*.* /q
```

The preceding command searches for all files starting with the letters "My" and ending with any extension. The output displayed is:

```
C:\Documents and Settings\Administrator\mybatch.bat
C:\Documents and Settings\Administrator\myfile.txt
C:\Program Files\Support Tools\mytext.txt
C:\WINDOWS\system32\mycomput.dll
C:\WINDOWS\system32\mydocs.dll
C:\WINDOWS\system32\mys.dll
```

You can add the */t* parameter to the preceding command to also display the file size, time, and date stamps:

```
140    6/7/2006    2:01:48 PM  C:\Documents and
Settings\Administrator\mybatch.bat
       60    6/8/2006    2:49:31 PM  C:\Documents and
Settings\Administrator\myfile.txt
       69    6/14/2006    9:28:38 AM  C:\Program Files\Support Tools\mytext.txt
    98816    3/25/2003    5:00:00 AM  C:\WINDOWS\system32\mycomput.dll
    90112    3/25/2003    5:00:00 AM  C:\WINDOWS\system32\mydocs.dll
   220160    3/25/2003    5:00:00 AM  C:\WINDOWS\system32\mys.dll
```

To locate all files in the D:\Reports directory with a .doc extension, you can use the following command:

```
Where /r D:\Reports *.doc /t
```

To locate all files in the D: drive of a remote computer named *HRSrv01*, you can use the following command:

```
Where /r \\HRSrv01\D
```

NOTE

The *Where* command is available only with the Windows Server 2003 operating system. Windows XP does not support this command.

Checking the System Date and Time

The *Now* command can be very useful when you want to check the current date and time on a computer. While the *Now* commands display only the current day, date, and time, you can use the *Date* and *Time* commands to individually display and set dates and times, respectively. To use this command, simply type **Now** at the command prompt and press **Enter**. The current date and time on the system is displayed as follows:

```
C:\Documents and Settings\Administrator>Now
Wed June 28 10:54:38 2006
```

> **NOTE**
>
> It is interesting to note that the *Now* command is not listed in the Windows Server 2003 command reference, but it *is* supported and you can use it to quickly view the current day, date, and time on a computer. However, Windows XP does not support this command.

Changing the System Date with the Date Command

The *Date* command displays the current system date and allows you to change it using any of the supported formats. The syntax of this command is:

```
date [MM-DD-YY[YY]] [/t]
```

When you use this command without any parameters, the current system date is displayed and you are prompted to enter a new date as follows:

```
C:\Documents and Settings\Administrator>date
The current date is: Wed 06/28/2006
Enter the new date: (mm-dd-yy)
```

If you press the **Enter** key, the command retains the current date without changing it. If you want to display just the current date, you can use the */t* parameter. You are not prompted to enter a new date.

When specifying a new date, make sure that the *MM* (month) parameter is between 1 and 12 and the *DD* (date) parameter is between 1 and 31. The *Date* command accepts the following formats for the system date:

- **MM-DD-YY** For example, 09-25-06.
- **MM/DD/YY** For example, 09/25/06.
- **MM.DD.YY** For example, 09.25.06.

To specify the year you can use either the *YY* or the *YYYY* format. This means that 06 stands for 2006, 99 stands for 1999, and 20 stands for 2020. The valid values for the *YYYY* format are from 1980 to 2099.

Changing the System Clock with the Time Command

You can use the *Time* command to view or change the system clock. The syntax of this command is:

```
Time [/t] [/time] [Hours:[Minutes[:Seconds[.Hundredths]]][{A | P}]]
```

When used without parameters, the command displays the current system time and prompts you to enter a new time, as shown in the following output:

```
C:\Documents and Settings\Administrator>time

The current time is: 10:58:01.23
Enter the new time:
```

If you press the **Enter** key, the command retains the current time without changing it. You can use the */t* or the */time* parameter to just display the current time. You are not prompted to enter a new time. The other parameters of this command are:

- **Hours** Specifies hours. The valid values for this parameter are from 0 to 23.
- **Minutes** Specifies minutes. The valid values for this parameter are from 0 to 59.
- **Seconds** Specified seconds. The valid values for this parameter are from 0 to 59.
- **Hundredths** Specifies one-hundredths of a second. The valid values for this parameter are from 0 to 99.
- **A** Specifies that the current time is during morning hours (A.M.). This parameter is required when using the 12-hour time format.
- **P** Specifies that the current time is during the afternoon or evening hours (P.M.). This parameter is required when using the 12-hour time format.

With the 12-hour time format, you must use either the *A* (A.M.) or the *P* (P.M.) parameter. If you do not specify either of these, the system considers it *A* (for A.M.) by default. The following examples illustrate the correct use of the *Time* command:

```
Time 8:30a
Time 15:55
Time 1:25:40:76
```

> **WARNING**
>
> Changing a computer's system clock seems to be a very simple process, and it is. Although the *Time* command is easy to use, you should use it cautiously on production servers. If you do not have a reason to change the system clock, do not change it. Several tasks depend on the system clock in an Active Directory-based network. System clock synchronization on all client and server computers is very critical to the way a network functions. For example, if a time mismatch exists between a client computer and the domain controller, the user may not be allowed to log on to the domain. If you still need to perform an experiment with the *Time* command, do it on a test computer.

Obtaining Information on the Logged-On User

You use the *Whoami* command to obtain information on the currently logged-on user, the name of the computer, group and domain membership, and privileges associated with the user. This command does not work on the Windows XP operating system. The syntax of this command is:

```
Whoami {/upn | /fqdn | /logonid}
Whoami [{/user | /groups | /priv}] [/fo Format]
Whoami /all [/fo Format]
```

Table 7.2 explains the parameters of this command.

Table 7.2 Parameters of the Whoami Command

Parameter	Description
/upn	Displays the name of the user in User Principle Name (UPN) format.
/fqdn	Displays the fully qualified domain name (FQDN) of the logged-on user.
/logonid	Displays the *userid* of the logged-on user, along with its security identifier.
/user	Displays the current username.
/groups	Displays the names of all groups of which the user is a member.
/priv	Displays the access privileges associated with the currently logged-on user.
/all	Displays the username, security identifiers, and privileges associated with the current user.

Continued

Table 7.2 continued Parameters of the Whoami Command

Parameter	Description
/fo Format	Used to specify the format of the command output. Valid arguments for this parameter are *Table*, *List*, and *CSV* (Comma Separated Value). If this parameter is not used the output is displayed in *Table* format.

The following examples illustrate use of the *Whoami* command:

```
Whoami
Whoami /upn
Whoami /groups /fo Table
Whoami /all /fo List
```

Depending on the information you require for the currently logged-on user, you can use the command to obtain necessary information as a list, in table format, or in CSV format.

NOTE

You cannot use the */fo Format* parameter with the */upn*, */fqdn*, or */logonid* parameter. If you use this parameter, a syntax error is displayed.

The following sample listing shows output of the *Whoami* command when used with the */group* and */fo List* parameters:

```
GROUP INFORMATION
-----------------


Group Name: Everyone
Type:       Well-known group
SID:        S-1-1-0
Attributes: Mandatory group, Enabled by default, Enabled group

Group Name: BUILTIN\Administrators
Type:       Alias
SID:        S-1-5-32-544
Attributes: Mandatory group, Enabled by default, Enabled group, Group owner

Group Name: BUILTIN\Users
Type:       Alias
```

```
SID:          S-1-5-32-545
Attributes: Mandatory group, Enabled by default, Enabled group


Group Name: LOCAL
Type:          Well-known group
SID:          S-1-2-0
Attributes: Mandatory group, Enabled by default, Enabled group


Group Name: PKB-DOMAIN\Enterprise Admins
Type:          Group
SID:          S-1-5-21-3462721432-852952767-903361428-519
Attributes: Mandatory group, Enabled by default, Enabled group


Group Name: PKB-DOMAIN\Domain Admins
Type:          Group
SID:          S-1-5-21-3462721432-852952767-903361428-512
Attributes: Mandatory group, Enabled by default, Enabled group
```

Sometimes when you are working on a computer, you may need to perform a specific administrative task using the nonadministrative account you are currently using. In such a situation, you may want to know whether the privilege you want to use is enabled or disabled. The *Whoami /priv* command can provide a quick view of system privileges that are enabled for the current user account you are using.

NOTE

The Windows XP operating system does not support the *Whoami* command. You can use this command only on Windows Server 2003 systems.

Obtaining System Configuration Information

You use the *Systeminfo* command to obtain complete information about the system's configuration, including the basic input/output system (BIOS) version, processors, operating system, size of the page file(s), product ID, and hardware components such as memory, hard disks, and other hardware devices. The information also includes the name of the manufacturer and model number of the computer. You can use the command on both local and remote computers. The syntax of this command is:

Systeminfo [/s Computer [/u Domain\UserName [/p Password]]] [/fo Format] [/nh]

Here is an explanation of this command's parameters:

- **/s Computer** Specifies a remote computer defined by the computer name or an Internet Protocol (IP) address. By default, the command gathers and displays information about the local computer.

- **/u Domain\UserName** Used to specify the domain and username under whose privileges the command is to be run. If you omit this parameter, the currently logged on username is used by default.

- **/p Password** Used to specify the password of the username specified in the */u* parameter.

- **/fo Format** Specifies the output format. By default, the output is displayed in Table format. You can also display the output in List or CSV format.

- **/nh** Used to suppress the display of column headers in the output.

If you want to run the command on a remote computer, you must supply the */s Computer* parameter to define the remote computer by its name or IP address. The */u* and */p* parameters are valid only when you use the */s Computer* parameter. The following examples illustrate use of this command:

```
Systeminfo /s HRSrv01
```

```
Systeminfo /s NYSRV2 /u NYDomain\GaryB /p ********
```

```
Systeminfo /s 192.168.0.25 /u Mydomain\Garyb /p ******** /fo List
```

The first line of code displays system configuration information about the computer named *HRSrv01*. In the second example, the command is used to display system information about a computer named *NYSRV2* using the credentials of *GaryB* with its password. The computer is located in the *NYDomain*. The third command illustrates use of an IP address in place of the computer name and */fo* parameter to display the output in List format.

Checking Protected System Files with the SFC Command

The System File Checker (SFC) is a helpful utility that can scan protected system files and replace any corrupted files with their original versions. You can use this utility to scan files if you suspect that a virus or other malicious application has replaced a protected system file. In some situations, the Windows files may be accidentally deleted. When you run the command without any parameters, the system files are checked after the computer is restarted. The syntax of this command is:

```
SFC [/scannow] [/scanonce] [/scanboot] [/revert] [/purgecache] [/cachesize=x]
```

The parameters of this command are as follows:

- **/scannow** Used to scan the system files immediately.

- **/scanonce** Used to scan the system files only once.

- **/scanboot** Used to scan the system files every time the system is started or restarted.

- **/revert** Returns the *SFC* utility to its default operation behavior.

- **/purgecache** Used to purge the Windows File Protection (WFP) cache and scan all system files immediately. This is a required parameter if you used the */cache-size=x* parameter.

- **/cachesize=x** Specifies the size of the WFP cache in megabytes.

If the utility finds that a system file has been overwritten, accidentally or otherwise, it retrieves the correct version of the file from the %SystemRoot%\System32\Dllcache folder. If you find that the Dllcache folder itself has become corrupted, you can use the *SFC* utility with the */scannow*, */scanonce*, or */scanboot* option to replace files in the Dllcache folder. This utility actually invokes WFP, which in turn verifies that all protected Windows system files are intact and in their original versions. Remember that you must have administrative privileges to run the *SFC* command.

Master Craftsman...

Windows File Protection

The WFP feature in Windows XP and Windows Server 2003 prevents corruption and deletion of Windows system files accidentally or by a malicious application, such as a virus. Protected system files include critical system files that are installed as part of the operating system and that help Windows run properly. Windows supports replacement of critical and protected system files only by the following procedures:

- Through Windows Update or Windows Server Update Services (WSUS)

- When Service Packs are installed using the Update.exe utility

- When Hot Fixes are installed using the Hotfix.exe or Update.exe utility

- When the operating system is upgraded using the Winnt32.exe utility

In all other cases, WFP does not let any program replace any of the protected system files using any other method.

Shutting Down and Restarting the System

Windows XP and Windows Server 2003 support shutdown and restart of local and remote computers from the command line. You use the *Shutdown* command with appropriate parameters to shut down or restart the computer and to specify to the shutdown event tracker a reason for the action. You can specify a wait time before the system is shut down. If a system is scheduled to be shut down or restarted using the *Shutdown* command, you can also prevent the shutdown provided you execute the *Shutdown* command again before the waiting time expires. There are some differences in how the command is used on Windows Server 2003 and Windows XP computers. For Windows Server 2003, the command syntax is:

```
Shutdown [/i | /l | /s | /r | /a | /p | /h | /e] [/f] [/m \\ComputerName] [/t
XXX] [/d [p:] XX:YY [/c "Comment"]]
```

Table 7.3 explains this command's parameters on Windows Server 2003 systems.

Table 7.3 Parameters of the Shutdown Command for Windows Server 2003

Parameter	Description
/i	Used to shut down or restart a remote computer. When this parameter is used all remaining parameters in the command are ignored. You must use this parameter before any other parameter. Figure 7.2 shows the Remote Shutdown dialog box.
/l	Used to immediately log off the current user that is logged on to the computer, without giving a timeout period. You cannot use this parameter with the /m *ComputerName* or /t parameter.
/s	Specifies that the system is to be shut down.
/r	Specifies that the system be restarted after it is shut down. You can use either the /s or the /r parameter, but not both.
/a	Prevents the shutdown or restart of the computer. This is effective only if you use the command during the timeout period. You can use this parameter only with /m *ComputerName*.
/p	Used to shut down the local computer without displaying a warning or specifying a timeout period. You can use this parameter only with the /d parameter. If the local computer does not support the power-down feature, the system is shut down but the power to the system remains on.
/h	Used to put the computer in hibernation, if it is supported and enabled. You can use this parameter only with the /f parameter.
/e	Used to document the reason for the unexpected shutdown of a local or remote computer.

Continued

Table 7.3 continued Parameters of the Shutdown Command for Windows Server 2003

Parameter	Description
/f	Forces any running applications to close without displaying any warning to the user. Use of this parameter may result in loss of unsaved data.
/m \\ ComputerName	Specifies the computer. You cannot use the /l parameter with this parameter. You can specify the computer name or its IP address.
/t XXX	Sets the timeout before the system is shut down or restarted. A warning remains displayed on the computer during this time. The valid range of values is from 0 to 600 seconds. If no timeout is specified, the default timeout value of 30 seconds is assumed. You cannot use this parameter with the /l parameter.
/d [p:] XX:YY	Used to specify the reason for the system shutdown, restart, or power down. Table 7.4 lists valid values of this parameter.
/c "Comment"	Enables you to specify a reason for the shutdown or restart. The "Comment" must be specified in quotation marks and can have a maximum of 127 characters. You can use this parameter only if you have used the /d parameter.

Only those who have the *Shutdown the System* user right can shut down the local computer. Administrators are granted this right by default on local computers. When the computer is a member of a domain, only members of the *Domain Admins* group can shut down computers in the domain; members of the *Admins* group can shut down local computers regardless of their domain membership.

Specifying Reasons for the Event Tracker

You can use the *Shutdown* command to record reasons for the shutdown event tracker by using the /d parameter with valid options. You can specify custom-configured major and minor reasons in the *XX:YY* format, respectively. You must first define these custom reasons on the system. Table 7.4 lists valid values for the /d parameter.

Table 7.4 Valid Values for the /d [p:] XX:YY Parameter

Value	Description
p:	Specifies that the shutdown or restart is planned. If you omit this argument, the shutdown event tracker assumes this to be an unplanned shutdown or restart.
XX	Specifies a major reason number for the shutdown. This should be a positive integer less than 256.

Continued

Table 7.4 continued Valid Values for the /d [p:] XX:YY Parameter

Value	Description
YY	Specifies a minor reason number for the shutdown. This should be a positive integer less than 65,536.

Use of the *d* parameter can be a little tricky in Windows Server 2003. When you use the *d p:* parameter, the shutdown event tracker records the shutdown as planned. If you omit the *p:* parameter, the shutdown is assumed to be unplanned and you can specify the major and minor reason codes for unplanned shutdown in the *XX:YY* format. However, if you use the *p:* option and also specify the *XX:YY* codes for unplanned shutdown, the system will not be shut down or restarted at all! The same is true when you omit the *p:* option, but specify reason codes for planned shutdown; the system will not shut down. So, be careful!

Using the Shutdown Command on the Local Computer

The following examples illustrate use of the *Shutdown* command for shutting down or restarting the local computer.

```
Shutdown /s /t 60 /f
```

The preceding command will shut down (*/s*) the local computer in 60 seconds (*/t 60*) and after forcing the applications to close (*/f*).

```
Shutdown /a
```

This command will abort shutdown of the computer when used within the timeout period specified by the */t* parameter.

```
Shutdown /r /c "Planned Shutdown" /d p:10:15
```

This command will shut down and restart the local computer with a reason as *"Planned Shutdown"* specifying the planned reason codes with the */d p: XX:YY* parameter. Major and minor reason codes are specified as 10 and 15, respectively. Since we have not used the */t* option, the computer will shut down in 30 seconds, which is the default. If you use this command on a Windows XP computer, the default timeout will be 20 seconds.

Using the Shutdown Command on the Remote Computer

You use the *Shutdown* command with the */m \\Computer* parameter to shut down or restart a remote computer. The following examples illustrate use of the *Shutdown* command for remote computers.

```
Shutdown /s /t 45 /f /m \\HRSRV2
```

The preceding command will shut down the computer named *HRSRV2* in 45 seconds after forcing all applications to close.

```
Shutdown /r /t120 /c "Unplanned Restart" /f /m \\192.168.0.25 /d 12:5
```

This command restarts the remote computer whose IP address is 192.168.0.25 in 120 seconds (two minutes), specifying the reason as *"Unplanned Restart"* after forcing all applications to close. The major and minor reasons for the restart are specified by the */d XX:YY* parameter as 12 and 5, respectively. Note that when the reason is unplanned, you cannot use the *p* option with the */d* parameter. You can abort the restart of this computer by using the following command before the 120-second timeout period expires:

```
Shutdown /a /m \\192.168.0.125
```

As an alternative to using the *Shutdown* command-line parameters for shutting down or restarting a remote computer, you can use the */i* parameter to invoke the Remote Shutdown dialog box, shown in Figure 7.2.

Figure 7.2 Remote Shutdown Dialog Box

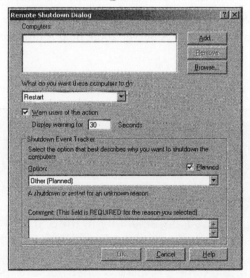

As you can see in Figure 7.2, you can select one or more remote computers to shut down or restart. The default timeout value is 30 seconds, but you can specify it to be anywhere between 0 and 600 seconds (10 minutes). The bottommost part of the dialog box allows you to enter a reason for the shutdown or restart.

Differences between the Windows XP and Windows Server 2003 Shutdown Commands

The *Shutdown* command syntax in Windows XP is a bit different from that in Windows Server 2003. The syntax for the Windows XP *Shutdown* command is:

```
Shutdown [{i| -l|-s|-r|-a}] [-f] [-m [\\ComputerName]] [-t xx] [-c "message"] [-d[u] [p]:xx:yy]
```

If you take a close look at both the Windows Server 2003 and Windows XP command syntax, you will notice the following differences:

- The /p, /h, and /e parameters are not supported in Windows XP.

- The default timeout value is 20 seconds. This value is 30 seconds for Windows Server 2003.

- The /d parameter supports the *u* option that specifies a user-defined reason for the shutdown or restart. In Windows Server 2003, the shutdown is assumed to be unplanned if you omit the *p* option. The reasons must be predefined; otherwise, the event tracker will not be able to record any reason for the shutdown.

- If you use the *Shutdown* command without parameters, the currently logged-on user is logged off. In Windows Server 2003, help is displayed when no parameter is used.

Swiss Army Knife...

Look for Differences

When you look at Windows XP documentation, the *Shutdown* command parameters are used with a hyphen (–) rather than a slash (/). In fact, you can use either of these signs. Also, the command-line reference in Help and Support does not show the *i* option, but the same is displayed when you use the *Shutdown /?* command at the command prompt. When we checked the *Shutdown* command without any parameters, help was displayed on both Windows Server 2003 and Windows XP computers and the current user was not logged off, as given in Help and Support. The moral here is that you must check the commands you are using on a test computer before you run them on a production server or include them in your batch files.

Managing System Services

You can manage Windows services from the command line using the *Service Control (SC)* utility. The *SC* utility interacts with the Windows Registry to control how services are started at system startup and how they run in the background. You can query a service to check its configuration information; start, stop, pause, and resume the service; and specify what action will be taken by default if a service fails. This utility consists of several subcommands for controlling the behavior of services and applications on local and remote computers. The main syntax of this command is:

```
SC \\Computer Subcommand [[Option1] [Option2]…]
```

In the preceding command, *Computer* is the name or IP address of the computer on which you want to manage the service, *Subcommand* is one of the subcommands, and *Option1* and *Option2* are the subcommand's parameters. Table 7.5 describes the *SC* utility's subcommands.

Table 7.5 Subcommands of the SC Utility

Subcommand	Description
SC Boot	Used to specify whether the last boot should be saved as *Last Known Good* configuration. This operation affects all services.
SC Config	Used to configure the service by modifying certain values in the Registry and Service Control Manager database.
SC Continue	Used to continue (resume) a paused service.
SC Control	Used to send a control code to the specified service. These control codes are either standard values or custom values defined by vendors.
SC Create	Used to create a service subkey as well as an entry in the Registry and in the Service Control Manager database.
SC Delete	Used to delete a service subkey from the Registry and the Service Control Manager database. If the service is running, it is marked for deletion.
SC Description	Used to configure a description string for a service.
SC EnumDepend	Used to specify the services that depend on the specified service.
SC Failure	Used to specify the actions to be taken if the service fails.
SC GetDisplayName	Used to obtain the display name of the specified service.
SC GetKeyName	Used to obtain the key name of a service by specifying the display name as input.

Continued

Table 7.5 continued Subcommands of the SC Utility

Subcommand	Description
SC Interrogate	Used to send an interrogate request to the service. The interrogate request updates the status of the service in the Service Control Manager.
SC Lock	Used to lock the Service Control Manager database. This operation affects all services.
SC Pause	Used to pause a running service.
SC QC	Used to query the configuration information of a service.
SC QDescription	Used to obtain the description string of a service by specifying its key name obtained from the GetKeyName subcommand.
SC QFailure	Used to display the actions that will be taken if the specified service fails.
SC Query	Used to obtain information about a service, type of service, driver, or driver type.
SC Queryx	Used to obtain extended information about a service, type of service, driver, or driver type.
SC QueryLock	Used to display the locked status of the Service Control Manager database.
SC SDSet	Used to set the Security Descriptor of a service using the Security Descriptor Definition Language (SDDL).
SC SDShow	Used to display the Security Descriptor of a service using SDDL.
SC Start	Used to start a stopped service.
SC Stop	Used to stop a running service.

As a system administrator, you will probably not need to use or even know most of the *SC* subcommands listed in Table 7.5. If you need help on any subcommand, you can simply type **SC Subcommand /?** at the command prompt and press **Enter** to obtain detailed information about the syntax and use of the specified subcommand. In the following sections, we will discuss some of the *SC* subcommands that are useful for everyday system administration tasks.

Obtaining Information about Services

Before you can use the *SC* utility to configure a service, you must have some information about the service. With some of the *SC* subcommands you might need the key name of the service and with others you may need the display name. You can get detailed information about one or more services configured on a computer using the *SC Query* command. The syntax of this command is:

```
SC [ServerName] query [ServiceName] [type= {driver | service | all}] [type= {own
| share | interact | kernel | filesys | rec | adapt}] [state= {active | inactive |
all}] [bufsize= BufferSize] [ri= ResumeIndex] [group= GroupName]
```

Here is a list of some of the parameters commonly used with the *SC* utility:

- **ServiceName** Specifies the name of the service obtained from the *SC GetKeyName* command.

- **Type** Specifies the type of the service. Valid arguments are *Driver, Service*, and *All*. When you select the *All* option, both services and drivers are displayed.

- **State** Used to display the state of the service. Valid parameters are *Active, Inactive*, and *All*. When you select the *All* option, both active and inactive services are displayed.

The following examples illustrate use of this command.

SC Query

The preceding command displays all configured services on the local computer. The output is displayed for each service as follows:

```
SERVICE_NAME: Schedule
DISPLAY_NAME: Task Scheduler
        TYPE              : 20   WIN32_SHARE_PROCESS
        STATE             : 4    RUNNING
                                 (STOPPABLE, PAUSABLE, ACCEPTS_SHUTDOWN)
        WIN32_EXIT_CODE   : 0    (0x0)
        SERVICE_EXIT_CODE : 0    (0x0)
        CHECKPOINT        : 0x0
        WAIT_HINT         : 0x0
```

The information provided includes the *Service_Name, Display_Name, Type* of service, *State* of the service, and *Service_Exit_Code*. In the given output, the name of the service is *Schedule*, the display name is *Task Scheduler*, and the state of the service is shown as running. Notice also that you can stop, pause, and shut down the service.

To obtain information about all services on a remote computer named *HRSRV1* that are *active*, use the following command:

```
SC \\HRSRV1 Query Type= service State= active
```

NOTE

As shown in this example, you must insert a space between the *Type* and *State* parameters (or any other parameter) and their values, after the equals (=) sign. If this space is missing, the command will not work. Hence, writing *Type= Service* (correct) is not the same as writing *Type=Service* (Wrong). This rule applies to all other parameters that use the equals sign.

If you need more information about a particular service, you can use the *SC QC* command. We are using the *Netlogon* service for the following example:

```
SC QC \\HRSRV1 Netlogon
```

Here is the output:

```
SERVICE_NAME: netlogon
        TYPE               : 20   WIN32_SHARE_PROCESS
        START_TYPE         : 2    AUTO_START
        ERROR_CONTROL      : 1    NORMAL
        BINARY_PATH_NAME   : C:\WINDOWS\system32\lsass.exe
        LOAD_ORDER_GROUP   : MS_WindowsRemoteValidation
        TAG                : 0
        DISPLAY_NAME       : Net Logon
        DEPENDENCIES       : LanmanWorkstation
                           : LanmanServer
        SERVICE_START_NAME : LocalSystem
```

You may notice from this sample output that the information includes the name of the service, the service type, its binary path name, its display name, its dependencies, and its service start name. The *binary name* of the service indicates the full path of the executable that runs the service. The *dependencies* are the services that cannot run unless this service is running. In this example, the *Workstation* and *Server* services are dependent on the *Netlogon* service. Notice that the service type of the *Netlogon* service is shown as *WIN_SHARE_PROCESS*. This is an important piece of information that shows that the service runs as a shared process. Some services run under their own context and are listed as *WIN_OWN_PROCESS*. The service start name indicates the account that the service uses to run, which in this case is the *LocalSystem* account.

Starting, Stopping, Pausing, and Resuming Services

You can stop and restart services on local and remote computers using the *SC Stop* and *SC Start* commands, respectively. Also, you can pause and resume services using the *SC Pause* and *SC Continue* commands, respectively. The syntax of these commands is:

```
SC [ServerName] Stop ServiceName
SC [ServerName] Start ServiceName [ServiceArguments]
SC [ServerName] Pause [ServiceName]
SC [ServerName] Continue [ServiceName]
```

The following examples illustrate use of these commands:

```
SC Stop Scheduler
SC Start Messenger
SC \\W3SRV5 Pause W3Svc
SC \\192.168.0.25 Continue NTfrs
```

In the first example, the *Scheduler* service is stopped on the local computer. The second example shows how the *Messenger* service is started on the local computer. The third example shows how to pause the Internet Information Service (*W3Svc*) on a computer named *W3SRV5*. The last example shows how you can resume the NT File Replication Service (*NTFrs*) on a computer with the IP address 192.168.0.25.

In all of the preceding examples, we used the abbreviated names for the services. If you are unsure about the abbreviated name of a service, you can simply run the *SC Query* command without any parameters. This will display all services currently configured on the computer. Look for the *SERVICE_NAME* parameter in the displayed output to determine the correct name of the service.

Configuring a Service's Startup Type

You can configure the startup type of the Windows services with the *SC Config* command. The syntax of this command when used for configuring startup types is:

```
SC Config \\Computer ServiceName Start= StartupType
```

In the preceding code, *Computer* specifies the name of a computer or its IP address, and *ServiceName* is the abbreviated name of the service as explained in the preceding section. The *StartupType* parameter specifies the startup type of the service. Table 7.6 describes different startup types for a service.

Table 7.6 Startup Types for Services

Startup Type	Description
Auto	Specifies that the service will automatically start when the system starts.
Demand	Specifies that the service will remain enabled but will start only when manually started or when called by an application or process. This is the default behavior of a service if the *StartupType* parameter is not defined.
Disabled	Specifies that the service is disabled and cannot be started. You must change the startup type of the service to some other value in order to start it.

The following examples will help you understand how you can change a service's startup types.

```
SC Config \\WWWSrv5 W3svc Start= Auto
```

The preceding command will configure the *W3svc* service to automatically start on system startup on a computer named *WWWSrv5*. If you want to configure the same service on the local computer, you can omit the *Computer* parameter.

```
Sc Config Scheduler Start= Demand
```

This command will configure the startup type of the *Task Scheduler* service on the local computer as manual. The service will stop until you start the service manually.

Managing Service Failures

If a Windows service fails for some reason, you can use the *SC Failure* command to configure how the system responds so that you can try to recover the service. The *SC QFailure* command displays what actions are currently configured on a computer if the specified service fails. You can use the commands on both local and remote computers. The syntax of the *SC QFailure* command is:

```
SC \\Computer QFailure ServiceName
```

In the preceding code, *Computer* specifies the name or the IP address of the remote computer. If you omit this parameter, the service configuration of the local computer is displayed. The *ServiceName* parameter specifies the abbreviated name of the service.

The output of this command includes the following information:

- **SERVICE_NAME** The abbreviated name of the service as it appears in the Registry subkey.

- **RESET_PERIOD** The time period in seconds after which the service will be reset.

- **REBOOT_MESSAGE** Displays the configured broadcast message when the service fails.

- **COMMAND_LINE** Displays the command or the script file that is configured to run when the service fails.

- **FAILURE_ACTIONS** Displays the configured actions on failure of the service and their delay times in milliseconds. Valid failure actions include *Run*, *Restart*, and *Reboot*.

Now, consider the following example that queries the system for configured actions on failure of the *NTFrs* service:

```
SC Qfailure NTFrs
```

Here is the output of this command:

```
[SC] QueryServiceConfig2 SUCCESS

SERVICE_NAME: ntfrs
        RESET_PERIOD (in seconds)    : 0
        REBOOT_MESSAGE               :
        COMMAND_LINE                 :
        FAILURE_ACTIONS              : RESTART -- Delay = 1800000 milliseconds.
                                       RESTART -- Delay = 1800000 milliseconds.
                                       RESTART -- Delay = 1800000 milliseconds.
```

If you want to configure the actions the system will take in an attempt to recover a failed service, you can use the *SC Failure* command. The syntax of this command is:

```
SC [ServerName] Failure [ServiceName] [Reset= ErrorFreePeriod] [Reboot=
BroadcastMessage] [Command= CommandLine] [Actions= FailureActionsAndDelayTime]
```

Here is a list of the new parameters for this command:

- **Reset= ErrorFreePeriod** Specifies the time period in seconds during which the service is without failure, after which the fail count is reset to zero. You use this parameter with the *Actions* parameter.

- **Reboot= BroadcastMessage** Specifies the broadcast message that is to be broadcast when the service fails.

- **Command= CommandLine** Specifies a command or a script file that should be run when the service fails.

- **Actions= FailureActionsAndDelayTime** Specifies the failure action and delay time (in milliseconds), separated by a forward slash (/). You must use this parameter with the *Reset* parameter. Valid values for *Action* are *Run*, *Restart*, and *Reboot*. If you do not want to specify an action, use the *Action= ""* parameter.

Note that the value of *Reset* is given in seconds and the value of *DelayTime* is specified in milliseconds. When specifying *FailureActionAndDelayTime*, you must enter it as a single entry without any spaces. For example, **Restart/5000** and **Run/1000** are correct entries. You should not write these as **Restart   /5000** and **Run   /1000**. Also, there should be a space after the equals sign but no space before or after *DelayTime*. It is possible to specify three different actions on first, second, and third failures, separated by forward slashes. Here is an example of how to do this:

```
SC Failure Messenger Reset= 60 Actions= Restart/10/Restart/10/Reboot/60000
```

This command will configure the *Messenger* service to restart 10 milliseconds after the first and second failures, and reboot the computer after the third failure in 60,000 milliseconds (one minute). The service failure counter is reset after 60 seconds if the service does not fail during this time. Now, look at another example:

```
SC Failure Scheduler Reset= 60 Reboot= "Since the Scheduler Service on this
computer has failed, it will reboot in 30 seconds." Actions= Reboot/30000
```

This command will configure the service to reboot the system after 30 seconds when the *Task Scheduler* service fails. The following message will be broadcast before the computer reboots:

```
Since the Scheduler Service on this computer has failed, it will reboot in 30
seconds.
```

You can also configure the service to run a command, a script, or a batch file when the service fails. Consider the following example:

```
SC Failure Scheduler Reset= 240 Actions= Restart/10/Restart/10/Run/30000 Command=
"D:\Mybatch.bat"
```

Configuring the Service Logon Type

By default, all services run under the *LocalSystem* account. If you want to change the account that the service should use, you can use the *SC Config* command with the *Obj* and *Password* parameters to specify a different account name and password, respectively. The *Password* parameter must follow the *Obj* parameter. The simplified syntax of this command is:

```
SC Config \\Computer ServiceName Obj= AccountName Password= Password
```

In the preceding code, the *Computer* parameter specifies the name of a computer or its IP address, and *ServiceName* is the abbreviated name of the service as explained in the previous section. The *AccountName* parameter is the account to be used by the service and the *Password* parameter specifies the password associated with the *AccountName* parameter. The following example shows how you can configure the logon account for the *Messenger* service on the local computer:

```
SC Config Messenger Obj= Garyb Password= ********
```

When you run this command, it will fail. This is because originally the service type was configured as a *WIN32_SHARED_PROCESS* process and it runs under the *LocalSystem* account. In order to change the account for this or any other service that runs as a shared Windows process, you must also use the *Type= Own* parameter to let the Service Control Manager know that the service will run under its own context using the specified account and password. The correct syntax for the preceding command is:

```
SC Config Messenger Obj= Garyb Password= ******** Type= Own
```

When you use the *SC QC* command for the *Messenger* service, you can also use the *Domain\UserName* format for specifying the account name for the service.

SC Subcommands That Affect All Services

The *SC* command set has several subcommands, as discussed in the previous sections. While most of the commands deal with a specified service, certain commands affect all services. These commands directly interact with the Service Control Manager database. Here is a list of these commands:

- *SC Boot*
- *SC Lock*
- *SC QueryLock*

We discuss these commands in the following sections.

SC Boot

The *SC Boot* command specifies whether the system should save the last boot information as the *Last Known Good Configuration*. The *Last Known Good Configuration* appears as one of the advanced boot options during system startup. Valid parameters for this command are *OK* and *Bad*. If you specify *OK*, the last boot information is saved as *Last Known Good Configuration* and if you specify *Bad* it is not saved.

SC Lock

The *SC Lock* command locks the Service Control Manager database. The database remains locked until you use the *U* parameter to unlock it. While the database is locked, the command prompt displays a message that the Service Control Manager database is locked. Locking the Service Control Manager database prevents services from running.

SC QueryLock

The *SC QueryLock* command can query the Service Control Manager database and let you know whether it is locked. You can use the *SC Lock* command with a *U* parameter to unlock the database.

Obtaining Driver Information

You can obtain a list of all device drivers currently installed on the system by using the *Driverquery* command. You can use this command on local or remote computers, and you can obtain the output of this command in *Table*, *List*, or *CSV* format. The syntax of this command is:

```
Driverquery  [/s Computer] [/u Domain\User /p Password] [/fo {TABLE | LIST |
CSV}] [/nh] [{/v | /si}]
```

Table 7.7 explains this command's parameters.

Table 7.7 Parameters of the Driverquery Command

Parameter	Description
/s Computer	Specifies the name or IP address of the computer.
/u Domain\User	Specifies the domain and user account name to be used to run the command.
/p Password	Specifies the password for the user specified with the /s Computer parameter.
/fo {Table | List | CSV}	Used to specify the format of the output. You can choose to display the output in Table, List, or CSV format.
/nh	Used to suppress the display of column headers in the output.
/v	Used to obtain detailed information about all device drivers installed on the specified computer.
/si	Used to obtain information about signed and unsigned device drivers.

You can display detailed information about drivers using the */v* parameter, and display signed and unsigned device drivers using the */si* parameter. Here is some sample output of the *Driverquery* command:

```
Driverquery /v /fo List


Module Name:      VIAudio
Display Name:     Vinyl AC'97 Audio Controller (WDM)
Description:      Vinyl AC'97 Audio Controller (WDM)
Driver Type:      Kernel
Start Mode:       Manual
State:            Running
Status:           OK
Accept Stop:      TRUE
```

```
Accept Pause:        FALSE
Paged Pool(bytes):   55,168
Code(bytes):         90,752
BSS(bytes):          0
Link Date:           2/1/2005 12:39:02 AM
Path:                C:\WINDOWS\system32\drivers\vinyl97.sys
Init(bytes):         1,664
```

The following example shows how you can use this command to obtain information on signed and unsigned device drivers on a remote computer named *PrnServ1* located in the *Mydomain* domain using the *Garyb* account and its password:

```
Driverquery \\PrnServ1 /u Mydomain\Garyb /p ******* /fo List
```

Here is some sample output of this command:

```
DeviceName:    Floppy disk drive
InfName:       flpydisk.inf
IsSigned:      TRUE
Manufacturer:  (Standard floppy disk drives)

DeviceName:    Communications Port
InfName:       msports.inf
IsSigned:      TRUE
Manufacturer:  (Standard port types)

DeviceName:    VIA AC'97 Audio controller
InfName:       oem7.inf
IsSigned:      FALSE
Manufacturer:  Unknown

DeviceName:    ECP Printer Port
InfName:       msports.inf
IsSigned:      TRUE
Manufacturer:  (Standard port types)

DeviceName:    Printer Port Logical Interface
InfName:       machine.inf
IsSigned:      TRUE
Manufacturer:  (Standard system devices)
```

It is clear from this sample output that the signed drivers are flagged as *TRUE* and the unsigned device drivers are flagged as *FALSE*.

Managing the Windows Registry

Windows saves a system's entire configuration information in the Registry. Windows cannot function without the Registry. The contents of the Registry vary from computer to computer depending on what devices, applications, and other components are installed on the system. The Registry is a hierarchical database of keys, subkeys, and entries. These components appear as folders in the Registry structure. The actual data is stored in *entries*, the lowermost element of the Registry. The Registry Editor displays the Registry data in a hierarchical fashion in order to make it easy for administrators and programmers to find appropriate keys, subkeys, and values in particular entries.

The Registry is composed of mainly two subtrees: HKEY_LOCAL_MACHINE and HKEY_USERS. But in order to make it easy to find a particular subtree, they are displayed as five subtrees in the Registry Editor, three of which are actually aliases of the other subtrees. Here are the contents of the main subtree of the Registry, as displayed in the Registry Editor:

- **HKEY_LOCAL_MACHINE** Stores information about the hardware, operating system, and other information such as the device drivers and startup configuration of the local computer.

- **HKEY_CLASSES_ROOT** Contains information used by various object linking and embedding (OLE) technologies and file class associations.

- **HKEY_CURRENT_USER** Contains the profile of the currently logged-on user.

- **HKEY_USERS** Contains information about all user profiles and the default profile on the computer. Profiles of users connected remotely are not included in this subtree.

- **HKEY_CURRENT_CONFIG** Contains information about the hardware profile that the local computer loaded at startup.

You can perform most of the administrative tasks related to the Registry without using the Registry Editor or the command line. You may find that, in some cases, it is necessary to directly edit the Registry on a computer to make changes to a particular key or a subkey. You can use the *Reg* command-line utility to add, change, import, and export values in Registry subkeys. The *Reg* command-line utility consists of several subcommands, each used for a particular task related to the Registry. Table 7.8 lists these subcommands.

Table 7.8 Subcommands for Managing the Windows Registry

Command	Description
Reg Add	Used to add a new subkey or an entry to the Registry.
Reg Compare	Used to compare subkeys or entries in the Registry.
Reg Copy	Used to copy a Registry entry to a specified location on a local or remote computer.
Reg Delete	Used to delete a subkey or an entry from the Registry.
Reg Export	Used to copy a subkey, a Registry entry, or a value on the local computer into a file so that it can be transferred to other computers.
Reg Import	Used to copy the contents of a file containing an exported subkey, a Registry entry, or a value from another computer to the Registry of the local computer.
Reg Load	Used to write saved subkeys of the Registry into a different subkey in the Registry. This command is intended for use in troubleshooting Registry problems.
Reg Query	Used to display a list of the next tier of subkeys located directly under the specified subkey in the Registry.
Reg Restore	Used to restore saved copies of Registry subkeys.
Reg Save	Used to save a copy of the specified subkeys, entries, and values of the Registry to a specified file.
Reg Unload	Used to delete a part of the Registry that was previously loaded with the Reg Load command.

As an administrator, you will find that at some point, you will need to work with the Registry from the command line or by using the Regedit.exe or Regedit32.exe utilities. While it is not recommended that you edit the Registry directly, you must be familiar with command-line utilities. In this section, we will discuss the *Reg* commands that are used to perform the most common tasks related to the Registry.

When working with the *Reg* commands, different keys of the Registry are referenced by predefined notations. Table 7.9 lists these notations.

Table 7.9 Command-Line Notations of Registry Root Keys

Root Key	Notation
HKEY_LOCAL_MACHINE	HKLM
HKEY_CLASSES_ROOT	HKCR
HKEY_CURRENT USER	HKCU
HKEY_USERS	HKU
HKEY_CURRENT_CONFIG	HKCC

NOTE

Microsoft has limited the functionality of certain *Reg* commands on remote computers. While all commands work on local computers, certain commands can be used to view Registry information on remote computers but not to configure the Registry settings. Even if some commands seem to work on remote computers, the parameters you can use with those commands would be limited. Check the syntax of the *Reg* command if you want to confirm that it will work on a remote computer. In most of the *Reg* commands, the *KeyName* parameter is limited to HKLM (HKEY_LOCAL_MACHINE) and HKU (HKEY_USERS) on remote computers.

Data Types Supported in the Windows Registry

The Windows Registry stores values of keys as data. Data types define what kind of data can be stored in the Registry. There are five main data types:

- **REG_BINARY** Stores the value as binary data of *0*'s and *1*'s but displayed in hexadecimal format. Information about most hardware components is stored as binary data.

- **REG_DWORD** Represents the data as a four-byte number and is commonly used for Boolean values—for instance, *0* is disabled and *1* is enabled. The data is displayed as a 32-bit (four-byte) long hexadecimal number.

- **REG_EXPAND_SZ** A variable-length data string. It is replaced by applications or services when they use this data. This value usually contains the file path associated with the application or service.

- **REG_MULTI_SZ** A multiple string used to represent values that contain lists or multiple values; each entry is separated by a *NULL* character.

- **REG_SZ** A standard fixed-length string, used to represent human-readable text values.

WARNING

Microsoft recommends that you not edit the Registry unless you have no other way of changing the system configuration. You can perform most configuration changes using alternative methods. Incorrectly editing the Registry can result in an unstable system, or a system that won't even start. Use of the *Reg* command

and the Regedit.exe or Regedit32.exe utilities should be left to experienced administrators or programmers only. Even if you need to change something in the Registry, first test the effects of these changes in a test lab.

When working with the Windows Registry from the command line, you will need to understand the notations for Registry keys and data types. The commands for the *Reg* utility also require that you know the correct path to the Registry subkey in order to view or change the stored values. For example, if you want to work with the *Print Spooler* service, you should know where it is located in the Registry structure. The correct path to the Print Spooler service is HKEY_LOCAL_MACHINE\System\CurrentControlSet\ Services\Spooler. The path you would use with a particular *Reg* command would be HKLM\ System\CurrentControlSet\Services\Spooler. We will discuss some of the common tasks associated with the Windows Registry in the following sections.

Examining Values Stored in a Subkey

The *Reg Query* command allows you to obtain information about a specified subkey and entries in it. The syntax of this command is:

```
Reg Query KeyName [{/v ValueName | /ve}] [/s] [/f Data] [{/k | /d}] [/c] [/e] [/t
Type]
```

The command runs on the local computer by default. You can use the *Computer* parameter along with *KeyName* to specify the name or IP address of a remote computer. The *KeyName* parameter must be a valid root key name, such as HKLM, HKCR, HKCU, HKU, or HKCC. When used on a remote computer, the valid values for this parameter are limited to HKLM and HKU. Table 7.10 explains other parameters of this command.

Table 7.10 Parameters of the Reg Query Command

Parameter	Description
/v ValueName	Specifies the name of the Registry value to be queried. If this parameter is omitted, all values named for the specified *KeyName* are displayed.
/ve	Specifies that only empty value names be queried.
/s	Specifies that all subkeys and value names be queried.
/f Data	Specifies the data or pattern for which the query is to be run. You must use quotation marks if a string is used.
/k	Specifies that the query be done for key names only.
/d	Specifies that the query be done for data only.

Continued

Table 7.10 continued Parameters of the Reg Query Command

Parameter	Description
/c	Used for case-sensitive queries. By default, Registry queries are not case-sensitive.
/e	Used to display only exact matches. The default is to display all matches.
/t Type	Specifies the Registry data types to search. Valid values are REG_SZ, REG_MULTI_SZ, REG_EXPAND_SZ, REG_DWORD, REG_BINARY, and REG_NONE. The default is to search all types.

The following examples illustrate use of the *Reg Query* command:

```
Reg Query HKLM\System\CurrentControlSet\Services\Spooler

Reg Query HKLM\System\CurrentControlSet\Services\Spooler /v DependOnService

Reg Query \\Server1\HKLM\System\CurrentControlSet\Services\Spooler
```

In the first example, the Registry on the local computer is queried to display values of the *Spooler* key that is located in the *HKLM* root key. In the second example, we narrowed down the query to list only the value of the *DependOnService* key by using the */v* parameter. In the third example, we queried the *Spooler* subkey on a remote computer named *Server1*.

Comparing Subkeys

You can compare two subkeys in the Registry by using the *Reg Compare* command. This is useful when you want to make sure that values of certain Registry keys for a particular service or application are identical on two computers. This is an excellent tool for troubleshooting inconsistencies in Registry keys, subkeys, and other entries in the Registry. The syntax of this command is:

```
Reg Compare KeyName1 KeyName2 [{/v ValueName | /ve}] [{/oa | /od | /os | on}]
[/s]
```

In the preceding code, *KeyName1* and *KeyName2* are the two subkeys you want to compare. You can specify these two keys on two different computers. As shown in Table 7.10, you can use the */v ValueName* or the */ve* parameter to compare all value names or only empty value names, respectively. The */s* parameter specifies that all subkeys and value names are to be compared.

You can use four different formats to display the comparison results:

■ **/oa** Specifies that all matches and differences be displayed.

■ **/od** Specifies that only differences be displayed. This is the default display method.

- **/os** Specifies that only matches be displayed.
- **/on** Specifies that nothing should be displayed.

The following examples illustrate use of this command.

```
Reg Compare HLKM\Software\Microsoft\DeviceManager
HLKM\Software\Microsoft\DeviceManager1
```

The preceding command compares the *DeviceManager* subkey to the *DeviceManager1* subkey on the local computer.

```
Reg Compare HLKM\Software\Microsoft\DeviceManager
HLKM\Software\Microsoft\DeviceManager1 /os
```

This command will display only the differences found when comparing the values under the *DeviceManager* and *DeviceManager1* subkeys on the local computer. This is because the */od* parameter is assumed by default.

```
Reg Compare \\PrnServ1\HKLM\System\CurrentControlSet\Services\Spooler \\. /s
```

This command compares the *Spooler* subkey in a remote computer named *PrnServ1* to the same subkey in the local computer. After comparison, the results are displayed as *Identical* or *Different*. If we had used the */od* parameter, only the differences would be displayed. If we had used the */os* parameter, only the matches would be displayed. Even when you do not specify any parameter for matches or differences, the differences are displayed because the */od* parameter is assumed by default.

Adding and Deleting Subkeys

You use the *Reg Add* command to add new subkeys or entries to the Registry. The *Reg Delete* command deletes a specified subkey or an entry from the Registry. The syntax of these commands is:

```
Reg Add KeyName [{/v ValueName | /ve}] [/t DataType] [/s Separator] [/d Data]
[/f]
```

```
Reg Delete KeyName [{/v ValueName | /ve | /va}] [/f]
```

In both of these commands, the *KeyName* parameter specifies the subkey to be added or deleted. The */v ValueName* parameter specifies the value name. The */f* parameter specifies that the action should be performed without prompting for confirmation. In the *Reg Add* command, the */ve* parameter specifies that the new entry will have a null value (it will be an empty entry), and in the *Reg Delete* command, this parameter specifies that all entries with a null value should be deleted. The */va* parameter in the *Reg Delete* command specifies that all entries under the specified key should be deleted, but not the subkeys.

The following examples illustrate use of the *Reg Add* command.

```
Reg Add HKLM\System\CurrentControlSet\Services\Spooler\ /v ObjectName /t REG_SZ
/d "LocalSystem"
```

```
Reg Add \\Server1\HKLM\Software\NewKey /v Path /t REG_EXPAND_SZ /d ^%SystemRoot%^
```

The command in the first example adds a subkey named *ObjectName* to the *Spooler* key with a data type of *REG_SZ* and a data value of *LocalSystem*. In the second example, a key named *NewKey* is added with a data type of *REG_EXPAND_SZ* and a data value of *%SystemRoot%*. The key is added to the remote computer named *Server1*. Now, let us look at some examples of *Reg Delete*:

```
Reg Delete \HKLM\System\CurrentControlSet\Services\Spooler /v ObjectName
```

```
Reg Delete \\Server1\HKLM\ System\CurrentControlSet\Services\Spooler /v
DisplayName
```

The command in the first example will delete the *ObjectName* subkey under the *Spooler* key on the local computer. In the second example, the subkey named *DisplayName* is deleted from a remote computer named *Server1*. In order to delete all subkeys under a particular key, you can use the following command:

```
Reg Delete HKLM\Software\Google\Obsolete
```

This command will delete the *Obsolete* key and all subkeys under it on the local computer. In all of the preceding *Reg Delete* command examples, you will be prompted to confirm deletion of Registry entries. You can suppress this confirmation message by using the */f* parameter.

Saving and Restoring Registry Keys

If you work with the Windows Registry on a regular basis and you frequently change keys, subkeys, or other entries, it is a good idea to save the existing Registry information. Saved Registry keys are helpful when you make an unwanted change that does not work as expected. You can restore a working set of Registry keys to return to their correct, saved values. You can save and restore Registry keys using the *Reg Save* and *Reg Restore* commands, respectively. The syntax of these commands is:

Reg Save KeyName FileName **[/y]**
Reg Restore KeyName FileName

The *Reg Save* command saves a copy of the keys, subkeys, or other entries in the Registry to a specified file. Similarly, the *Reg Restore* command can replace a specified key, subkey, or entry with values taken from a specified file. You use the */y* parameter in the *Reg Save* command to overwrite an existing file without prompting you for a confirmation.

The following examples illustrate use of the *Reg Save* command.

```
Reg Save HKLM\System\CurrentControlSet\Services\Spooler SpoolBkUp.Hiv
```

```
Reg Save \\Server1\HKLM\System\ CurrentControlSet\Services\Spooler
\\Server1\RegBkUp\SpoolBkUp.Hiv
```

In the first example, the *Spooler* key and all subkeys under it are saved to a file named *SpoolBkUp.Hiv* on the local computer. In the second example, the same key is saved in the folder named *RegBkUp* on a remote computer named *Server1*. If a file with the same name already exists on the computer, you will be prompted to confirm whether you want to overwrite the existing file. You can suppress this confirmation warning by using the */y* parameter.

Now, let us look at some *Reg Restore* commands:

```
Reg Restore HKLM\System\CurrentControlSet\Services\Spooler SpoolBkUp.Hiv


Reg Restore \\Server1\HKLM\System\CurrentControlSet\Services\Spooler
\\Server1\RegBkUp\SpoolBkUp.Hiv
```

You may notice from these two commands that the syntax of the *Reg Save* and *Reg Restore* commands is fairly simple. With a little practice, you can learn to use these commands.

Copying Registry Keys

You can copy Registry keys from one location to another in the Registry hierarchy either on the local computer or from a remote computer to the local computer. The *Reg Copy* command makes it easy to copy Registry keys, subkeys, and other entries from a specified source location to a specified target location. The syntax of this command is:

```
Reg Copy KeyName1 KeyName2 [/s] [/f]
```

In the preceding code, *KeyName1* and *KeyName2* are the full paths of the source and target keys, respectively. Any of these keys can be on either the local or the remote computer. As you must with other *Reg* commands, you must include the name of the remote computer in *Computer*, and the *KeyName* parameter. The *Computer* parameter can be the name of the computer or its IP address. You use the */s* parameter to copy all subkeys and entries under the specified key, and the */f* parameter to force the command to copy the subkey without prompting for confirmation. The following example illustrates use of this command:

```
Reg Copy HKLM\System\CurrentControlSet\Services\Spooler
\\Server1\HKLM\System\CurrentControlSet\Services\Spooler
```

This command copies the subkey named *Spooler* from the local computer to the remote computer named *Server1*. The following example shows how to use the *Reg Copy* command on the local computer only:

```
Reg Copy HKLM\System\CurrentControlSet\Services\Spooler
HKLM\System\CurrentControlSet\Services\Spooler2 /s /f
```

This command will copy all subkeys and values under the *Spooler* key to the key named *Spooler1* on the local computer. The */s* parameter will enable the command to make a complete copy of all subkeys and values and the */f* parameter will suppress the confirmation prompt.

Summary

In this chapter, we discussed some of the key issues with the Windows operating system. The Windows operating system depends on some key services, drivers, and most importantly, the Registry, to operate properly. We discussed the command-line utilities required to maintain system services and the Windows Registry. We also discussed the *SC* and *Reg* command-line utilities which offer sets of several subcommands that are helpful in regular Windows operating system configuration and maintenance tasks. While you will rarely need to edit the Registry directly, either from the graphical user interface (GUI) or from the command line, it is good to understand how you can query, add, delete, save, and restore Registry entries. In the next chapter, we will discuss some other elements of Windows systems that enable you to monitor and manage events, tasks, and system performance.

Chapter 8

Monitoring System Events, Processes, and Performance

Topics in this chapter:

- **Managing Event Logs from the Command Line**
- **Creating New Events**
- **Working with Event Triggers**
- **Viewing Logged Events**
- **Monitoring Application Processes and Tasks**
- **Using Filters with the TaskList and TaskKill Commands**
- **Working with System Performance**

Introduction

In the preceding chapter, we learned about command-line utilities for managing system services, obtaining information about drivers and system configuration, and working with the Windows Registry. In this chapter, we will focus our discussion on some additional command-line utilities used for monitoring system events and performance logs. The ultimate goal of every system and network administrator is to keep the entire network running and to fine-tune it to provide optimum performance. Windows provides graphical utilities such as the Event Viewer, Task Manager, and Performance Console to help administrators monitor system events, application processes, and system performance. Although these tools are easy to use, they also can be time consuming. We will discuss the command-line equivalents of these tools in this chapter. As we did with other command-line utilities discussed in previous chapters, we will provide several examples of how to use these utilities to help you better understand the commands for monitoring and managing system events, processes, and performance.

Managing Event Logs from the Command Line

Monitoring and managing events on a system is essential for ensuring system maintenance and optimal system performance. Event logs record system status information as well as errors and warnings concerning the system, its security, and its applications, as these errors and warnings occur. Windows XP and Windows Server 2003 include the following three basic commands for monitoring and managing event logs on local and remote computers:

- **Eventcreate** Used to create custom events for the application and system logs. You cannot create custom events for security logs.

- **Eventtriggers** Used to monitor events written to the event logs. You can create event triggers to take a corrective action to resolve a known problem associated with a system service or an application.

- **Eventquery** Used to query event logs and display information taken from these logs based on specified search criteria. The results of the *Eventquery* command can either be displayed on the screen or be redirected to a file for review at a later time.

The following sections describe each command and include examples to help you understand the correct syntax and use.

Creating New Events

You can create custom events using the *Eventcreate* command. This utility adds new events to the event logs. It is interesting to note that the *Eventcreate* command runs on the local computer by default as soon as the system starts. This is why all system, application, and security events are constantly written to the event logs. The *Eventcreate* command can create custom events for application and system logs but not for security logs. This command runs with the account permissions of the currently logged-on user. The syntax of this command is:

```
Eventcreate [/s Computer [/u Domain\User [/p Password]] {[/l
{APPLICATION|SYSTEM}]|[/so SrcName]} /t
{ERROR|WARNING|INFORMATION|SUCCESSAUDIT|FAILUREAUDIT} /id EventID /d Description
```

Table 8.1 explains this command's parameters.

Table 8.1 Parameters of the Eventcreate Command

Parameter	Description
/s Computer	Specifies the remote computer, by its name or Internet Protocol (IP) address, where you want to create an event. If you omit this parameter, the local computer is assumed.
/u Domain\User	Specifies the domain and user account with whose account privileges the command is to be executed. By default, the account privileges of the currently logged-on user are used.
/p Password	Specifies the password of the user account specified by the /u parameter.
/l {Application | System}	Specifies the name of the category where the event log is to be created. You can choose from *Application* and *System* event logs.
/so SrcName	Specifies the source of the event. The value can be a string that specifies an application or a system component that generates the event.
/t {ERROR | WARNING | INFORMATION | SUCCESSAUDIT | FAILUREAUDIT}	Specifies the type of event to be created. Valid options for this parameter are *Error, Warning, Information, SuccessAudit, and FailureAudit.*
/id EventID	Specifies the ID for the event to be created. Valid values range from 1 to 65,535.
/d Description	Used to insert a description for the created event.

The following examples illustrate use of the *Eventcreate* command.

```
Eventcreate /t Information /id 100 /l Application /d "Creating an Entry in
Application Event Log"
```

In the preceding example, we used the *Eventcreate* command to create an information entry in the application event log on the local computer. The command uses the account permissions of the currently logged-on user to create the event entry. The event ID is specified as 100. Now, look at another example:

```
Eventcreate /t Error /id 2000 /so Winword /l Application /d "Error Event Written
by MS Word in Application Log"
```

In this example, the *Eventcreate* command is used to create an *Error* event that will be written to the *Application* log with an ID of *2000*. The source of the event is an application named *Winword* (Microsoft Word).

```
Eventcreate /t Warning /s PrnServ /u Mydomain\GaryB /p ******** /l Application /d
"Creating an Entry for Print Server in Application Log"
```

In this example, the *Eventcreate* command is executed on a remote computer named *PrnServ* with account permissions of a user named *GaryB* in the *Mydomain* domain. This command creates a *Warning* entry in the *Application* log.

In the preceding command, and in other commands associated with event logs, you may skip the */p Password* parameter. This will cause the command interpreter to prompt for a password of the user specified with the */u Domain\User* parameter.

> **NOTE**
>
> Windows does not allow you to create or write custom events to security logs. You can use events created with the *Eventcreate* command only to record events in the system and application categories.

Working with Event Triggers

In Windows XP and Windows Server 2003, you can set event triggers on event logs and track problems on local and remote computers. Depending on your settings, you can use event triggers to perform a variety of tasks when the specified criteria are met. For example, you may run a command, execute a script, run an application, or even send an e-mail message. You use the *Eventtriggers* command to create, delete, and view system events on a local or remote computer.

Administrators commonly use the *Eventtriggers* command to monitor event logs to resolve known issues with the system and problems with applications, and to maintain system security. You can create custom event triggers that will constantly monitor the event logs for a particular event entry. When an event trigger finds a predefined entry being written to the event logs, a script can be executed to take corrective action. For example, you can create an event trigger that monitors the event logs for an entry that indicates a service has stopped.

When the event trigger encounters this entry in the event logs, a script file can be used to restart the service. Similarly, you can write an event trigger to monitor the available disk space on a system's servers. You can write a script to delete unwanted or temporary files from servers as soon as disk space goes below a specified level.

When you use the *Eventtriggers* command without any parameters, a list of current event triggers is displayed as follows:

```
Trigger ID       Event Trigger Name                   Task
============     =========================      ==================================

        2       Myapp Errors                         D:\Programs\Errchks.bat
        1       Low Disk Space                       D:\Myfiles\DskClean.bat
```

If the command does not find any event triggers, the following message is displayed:

```
Info: No event triggers are found.
```

The *Eventtriggers* command consists of the following three subcommands, which you can use to create, delete, and query event triggers, respectively:

- *Eventtriggers /Create*

- *Eventtriggers /Delete*

- *Eventtriggers /Query*

In Chapters 5 and 7, we discussed the *DiskPart* and *SC* commands, respectively. As with the *Eventtriggers* command, these commands also consist of several subcommands. Unlike these commands, where you write the subcommands directly after the main command without using a hyphen (-) or a forward slash (/), the *Eventtriggers* commands use the forward slash before the subcommand. We explain these commands in the following sections.

Creating Event Triggers

You must create custom event triggers before you can use them. You can create custom event triggers using the *Eventtriggers /Create* command. The syntax of this command is:

```
Eventtriggers /create [/s Computer [/u Domain\User [/p Password]]] /tr
TriggerName [/l [APPLICATION] [SYSTEM] [SECURITY] ["DNS Server"] [LOG]
[DirectoryLogName] [*] ] {[/eid ID]|[/t
{ERROR|INFORMATION|WARNING|SUCCESSAUDIT|FAILUREAUDIT}]|[/so Source]} [/d
Description] /tk TaskName [/ru {[Domain\]User | "System"} [/rp Password]]
```

As with other commands, you can use the */s Computer*, */u Domain\User*, and */p Password* parameters to specify a remote computer by its name or its IP address, username, and password, respectively. When these parameters are omitted, the command is executed on the local computer with the account permissions of the currently logged-on user. Similarly, you can specify the type of event log to be monitored as *Error, Information, Warning, Success Audit,* or *Failure Audit* using the */t* parameter. You can use the */so Source* parameter to specify the source of the event in the event log.

You use the /l parameter with this command to specify the event log to be monitored. Valid options for this parameter include *Application, System, Security, DNS Server, Log*, and *DirectoryLog*. By default, an asterisk (*) is used as the event log type.

> **NOTE**
>
> With the *Eventtriggers /Create* command, you can use only one of the parameters out of /t, /so, and /eid to specify the event. These parameters are known as *event constraints* that limit the scope of the event triggers depending on the event ID, event source, and event type. If you use the /t parameter, you cannot use /so or /eid. Similarly, when you use /so, you cannot use /t or /eid.

Table 8.2 lists additional parameters associated with this command.

Table 8.2 Additional Parameters of the Eventtriggers Command

Parameter	Description
/tr TriggerName	Specifies a friendly name for the event trigger. A maximum of 63 characters are allowed.
/tk TaskName	Specifies a task, a command, a script file, or an application to be executed when the event trigger conditions are met. You must specify the full path of the task, command, or script file.
/ru Domain\User | "System"	Specifies a username whose account permissions are to be used to execute the task specified by the /tk TaskName parameter. You can use the "System" (or " ") option to specify the "NT Authority\System" account. By default, a specified task or command is executed with the permissions of the currently logged-on user.
/rp Password	Specifies the password for the user specified with the /ru parameter. When the System account is used, this parameter is ignored.

When you create event triggers, you must thoroughly understand the various known issues regarding the network and/or individual servers. Depending on your requirements, you may need to define issues for which you need to create event triggers that will monitor the event logs and run a task, command, or script file to take corrective action. The following examples will help you understand how to use the *Eventtriggers /Create* command.

```
Eventtriggers /Create /tr "Low Disk Space" /l System /t Error /tk D:\Myfiles\
DskClean.bat
```

In the preceding example, the *Eventtriggers /Create* command is used to create an event named *Low Disk Space* on the local computer to monitor *Error* events in the *System* event logs. The command will run a batch file named DskClean.bat from the D:\Myfiles folder to delete unwanted and temporary files from the disk to free up space. The command uses the account permissions of the locally logged-on user.

```
Eventtriggers /Create /s PrnServ /u Mydomain\GaryB /p ******** /tr "Low Disk
Space" /eid 4133 /tk \\FileSrv\Myfiles\DskClean.bat
```

In this example, the *Eventtriggers /Create* command is used to create an event trigger named *Low Disk Space* that monitors the event logs for event ID *4133*. The command is executed on a remote computer named *PrnServ* with the account permissions of *GaryB* in a domain named *Mydomain*. A file named DskClean.bat is run from the Myfiles folder on the network share located on a file server named *FileSrv*.

Master Craftsman...

Using Correct Path and Quotation Marks

Some parameters for the commands discussed in this chapter require you to enclose the options in quotation marks. For example, you must specify the *TriggerName* and *Description* parameters using quotation marks.

Similarly, the command interpreter does not check for accuracy of the path of the command, application program, or script file specified with the *Eventtriggers /Create /tk TaskName* parameter. You must make sure that the full path is specified with the correct syntax. When you need to pass the arguments to a script file, enclose the file path and command arguments in quotation marks. This rule applies not only to the commands in this chapter, but also to all commands discussed in the book. Any argument that contains spaces must be enclosed in quotation marks.

Deleting Event Triggers

You can remove unwanted event triggers using the *Eventtriggers /Delete* command. The trigger identifier identifies the event trigger that is to be deleted. You cannot restore deleted event triggers. If you need the deleted event triggers again, you will need to create them again. The syntax of this command is:

```
Eventtriggers /Delete [/s Computer [/u Domain\User [/p Password]]] /tid {ID|*}
```

As with other commands, you use the */s Computer*, */u Domain\User*, and */p Password* parameters to specify a remote computer, username, and password, respectively. When you omit these parameters, the command is executed on the local computer with the account permissions of the currently logged-on user.

The */tid* specifies the trigger identifier for the event trigger that is to be deleted. The trigger identifier is a number representing the event trigger as it appears when the configured event triggers are displayed using the *Eventtriggers /Query* command. You can also use an asterisk (*) to delete all event triggers on a specific computer. The following examples illustrate use of this command.

```
Eventtriggers /Delete /tid 3
Eventtriggers /Delete /tid * /s PrnServ /u Mydomain\GaryB /p ********
Eventtriggers /Delete /tid 5 /s 192.168.0.25 /u Mydomain\GaryB /p ********
```

In the first example, the *Eventtriggers /Delete* command deletes the event trigger *3* that is identified by the */tid* parameter. In the second example, all event triggers on a remote computer named *PrnServ* located in the *Mydomain* domain are deleted and the command is executed with the account permissions of a user named *GaryB*. In the third example, event trigger *5* is deleted from a remote computer whose IP address is 192.168.0.25, located in the *Mydomain* domain.

Querying Event Triggers

When you need information on event triggers currently configured on a local or remote computer, you can use the *Eventtriggers /Query* command to display the event triggers in a desired output format. The syntax of this command is:

```
Eventtriggers /Query [/s Computer [/u Domain\User [/p Password]]] [/fo
{TABLE|LIST|CSV}] [/nh] [/v]
```

As with other commands, you use the */s Computer, /u Domain\User,* and */p Password* parameters to specify a remote computer, username, and password, respectively. When you omit these parameters, the command is executed on the local computer with the account permissions of the currently logged-on user.

You can specify the format of the output using the */fo* parameter. By default, the output is displayed in a *Table* format but you can also display it in *List* or *CSV* (Comma Separated Value) format. When the output is to be redirected to a file rather than the command shell window, you should use the *CSV* format. You may use the */nh* parameter if you do not want the column headers to appear in the output. You cannot use this parameter with the *List* format.

When you use the */v* (verbose mode) parameter, the output includes detailed information about each of the currently configured event triggers. This parameter forces the command to include the following additional information about each event trigger:

- **Host name** The name or IP address of the computer where the event trigger is configured.

- **Query** The text of the complete command used to create the event trigger.

- **Description** The description of the event trigger. This is the description specified with the */d Description* parameter in the *Eventtriggers /Create* command.

- **Username** The user account whose permissions are used to create and run the task associated with the event trigger.

The following examples illustrate use of the *Eventtriggers /Query* command.

```
Eventtriggers /Query
Eventtriggers /Query /fo List
Eventtriggers /Query /s 192.168.0.25 /u Mydomain\GaryB /p ******** /nh /v
```

In the first example, the local computer is queried to display all event triggers currently configured on the system. In the second example, the output is displayed using the *List* format as specified by the */fo* parameter. In the third example, a remote computer with an IP address of 192.168.0.25, which is located in the *Mydomain* domain, is queried for currently configured event triggers. The output contains detailed information about each event trigger because the */v* parameter is used. The */nh* parameter forces the command to suppress column headers from the output.

Viewing Logged Events

You use the *Eventquery* command to view events recorded in event logs. This is a helpful tool for monitoring events on local and remote computers and for resolving problems arising from malfunctioning system services or applications. You can also search the event logs in the security category to look for security breaches or traces of malicious code circulating around the systems in the network. You must carefully examine event logs on a regular basis to prevent problems from occurring. If a problem occurs, you can query the event logs to diagnose the cause of the problem and to find an appropriate resolution. Further, you can use the *Eventquery* command with appropriate filters based on event category, source, and event ID to shortlist the events. The syntax of this command is:

```
Eventquery[.vbs] [/s Computer [/u Domain\User [/p Password]]] [/fi FilterName]
[/fo {TABLE|LIST|CSV}] [/r EventRange [/nh] [/v] [/l [APPLICATION] [SYSTEM]
[SECURITY] ["DNS server"] [UserDefinedLog] [DirectoryLogName] [*] ]
```

> **NOTE**
>
> The *Eventquery* command is a little different from other commands, and you must run it using the *CScript* scripting host. This is because the *Eventquery* command is configured as a Windows script. Since Windows uses WScript as the default scripting host, you must switch to CScript by using the following command at the command prompt:

```
CScript //h:cscript //s //nologo
```
When you run this command, the following message appears:
```
Command line options are saved.
The default script host is now set to cscript.exe.
```
After running the preceding command, you can use the *Eventquery* command without including the .vbs extension.

As with other commands, you use the */s Computer*, */u Domain\User*, and */p Password* parameters to specify a remote computer, username, and password, respectively. When you omit these parameters, the command is executed on the local computer with the account permissions of the currently logged-on user.

You can specify the format of the output using the */fo* parameter. By default, the output is displayed in a *Table* format but you can also display it in *List* or *CSV* format. When the output is to be redirected to a file rather than the command shell window, you should use the *CSV* format. You may use the */nh* parameter if you do not want the column headers to appear in the output. You cannot use this parameter with the *List* format. When you use the */v* (verbose mode) parameter, the output includes detailed information about each of the currently configured event triggers.

Table 8.3 explains additional parameters of this command.

Table 8.3 Additional Parameters of the Eventquery Command

Parameter	Description
/fi FilterName	Specifies the types of events that should be included in or excluded from the event query. Table 8.4 lists the types of filters that you can use along with valid filter operators.
/r EventRange	Specifies the range of events to be included in the output of the event query command.
/l LogType	Used to specify the event log to be monitored. Valid options for this parameter include *Application*, *System*, *Security*, *"DNS Server"*, *UserDefinedLog*, and *DirectoryLog*. By default, an asterisk (*) is used as the event log type.

NOTE

You can use the *"DNS Server"* option with the */l* parameter only if the local computer or the computer specified with the */s Computer* parameter is running the domain name system (DNS) service.

Using Filters to View Specific Events

Event logs are huge files containing thousands of events recorded by different system services, drivers, applications, and security mechanisms implemented on a particular computer.
It is not possible to go through this big list of events to search for a particular event that you
may need to examine to resolve a certain issue. The *Eventquery* command allows you to
specify filters with the */fi FilterName* parameter so that the output of the command contains
only those events that meet certain search criteria based on specified filters. Filters further
use filter operators to sort the output. You can also cut short the output of this command by
specifying a range of events. The following sections explain how to use filters with the
Eventquery command.

Filter Names and Filter Operators

You filter events in event logs by using filter names and filter operators. These operators sort
the output of the query to display only the desired results. You can use the */fi FilterName*
parameter to specify the filter names with the following valid filter operators:

- **eq** Stands for equal to.
- **ne** Stands for not equal to.
- **gt** Stands for greater than.
- **lt** Stands for less than.
- **ge** Stands for greater than or equal to.
- **le** Stands for less than or equal to.
- **or** Allows you to use the *Type* and the *ID* filters in a single command.

Table 8.4 lists filter names, filter operators, and their valid values.

Table 8.4 Filters for the Eventquery Command

Filter Name	Description	Operators	Valid Values
Computer	Specifies the name of the computer that generated the event.	*eq, ne*	Any valid character string.
Category	Specifies the category of the event. The event category depends on the source of the event.	*eq, ne*	Any valid character string.

Continued

www.syngress.com

Table 8.4 continued Filters for the Eventquery Command

Filter Name	Description	Operators	Valid Values
Datetime	Specifies the date and time when the event occurred.	*eq, ne, gt, lt, ge, le*	Date and time in the format *mm/dd/yy(yyyy), hh:mm:ssAM* or *mm/dd/yy (yyyy), hh:mm:ssPM.*
ID	Specifies the numeric identifier of the event. Each event in the event log has a numeric ID.	*eq, ne, or, gt, lt, ge, le*	Any positive integer between 1 and 65,535.
Source	Specifies the source of the event such as application, system, or service.	*eq, ne*	Any valid character string.
Type	Specifies the type of event, such as *Error, Information, Warning, SuccessAudit*, or *FailureAudit*.	*eq, ne, or*	*Error, Information, Warning, SuccessAudit, FailureAudit*
User	Specifies the user account that generated the event. This can be an actual user account or a special account such as the *LocalSystem* account, a network service, and so on. If N/A appears in this column, this means the user account is not applicable.	*eq, ne*	Any valid username only or a username in the *Domain\Username* format.

NOTE

You can also use the *DateTime* filter with the */fi* parameter in the "FromDate-ToDate" or "FromDate/ToDate" format. In this case, you will only be able to use the *eq* filter operator. Here is an example:

```
Eventquery /fi "DateTime Eq
07/20/06,01:30:45AM/07/20/06,05:30:59PM"
```

Note that you can use either a forward slash (/) or a hyphen (-) between *FromDate* and *ToDate* values.

Range of Events

When using the *Eventquery* command, you can specify a range of events with the */r EventRange* parameter. This parameter specifies the number of events to include in the output. The following are valid options for this parameter:

- **/r N** Displays the *N* number of most recent events. For example, */r 20* will display the 20 most recent events.

- **/r -N** Displays the *N* number of oldest events. For example, */r -50* will display the 50 oldest events.

- **/r N1-N2** Displays events in the range from *N1* to *N2*, with *N1* being the most recent event. For example, */r 100-150* will display events with numbers 100 to 150. In this case, the 100th event will be the most recent event.

Examples of the Eventquery Command

With so many parameters, filter types, and filter operators, it might seem like it's difficult to use the *Eventquery* command. Actually, it is not as difficult as you might think. A little practice with dummy commands at the command prompt will help you understand the correct syntax and use of this command. Now that you have an idea of what filter names and filter operators are, let us take a look at some examples to illustrate use of the *Eventquery* command.

```
Eventquery /r 10 /1 Application
```

The preceding command queries the application event logs to list the 10 most recent events (specified by */r 10*) on the local computer. Since we did not use any filters or formatting parameters, the output contains all types of events and is displayed in a *Table* format. The output of this command is:

```
-----------------------------------------------------------------------
Listing the events in 'application' log of host 'PrnServ1'
-----------------------------------------------------------------------

Type          Event   Date Time                 Source            ComputerName
------------- ------  -------------------------  ----------------  --------------
information   1000    7/11/2006 6:16:34 AM       LoadPerf          PrnServ1
information   1001    7/11/2006 6:16:34 AM       LoadPerf          PrnServ1
information   1800    7/11/2006 6:12:32 AM       SecurityCenter    PrnServ1
information   105     7/11/2006 6:12:31 AM       dcfssvc           PrnServ1
warning       1517    7/11/2006 3:47:20 AM       Userenv           PrnServ1
information   1000    7/11/2006 2:45:12 AM       LoadPerf          PrnServ1
information   1001    7/11/2006 2:45:12 AM       LoadPerf          PrnServ1
information   1800    7/11/2006 2:41:09 AM       SecurityCenter    PrnServ1
information   105     7/11/2006 2:41:08 AM       dcfssvc           PrnServ1
warning       1517    7/11/2006 2:10:10 AM       Userenv           PrnServ1
```

Now, look at another example:

```
Eventquery /s 192.168.0.25 /u Mydomain\GaryB /p ******** /fi "Type Eq Warning" /l
Application
```

This command queries the *Application* event logs on a remote computer with an IP address of 192.168.0.25 with the account permissions of user *GaryB* in the *Mydomain* domain. The */fi* parameter specifies the filter as *"Type Eq Warning"* to list only warning events. Here is another example with multiple filters:

```
Eventquery /r 15-25 /fi "Datetime Ge 07/20/06,01:30:45AM" /fi "Type Eq Error" /fi
"ID Eq 1000 or ID Eq 2000" /l System
```

This command looks a bit complex, but it's easy to understand. The command specifies a range of the 15 to 25 most recent events using the */r 15-25* parameter in the *System* category. The first filter specifies that only events with a *Datetime* greater than or equal to *20th* July 2006, 1:30:55 AM be listed (*/fi "Datetime Ge 07/20/06, 01:30:45AM"*). Another filter specifies that only events of type *Error* be listed, and a third filter specifies that the event ID must be either *1000* or *2000* (*/fi "ID Eq 1000 or ID Eq 2000"*). It is notable that you can use the *Or* operator with *Type* and ID filters only, and not with any other *FilterName*.

Monitoring Application Processes and Tasks

Administrators need to monitor running processes, services, and applications on critical and noncritical servers in order to make sure things are working as expected. Even a small component on a system may cause the system to become slow or nonresponsive if it takes up the entire CPU time or a big chunk of available system memory. Nonresponding applications may bring down or even shut down a critical server without even being noticed. It is essential to keep an eye on applications and services running on critical servers in order to avoid downtime. Windows includes the Task Manager to help you quickly identify nonresponsive components and terminate them, if necessary. In this section, we will discuss two important command-line utilities known as *TaskList* and *TaskKill* that you can use in your batch files or scripts to administer and maintain Windows servers.

Viewing Running Processes and Applications

You use the *TaskList* command-line utility to get information on all processes currently running on the computer. You can use the command on the local computer as well as on a remote computer with appropriate credentials. Processes currently running on a computer include both *system* and *user* processes and the *TaskList* utility can display these processes in the desired format. You can also use filters to include or exclude certain processes from the output. The syntax of this command is:

```
TaskList [/s computer] [/u domain\user [/p password]] [/fo {TABLE|LIST|CSV}]
[/nh] [/fi FilterName [/fi FilterName2 [ ... ]]] [/m [ModuleName] | /svc | /v]
```

Table 8.5 explains this command's parameters.

Table 8.5 Parameters of the TaskList Command

Parameter	Description
/s Computer	Specifies the name or IP address of a remote computer where the command is to be executed. If you omit this parameter, the command is run on the local computer.
/u Domain\User	Specifies the name of the domain and user whose account permissions are to be used to run the command. If you omit this parameter, the account permissions of the currently logged-on user are used.
/p Password	Specifies the password for the user account specified with the /u parameter.
/fo Format	Specifies the output format. Valid options are *Table, List*, and *CSV*. If no format is specified, the output is displayed in *Table* format.
/nh	Used to suppress column headers from the output. You can use this parameter only when the *Table* or *CSV* option is used with the */fo Format* parameter. You cannot use it with the *List* output format.
/fi FilterName	Specifies a filter to include or exclude processes or tasks in the query. Table 8.7 explains different filters, filter operators, and their valid values. You can use multiple filters in a single command.
/m ModuleName	Specifies the name of the module for which detailed information should be included in the output. By default, all the processes for all the running modules are included in the output. You cannot use this parameter with the */svc* or */v* parameter.
/svc	Specifies that the service information for each process in the module be included in the output without any truncation. You can use this parameter only with the *Table* output format. You cannot use it with the */m ModuleName* or */v* parameter.
/v	Specifies the verbose mode. The output includes additional columns containing information such as the status of the running process, the name of the user running the process, the CPU time used by the process, and, if available, the display name of the process. The status information tells you whether the process status is *Running, Not Responding*, or *Unknown*.

When you use the *TaskList* command without any parameters on a local or remote computer, the processes currently running on the computer are displayed as shown in the following listing:

```
Image Name                   PID  Session Name        Session#     Mem Usage
=========================  ======  ================  ========  ============
System Idle Process            0  Console                   0         28 K
System                         4  Console                   0        236 K
smss.exe                     604  Console                   0        388 K
csrss.exe                    668  Console                   0      4,264 K
winlogon.exe                 692  Console                   0      3,608 K
services.exe                 736  Console                   0      3,840 K
lsass.exe                    748  Console                   0      1,396 K
svchost.exe                  896  Console                   0      4,392 K
svchost.exe                  952  Console                   0      4,028 K
svchost.exe                  988  Console                   0     17,380 K
svchost.exe                 1052  Console                   0      2,612 K
svchost.exe                 1164  Console                   0      4,156 K
WLTRYSVC.EXE                1484  Console                   0      1,396 K
BCMWLTRY.EXE                1496  Console                   0      6,836 K
explorer.exe                1584  Console                   0     22,720 K
spoolsv.exe                 1620  Console                   0      4,436 K
soundman.exe                1772  Console                   0      2,832 K
SynTPLpr.exe                1780  Console                   0      3,080 K
SynTPEnh.exe                1792  Console                   0      4,328 K
```

You can use filters and other parameters to limit the output to view only selected processes. By default, the output is displayed in *Table* format. If you want to redirect the output to a database file, you can use the */fo* parameter with the *CSV* format. By default, only the following columns appear in the output:

- **Image Name** The name of the process, application, or service running on the computer. Image names of applications and services usually appear as executables or other filenames.

- **PID** The identification number of the process.

- **Session Name** The name of the active session for the process. Local sessions are denoted by *Local*.

- **Session#** The identification number of the current session.

- **MemUsage** The total amount of memory currently used by the process.

You can use the */v* parameter to get detailed information about each process. Consider the following command:

```
TaskList /fo List /v
```

The output of this command is:

```
Image Name:    HelpCtr.exe
PID:           2620
Session Name:  Console
Session#:      0
Mem Usage:     2,860 K
Status:        Running
User Name:     PrnServ\User
CPU Time:      0:00:01
Window Title:  Help and Support Center

Image Name:    spoolsv.exe
PID:           1620
Session Name:  Console
Session#:      0
Mem Usage:     4,412 K
Status:        Running
User Name:     NT AUTHORITY\SYSTEM
CPU Time:      0:00:00
Window Title:  N/A
```

You may notice that the */v* parameter adds the following additional columns of information for each process:

- **Status** The current status of the process that may be *Running* or *Not Responding.*
- **User Name** The name of the user who started the process. For system processes, it shows *NT AUTHORITY\SYSTEM.*
- **CPU Time** The total amount of CPU time used by the process since it started.
- **Window Title** The name of the process as it appears to the user.

Here are some additional examples of the *TaskList* command.

```
TaskList /v /fo CSV /nh
```

In the preceding example, the *TaskList* command is executed on the local computer. The */v* parameter is used to get detailed information about each process and the output format is specified as *CSV.* The */nh* parameter is used to suppress the display of column headers from the output. You can also redirect the output of this command to a file by using the >> redirection parameter. For example, you can write this command as follows to redirect the output to a file named *PrnServTasks.log*:

```
TaskList /v /fo CSV /nh >>PrnServTasks.log
```

Now, let us look at two more examples:

```
TaskList /fi "PID Lt 2000" /fi "Status Eq Running"
```

```
TaskList /s PrnServ /u Mydomain\GaryB /fi "UserName Eq NTAUTHORITY\SYSTEM" /fi
"Status Eq Not Responding"
```

In the first example, we used the */fi* parameter to specify a filter that will include only processes that have a process ID (PID) that is less than 2,000 (*/fi "PID Lt 2000"*). Another filter limits the output to only processes that have their current status as *Running* (*/fi "Status Eq Running"*). You can use multiple filters in a single command. We explain filters in more detail later in this book.

In the second example, the *TaskList* command is executed on a remote computer named *PrnServ* with the account permissions of a user named *GaryB* in the *Mydomain* domain. We used two filters in this command to view the processes that were started with the *"NT AUTHORITY\SYSTEM"* account and are not responding. The first filter limits the output to only processes that are started by the *"NT AUTHORITY\SYSTEM"* user (*/fi "UserName Eq NT AUTHORITY\SYSTEM"*) and the second filter limits the output to only processes that have their current status as *"Not Responding"* (*/fi "Status Eq Not Responding"*). In the next section, you will learn how to filter out nonresponding processes and terminate them using the *TaskKill* command.

> **NOTE**
>
> The *TaskList* and *TaskKill* commands included with Windows XP and Windows Server 2003 are much more powerful than their graphical user interface (GUI) equivalent, the Task Manager. These commands seem to be complex due to the large number of associated filters and filter operators, but once you learn how to use them, you will certainly find that they are not as difficult as they seem to be and are much more helpful in troubleshooting and maintaining systems than the Task Manager.

Viewing Service Information

When you use the *TaskList* command with the */svc* parameter, the output includes information about the currently configured services and their associated processes. You can use this parameter only with the *Table* output format. Additionally, you cannot use the */m ModuleName* parameter with this parameter. Consider the following example:

```
TaskList /svc
```

This command lists all the currently configured services on the local computer, along with their associated image names and PIDs. Since the default output format is *Table*, you need not use the */fo Format* parameter. The output of this command appears as follows:

```
Image Name                     PID Services
========================= ====== =============================================
System Idle Process              0 N/A
System                           4 N/A
smss.exe                       604 N/A
csrss.exe                      668 N/A
winlogon.exe                   692 N/A
services.exe                   736 Eventlog, PlugPlay
lsass.exe                      748 PolicyAgent, ProtectedStorage, SamSs
svchost.exe                    896 DcomLaunch, TermService
svchost.exe                    952 RpcSs
svchost.exe                    988 AudioSrv, CryptSvc, Dhcp, dmserver, ERSvc,
                                   EventSystem, FastUserSwitchingCompatibility,
                                   helpsvc, lanmanserver, lanmanworkstation,
                                   Netman, Nla, RasMan, Schedule, seclogon,
                                   SENS, SharedAccess, ShellHWDetection,
                                   srservice, TapiSrv, Themes, TrkWks, W32Time,
                                   winmgmt, wscsvc, WZCSVC
svchost.exe                   1052 Dnscache
svchost.exe                   1164 LmHosts, RemoteRegistry, SSDPSRV, WebClient
WLTRYSVC.EXE                   1484 wltrysvc
explorer.exe                  1584 N/A
spoolsv.exe                   1620 Spooler
SynTPLpr.exe                  1780 N/A
SynTPEnh.exe                  1792 N/A
AGRSMMSG.exe                  1800 N/A
rundll32.exe                  1808 N/A
sistray.exe                   1948 N/A
ScsiAccess.EXE                 628 ScsiAccess
svchost.exe                    672 stisvc
xcommsvr.exe                  1016 XCOMM
livesrv.exe                   1032 LIVESRV
vsserv.exe                    1392 VSSERV
alg.exe                       2308 ALG
HelpCtr.exe                   2620 N/A
HelpSvc.exe                   2752 N/A
HelpHost.exe                  2804 N/A
cmd.exe                       2872 N/A
```

```
WINWORD.EXE                    3648 N/A
tasklist.exe                    184 N/A
wmiprvse.exe                   2584 N/A
```

You can run this command on a remote computer by using the /s *Computer* parameter and limit the output by specifying an appropriate filter.

Viewing Process Modules

You can view the modules associated with processes currently running on a computer by using the /m *ModuleName* parameter with the *TaskList* command. These modules are also known as dynamic link libraries (DLLs). Most of the modules (or DLLs) are used by multiple processes. You cannot use this parameter with the /svc or /v parameter. To view a complete list of processes and their associated modules, use the /m parameter without using the *ModuleName* option, as follows:

```
TaskList /m
```

The output will include all the currently running processes and the modules associated with each process. The following listing shows partial output of this command:

```
Image Name                   PID Modules
============================ ====== =================================================
System Idle Process            0 N/A
System                         4 N/A
smss.exe                     604 ntdll.dll
csrss.exe                    668 ntdll.dll, CSRSRV.dll, basesrv.dll,
                                 winsrv.dll, USER32.dll, KERNEL32.dll,
                                 GDI32.dll, sxs.dll, ADVAPI32.dll, RPCRT4.dll
winlogon.exe                 692 ntdll.dll, kernel32.dll, ADVAPI32.dll,
                                 RPCRT4.dll, AUTHZ.dll, msvcrt.dll,
                                 CRYPT32.dll, USER32.dll, GDI32.dll,
                                 MSASN1.dll, NDdeApi.dll, PROFMAP.dll,
                                 NETAPI32.dll, USERENV.dll, PSAPI.DLL,
                                 REGAPI.dll, Secur32.dll, SETUPAPI.dll,
                                 VERSION.dll, WINSTA.dll, WINTRUST.dll,
                                 IMAGEHLP.dll, WS2_32.dll, WS2HELP.dll,
                                 MSGINA.dll, SHELL32.dll, SHLWAPI.dll,
                                 COMCTL32.dll, ODBC32.dll, comdlg32.dll,
                                 comctl32.dll, odbcint.dll, SHSVCS.dll,
                                 sfc.dll, sfc_os.dll, ole32.dll, Apphelp.dll,
                                 WINSCARD.DLL, WTSAPI32.dll, sxs.dll,
                                 uxtheme.dll, WINMM.dll, rsaenh.dll,
                                 cscdll.dll, WlNotify.dll, WINSPOOL.DRV,
                                 MPR.dll, SAMLIB.dll, BCMLogon.dll,
```

```
                              iphlpapi.dll, MFC42.DLL, OLEAUT32.dll,
                              msv1_0.dll, cscui.dll, xpsp2res.dll,
                              NTMARTA.DLL, WLDAP32.dll, wdmaud.drv,
                              msacm32.drv, MSACM32.dll, midimap.dll,
                              COMRes.dll, CLBCATQ.DLL
```

You can search all the processes that use a particular module by specifying the *ModuleName*. Consider the following example:

```
TaskList /m DNSAPI.DLL
```

This command will list all the processes that use the *DNSAPI.DLL* module. The output will be similar to the following listing:

```
Image Name                   PID Modules
========================== ====== =================
lsass.exe                    748 DNSAPI.dll
svchost.exe                  952 DNSAPI.dll
svchost.exe                  988 DNSAPI.dll
svchost.exe                 1052 DNSAPI.dll
spoolsv.exe                 1620 DNSAPI.dll
backWeb-7288971.exe         1916 DNSAPI.dll
livesrv.exe                 1032 DNSAPI.dll
vsserv.exe                  1392 DNSAPI.dll
wmiprvse.exe                3820 DNSAPI.dll
tasklist.exe                2884 DNSAPI.dll
```

You can run this command on a remote computer by using the */s Computer* parameter and limit the output by specifying an appropriate filter.

Terminating Applications and Processes

Sometimes when you are working on a computer an application will stop responding. It is easy to terminate the application by opening the Task Manager, locating the application, and clicking the **End Process** button. You can perform this action from the command line by using the *TaskKill* utility. You use the *TaskKill* command to terminate one or more running or nonresponding processes on a local or remote computer. The syntax of this command is:

```
TaskKill [/s Computer] [/u Domain\User [/p Password]]] [/fi FilterName] [/pid
ProcessID]|[/im ImageName] [/f][/t]
```

Table 8.6 explains this command's parameters.

Table 8.6 Parameters of the TaskKill Command

Parameter	Description
/s Computer	Specifies the name or IP address of a remote computer where the command is to be executed. If you omit this parameter, the command is run on the local computer.
/u Domain\User	Specifies the name of the domain and user whose account permissions are to be used to run the command. If you omit this parameter, the account permissions of the currently logged-on user are used.
/p Password	Specifies the password for the user account specified with the /u parameter.
/fi FilterName	Specifies a filter to include or exclude processes or tasks in the query. Table 8.7 explains different filters, filter operators, and their valid values. You can use multiple filters in a single command.
/pid ProcessID	Specifies the PID of the process that is to be terminated.
/im ImageName	Specifies the image name of the process or processes to be terminated. You can use wildcards to specify multiple processes.
/f	Used to forcefully terminate all processes. This parameter is ignored for remote processes, which are terminated forcefully by default.
/t	Used to terminate all child processes associated with the parent process. The operation is also known as a Tree Kill operation.

The following examples show how to use the *TaskKill* command.

```
TaskKill /pid 1020
TaskKill /im Winword.exe
TaskKill /s PrnServ /u Mydomain\GaryB /pid 1748 /pid 1756 /pid 1764
TaskKill /s PrnServ /u Mydomain\GaryB /fi "Status Eq Not Responding"
```

In the first example, the *TaskKill* command is used to terminate a process with a PID of *1020* on the local computer. In the second example, the process to be terminated is identified by its *ImageName* (*/im Winword.exe*). In the third example, the command is used to terminate three processes with the PIDs 1748, 1756, and 1764 on a remote computer named *PrnServ* with the account permissions of a user named *GaryB* in the *Mydomain* domain. In the last example, we used a filter to terminate all processes that are not responding by using a filter (*/fi "Status Eq Not Responding"*).

In some cases, applications start multiple processes. Terminating a single process does not completely shut down the application. You may need to terminate the application by using the */t* parameter. The */t* parameter forces the application to terminate all child processes.

Sometimes a process will as a result of the *TaskKill* command. In such cases, you may need to use the */f* parameter to forcefully terminate the process. On remote computers, the *TaskKill* command terminates all processes by default when the parent process is terminated and you need not use the */f* parameter.

NOTE

It is a common practice to terminate processes by using their PIDs. This simply means that you will need to use the *TaskList* command to obtain the PID for a particular process.

Using Filters with the TaskList and TaskKill Commands

We discussed filter operators during our discussion of the *Eventquery* command in the section titled "Using Filters to View Specific Events." You can use the same filter operators with the *TaskList* and *TaskKill* commands also. Table 8.7 lists filter names, their description, valid filter operators, and valid values that you can use with the *TaskList* and *TaskKill* commands.

Table 8.7 Filters for the TaskList and TaskKill Commands

Filter Name	Description	Operators	Valid Values
Status	Helps in locating applications or processes that are not responding.	*eq, ne*	*Running* or *Not Responding*
ImageName	Helps in locating a particular application based on the name of the executable or filename.	*eq, ne, gt, lt, ge, le*	Any valid character string identifying the executable or filename.
PID	Used to locate an instance of the application or process when multiple copies are running on the computer.	*eq, ne, gt, lt, ge, le*	Any valid positive integer identifying the process with a PID.
Session	Used for shared applications such as Terminal Services.	*eq, ne*	Any valid session number.
SessionName	Used for shared applications such as Terminal Services.	*eq, ne*	Any valid session name.

Continued

www.syngress.com

Table 8.7 continued Filters for the TaskList and TaskKill Commands

Filter Name	Description	Operators	Valid Values
CPUTime	Used to determine the applications that have been running for a particular amount of time. For example, applications or processes that have been running for over an hour can be filtered out. Similarly, you can filter processes that have just started.	eq, ne, gt, lt, ge, le	CPU time in the format hh:mm:ss. Valid values for mm and ss range from 00 to 59.
MemUsage	Used to identify applications that take up more system memory that can currently be supported. Applications or processes taking up significant memory can be terminated.	eq, ne, gt, lt, ge, le	Any valid positive integer specifying the amount of memory used by the process in kilobytes (KB).
UserName	Used to identify the processes started by a particular user. You can distinguish the processes started by the users from the system.	eq, ne	Any valid character string identifying the user or domain and user in Domain\User format.
Services	Used to identify the application that starts a particular service.	eq, ne	Any valid character string identifying the service.
WindowsTitle	Used to locate an application or process by specifying the displayed Windows title.	eq, ne	Any valid character string identifying the Windows title for the process.
Modules	Used to identify applications that use different modules.	eq, ne	Any valid character string identifying the module.

You can use multiple filters in a single command to include or exclude certain processes from the output. Here are some additional examples of how you can use the *TaskList* and *TaskKill* commands.

To list all processes on a remote computer which have an *ImageName* starting with *Note*, such as Notepad.exe, use this command:

```
TaskList /s PrnServ /u Mydomain\GaryB /p ******** /fi "ImageName Eq Note*"
```

To list all processes on a remote computer which are using more than 30,000 KB (30 MB) of memory, use this command:

```
TaskList /s PrnServ /u Mydomain\GaryB /p ******** /fi "Memusage Gt 30000"
```

To list all processes on a local computer which are using more than 30,000 KB (30 MB) of memory and are running for more than 40 minutes, use this command:

```
TaskList /fi "Memusage Gt 30000" /fi "CPUTime Gt 00:40:00"
```

To terminate all processes on the local computer which are using a module named *Winspool.dll*, use this command:

```
TaskKill /fi "Modules Eq Winspool.dll"
```

To terminate all processes on a local computer which have been running for more than 30 minutes and are not responding, use this command:

```
TaskKill /fi "PID Gt 10" /fi "CPUTime Gt 00:30:00" /fi "Status Eq Not Responding"
```

WARNING

You must be careful when terminating processes. It is a good practice to first get a list of running processes and their associated PIDs before proceeding with the *TaskKill* command. Exercise extreme caution, as an incorrectly terminated process may cause the system to stop responding or even shut down.

Working with System Performance

Microsoft recommends that the best tool for monitoring and managing system performance is the Performance Console. This is true. The Performance Console is indeed a powerful tool and is easy to configure. However, command-line utilities are available that help make the Performance Console an even better tool. In this section, we will discuss some commands related to system performance. These utilities include *TypePerf, Lodctr, Unlodctr,* and *Relog.* Each utility has its own importance and any administrator who loves to work with the Windows command line must not ignore them.

Viewing Performance Data

The *TypePerf* command allows you to view performance counter data on the screen or send it to a supported log file for later review. You can use this command on a local or remote computer. Once the command is executed, all performance data is sent to the specified destination. You can terminate the process by using the **Ctrl+C** key combination or by using the */sc Samples* parameter. The syntax of this command is:

```
TypePerf [Counter [Counter ...]] [-cf FileName] [-f {CSV|TSV|BIN}] [-si Interval]
[-o FileName] [-q [object]] [-qx [object]] [-sc Samples] [-config FileName] [-s
ComputerName] [-y]
```

Table 8.8 explains this command's parameters.

Table 8.8 Parameters of the TypePerf Command

Parameter	Description
Counter	Specifies one or more performance counters to display. Each performance counter is specified using a supported counter path. Counter paths are explained in the section "Specifying the Counter Path."
-cf FileName	Used to specify the name of the file that contains the performance counters that are to be monitored. The counters must be written one per line in the specified file.
-f {CSV | TSV | BIN | SQL}	Used to specify the output file format. Valid options are CSV, TSV, BIN, and SQL. If no format is specified, the command uses the CSV output format by default.
-si Interval	Specifies the sampling interval for collecting performance data. The default interval is one second. The format is [[hh:]mm:]ss.
-o FileName	Specifies the name of the output file or the Structured Query Language (SQL) database. By default, the output is displayed in the command shell window (STDOUT).
-q [Object]	Used to display all available counters for the specified object. If the object name is omitted, all available counters for all objects are displayed. The instances of the counters are not included in the output.
-qx [Object]	Used to display all available counters and their instances for the specified object. If the object name is omitted, all available counters and their instances for all objects are displayed.
-sc Samples	Specifies the number of samples to collect. By default, sample collection continues until you press the **Ctrl + C** key combination.
-config FileName	Used to specify the name of the file that contains the configuration settings of the command.
-s ComputerName	Specifies the name or the IP address of a remote computer. By default, the command is executed on the local computer.
-y	Used to answer Yes to all questions during the execution of the command without prompting.

Specifying the Counter Path

The *TypePerf* command supports counter paths in a variety of formats. Each counter path includes the parent object, counter, and instance of the counter. If the performance counter resides on a remote computer, the name of the remote computer precedes the counter path. Here is a list of formats for specifying counter paths:

- \\machine\object(parent/instance#index)\counter

- \\machine\object(parent/instance)\counter

- \\machine\object(instance#index)\counter

- \\machine\object(instance)\counter

- \\machine\object\counter

- \object(parent/instance#index)\counter

- \object(parent/instance)\counter

- \object(instance#index)\counter

- \object(instance)\counter

- \object\counter

Using Wildcards with Counter Paths

You can also use wildcards (*) while specifying counter paths. The following general rules apply when using wildcards:

- If you use a wildcard character in the parent name, all instances of the specified object that match the instance and counter will be displayed.

- If you use a wildcard character in the instance name, all instances of the specified object and parent object will be displayed if all instance names corresponding to the specified index match the wildcard character.

- If you use a wildcard character in the counter name, all counters of the specified object are displayed.

NOTE

You cannot use wildcards that specify only a partial counter path string. For example, you cannot use *Pro** to specify the *Process* or *Processor* object. Also, if any counter path contains a character string with spaces, you must enclose the entire string within quotation marks.

The following examples illustrate use of the *TypePerf* command.

```
TypePerf "\Processor(_Total)\% Processor Time"
```

The preceding command is used to display *%Processor Time* for the *Processor* object on the local computer. When the command is executed the performance data is displayed in the command shell window. Since the number of samples is not specified, you must terminate the command by pressing the **Ctrl + C** key combination. Here is the output of this command:

```
"(PDH-CSV 4.0)","\\PrnServ\Processor(_Total)\% Processor Time"

"07/12/2006 06:17:51.250","0.000000"
"07/12/2006 06:17:52.250","0.000000"
"07/12/2006 06:17:53.250","0.000000"
"07/12/2006 06:17:54.250","0.000000"
"07/12/2006 06:17:55.250","0.000000"
```

The following command displays the performance data for two counters on the local computer. These are *Available Bytes* for the *Memory* object and *%Processor Time* for the *Processor* object:

```
TypePerf "\Memory\Available bytes" "\Processor(_total)\% Processor Time"
```

Here is the output of the preceding command:

```
"(PDH-CSV 4.0)","\\PrnServ\Memory\Available bytes",
"\\PrnServ\Processor(_total)\% Processor Time"
"07/12/2006 06:25:52.375","126562304.000000","1.538462"
"07/12/2006 06:25:53.375","126234624.000000","0.000000"
"07/12/2006 06:25:54.375","126562304.000000","0.000000"
"07/12/2006 06:25:55.375","126554112.000000","0.000000"
"07/12/2006 06:25:56.375","126672896.000000","0.000000"
"07/12/2006 06:25:57.375","126672896.000000","0.000000"
"07/12/2006 06:25:58.375","126337024.000000","1.470588"
"07/12/2006 06:26:00.500","126660608.000000","0.000000"
"07/12/2006 06:26:01.500","126558208.000000","0.000000"
"07/12/2006 06:26:02.500","126566400.000000","0.000000"
"07/12/2006 06:26:03.500","126222336.000000","0.000000"
"07/12/2006 06:26:04.500","126328832.000000","0.000000"
```

The following example takes a list of performance counters to be monitored from a file named *Perfctr.txt* and sends the output to a file named *Perfdata.tsv*. The data is collected in intervals of five seconds (*-si 5*) and only 50 samples (*-sc 50*) are collected. The output format is specified as *TSV*:

```
TypePerf -cf Perfctr.txt -si 5 -sc 50 -f TSV -o Perfdata.tsv
```

The following command queries the system Registry to display a list of counters and their associated instances for the *PhysicalDisk* object. The output of the command is sent to a file named *Ctrdata.txt*:

```
TypePerf -qx PhysicalDisk -o Ctrdata.txt
```

You can run any of the preceding commands on a remote computer by including the computer name before the counter path. Here is an example:

```
TypePerf "\\PrnServ\Processor(_Total)\% Processor Time"
```

Since the counter path contains a space, we have used quotation marks in all of the preceding commands.

Adding New Performance Counters

Windows-based operating systems rely on performance counters to keep track of different system services and components. Although the built-in counters are sufficient for monitoring different components of a system, you may need to add custom counters at some point in time. The *Lodctr* command allows you to add new counters to a system so that these counters are available when you use the Performance Console. This command has options for registering the counters and associated explanation text as well as saving these counters in a file for later use. The syntax of this command is:

```
Lodctr [\\ComputerName] FileName [/s:FileName] [/r:FileName]
```

Here are the parameters of this command:

- **ComputerName** Used if the command is to be executed on a remote computer. You can also use the IP address of the remote computer. You must insert two backslashes (\\) before the computer name or the IP address, whichever you use. If you do not use this parameter, the command is executed on the local computer.

- **FileName** The name of the initialization file that contains the data for the new performance counter and the associated explanation text.

- **/s: FileName** Used when you want to save the current performance Registry settings and explanation text to the specified file. The file has a .ini extension.

- **/r: FileName** Used when you want to restore the performance Registry settings data from the specified file.

> **NOTE**
>
> Since there is no provision for the */u UserName* or */p Password* parameter in this command, you must have access to the remote computer. If any of the arguments for the parameters contains spaces, you must enclose them in quotation marks.

Removing Performance Counters

You can remove performance counters from a system by using the *Unlodctr* command. This command removes the names of the performance counters and their associated explanation text for the specified service or the driver from the system Registry. The syntax of this command is:

```
Unlodctr [\\ComputerName] DriverName
```

You use the *ComputerName* parameter to specify a remote computer. If you omit this parameter, the command is executed on the local computer. The *DriverName* parameter specifies the name of the service or the driver for which you want to remove the performance counters from the system. When you use the command without any parameters, help is displayed for the command.

Extracting Performance Counters from Existing Logs

The *Relog* command-line utility allows you to extract performance counters from existing performance logs. You can create new performance logs as well as change the configuration of the command, such as the format and sampling rate. This command supports all types of log file formats, including Windows NT 4.0 compressed logs. The syntax of this command is:

```
Relog [FileName [filename ...]] [-a] [-c Path [path ...]] [-cf FileName] [-f {BIN
| TSV | CSV |SQL}] [-t value] [-o FileName] [-b M/d/yyyy [[hh:]mm:]ss] [-e
M/d/yyyy [[hh:]mm:]ss] [-config FileName] [-q] [-y]
```

Table 8.9 explains the parameters used with this command.

Table 8.9 Parameters of the Relog Command

Parameter	Description
FileName	Specifies the name of the existing performance log file. You can include multiple files in a single command.
-a	Used to append output to the file instead of over-writing it. For SQL format, this parameter is ignored, as the default is to always append the output to the file.
-c Counter	Specifies the path to the counter logs. You can use multiple counters in a single command, separated by commas. If the counter path contains spaces, the path must be enclosed in quotation marks.
-cf FileName	Specifies the name of the text file that contains the list of the counters to be included in the Relog file.
-f {CSV | TSV | BIN | SQL}	Used to specify the output file format. Valid options are CSV, TSV, BIN, and SQL. If no format is specified, the command uses the BIN output format by default.
-t Value	Specifies that every nth record be written to the output Relog file. The Value option sets the sampling interval for the records. By default, every record is written to the Relog file.
-o FileName	Specifies the name of a file or the SQL database where the output is to be written.
-b M/d/yyyy [[hh:]mm:]ss]	Specifies the starting time when the first record is collected from the input performance log file.
-e M/d/yyyy [[hh:]mm:]ss]	Specifies the ending time when the last record is collected from the input performance log file.
-config FileName	Used to specify the name of the file that contains the configuration settings of the command.
-q	Used to display the performance counters and time ranges of log files specified in the input file.
-y	Used to answer Yes to all questions during execution of the command without prompting.

You must specify the counter paths using the correct syntax and supported format. Refer to the section titled "Specifying the Counter Path," earlier in this chapter, for a list of supported formats. Here are some examples of this command.

The following command resamples a performance log file named C:\Logfiles\Perflog.csv and sends the output to another file named C:\Logfiles\Perflog.blg. The −c parameter specifies that only the "Processor (-Total)\%Processor Time" counter be included in the output file:

```
Relog C:\Logfiles\Perflog.csv -c "\Processor(_Total)\% Processor Time" -o
C:\Logfiles\Perflog.blg
```

The following command resamples a performance log file named
C:\Logfiles\PerfLog.txt and sends the output to another file named C:\Logfiles\PerfLog.blg
in *CSV* format. The sampling value has been set at 3, which causes the command to read
every third record from the input file:

```
Relog C:\Logfiles\Perflog.blg -f CSV-o C:\Logfiles\Perflog.blg -t 3
```

The following command resamples an existing trace log file named
C:\Logfiles\TraceLog.txt at fixed intervals of 30, and lists counter paths, output files, and formats:

```
Relog C:\Logfiles\TraceLog.blg -cf C:\Logfiles\Counters.txt -o
C:\Logfiles\\Newlog.csv -t 30 -f CSV
```

Summary

In this chapter, we discussed some command-line utilities for monitoring and managing
event logs, processes, and performance logs. Monitoring is an important aspect of system and
network administration and you cannot ignore it. Windows includes several GUI utilities for
monitoring system services, application processes, and other tasks. But a set of utilities that
are equally if not more powerful is also included for working from the command line. In this
chapter, we discussed those utilities—*Eventcreate*, *Eventtriggers*, and *Eventquery*—that you can
use to monitor and manage event logs. You learned how you can view system services and
applications using the *TaskList* command and how to terminate nonresponsive processes
using the *TaskKill* command. Both of these commands seem complex because of their large
number of optional filters and filter operators, but we provided several examples to help you
understand how to use these commands. This chapter also included some command-line
utilities for monitoring and managing performance logs. These utilities included *TypePerf* for
displaying performance data in the command shell window; *Lodctr* for registering new performance counters in the Windows Registry; and *Relog* for extracting and resampling stored
performance data. In the next chapter, we will discuss some utilities for managing local and
network printers.

Chapter 9

Managing Printing Services

Topics in this chapter

- **Working with Printer Commands**

- **Installing a Local Printer**

- **Configuring and Renaming Printers**

- **Managing Printer Drivers**

- **Creating and Configuring TCP/IP Printer Ports**

- **Managing Print Queues and Print Jobs**

Introduction

Managing printers, printer drivers, and print jobs is full-time work in some large organizations where printing is considered an essential part of everyday business. Where there are a large number of printers and several departments are using them via multiple print servers, administrators must be prepared to tackle different types of printing problems on a regular basis. Having your organization's printers and print servers centrally located can make things easier for you, but even if they are spread across different sections or floors of your building, as long as there are no physical problems with the printers, you can manage them and their print jobs from a central location, by using Windows command-line utilities. Perhaps the only thing you cannot do using command-line printer utilities is to set permissions for an installed printer. In this chapter, we will discuss some utilities that will help you manage printers from the command line.

Working with Printer Commands

The commands related to printer management in Windows XP and Windows Server 2003 are provided as Windows scripts. By default, Windows assumes WScript as the scripting host for the computer. If this is your first time using printer commands, you will need to change the scripting host from WScript to CScript. You can do this from the command prompt by following these steps:

1. Start the command interpreter by running **cmd** from the **Start** menu.

2. Type **CScript //h:cscript //s** and press the **Enter** key.

When you run this command, the following message appears:

```
Command line options are saved.
The default script host is now set to "cscript.exe".
```

After running the preceding command, you can use the printer commands without including the .vbs extension. The scripting host is changed on a per-user basis. If you are using the printer commands for another user in a batch file, you must include the preceding command before other printer commands.

Instead of changing the scripting host from WScript to CScript, you can use these commands with the .vbs extension. However, you still must type **CScript** before each command. The following example shows how you can use the *Prnmngr* command to list all printers installed on the local computer without changing the scripting host:

```
Cscript Prnmngr.vbs -l
```

Since the Cscript.exe file is located in the %SystemRoot%\System32 folder of the local computer, you must make sure that the path exists in the *%path%* environment variable in the command shell to successfully run the command. For more information on how you can change the command path or add a path to the command shell, refer to the section titled "Changing the Command Path" in Chapter 2.

Working with Remote Computers

You can use printer commands on the local computer as well as on a remote computer. For most of the commands discussed in this chapter, you can specify a remote computer by adding the following parameters to the command you are using:

- **-s Computer** Specifies a remote computer. If you omit this parameter, all commands are run on the local computer.

- **-u UserName** Specifies a user account that has permissions to connect to the remote computer by using Windows Management Instrumentation (WMI) services in order to run the command. Members of the local Administrators group on every computer are granted this permission by default.

- **-w Password** Specifies the password for the user specified with the *-u UserName* parameter.

Later in this chapter, we will provide some examples to illustrate use of printer commands that are executed on remote computers.

NOTE

Not all commands discussed in this chapter will allow you to use the *-u, -p,* and *-w* parameters to specify a remote computer, username, and password, respectively. Moreover, if you try to use the *-u* and *-p* parameters on the local computer, you will get an error message. If you need to use another user account for the local computer, you must log off and log on again using the account that has sufficient permissions to manage printers.

Installing a Local Printer

You can install a printer and configure its properties using the *Prnmngr* command. You can install a local printer on the local computer or on a remote computer. In addition, you can display a detailed listing of all the printers installed on a computer and set the default printer. When you use the *Prnmngr* command without using any of its parameters, the command interpreter will display help for the command. The following sections explain different parameters of this command.

Listing All Printers Installed on a Computer

You use the *Prnmngr* command with the *-l* parameter to display a list of all printers installed on the local computer or a remote computer. The syntax of this command when used to list printers is:

```
Prnmngr -l [-s ComputerName] [-u UserName -w Password]
```

-l is a required parameter that specifies that the command is being used to list installed printers on the computer. For example, the following command lists all printers installed on the local computer:

```
Prnmngr -l
```

Here is the output of this command:

```
Server name PrnServ1
Printer name HP OfficeJet V40
Share name HPOJ40
Driver name HP OfficeJet V40
Port name LPT1:
Comment
Location Office Jet Printer for Managers
Print processor WinPrint
Data type RAW
Parameters
Attributes 580
Priority 1
Default priority 0
Status Idle
Average pages per minute 0
```

As shown in the preceding code listing, the output includes such information as the name of the print server (the name of the computer where the printer is installed), the name of the printer, the name of the printer share (if the printer is shared), the port the printer uses, the printer priority, and its current status, among other things.

If you want to list printers installed on a remote computer, you can add the *-s ComputerName*, *-u UserName*, and *-w Password* parameters, as illustrated in the following example:

```
Prnmngr -l -s PrnServ2 -u GaryB -w ********
```

You can omit the *-u Username* and *-w Password* parameters if you are executing the command with sufficient permissions on the remote computer. The command does not allow you to use the *-u* and *-w* parameters on the local computer.

Adding a Local Printer

You can add a local printer to the local computer or a remote computer by using the *Prnmngr* command and the *-a* parameter. The syntax of this command when used for adding printers is:

```
Prnmngr -a -p PrinterName [-s ComputerName] -m DriverName -r PortName [-u
UserName -w Password]
```

All parameters listed with the command are required parameters. Table 9.1 explains the purpose of these parameters.

Table 9.1 Parameters of the Prnmngr Command for Adding Printers

Parameter	Description
-a	Specifies that the command is being used to add a printer.
-p PrinterName	Specifies the name of the printer.
-s ComputerName	Specifies a remote computer. If you omit this parameter, the command is executed on the local computer. You cannot use the Internet Protocol (IP) address of the computer.
-m DriverName	Specifies the name of the printer driver.
-r PortName	Specifies the name of the port that the new printer will use. You can use parallel ports such as LPT1, LPT2, and so on; serial ports such as COM1, COM2, and so on; or Universal Serial Bus (USB) ports such as USB001, USB002, and so on. You can also specify the name of a Transmission Control Protocol/Internet Protocol (TCP/IP) network port. You must create the port before adding the printer. Refer to the section titled "Managing TCP/IP Printer Ports," later in this chapter, for more information on network printers.
-u UserName	Specifies the user whose account permissions are used to execute the command.
-w Password	Specifies the password for the user account used with the *-u UserName* parameter.

The following examples illustrate how you can add new printers using the *Prnmngr* command.

```
Prnmngr -a -p "HP OfficeJet" -m "HP Office Jet V40" -r COM1:
```

The preceding command installs a printer named *"HP OfficeJet"* using the driver named *"HP Office Jet V40"* on the COM1 local parallel port. Note that a colon (*:*) must follow the port name.

> **NOTE**
>
> As shown in this example, if a command argument contains any spaces, you must enclose the argument in quotation marks. For example, the argument for the *-p PrinterName* parameter in this example appears as *-p "HP OfficeJet"* since this argument contains a space. We can also use this argument without quotation marks—as *-p HP_OfficeJet*—since the argument does not contain a space.

If you were to use the same command to install a local printer on a remote computer, you would write it as follows:

```
Prnmngr -a -p HP_OfficeJet -s PrnServ2 -m "HP Office Jet V40" -r USB001: -u GaryB
-w ********
```

This command adds the printer named *HP_OfficeJet* on the USB001 port of a remote computer named *PrnServ2* using a printer driver named *"HP Office Jet V40."* When the command is executed successfully, the following message is displayed:

```
Added Printer HP OfficeJet.
```

If the user executing the command does not have sufficient permissions to delete the printer, the command interpreter will return an error message saying that it is unable to execute the command due to user credentials. You must make sure you are using the correct user credentials when adding a printer.

Deleting an Installed Printer

You can delete an installed printer by using the *Prnmngr* command with the *-d* parameter. The syntax of this command when used for deleting printers on the local computer or a remote computer is:

Prnmngr -d -p PrinterName [**-s** ComputerName] [**-u** UserName **-w** Password]

-d is a required parameter that specifies that the command is being used to delete a printer. You specify the target printer using the *-p PrinterName* parameter. The following is an example of this command:

```
Prnmngr -d -p Xerox_Color
```

This command will delete the printer named *Xerox* from the local computer. When the command is executed successfully, the following message is displayed:

```
Deleted printer (connection) Xerox
```

If the name of the printer specified with *-p PrinterName* is not a valid name or if the printer does not exist on the specified computer, an error message is displayed:

```
Unable to delete printer (connection) Xerox Error 0x80041002 Not found
Operation GetObject
Provider CIMWin32
Description
Win32 error code
```

If the user executing the command does not have sufficient permissions to delete the printer, the command interpreter will return an error message saying that it is unable to execute the command due to user credentials. You must make sure you are using the correct printer name and user credentials.

> **NOTE**
>
> When you delete a printer, its share is also deleted from the computer. You must exercise caution when deleting printers that are shared on a network. Before you delete a printer, make sure that no one on the network is using it and that no documents are waiting to print in the print spooler.

Displaying All Printers Configured on a Computer

In some situations you may need to get information on all printers installed on a particular computer, whether it is the local computer or a remote print server. It is usually helpful to view a list of installed printers on a computer before setting the default printer or when adding new printers. You can use the *Prnmngr* command with the -*x* parameter to view all of the printers installed on a computer. The basic syntax of this command is:

```
Prnmngr -x [-s ComputerName] [-u UserName] [-w Password]
```

-*x* is a required parameter that tells the command to list installed printers. You can specify a remote computer by using the -*s ComputerName* parameter. The following example illustrates use of this command:

```
Prnmngr -x -s PrnServ2 -u GaryB -w ********
```

This command displays a list of all printers installed on the remote computer named *PrnServ2* using the account permissions of a user named *GaryB*.

Displaying the Default Printer

To display the default printer on the local computer, you can use the following command:

```
Prnmngr -g
```

The output of this command is displayed as follows:

```
The default printer is HP OfficeJet V40
```

Setting the Default Printer

You can change the default printer by using the *Prnmngr* command with the *-t* parameter. The syntax of this command is:

Prnmngr -t -p PrinterName

-t is a required parameter that tells the command to set the default parameter. The *-p PrinterName* parameter specifies the name of the new default printer. You must make sure that you are specifying the correct printer name as it appears in the list of installed printers. Here is an example of this command:

```
Prnmngr -t -p "Xerox Color"
```

This command sets the new default printer to *"Xerox Color."* If the specified printer name is incorrect, an error message will be displayed. You might have noticed that this command does not allow you to use the *-u*, *-p*, and *-w* parameters to specify a remote computer, username, and password, respectively.

> **NOTE**
>
> The default printer for a user is defined in the user profile. This means that on the same local or remote computer, you may find a different default printer when logged on using the administrator account and when logged on using a normal user account. This is particularly significant when working on print servers that have several printers installed on them. But for a normal desktop with only one installed printer the default printer would be the same for all users.

Configuring and Renaming Printers

You can configure printers installed on the local computer or a remote computer by using the *Prncnfg* command. Three different parameters work with this command for viewing, configuring, and renaming installed printers. You can display configuration information about a printer using the *Prncnfg -g* command, configure the properties of a printer using the *Prncnfg -t* command, and rename a printer using the *Prncnfg -x* command. The *Prncnfg -t* command also allows you to share a printer and publish it in Active Directory. A shared printer that is published in Active Directory is available to network users, and users can search for the printer using its name or any of its attributes.

We will discuss the *Prncnfg* command for each of these functions in the following sections.

Displaying the Printer Configuration

You can use the *Prncnfg* command with the *-g* parameter to display configuration information about a specified printer. This information is useful if you want to view an installed printer's properties. The syntax of this command when used for this purpose is:

Prncnfg -g [**-s** ComputerName] **-p** PrinterName [**-u** UserName **-w** Password]

-g is a required parameter that tells the *Prncnfg* command to get configuration information for the printer specified by the *-p PrinterName* parameter. You must make sure that you have correctly specified the name of the printer. Otherwise, the command interpreter will return an error message. Let's look at an example of this command:

Prncnfg –g –p "HP OfficeJet V40"

Here is the output of the preceding command:

```
Server name PrnServ1
Printer name HP OfficeJet V40
Share name HPOJV40
Driver name HP OfficeJet V40
Port name LPT1:
Comment Multifunction Printer for HRDept.
Location NY Bldg Second Flr
Separator file C:\WINDOWS\system32\sysprint.sep
Print processor WinPrint
Data type RAW
Parameters
Priority 1
Default priority 0
Start time 09h00
Until time 18h00
Attributes local default do_complete_first
```

The output of this command includes configuration information concerning the name of the print server, the name of the printer, the printer's share name, the name of the printer driver, the port to which it is attached, and advanced settings such as its availability and separator page. You can execute the same command on a remote computer or a print server to view detailed configuration information about any installed printer.

> **N**OTE
>
> When working with commands used to manage printers, you will need to specify the remote computers by name. These commands do not allow you to use the IP address of a remote computer in place of the computer name. This is different from most other commands in Windows XP and Windows Server 2003, where you can specify the remote computer by either its name or its IP address.

Configuring Printer Properties

You can use the *Prncnfg* command with the *-t* parameter to configure the properties of a printer attached to the local computer or a remote computer. You can use this command with a number of optional parameters to configure a variety of printer properties. We divided our discussion of these commands into four different sections. We will start with configuring the basic properties of a printer and then discuss other properties such as sharing the printer, publishing it in Active Directory, and configuring its spooler properties.

Configuring Basic Printer Properties

You can configure the basic properties of a printer attached to the local computer or to a remote computer by using the *Prncnfg -t* command. These properties include the printer location, the file containing the text for the separator page, its hours of availability, its priority, and data types it can accept. The command syntax is:

```
Prncnfg -t [-s ComputerName] -p PrinterName [-u UserName -w Password] [-r
PortName] [-l Location] [-m Comment] [-f SeparatorText] [-st StartTime] [-ut
EndTime] [-o Priority] [-i DefaultPriority] [-y DataType] [{+ | -}rawonly]
```

You use the *-s ComputerName*, *-u UserName*, and *-w Password* parameters to specify a printer attached to a remote computer, user account, and password, respectively. Here is a list of additional parameters of this command:

- **-t** A required parameter that tells the *Prncnfg* command to configure the specified printer.

- **-p PrinterName** Specifies a printer attached to the local computer or to a remote computer.

- **-r PortName** Specifies the port to which the printer is attached. You must use a correct port name, such as LPT1, COM1, and so on. If the printer is attached to a TCP/IP port, the port name must be exactly the same as that used when creating the TCP/IP port.

- **-l Location** Specifies the location of the printer, such as "Third Floor Color Printer."

- **-m Comment** Specifies the comments string as it appears to users. The string must be enclosed in quotation marks.

- **-f SeparatorText** Specifies a file that contains the text that appears on the separator page. Separator pages are used between different print jobs to separate one print job from another where a large number of documents are printed on a heavily used printer.

- **-st StartTime** Specifies the start time when the printer becomes available. You use this parameter with the *-ut EndTime* parameter to limit the printer's availability. You must specify the time using the 24-hour time format. For example, to specify 9:00 A.M., you should type **0900**. If print jobs are sent to the printer before or after the availability time, they are held in the print spooler until the printer becomes available.

- **-ut EndTime** Specifies the end time after which the printer becomes unavailable. You use this parameter with the *-st StartTime* parameter to limit the printer's availability. You must specify the time using the 24-hour time format. For example, to specify 5:00 P.M., you should type **1700**.

- **-o Priority** Specifies the priority that the print spooler uses to route spooled print jobs. Print queues with higher priority are routed to the printer before print queues with lower priority.

- **-i DefaultPriority** Defines the default priority that is to be assigned to each print job.

- **-y DataType** Specifies the data types that the printer can accept.

- **{ + | -}rawonly** Specifies that only raw-data print jobs can be sent to this printer.

The following examples illustrate use of the printer configuration command.

```
Prncnfg -t -p "HP OfficeJet V40" -l "Second Floor"-st 0900 -ut 1800
```

The preceding command configures the location as *"Second Floor"* for a printer named *"HP OfficeJet V40"*. The printer is made available from 9:00 A.M. to 6:00 P.M.

```
Prncnfg -t -p "HP OfficeJet V40" -m "Multifunction Color Printer" -f PrintSep.Sep
```

This command configures a printer named *"HP OfficeJet V40"* to use a text file named *PrintSep.sep*. Note that the separator files are text files but they have the .sep extension. The *-m* parameter sets the comments for the printer as *"Multifunction Color Printer."*

```
Prncnfg -t -p "Xerox Color" -s PrnServ2 -u GaryB -w ******** -o 1
```

This command sets the priority as *1* for a printer named *"Xerox Color"* that is attached to a remote computer named *PrnServ2* using the account permissions of a user named *GaryB.*

Master Craftsman...

Separator Pages

Windows provides three separator pages that you can use with printing devices. One function of a separator page is to provide a separation between different print jobs on a printer with heavy printing loads, to enable users to locate the pages they have printed. A separator page looks like a banner page that contains such information as the name of the user who sent the print job, and the date and time of printing.

Another function of a separator page is to switch the printing modes. Separator pages used for this task are located in the %SystemRoot%\System32 folder of Windows XP and Windows Server 2003 computers. Here is a brief description of each of these separator pages:

- **PCL.sep** Switches the printer to Printer Control Language (PCL) mode and prints a banner page. Hewlett-Packard developed PCL, but it has become an industry standard. PCL mode requires that the printers be compatible with PCL printing and that they support the Printer Job Language (PJL).

- **PSCRIPT.sep** Does not print a banner page, but switches the printer to PostScript mode. The printer must support PostScript to use this separator file.

- **SYSPRINT.sep** Switches the printer to PostScript mode and prints a banner page before each document.

Depending on the printer you are using, you can use any of these files as separator pages. You can also customize these files to fit your requirements.

Sharing a Printer

You use the *Prncnfg* command with the *-t* parameter and other optional parameters to share a printer and set its share name. Shared printers become available to network users who have appropriate permissions to use the printer. When working in a domain environment, you can also publish the printer in Active Directory while sharing it, as discussed later in this section. The syntax of this command is:

```
Prncnfg -t [-s ComputerName] -p PrinterName [{+ | -}shared] [-h ShareName] [-u
UserName -w Password]
```

Here is a list of the parameters of the *Prncnfg -t* command for sharing a printer:

■ **+shared** Specifies that the printer is shared on the network. The plus sign (+) indicates that the printer is shared.

■ **-shared** Is used to stop sharing a printer on the network. The minus sign (-) indicates that the printer is not shared.

■ **-h ShareName** Specifies the share name of the printer. Network users will specify this name when browsing for shared printers.

The following examples illustrate use of this command.

```
Prncnfg -t -p "Xerox Color" +shared -h Xerox_Color
```

The preceding command shares the printer named *"Xerox Color"* on the network and sets its share name as *Xerox_Color*. Note that we did not use quotation marks for the *-h ShareName* parameter, as the argument did not contain any spaces. Now, let's look at another example:

```
Prncnfg -t -p "Xerox Color" -s PrnServ2 -shared
```

This command stops sharing the printer named *"Xerox Color"* on a remote computer named *PrnServ2*. Notice that you need not specify the share name of the printer when you want to stop sharing it.

Configuring Advanced Printer Properties

Print jobs are usually spooled on network print servers before they are sent to the printer. Print spoolers help you better manage print jobs. These are advanced printer configurations that you can perform using the *Prncnfg -t* command with appropriate optional parameters, as shown in the following command syntax:

```
Prncnfg -t [-s ComputerName] -p PrinterName [-u UserName -w Password] [{+ | -
}direct] [{+ | -}queued] [{+ | -}keepprintedjobs] [{+ | -}workoffline] [{+ | -
}enabledevq] [{+ | -}docompletefirst] [{+ | -}enablebidi]
```

You may notice that all of these optional parameters use a + sign to configure or enable a particular printer property and a - sign to remove or disable that property. The following list explains the advanced spooler configuration parameters:

■ **+direct** Specifies whether the print jobs are sent directly to the printer without being spooled first.

■ **-direct** Specifies whether the print jobs are not sent directly to the printer but are sent to the spooler from which they will be sent to the printer.

- **+queued** Specifies that the printer will not start printing the job until the last page of the document is spooled. This parameter ensures that once the printer starts printing, the entire document is available to the printer. With this parameter, administrators can cancel a print job while it is in the spooler and has not started printing. Control is not returned to the application that sent the print job until the entire print job is printed.

- **–queued** Specifies that the print job will start printing as soon as the spooler receives it. This parameter helps speed up the printing process if the printer is available when the job is sent for printing. Control is returned to the application as soon as the job starts printing.

- **+keepprintedjobs** Specifies that the print spooler should retain the jobs after they have been sent to the printer. This helps when resending the jobs to the printer from the spooler itself, instead of from the application that originally sent the print job.

- **+keepprintedjobs** Specifies that the print jobs are deleted from the print spooler as soon as printing finishes. If you need to reprint the jobs, you must send the print jobs from the original application.

- **+workoffline** Enables you to use the printer even if the computer is not connected to the printer or the printer is not available. The print jobs are stored in the printer until the printer becomes available.

- **–workoffline** Specifies that the printer is not to be used offline.

- **+docompletefirst** Specifies that the print jobs that have completed spooling will start printing before any jobs that are still in the process of spooling. The spooled jobs will start printing regardless of the priority of the jobs. This parameter is helpful when the print jobs with higher priority take longer to spool than smaller jobs with lower priority.

- **–docompletefirst** Specifies that the print spooler will wait for a job with higher priority to complete spooling and will not print jobs with lower priority even if these jobs are very small.

- **+enabledevq** When used, the computer checks the printer setup before sending the jobs to the printer. The print jobs that do not match the printer setup are not sent to the printer but are held in the print queue. This feature is helpful when users are sending print jobs to a printer that does not support some features. For example, if a user sends a PostScript print job to a non-PostScript printer, the job will be held in the print spooler instead of being sent to the printer.

- **–enabledevq** When used, the computer does not check the printer setup before sending the print jobs to the printer. Mismatched jobs are sent directly to the printer even if they do not match the printer setup.

- **+enableidi** Used to enable the printer to send its status information to the print spooler. This parameter is used by default.

- **-enableidi** When used, the printer does not send its status information back to the print spooler.

The following examples illustrate use of some of the commands used to configure a printer's spooler configuration properties.

```
Prncnfg -t -p "Xerox Color" +keepprintedjobs
```

You use the preceding command to configure a printer named *"Xerox Color"* to keep printed jobs in the print spooler after they have been printed. With this configuration, any jobs that have completed printing are held in the spooler and you may resend a particular job to the printer from the spooler instead of using the application that originally sent the print job. You can disable this feature by using the *-keepprintedjobs* parameter.

```
Prncnfg -t -p "HP OfficeJet V40" +docompletefirst
```

This command configures a printer named *"HP OfficeJet V40"* to wait until the entire print job is sent to the print spooler. The print job will be sent to the printer only when the entire job is spooled. You can disable this feature by using the *-docompletefirst* parameter.

Swiss Army Knife...

Checking the Spooler Service

Printers use the spooler service to spool and send print jobs to installed printers on a computer. It is essential for an administrator to check that the spooler service is functioning properly in order for the computer to spool print jobs and send them to the printer. In addition, the print spooler on a print server needs sufficient hard-disk space to hold spooled print jobs. If there is insufficient hard-disk space, the print server will become slow, causing delays in printing. If you feel that the spooler service is not behaving as it should, you can stop and restart this service by using the following commands:

```
SC Stop Spooler
SC Start Spooler
```

For more information on how to check the spooler service, start and stop this service, and configure its recovery options, refer to the *SC* commands discussed in the section titled "Managing System Services" in Chapter 7.

Publishing a Printer in Active Directory

The *Prncnfg -t* command allows you to publish a printer in Active Directory. When a printer is published in Active Directory, users on the network can search for the printer using its share name, its location, or one of its attributes, such as whether it can print in color. The syntax of this command is:

```
Prncnfg -t [-s ComputerName] -p PrinterName [{+ | -}published] [-u UserName -w
Password]
```

To publish a printer in Active Directory, you use the *+published* parameter. If you want to remove a printer from Active Directory, you use the *-published* parameter, specifying the correct printer name. You must specify a correct printer name; otherwise, the command will return an error message. For example, to publish a printer named *"HP OfficeJet V40"* in Active Directory, you can use the following command:

```
Prncnfg -t -p "HP OfficeJet V40" +published
```

To remove a printer named *"Xerox Color"* configured on a remote computer named *PrnServ2* from Active Directory, you can use the following command:

```
Prncnfg -t -p "Xerox Color" -s PrnServ2 -u GaryB -w ******** -published
```

When the printer is successfully published in Active Directory, a success message is displayed. However, this command does not report an error if the printer is already published in Active Directory or is removed from Active Directory.

As with other commands, the *-s ComputerName* parameter specifies a remote computer. If you omit this parameter, the command is executed on the local computer with the account permissions of the currently logged-on user. The *-u UserName* and *-w Password* parameters specify the username and password whose account permissions are to be used for executing the command.

Master Craftsman...

Searching for Printers Published in Active Directory

In Windows XP and Windows Server 2003, printers can be published in Active Directory when they are shared on the network, provided that the computer where the printer is installed is a member of the Active Directory domain. However, printers are not shared by default when they are installed. You must share the printer manually from the Printers and Faxes Wizard or from the command line.

Continued

Active Directory makes it easy to search for shared printers on the network for users who are looking for specific printers. Find Printers is a powerful search utility that can locate printers published in Active Directory based on different types of search criteria. This utility is a part of the Search Companion, a feature of Active Directory. In order to use this utility, you must be logged on to the domain. This utility includes the following three tabs:

- **Printers** Allows you to specify the name, location, and model of the printer you are looking for.

- **Features** Allows you to specify any of the features of the printer, such as its resolution, and whether it can print in color and can handle single-sided printing.

- **Advanced** Allows you to specify advanced features of the printer, such as whether the printer supports collation of pages.

When you run the search, a list of printers is displayed. You can sort the list or filter the list to view only the printers you are interested in. You can also save the search results for future use. Connecting to a particular printer from the search results is as easy as right-clicking the printer and selecting **Connect**.

Search Companion and the Find Printers utility are available only when you are logged on to an Active Directory domain. They are not available when the computer you are working on is in a workgroup environment.

Renaming a Printer

You can use the *prncnfg -x* command to change the name of an installed printer. You can use this command on the local computer or a remote computer. The syntax of this command is:

```
Prncnfg -x [-s ComputerName] -p PrinterName -z NewPrinterName [-u UserName -w
Password]
```

Here are the parameters of this command:

- **-x** A required parameter that tells the *Prncnfg* command to change the name of the printer.

- **-p PrinterName** Specifies the name of an existing printer.

- **-z NewPrinterName** Specifies the new name for the printer specified with the *-p PrinterName* parameter.

As with other commands, the *-s ComputerName* parameter specifies a remote computer. If you omit this parameter, the command is executed on the local computer with the account permissions of the currently logged-on user. The *-u UserName* and *-w Password* parameters specify the username and password whose account permissions are to be used for executing the command.

The following example illustrates use of the *Prncnfg* command for renaming a printer:

```
Prncnfg -x "Xerox Color" -z "Xerox Phaser"
```

This command changes the name of the printer from *"Xerox Color"* to *"Xerox Phaser"* on the local computer.

NOTE

Changing the name of a printer using *Prncnfg -x* does not change its share name. You must change the share name of the printer separately using the *Prncnfg -t* command or from the Sharing tab of Printer Properties.

Managing Printer Drivers

You manage printer drivers using the *Prndrvr* command. You can display information about all the printer drivers installed on the local computer or a remote computer, install printer drivers, delete a particular printer driver, and delete all printer drivers that are not in use by any of the printers. When you use the *Prndrvr* command without using any of its parameters, the command interpreter displays help for the command, as you would use the *Prndrvr /?* command to obtain help for the command. The following sections discuss different parameters of this command used for functions related to viewing, installing, and deleting printer drivers.

Displaying Driver Information for All Printers on a Computer

You can obtain detailed information about the drivers of all the printers installed on the local computer or a remote computer by using the *Prndrvr -l* command. By default, the command runs on the local computer with the account permissions of the currently logged-on user. You can use the *-s ComputerName* parameter to specify a remote computer. Optionally, you can use the *-u UserName* and *-w Password* parameters to specify user credentials that are different from those of the currently logged-on user. The syntax of this command is:

```
Prndrvr -l [-s ComputerName] [-u UserName -w Password]
```

The following listing shows sample output of this command:

```
Server name PrnServ1
Driver name HP OfficeJet V40,3,Windows NT x86
Version 3
Environment Windows NT x86
```

```
Monitor name
Driver path C:\WINDOWS\System32\spool\DRIVERS\W32X86\3\UNIDRV.DLL
Data file C:\WINDOWS\System32\spool\DRIVERS\W32X86\3\HPOJV40.GPD
Config file C:\WINDOWS\System32\spool\DRIVERS\W32X86\3\UNIDRVUI.DLL
Help file C:\WINDOWS\System32\spool\DRIVERS\W32X86\3\UNIDRV.HLP
Dependent files
 C:\WINDOWS\System32\spool\DRIVERS\W32X86\3\HPFUD50.DLL
 C:\WINDOWS\System32\spool\DRIVERS\W32X86\3\UNIRES.DLL
 C:\WINDOWS\System32\spool\DRIVERS\W32X86\3\HPFDJ50.INI
 C:\WINDOWS\System32\spool\DRIVERS\W32X86\3\HPFUI50.DLL
 C:\WINDOWS\System32\spool\DRIVERS\W32X86\3\HPFIMG50.DLL
 C:\WINDOWS\System32\spool\DRIVERS\W32X86\3\HPF900AL.DLL
 C:\WINDOWS\System32\spool\DRIVERS\W32X86\3\HPFDJ95X.GPD
 C:\WINDOWS\System32\spool\DRIVERS\W32X86\3\HPFDJ97X.GPD
 C:\WINDOWS\System32\spool\DRIVERS\W32X86\3\HPFDJ200.HLP
 C:\WINDOWS\System32\spool\DRIVERS\W32X86\3\HPFNAM50.GPD
 C:\WINDOWS\System32\spool\DRIVERS\W32X86\3\STDNAMES.GPD


Server name PrnServ1
Driver name Xerox Phaser 1235 PS,3,Windows NT x86
Version 3
Environment Windows NT x86
Monitor name
Driver path C:\WINDOWS\System32\spool\DRIVERS\W32X86\3\PSCRIPT5.DLL
Data file C:\WINDOWS\System32\spool\DRIVERS\W32X86\3\XRPH1235.PPD
Config file C:\WINDOWS\System32\spool\DRIVERS\W32X86\3\PS5UI.DLL
Help file C:\WINDOWS\System32\spool\DRIVERS\W32X86\3\PSCRIPT.HLP
Dependent files
 C:\WINDOWS\System32\spool\DRIVERS\W32X86\3\PSCRIPT.NTF
 C:\WINDOWS\System32\spool\DRIVERS\W32X86\3\XXPSINI1.INI
 C:\WINDOWS\System32\spool\DRIVERS\W32X86\3\XXPSRU1.DLL
 C:\WINDOWS\System32\spool\DRIVERS\W32X86\3\XXUI1.DLL
 C:\WINDOWS\System32\spool\DRIVERS\W32X86\3\XXWH1HLP.HLP
```

When examining the sample output, you may notice that detailed information is displayed about each printer driver, including the names of the driver files, data files, configuration files, and other files, such as help files and dependent files.

Installing a Printer Driver

You install printer drivers using the *Prndrvr -a* command. This command allows you to install a printer driver on a remote print server by using the *-s ComputerName* parameter. The syntax of this command is:

```
Prndrvr -a [-m DriverName] [-v {0 | 1 | 2 | 3}] [-e Environment] [-s
ComputerName] [-h Path] [-i FileName.inf] [-u UserName -w Password]
```

Table 9.2 explains this command's parameters.

Table 9.2 Parameters of the Prndrvr Command for Installing Printer Drivers

Parameter	Description
-a	A required parameter that tells the *Prncnfg* command to install a printer driver.
-m DriverName	Specifies the name of the printer driver. The printer driver is usually named after its model number for a particular manufacturer.
*-v {0	1	2	3 }*	Specifies the version of the printer driver you want to install. We discuss version numbers later in this section.
-e Environment	Specifies the environment for the printer driver you want to install. We discuss the printer driver environment later in this section.
-h Path	Specifies the path to the printer driver file. If you omit this parameter, the command assumes that the driver is located in the location from where Windows was installed.
-i FileName.inf	Specifies the name of the INF file for the printer driver.

By default, the command runs on the local computer with the account permissions of the currently logged-on user. You can use the *-s ComputerName* parameter to specify a remote computer. You must specify the remote computer by its name, as the command does not allow you to use the computer's IP address. Optionally, you can use the *-u UserName* and *-w Password* parameters to specify user credentials that are different from those of the currently logged-on user.

You can specify a version number for the printer driver you are installing by using the *-v* parameter. This parameter works in conjunction with the *-e Environment* parameter to set the environment for the printer driver. The following version numbers are available:

- **Version 0** Supports Windows 95, Windows 98, and Windows ME operating systems.

- **Version 1** Supports the Windows NT 3.51 operating system.

- **Version 2** Supports the Windows NT 4.0 operating system.

- **Version 3** Supports the Windows XP and Windows 2000 operating systems.

You can also specify a printer driver environment for the printer driver using the *-e Environment* parameter. Table 9.3 lists the driver environments and their available version numbers.

Table 9.3 Printer Driver Environments and Their Available Version Numbers

Environment	Available Version Numbers
Windows NT X86	1, 2, and 3
Windows NT Alpha_AXP	1 and 2
Windows IA64	3
Windows NT R4000	1
Windows NT PowerPC	1
Windows NT4.0	0

If you do not specify a version or the environment, the command assumes that the printer driver is installed for the environment where the command is being executed.

The following example illustrates use of the *Prndrvr* command to install a printer driver:

```
Prndrvr -a -m " Xerox Phaser 1235PS " -v 2 -e "Windows NT x86"
```

This command installs a printer driver named *"Xerox Phaser 1235PS"* on the local computer. The version number and environment for the driver are configured as *2* and *"Windows NT x86"* using the *-v* and *-e* parameters, respectively.

Deleting a Printer Driver

You can use the *Prndrvr -d* command to delete a printer driver installed on the local computer or a remote computer. The syntax of this command is:

```
Prndrvr -d [-s ComputerName] -m DriverName -v {0 | 1 | 2 | 3} -e Environment [-u
UserName -w Password]
```

The parameters of this command are similar to the parameters of the *Prndrvr -a* command. The only difference is that you need not specify the path or the INF file for the driver file. The following example illustrates use of this command:

```
Prndrvr -d -m "Xerox Phaser 1235PS" -v 2 -e "Windows NT x86"
```

This command deletes version *2* of a printer driver named *"Xerox Phaser 1235PS"* from the local computer.

Deleting All Printer Drivers from a Computer

You can delete all printer drivers from a computer by using the *Prndrvr -x* command. This is particularly helpful when unused drivers remain on a print server after physical printers have been removed. The syntax of this command is:

```
Prndrvr -x [-s ComputerName] [-u UserName -w Password]
```

For example, to remove all printer drivers from a computer named *PrnServ2* using the account permissions of a user named *GaryB* you can use the following command:

```
Prndrvr -x -s PrnServ2 -u GaryB -w ********
```

Creating and Configuring TCP/IP Printer Ports

Network printers are usually attached directly to one of the ports on the network. These printers are assigned an IP address. In smaller organizations, you can assign the IP address to a printer manually. In large organizations, however, Dynamic Host Configuration Protocol (DHCP) servers handle IP address assignment. Network devices such as printers usually obtain the same IP address from the DHCP server regardless of the duration of their lease. In this section, we will discuss the *Prnport* command that is used to manage TCP/IP ports. We will begin by displaying the information about the TCP/IP ports currently configured on a computer, and then we will discuss how to create and configure TCP/IP ports on local and remote computers.

Viewing TCP/IP Printing Ports Configured on a Computer

You can display detailed information about all TCP/IP printer ports configured on a computer by using the *Prnport -l* command. This information is useful when you need to view or change the configuration of one or more TCP/IP printing ports. The syntax of this command is:

```
Prnport -l [-s ComputerName] [-u UserName -w Password]
```

In the preceding command, *-l* is a required parameter that tells the *Prnport* command to list all TCP/IP ports configured on the local computer or a remote computer. The following example illustrates use of this command:

```
Prnport -l -s PrnServ2
```

This command displays all TCP/IP ports on a remote computer named *PrnServ2*. The output of this command is:

```
Server name PrnServ2
Port name IP_192.168.0.18
Host address 192.168.0.18
Protocol RAW
Port number 9100
SNMP Enabled
Community public
Device index 1

Server name PrnServ2
Port name IP_192.168.0.20
Host address 192.168.0.20
Protocol LPR
Queue HPQueue
Byte Count Enabled
SNMP Enabled
Community public
Device index 1

Number of ports enumerated 2
```

The output displays the name of the computer, the name of the port, the output protocol (RAW or LPR), and whether SNMP is enabled or disabled for a particular port. The community name is usually configured as *public* for managing the printer using a network management application such as Microsoft Systems Management Server (SMS). If the command is executed in the local computer, the *Server Name* column is blank.

Viewing the Configuration of a TCP/IP Printing Port

Once you have created a standard TCP/IP port on a computer, you can view its configuration using the *Prnport -g* command, specifying the name of the port. You can also view the configuration of any other TCP/IP printing port using this command. The command works on the local computer as well as on a remote computer. The syntax of this command is:

Prnport -g -r PortName [**-s** ComputerName] [**-u** UserName **-w** Password]

In the preceding command, *-r PortName* is a required parameter that specifies the TCP/IP port for which you want to view configuration information. The following example illustrates use of this command:

```
Prnport -g -r IP_192.168.0.20 -s PrnServ
```

This command displays configuration information about the TCP/IP port named *IP_192.168.0.20* on a remote computer named *PrnServ.* You must specify a correct port name with the *-r PortName* parameter. If the port name is incorrect or the port does not exist, the command will return an error message saying that the specified port could not be found. The output of this command is:

```
Server name PrnServ2
Port name ip_192.168.0.20
Host address 192.168.0.20
Protocol RAW
Port number 9100
SNMP Enabled
Community Public
Device index 1
```

NOTE

With all *Prndrvr* commands that require specifying a TCP/IP port name, you must make sure that the port name you are specifying is correct. If the specified port name is incorrect, or the port does not exist on the computer, the following error message is displayed:

Unable to get port Error 0x80041002 Not found
Operation
Provider Win32 Provider
Description The printer name is invalid.

Creating and Configuring a Standard TCP/IP Printing Port

Two similar *Prnport* commands are included with Windows XP and Windows Server 2003 operating systems for creating and configuring TCP/IP printer ports. When used with the *-a* parameter, the *Prnport* command creates a TCP/IP printer port. When you use the *Prnport* command with the *-t* parameter, you can configure an existing TCP/IP printer port. You can use the same command to create a TCP/IP RAW port or a TCP/IP LPR port, and you can use the commands on the local computer or on a remote computer. The syntax of these commands is:

```
Prnport -a -r PortName  [-s ComputerName] [-u UserName -w Password] -h IPAddress
[-o {raw -n PortNumber | lpr}] [-q QueueName] [-m{e | d}] [-i IndexName] [-y
CommunityName] [-2{e | d}]
```

```
Prnport -t -r PortName  [-s ComputerName] [-u UserName -w Password] -h IPAddress]
[-o {raw -n PortNumber | lpr}] [-q QueueName] [-m{e | d}] [-i IndexName] [-y
CommunityName] [-2{e | d}]
```

You might have noticed that the syntax for both of these commands is similar, but that you use the *-a* parameter to create the port and the *-t* parameter to configure it. As you can with other commands, you can use the *-s ComputerName, -u UserName*, and *-w Password* parameters to specify a remote computer, username, and password, respectively. The user specified with the *-u UserName* parameter must have sufficient permissions to create or configure printer ports on the computer where the command is to be executed.

Table 9.4 explains additional parameters of this command.

Table 9.4 Parameters of the Prnport Command for Creating a TCP/IP Port

Parameter	Description
-a	A required parameter that tells the *Prnport* command to create the specified TCP/IP port.
-r PortName	A required parameter that specifies the name of the TCP/IP port to which you want to connect the printer.
-h IPAddress	A required parameter that specifies the IP address of the port that you want to assign to the port.
*-o {RAW – n PortNumber	LPR}*	Specifies the TCP/IP port—either TCP/IP RAW or TCP/IP LPR. Most printers use the TCP/IP RAW port with a default port number of 9100. UNIX printers use the TCP/IP LPR port.
-q QueueName	Specifies the queue name for the TCP/IP RAW port.
*-m{e	d}*	Enables (*-me*) or disables (*-md*) SNMP support for the TCP/IP port.
-i IndexName	Specifies an SNMP index number when SNMP support is enabled.
-y CommunityName	Specifies the SNMP community name when SNMP support is enabled.
*-2{e	d}*	Used to enable double spools with TCP/IP LPR ports (also known as respooling). The *-2e* parameter enables this feature and the *-2d* parameter disables it.

The following examples show how you can use the *Prnport* command to create and configure TCP/IP ports.

```
Prnport -a -r IP_192.168.0.20 -h 192.168.0.20 -o RAW -n 9100
```

The preceding command creates a TCP/IP port named *IP_192.168.0.20* using an IP address of *192.168.0.20* on the local computer. The port type is *RAW* and it uses the port number *9100* by default. You can, however, specify a different port number for a RAW TCP/IP port. If you replace the *-n PortNumber* parameter with the *-o* parameter, the new

TCP/IP port will use TCP/IP RAW port number 9100 by default. Note that you can use the *-n PortNumber* parameter only with TCP/IP RAW ports. Let's consider another example:

```
Prnport -a -r IP_192.168.0.18 -s PrnServ2 -h 192.168.0.18 -o LPR -q Queue2
```

This command creates a TCP/IP LPR port named *IP_192.168.0.18* connected to the IP address *192.168.0.18* on a remote computer named *PrnServ2*. The name of the LPR queue is specified as *Queue2*.

The following example illustrates how you can configure TCP/IP ports using the *Prnport -t* command:

```
Prnport -t -r IP_192.168.0.18 -h 192.168.0.20 -me -i 1 -y Public
```

This command enables SNMP support for the TCP/IP port named *IP_192.168.0.20*. The index number for the SNMP community named *Public* is specified as *1*. Specifying the community name as *Public* allows any network management application to use and manage the printer connected to this TCP/IP port.

Deleting a Standard TCP/IP Printing Port

You can use the *Prnport -d* command to delete a particular TCP/IP port from the local computer or a remote computer. Unused TCP/IP ports are usually removed from print servers. The syntax of this command is:

```
Prnport -d -r PortName [-s ComputerName] [-u UserName -w Password]
```

-d is a required parameter for the *Prndrvr* command; it tells the command to delete the specified TCP/IP port. You can specify a remote computer by using the *-s ComputerName* parameter. You can use the *-u UserName* and *-w Password* parameters to specify a user account whose permissions are to be used to delete the specified TCP/IP port. The following example illustrates use of this command:

```
Prnport -d -r IP_192.168.0.20 -s PrnServ -u Garyb -w ********
```

This command deletes a TCP/IP port named *IP_192.168.0.20* from a remote computer named *PrnServ* using the account permissions of a user named *Garyb*.

Managing Print Queues and Print Jobs

Managing print queues and print jobs are common print management tasks. Windows XP and Windows Server 2003 include two command-line utilities that you can use to manage print jobs on printers attached to the local computer or a remote computer. You use the *Prnqctl* utility to manage print queues and the *Prnjobs* utility to manage individual print jobs. In this section, we will discuss how you can use these utilities to perform a number of tasks.

Printing a Test Page

One way to test the installation and configuration of a printer is to send a test page to the printer. You can use the *Prnqctl* command with the *-e* parameter to print a test page on a printer. The syntax of the command is:

```
Prnqctl -e [-s ComputerName] -p PrinterName [-u UserName -w Password]
```

-e is a required parameter that tells the *Prnqctl* command to print a test page on the printer specified by the *-p PrinterName* parameter. Here is an example of how to use this command:

```
Prnqctl -e -s PrnServ2 -p "Xerox Color"
```

This command prints a test page to a printer named *"Xerox Color"* connected to a remote computer named *PrnServ2*. The test page usually tests most of the functions supported by a particular model of a printer. You can tell by the test page whether the printer is not configured properly. For example, an incorrect driver will result in garbled output and you will not be able to read the text printed on the page.

Pausing and Resuming a Printer

At times, you may need to resolve a printer problem by pausing all the print jobs running on the printer. Pausing a printer does not delete or cancel any printing jobs; rather, the jobs are held in the print spooler until the printer becomes available again. You can pause and resume printing of printers attached to local or remote computers by using the *Prnqctl* command. You use the *-z* and *-m* parameters with the *-p PrinterName* parameter to pause and resume the printer, respectively. Here is the syntax of these commands:

```
Prnqctl -z [-s RemoteComputer] -p PrinterName [-u UserName -w Password]
Prnqctl -m [-s RemoteComputer] -p PrinterName [-u UserName -w Password]
```

These commands are identical, apart from the fact that the *-z* parameter pauses the specified printer and the *-m* parameter resumes printing. The following examples illustrate use of these commands.

```
Prnqctl -z -s PrnServ2 -p "Xerox Color"
```

The preceding command pauses the printer named *"Xerox Color"* on a remote computer named *PrnServ2*. When the command is executed, the print job currently running on the printer is completed before the printer is paused. Only the print jobs that have not yet been sent to the printer are held up. You can resume printing on this printer by using the following command:

```
Prnqctl -m -s PrnServ2 -p "Xerox Color"
```

Remember that you cannot use the *-z* and *-m* parameters together on a single command line. You must use them in individual commands.

Canceling All Print Jobs in the Print Spooler

If you need to take a printer offline for a while, you can cancel all print jobs that are currently waiting to print in the print spooler for a specified printer, by using the *Prnqctl -x* command. The syntax of this command is:

```
Prnqctl -x [-s ComputerName] -p PrinterName [-u UserName -w Password]
```

-x is a required parameter that tells the *Prnqctl* command to cancel print jobs for the print spooler for the printer specified with the *-p PrinterName* parameter. Here is an example of how to use this command:

```
Prnqctl -x -s PrnServ2 -p "HP OfficeJet V40"
```

This command cancels all print jobs in the print spooler for the printer named *"HP OfficeJet V40"* on a remote computer named *PrnServ2*.

WARNING

Remember that you cannot recall jobs you have canceled. You must resend the print jobs to the printer if you want to print the canceled jobs. If you are troubleshooting a printer problem, try to resolve the problem by first pausing the print jobs. Canceling jobs in the print spooler should be your last resort when troubleshooting a problem. You can also try to redirect print jobs to another similar printer instead of canceling them. On heavily used printers in a corporate environment, you must exercise caution when canceling print jobs.

Listing All the Print Jobs in a Print Queue

Print jobs are held in the spooler while they wait for their turn to print on a particular printer. The jobs are held in the print spooler in a queue, and the jobs are printed according to their priority and on a first-in, first-out basis. You can view the print jobs in the print spooler by using the *Prnjobs -l* command. The syntax of this command is:

```
Prnjobs -l [-s ComputerName ] [-p PrinterName] [-u UserName -w Password]
```

-l is a required parameter that tells the *Prnjobs* command to list all print jobs in the print spooler for the printer specified with the *-p PrinterName* parameter. If you do not use the *-p PrinterName* parameter, the command lists all jobs in all printer queues on the specified computer. The following example illustrates use of this command:

```
Prnjobs -l -s PrnServ2
```

This command lists all print jobs in all print queues on a remote computer named *PrnServ2*. You can narrow down the listing by specifying a particular printer, as shown in the following example:

```
Prnjobs -l -s PrnServ2 -p "HP OfficeJet V40"
```

The output of this command will show only the jobs in the spooler for the printer named *"HP OfficeJet V40"* on the remote computer named *PrnServ2*. The output of this command is:

```
Job ID 2
Printer HP OfficeJet V40
Document Microsoft Word - Ch09-Managing Printing Services.doc
Data type NT EMF 1.008
Driver name HP OfficeJet V40
Description HP OfficeJet V40, 2
Elaspsed time 00:00:10
Machine name PrnServ2
Job status
Notify User
Owner User
Pages printed 4
Parameters
Size 911296
Start time 09h00
Until time 18h00
Status Online
Status mask 0
Time submitted 07/19/2006 04:24:14
Total pages 22

Number of print jobs enumerated 1
```

As you can see, the listing contains detailed information about each job in the spooler waiting to print. You may need to write down the job ID number if you want to pause, resume, or cancel a particular print job from the command line. The output also contains some information about the printer configuration, such as the name of the printer and the hours it is available.

Pausing, Resuming, and Canceling a Print Job

You use the *Prnjobs* command to pause, resume, and cancel a print job. You can use the command on the local computer or on a remote computer. When working on the local computer, you must have sufficient permissions to manage print jobs. If the user account with which you are logged on does not have permissions to manage print jobs, you must log off and log on again using another user account that has permissions to manage print jobs. Here are some examples of how to use this command:

Prnjobs -z [**-s** RemoteComputer] **-p** PrinterName **-j** JobNumber [**-u** UserName **-w** Password]

Prnjobs -m [**-s** RemoteComputer] **-p** PrinterName **-j** JobNumber [**-u** UserName **-w** Password]

Prnjobs -x [**-s** RemoteComputer] **-p** PrinterName **-j** JobNumber [**-u** UserName **-w** Password]

Here is an explanation of the parameters of these commands:

- **-z** Required when you want to pause a print job identified by its job number.

- **-m** Required when you want to resume a print job identified by its job number. Note that you can only resume a print job that has been paused. If a print job has not been paused, you cannot resume it.

- **-x** Required when you want to cancel a print job identified by its job number.

- **-p PrinterName** A required parameter that specifies the name of the printer where you want to manage the print jobs. This parameter is required with all three commands.

- **-j JobNumber** A required parameter that identifies the print job that you want to pause, resume, or cancel. This parameter is required with all three commands. You must specify a correct job number to avoid pausing or canceling an incorrect job. The job number appears as *Job ID* when you list the print jobs in the print queue using the *Prnjobs -l* command.

Remember that you can use only one of the parameters from *-z*, *-m*, and *-x* in a single command line. You must use these parameters individually. You cannot combine any two parameters. The following examples illustrate use of these commands:

```
Prnjobs -z -p "Xerox Color" -j 27
Prnjobs -z -s PrnServ2 -p "HP OfficeJet V40" -j 8
```

The first command pauses a print job with job ID number *27* on a printer named *"Xerox Color"* attached to the local computer. The second command pauses a print job with job ID number *8* on the printer named *"HP OfficeJet V40"* on a remote computer named *PrnServ2*. You can use the following commands to resume printing of these two jobs, respectively:

```
Prnjobs -m -p "Xerox Color" -j 27
Prnjobs -m -s PrnServ2 -p "HP OfficeJet V40" -j 8
```

To cancel these jobs, you can use these commands:

```
Prnjobs -x -p "Xerox Color" -j 27
Prnjobs -x -s PrnServ2 -p "HP OfficeJet V40" -j 8
```

When working on a remote computer, you use the *-u UserName* and *-w Password* parameters to use an account that has permissions to manage print jobs on that computer.

Summary

In this chapter, we discussed some of the command-line utilities used to manage printers and print jobs. It is interesting to note that the syntax for most of these commands is easy to understand and use. The commands included with Windows XP and Windows Server 2003 for managing printers are provided as scripts (with a .vbs extension) and use the CScript scripting host rather than the WScript scripting host that is the default scripting host for Windows operating systems. We also learned that to view and install printers we use the *Prnmngr* command, and to view and configure installed printers we use the *Prncnfg* command. Other commands we discussed in this chapter include *Prndrvr*, *Prnport*, *Prnqctl*, and *Prnjobs*, which enable you to manage printer drivers, create and configure TCP/IP ports, manage print queues, and manage print jobs, respectively. Finally, when working with printers attached to remote computers, you must use an account that has permissions to connect to them using Windows Management Instrumentation (WMI) services.

Part IV
Working with
Active Directory

Chapter 10

Overview of Directory Services Commands

Topics in this chapter:

- **Getting Started with DS Commands**

- **Types of Objects for DS Commands**

- **Querying the Directory Database with DSQuery**

- **Adding New Objects with DSAdd**

- **Displaying Object Properties with DSGet**

- **Modifying Objects with DSMod**

- **Moving and Renaming Objects with DSMove**

- **Deleting Directory Objects with DSRm**

Introduction

Windows Server 2003 includes a powerful set of command-line utilities for managing objects in the Active Directory database. These commands are handy for everyday directory database administration. Active Directory stores complete information about all types of objects, or *object classes*, in the network. These object classes include computers, servers, sites, subnets, users, groups, quotas, and directory partitions. Managing this wide variety of objects from the graphical interface can be a time-consuming job for a common administrator. Although managing Active Directory from the command line isn't necessarily easy, once you learn the basics of the command-line utilities available for managing directory objects, you will find that these utilities can really save you time and effort in the long run. In this chapter, we will introduce you to the Directory Services command-line utilities (also known as *DS commands*). In the next chapter, you will learn how to use these commands to manage Active Directory objects such as users, groups, and computers.

Getting Started with DS Commands

This chapter provides an overview of the DS commands for managing objects in the Active Directory database. The DS commands included with the Windows Server 2003 operating system are as follows:

- **DSAdd** Used to add new objects to Active Directory.
- **DSGet** Used to display properties of the objects in Active Directory.
- **DSMod** Used to modify the properties of objects in Active Directory.
- **DSMove** Used to move objects from one container to another in Active Directory.
- **DSQuery** Used to search for objects in Active Directory.
- **DSRm** Used to remove (delete) objects from Active Directory.

NOTE

You can use either a hyphen (-) or a forward slash (/) with the parameters of any of the DS commands. We used the hyphen in this and the following chapter.

Types of Objects for DS Commands

The Directory Services commands discussed in this chapter work with a variety of object classes stored in Active Directory. These object classes are used with each DS command as target objects and are identified by their respective distinguished names (DNs). These objects include computers (desktops and member servers), contacts, groups, organizational units (OUs), servers (domain controllers), sites, subnets, quotas, and partitions. For example, when working with the *User* object class, the *DSQuery* command becomes *DSQuery User*. This is followed by command-line parameters to identify the object by its DN.

Table 10.1 gives an overview of the DS commands and the object types you can use with them.

Table 10.1 DS Commands and Object Types

Object	DSQuery	DSAdd	DSGet	DSMod	DSMove	DSRm
Computer	Yes	Yes	Yes	Yes	Yes	Yes
Contact	Yes	Yes	Yes	Yes	Yes	Yes
Group	Yes	Yes	Yes	Yes	Yes	Yes
Site	Yes	No	Yes	No	Yes	Yes
Server	Yes	No	Yes	Yes	Yes	Yes
Subnet	No	No	Yes	No	Yes	Yes
OU	Yes	Yes	Yes	Yes	Yes	Yes
User	Yes	Yes	Yes	Yes	Yes	Yes
Quota	Yes	Yes	Yes	Yes	Yes	Yes
Partition	Yes	No	Yes	Yes	Yes	Yes

It is clear from Table 10.1 that the *DSMove* and *DSRm* commands work with all types of objects in Active Directory. In addition, you can use the *DSQuery* * command to search for any type of object in the directory database.

> **NOTE**
>
> The *Computer* and *Server* object classes in Directory Services may be a little confusing at first. Remember that the *Computer* object in Directory Services refers to desktop computers and servers that are members of the domain (also called member servers), and the *Server* object refers to domain controllers in the domain. Do not assume that the *Server* object refers to any kind of server hardware installed on the network.

You specify the target objects for DS commands using their DNs. If the command syntax uses the *ObjectDN* parameter, it means you can specify the DN of a single object. On the other hand, if the command syntax uses the *ObjectDN …* parameter (note the three dots after *ObjectDN*), you can specify DNs for multiple objects. When you specify multiple objects, you must leave a space between the DN of each object.

Swiss Army Knife...

Distinguished Names

It is important to understand what the distinguished name (DN) and relative distinguished name (RDN) are when working with DS commands. Each object in Active Directory is identified by its DN, which correctly describes its position within the Active Directory hierarchy. The following is an example of a user's DN:

```
CN=Paul Smith, OU=Books, DC=Syngress, DC=com
```

In the preceding code, *CN* stands for the *common name* of the user object *Paul Smith*. The common name is also known as the RDN of the object. The location of this user object is in the *OU* named *Books*. Thus, *Books* is the container object for the user object *Paul Smith*. The domain components of this user object are identified by the *DC*. Each level of the domain hierarchy is identified by a *DC* component. In this example, the *Syngress* domain is a second-level domain of the *.com* top-level domain.

When using DNs with the DS commands, it is recommended that you enclose the DN within quotation marks. Although quotation marks are required only when the DN contains spaces, it is good to always enclose a DN in quotation marks to avoid mistakes. Thus, the preceding example would be written as follows:

```
"CN=Paul Smith, OU=Books, DC=Syngress, DC=com"
```

Working on Remote Computers

By default, the DS commands are executed on the local computer (server) if you do not specify a remote server on the network. With each DS command discussed in this and the following two chapters, you can use the following parameters to specify a remote computer (or a remote network server):

- **-s Server | -d Domain** Specifies a remote server or a domain. You can use either the name of the server or the name of the domain, but not both. If the domain name is not specified, the domain where you have logged on is assumed by default.

- **-u UserName** Specifies the name of the user whose account permissions are to be used to execute the DS command on the remote server. If you omit this parameter, the account permissions of the currently logged-on user are used by default.

- **-p Password** Specifies the password for the user account. You can use an asterisk (*) as an argument for the *-p Password* parameter (*-p **). When the command is executed you will be prompted to type the password. This option is good to use when you are concerned with Active Directory security.

You can specify the username in any of the following formats:

- **UserName** This is the simplest form of the username. We have been using this format with most of the commands discussed in previous chapters.

- **Domain\User** Using this format, you can specify a domain name along with the username. For example, you would specify a user named *GaryB* in the domain named *Syngress* as *Syngress\GaryB*.

- **User Principal Name (UPN)** The UPN name of a user includes the at sign (@) after the username. Examples of UPN names are *GaryB@Syngress.com* and *JohnS@Books.Syngress.com*.

Querying the Directory Database with DSQuery

The *DSQuery* commands search the Active Directory database according to specified search criteria. You can search for computers, users, groups, contacts, sites, servers, partitions, and quotas using the *DSQuery* commands. Most of these commands share a common syntax. You can use the *DSQuery ** command to search all types of objects in Active Directory.

The syntax of these commands looks very complex, but once you understand the basic syntax and parameters of these and other DS commands, you may find that they are not as difficult to use as they seem to be. The following sections describe each *DSQuery* command. Wherever possible, we will try to provide examples to help you understand the use of these commands. First we'll look at the parameters that are common to all of the *DSQuery* commands.

Parameters Common to All DSQuery Commands

All of the *DSQuery* commands use a large number of parameters. When you look at the syntax of these commands, you will find that a number of parameters are common to all *DSQuery* commands. Here is a list of the common parameters:

- **{StartNode | forestroot | domainroot}** Specifies the starting point or node of the search. You can specify a *forestroot*, a *domainroot*, or the DN of a node. When you use the *forestroot* as the start node, the search is performed using the Global Catalog (GC). By default, the search is started from the *domainroot*.

- **-o {dn | rdn | samid}** Specifies the format that will be used to display the results of the search. You can choose from *dn* (distinguished name), *rdn* (relative distinguished name), and *samid* (security accounts manager account name) to display the names of the entries found in the search. By default, the *dn* format is used.

- **-scope {subtree | onelevel | base}** Specifies the scope of the search. This parameter is useful for defining how far the search will be conducted in the object hierarchy in Active Directory. The *subtree* argument tells the command that the scope is a subtree with its root at the start node. The *onelevel* argument specifies that the search is to be conducted one level down the object hierarchy. The *base* argument specifies that the search is to be conducted only for the single object specified by the start node. When you have used the *forestroot* option as the start node, you can use only the *subtree* option as the scope. By default, the *subtree* option is used as the scope for the search.

- **-name Name** Used to search for objects whose name attribute matches the value specified by the *–name* parameter. The *Name* option is the common name (CN) attribute used with the DN of an object. You can use wildcards with this option. For example, if you want to search for all computers whose name starts with *NYC*, you can specify the value of the *–name* parameter as *NYC**.

- **-desc Description** Used to search for objects whose description attributes match the value specified by the *-desc* parameter. You can use wildcards with this option. For example, if you want to search for all helpdesk users whose description starts with *Help*, you can specify a value of *Help** for the *–desc* parameter.

- **-q** Used to perform a quiet search. The results of the search are not displayed in the command shell window.

- **-r** Used to perform the search using recursion or use referrals. By default, recursion is disabled for performing searches.

- **-gc** Specifies that the search is to be performed using the GC. The GC is searched only if the start node is specified as *forestroot*.

- **-limit NumberOfObjects** Specifies the number of objects to be included in the search results. By default, only 100 objects are displayed. If you specify a value of *0* for the *-limit* parameter, all objects matching the search criteria are included in the output.

- **{-uc | -uco | -uci}** Specifies that the command will use the Unicode character set for input or output. If the command input is taken from a pipe or the output is sent to a pipe, you use the *-uc* parameter. If only the output to a pipe or file is to use the Unicode format, you use the *-uco* parameter. If only the input from a pipe or file is to use the Unicode format, you use the *-uci* parameter.

The following sections discuss the purpose and syntax of each DSQuery command.

DSQuery Computer

You use the *DSQuery Computer* command to search for computer objects in the Active Directory database that match the specified search criteria. These objects include member servers and desktops. The syntax of this command is:

```
DSQuery Computer [{StartNode| forestroot | domainroot}] [-o {dn | rdn | samid}]
[-scope {subtree | onelevel | base}] [-name Name] [-desc Description] [-samid
SAMName] [-inactive NumberOfWeeks] [-stalepwd NumberOfDays] [-disabled] [{-s
Server| -d Domain}] [-u UserName] [-p {Password|*}] [-q] [-r] [-gc] [-limit
NumberOfObjects] [{-uc | -uco | -uci}]
```

Some of the parameters of this command are common to other *DSQuery* commands. Table 10.2 explains the parameters that are specific to the *DSQuery Computer* command.

Table 10.2 Parameters of the *DSQuery* Command

Parameter	Description
-samid	Specifies that the search be conducted using the Security Account Manager (SAM) account name of the object.
-inactive NumberOfWeeks	Used to search for computer accounts that have been inactive for the specified number of weeks. Even if a computer is being used regularly, the account is considered inactive if no one has logged on to the domain.
-stalepwd NumberOfDays	Used to search for computer accounts whose passwords have not been changed for a specified number of days.
-disabled	Used to search for computers that have disabled accounts.

For a description of other parameters, please refer to the section "Parameters Common to All DSQuery Commands," earlier in this chapter. You can pipe the output of the *DSQuery Computer* command as input to other DS commands, such as *DSGet*, *DSMove*, *DSMod*, and *DSRm*.

DSQuery Contact

You use the *DSQuery Contact* command to search for contact objects in the Active Directory database that match the search criteria. The syntax of this command is:

```
DSQuery Contact [{StartNode| forestroot | domainroot}] [-o {dn | rdn}] [-scope
{subtree | onelevel | base}] [{-s Server| -d Domain}] [-u UserName] [-p
{Password|*}] [-q] [-r] [-gc] [-limit NumberOfObjects] [{-uc | -uco | -uci}]
```

This command does not use any special parameters. For a description of common parameters, please refer to the section "Parameters Common to All DSQuery Commands," earlier in this chapter. You can pipe the output of the *DSQuery Contact* command as input to other DS commands, such as *DSGet*, *DSMove*, *DSMod*, and *DSRm*.

DSQuery Group

You use the *DSQuery Group* command to search for groups in Active Directory that match the specified search criteria. The output includes names of all types of groups, such as local groups, global groups, and universal groups. The syntax of this command is:

```
DSQuery Group [{StartNode| forestroot | domainroot}] [-o {dn | rdn | samid}] [-
scope {subtree | onelevel | base}] [-name Name] [-desc Description] [-samid
SAMName] [{-s Server| -d Domain}] [-u UserName] [-p {Password|*}] [-q] [-r] [-gc]
[-limit NumberOfObjects] [{-uc | -uco | -uci}]
```

This command does not use any special parameters. If the search criteria you specify do not return any results or return incorrect results, you can use the *DSQuery* * command. This command provides a more generalized search of the Active Directory groups. For a description of common parameters, please refer to the section "Parameters Common to All DSQuery Commands," earlier in this chapter. You can pipe the output of the *DSQuery Contact* command as input to other DS commands, such as *DSGet*, *DSMove*, *DSMod*, and *DSRm*.

DSQuery OU

You use the *DSQuery OU* command to search Active Directory for OUs that match the specified search criteria. The syntax of this command is:

```
DSQuery OU [{StartNode| forestroot | domainroot}] [-o {dn | rdn | samid}] [-
scope {subtree | onelevel | base}] [-name Name] [-desc Description] [-samid
SAMName] [{-s Server| -d Domain}] [-u UserName] [-p {Password|*}] [-q] [-r] [-gc]
[-limit NumberOfObjects] [{-uc | -uco | -uci}]
```

This command does not use any special parameters. For a description of common parameters, please refer to the section "Parameters Common to All DSQuery Commands," earlier in this chapter. You can pipe the output of the *DSQuery OU* command as input to other DS commands, such as *DSGet*, *DSMove*, *DSMod*, and *DSRm*.

DSQuery Site

You use the *DSQuery Site* command to search the Active Directory database for site objects that match the specified search criteria. The syntax of this command is:

```
DSQuery Site [-o {dn | rdn}] [-name Name] [-desc Description] [{-s Server| -d
Domain}] [-u UserName] [-p {Password|*}] [-q] [-r] [-gc] [-limit
NumberOfObjects] [{-uc | -uco | -uci}]
```

Because this command searches for Active Directory site objects, you cannot specify the scope of the search. You also cannot use the *StartNode* parameter with this command. This command does not use any special parameters. If the search criteria you specify do not return any results or return incorrect results, you can use the *DSQuery ** command. This command provides a more generalized search of Active Directory sites. For a description of common parameters, please refer to the section "Parameters Common to All DSQuery Commands," earlier in this chapter. As with other DS commands, you can pipe the output of this command to other DS commands, such as *DSGet*, *DSMove*, *DSMod*, and *DSRm*.

DSQuery Server

You use the *DSQuery Server* command to search for server objects (domain controllers) in the Active Directory database that match the specified search criteria. The syntax of this command is:

```
DSQuery Server [-o {dn | rdn}] [-forest] [-domain DomainName] [-site SiteName]
[-name Name] [-desc Description] [-hasfsmo {schema | name | infr | pdc | rid}]
[-isgc] [{-s Server| -d Domain}] [-u UserName] [-p {Password|*}] [-q] [-r] [-gc]
[-limit NumberOfObjects] [{-uc | -uco | -uci}]
```

This command uses the following special parameters for the search:

- **–forest** Used to search for all domain controllers (server objects) in the current forest.

- **–domain DomainName** Used to search for all domain controllers (server objects) in the domain specified by *DomainName*. The *DomainName* parameter is specified in the DNS name format. By default, the search is conducted using the current domain. Hence, if you want to search for all server objects that are domain controllers in the current domain, you need not use this parameter.

- **–site SiteName** Used to search for all domain controllers (server objects) that are located in the site specified by *SiteName*.

- **-isgc** Limits the search to domain controllers that have been assigned the role of GC servers in the scope specified by the *–forest, -domain,* or *–site* parameter. If none of these parameters is used with the *DSQuery Server* command, the command searches for all GC servers in the current domain.

- **–hasfsmo** Allows you to search for domain controllers that have been assigned Flexible Operations Master roles in the Active Directory network. The parameter can use *schema, name, infr, pdc,* and *rid* as its values.

Table 10.3 explains the options available with the *–hasfsmo* parameter.

Table 10.3 Options Available with the –hasfsmo Parameter

Option	Description
schema	Specifies that the search be conducted for domain controllers that have been assigned the Schema Master role for the forest.
name	Specifies that the search be conducted for domain controllers that have been assigned the Domain Naming Master role for the forest.
infr	Specifies that the search be conducted for domain controllers that have been assigned the Infrastructure Master role for the domain used with the *–domain* parameter or for the current domain.
pdc	Specifies that the search be conducted for domain controllers that have been assigned the Primary Domain Controller (PDC) Emulator role for the domain used with the *–domain* parameter or for the current domain.
rid	Specifies that the search be conducted for domain controllers that have been assigned the Relative ID (RID) Master role for the domain used with the *–domain* parameter or for the current domain.

If you do not use the *-domain* parameter with the *DSQuery Server* command, the current domain is used for the search. For a description of other parameters, please refer to the section "Parameters Common to All DSQuery Commands," earlier in this chapter. As with other DS commands, you can pipe the output of this command to other DS commands, such as *DSGet, DSMove, DSMod,* and *DSRm.*

DSQuery User

You use the *DSQuery User* command to search for user objects (user accounts) in the Active Directory database that match the specified search criteria. You will frequently need this command for your regular administrative jobs, to search for user accounts as well as to search for inactive or disabled user accounts. You can also search for user accounts that have *stale passwords.* Stale passwords are passwords that have not been changed for a specific number of days. The syntax of this command is:

```
DSQuery User [{StartNode| forestroot | domainroot}] [-o {dn | rdn | samid}] [-
scope {subtree | onelevel | base}] [-name Name] [-desc Description] [-upn UPN]
[-samid SAMName] [-inactive NumberOfWeeks] [-stalepwd NumberOfDays] [-disabled]
[{-s Server| -d Domain}] [-u UserName] [-p {Password|*}] [-q] [-r] [-gc] [-limit
NumberOfObjects] [{-uc | -uco | -uci}]
```

Table 10.4 explains the parameters that are special to the *DSQuery User* command.

Table 10.4 Parameters of the *DSQuery User* Command

Parameter	Description
-upn UPN	Specifies the UPN name of the user account for which you are conducting the search. An example of the UPN name is *garyb@books.syngress.com*.
-samid	Specifies that the search be conducted using the SAM account name of the user object.
-inactive NumberOfWeeks	Used to search for user accounts that have been inactive for the specified number of weeks. Inactive user accounts are those that have not logged on to the domain.
-stalepwd NumberOfDays	Used to search for user accounts whose passwords have not been changed for the specified number of days. Passwords for user accounts in a domain must be changed regularly according to the configured password policy for the domain.
-disabled	Used to search for disabled user accounts in the domain.

If the search criteria you specify do not return any results or return incorrect results, you can use the *DSQuery ** command. This command provides a more generalized search of the user accounts stored in the Active Directory database. For a description of common parameters, please refer to the section "Parameters Common to All DSQuery Commands," earlier in this chapter. You can pipe the output of the *DSQuery User* command as input to other DS commands, such as *DSGet, DSMove, DSMod,* and *DSRm.*

NOTE

You can use the *upn* option for the *–o* parameter only with the *DSQuery User* command. Other *DSQuery* commands do not allow you to use this option. This is because the UPN format is valid only with usernames. Moreover, the *DSQuery Contact, DSQuery OU, DSQuery Site, DSQuery Server, DSQuery Quota,* and

DSQuery Partition commands do not support use of the *samid* option for the *–o* parameter. The only options supported with these commands are *dn* and *rdn*.

If you want to use the *DSQuery* * command to search for all types of objects in Active Directory using specified search criteria, you are not allowed to use the *–o* parameter at all.

DSQuery Quota

You use the *DSQuery Quota* command to search for quota entries for security principals in the Active Directory database according to the specified search criteria. *Quota* refers to the maximum number of objects that a *security principal* (user, group, computer, or *InetOrgPerson*) can own in an Active Directory partition. The syntax of this command is:

```
DSQuery Quota {domainroot |ObjectDN} [-o {dn | rdn}] [-acct Name] [-qlimit
Filter] [-desc Description] [{-s Server| -d Domain}] [-u UserName] [-p
{Password|*}] [-q] [-r] [-gc] [-limit NumberOfObjects] [{-uc | -uco | -uci}]
```

This command does not allow you to use the *scope* parameter for the search. You are also not allowed to use the *samid* option with the *–o* parameter. Table 10.5 explains the parameters special to the *DSQuery Quota* command.

Table 10.5 Parameters of the *DSQuery Quota* Command

Parameter	Description
*{domainroot	ObjectDN}*	A required parameter that specifies where the command should begin the search. You can use the *domainroot* option to specify the root of the current domain or you can use the *ObjectDN* option to specify the DN of the object.
-acct Name	Used to search for quota specifications for the security principal (user, group, computer, or *InetOrgPerson*) specified by the *Name* option.
-qlimit Filter	Used to search for quota specifications whose limits match the value given in the *Filter* option. If you want to find quota specifications that do not have any limits, you can use this parameter as *-qlimit "-1"*.

If the search criteria you specify do not return any results or return incorrect results, you can use the *DSQuery* * command. This command provides a more generalized search of the user accounts stored in the Active Directory database. For a description of common parameters, please refer to the section "Parameters Common to All DSQuery Commands," earlier in this chapter. You can pipe the output of the *DSQuery Quota* command as input to other DS commands, such as *DSGet, DSMove, DSMod,* and *DSRm*.

> **NOTE**
>
> The command interpreter reads as a string the value specified with the *–qlimit Filter* parameter used with the *DSQuery Quota* command. You must always enclose the value of the *Filter* option in quotation marks. Thus, valid values for the *Filter* option should read as *–qlimit "=100", -qlimit "<=49", -qlimit ">=500"*, and so on. Note that even mathematical operators, such as =, <=, and >=, are to be enclosed in quotation marks. There should be no space between the mathematical operator and the numerical value.

DSQuery Partition

You use the *DSQuery Partition* command to search for *partition* objects in the Active Directory database that match the specified search criteria. The *partition* object refers to the Active Directory partition. The syntax of this command is:

```
DSQuery Partition [-o {dn | rdn}] [-part Filter] [{-s Server| -d Domain}] [-u
UserName] [-p {Password|*}] [-q] [-r] [-gc] [-limit NumberOfObjects] [{-uc | -
uco | -uci}]
```

You use the *–part Filter* parameter to search for objects in the directory partition whose CNs match the value given in the *Filter* option. For a description of common parameters, please refer to the section "Parameters Common to All DSQuery Commands," earlier in this chapter. You can pipe the output of the *DSQuery Partition* command as input to other DS commands, such as *DSGet, DSMove, DSMod,* and *DSRm*.

DSQuery *

The *DSQuery *** command is a special *DSQuery* command that can search for all types of objects in the Active Directory database according to the specified search criteria. The * in this command refers to *all objects*. For example, if you want to search for all user and computer accounts that match specific search criteria using a single command line, you can use a single *DSQuery *** command. This is equivalent to using the *DSQuery User* and *DSQuery Computer* commands separately. The syntax of this command is:

```
DSQuery * [{ObjectDN| forestroot | domainroot}] [-scope {subtree | onelevel |
base}] [-filter LDAPFilter] [-attr {AttributeList|*}] [-attrsonly] [-l] [{-s
Server| -d Domain}] [-u UserName] [-p {Password|*}] [-q] [-r] [-gc] [-limit
NumberOfObjects] [{-uc | -uco | -uci}]
```

It is evident from the command syntax that this command relies on the Lightweight Directory Access Protocol (LDAP) to search for the objects in Active Directory. This is different from other *DSQuery* commands, where you can use a direct approach to finding objects. Table 10.6 explains the special parameters used for the *DSQuery *** command.

www.syngress.com

Table 10.6 Parameters of the *DSQuery* * Command

Parameter	Description
-filter LDAPFilter	Defines a search filter that relies on LDAP. This filter must be specified in the LDAP filter format. An example of an LDAP filter is *(&(ObjectClass=Person) (sn=smith*))*. This value would search for a person in Active Directory who has any form of the name *smith*. By default, the command uses the LDAP filter *(ObjectClass=*)* that returns all objects in the Active Directory database.
*-attr {AttributeList | *}*	Specifies the attributes that should be included as part of the search results. The attributes displayed are separated by a semicolon. When the * option is used for this parameter, all attributes are displayed in the *List* format. By default, only the DNs are included in the displayed output attributes.
-attrsonly	Specifies that the search results should include only the attributes of the objects but not the values of these attributes. By default, the command returns both the attributes and their respective values.
-l	Specifies that the output be displayed in the *List* format. By default, the output is displayed in the *Table* format.

For a description of common parameters, please refer to the section "Parameters Common to All DSQuery Commands," earlier in this chapter. You can pipe the output of the *DSQuery* * command as input to other DS commands, such as *DSGet*, *DSMove*, *DSMod*, and *DSRm*.

NOTE

The *Partition* and *Quota* subcommands used with the *DSQuery*, *DSAdd*, *DSGet*, and *DSMod* commands have nothing to do with hard-disk partitions and disk quotas. *Partition* in these commands refers to the Active Directory partition and *Quota* refers to the number of objects that a security principal (user, group, computer, or *InetOrgPerson*) is allowed to own in the specified directory partition. Do not confuse these terms with disk partitions and disk quotas. You manage disk partitions using the *DiskPart* command-line utility discussed in Chapter 6.

Adding New Objects with DSAdd

You use the *DSAdd* utility to add new objects to the Active Directory database. You can add new objects that fall into categories such as users, groups, computers, OUs, quotas, and contacts. The syntax of these commands looks very complex, but once you understand the basic syntax and parameters of these and other DS commands, you may find that they are not as difficult to use as they seem to be. The following sections describe each *DSAdd* command. Let's first look at the parameters that are common to all of the *DSAdd* commands.

Parameters Common to All DSAdd Commands

All of the *DSAdd* commands use a large number of parameters. When you look at the syntax of these commands, you will find that a number of parameters are common to all *DSAdd* commands. Here is a list of those parameters; we will discuss the parameters that are unique to each *DSAdd* subcommand in their respective sections:

- **ObjectDN** Specifies the DN of the object that you want to add to Active Directory. In the syntax of the *DSAdd* commands you will notice that this parameter is replaced by such parameters as *ComputerDN*, *ContactDN*, and *UserDN*, among others, making it easy for you to understand the command syntax. If you omit this parameter, the command interpreter will attempt to obtain this parameter from the standard input (STDIN). This standard input can be from the keyboard, redirected input from a file, or piped output from another command. If you decide to use the keyboard or a redirected file for the *ObjectDN* parameter, you can use the **Ctrl + Z** (^Z) key combination to mark the end of the input.

- **-Desc Description** Specifies the description for the Active Directory object you want to add. In most cases, the object description contains spaces. So, you must enclose the *Description* argument in quotation marks.

- **-q** Used to put the command interpreter in quiet mode so that no output is displayed when the command is executed.

- **{-uc | -uco | -uci}** Specifies that the command will use the Unicode format for input or output. If the command input is taken from a pipe or the output is sent to a pipe, you use the *–uc* parameter. If only the output to a pipe or file is to use the Unicode format, you use the *–uco* parameter. If only the input from a pipe or file is to use the Unicode format, you use the *–uci* parameter.

In addition to the preceding parameters, you can also use the following parameters when working on remote computers. If you omit the following parameters, the commands are executed on the local computer:

- **S Server | -d Domain** Specifies a remote server or a domain. You can use either the name of the server or the name of the domain, but not both. If you do not specify the domain name, the domain where you have logged on is assumed by default.

- **-u UserName** Specifies the name of the user whose account permissions are to be used to execute the DS command on the remote server. If you omit this parameter, the account permissions of the currently logged-on user are used by default.

- **-p Password** Specifies the password for the user account. You can use an asterisk (*) as an argument for the *-p Password* parameter (*-p ***). When the command is executed you will be prompted to type the password. This option is good to use when you are concerned with Active Directory security.

You can specify the username in any of the following formats:

- **UserName** This is the simplest form of the username. We have been using this format with most of the commands discussed in previous chapters.

- **Domain\User** Using this format, you can specify a domain name along with the username. For example, you would specify a user named *GaryB* in the domain named *Syngress* as *Syngress\GaryB*.

- **UPN** The UPN name of a user includes the at sign (@) after the username. Examples of UPN names are *GaryB@Syngress.com* and *JohnS@Books.Syngress.com*.

The following sections discuss the purpose and command syntax of the *DSAdd* commands.

DSAdd Computer

You use the *DSAdd Computer* command to add computer objects to Active Directory. Computer objects refer to desktops and member servers that are part of the Active Directory domain. The syntax of this command is:

```
DSAdd Computer ComputerDN [-samid SAMName] [-desc Description] [-locLocation] [-
memberof GroupDN ...] [{-s Server | -d Domain}] [-uUserName] [-p {Password | *}]
[-q] [{-uc | -uco | -uci}]
```

The following list explains the parameters that are specific to the *DSAdd Computer* command:

- **-samid SAMName** Specifies the SAM account name of the computer you want to add. If you omit this parameter, the command derives the *SAMName* from the value of the CN part of the *ComputerDN*.

- **-loc Location** Specifies the location of the computer.

- **-memberof GroupDN …** Specifies the group or groups to which you want the computer to be a member. The *GroupDN* argument specifies the name of the group. To specify more than one group put a space between each *GroupDN* argument.

For a description of other parameters, please refer to the section "Parameters Common to All DSAdd Commands," earlier in this chapter.

DSAdd Contact

You use the *DSAdd Contact* command to add a contact object to the Active Directory database. The syntax of this command is:

```
DSAdd Contact ContactDN [-fn FirstName] [-mi Initial] [-ln LastName] [-display
DisplayName] [-desc Description] [-office Office] [-tel PhoneNumber] [-email
Email] [-hometel HomePhoneNumber] [-pager PagerNumber] [-mobile CellPhoneNumber]
[-fax FaxNumber] [-iptel IPPhoneNumber] [-title Title] [-dept Department] [-
company Company] [{-s Server | -d Domain}] [-u UserName] [-p {Password | *}] [-
q] [{-uc | -uco | -uci}]
```

The *ContactDN* parameter specifies the DN of the contact you want to add. If you omit this parameter, the command will attempt to obtain the value of the *ContactDN* parameter from STDIN. Table 10.7 explains the parameters specific to the *DSAdd Contact* command.

Table 10.7 Parameters of the *DSAdd Contact* Command

Parameter	Description
-fn FirstName	Specifies the contact's first name.
-mi MiddleName	Specifies the contact's middle name.
-ln LastName	Specifies the contact's last name.
-display DisplayName	Specifies the contact's display name.
-office Office	Specifies the location of the contact's office.
-tel PhoneNumber	Specifies the contact's telephone number.
-email Email	Specifies the contact's e-mail address.
-hometel HomePhoneNumber	Specifies the contact's home telephone number.
-pager PagerNumber	Specifies the contact's pager number.
-mobile CellPhoneNumber	Specifies the contact's cell/mobile phone number.
-fax FaxNumber	Specifies the contact's fax number.
-iptel IPPhoneNumber	Specifies the contact's Internet Protocol (IP) telephone number.
-title Title	Specifies the contact's title.

Continued

Table 10.7 continued Parameters of the *DSAdd Contact* Command

Parameter	Description
-dept Department	Specifies the contact's department.
-company Company	Specifies the name of the company where the contact works.

At first, the overwhelming number of parameters seems to make the command syntax very complex. But once you use the command a number of times, you will learn that it is not difficult to remember or use these parameters. For a description of common parameters, please refer to the section "Parameters Common to All DSAdd Commands," earlier in this chapter.

DSAdd Group

You use the *DSAdd Group* command to add a single group object to the Active Directory database. This group can be a security group or a distribution group. You can also define whether the group you want to add is a domain local group, a universal group, or a global group. The syntax of this command is:

```
DSAdd Group GroupDN [-secgrp {yes | no}] [-scope {l | g | u}] [-samid SAMName]
[-desc Description] [-memberof Group ...] [-members Member ...] [{-s Server | -d
Domain}] [-u UserName] [-p {Password | *}] [-q] [{-uc | -uco | -uci}]
```

The parameters specific to this command are as follows:

- **-secgroup {yes | no}** Specifies whether the new group in Active Directory will be created as a security group (*yes*) or as a distribution group (*no*). By default, the new group is created as a security group.

- **-scope {l | g | u}** Specifies the scope of the new group. You can choose from local group (*l*), global group (*g*), or universal group (*u*). By default, the new group is created as a global group (*g*).

- **-samid SAMName** Used to specify a SAM name for the new group.

- **-memberof Group ...** Used to specify the groups that the new group will be a member of. You can specify multiple groups with this parameter by using spaces between object DNs.

- **-members Member ...** Used to specify the objects that will become members of the newly created group. You can specify multiple objects with this parameter by using spaces between object DNs.

For a description of common parameters, please refer to the section "Parameters Common to All DSAdd Commands," earlier in this chapter.

Master Craftsman...

Group Types and Scope of a Group

In Windows Server 2003 domains, you can create two types of groups: *security groups* and *distribution groups*. Distribution groups are used for mailing lists and do not have any associated security descriptors. Security groups have associated security descriptors and are mainly used for managing user accounts and assigning permissions to network resources. With each group type, you can define the scope of the group in one of the following three types:

- **Domain Local** You primarily use the Domain Local groups to assign access permissions to network resources within a domain. Domain Local groups contain global and universal groups from the same domain or from any domain within the forest.

- **Global** You use the Global groups to group users that have similar job functions. Global groups typically include users and groups from within the same domain.

- **Universal** You use Universal groups to club users that need to have a wide variety of access permissions throughout the domain or across domains in a forest. Universal groups contain users and groups from any domain in the forest.

The type of group scope depends on the domain's functional level. If all of the domain controllers in the network are running the Windows Server 2003 operating system, the domain is considered to be at Windows Server 2003 domain functional level. This level allows you to use all of the features of Windows Server 2003 Active Directory.

DSAdd OU

You use the *DSAdd OU* command to add a new OU object to the Active Directory hierarchy. The syntax of this command is:

```
DSAdd OU OrganizationalUnitDN [-desc Description] [{-s Server | -d Domain}] [-u
UserName] [-p {Password | *}] [-q] [{-uc | -uco | -uci}]
```

OrganizationalUnitDN is a required parameter that specifies the DN of the OU you want to create with the *DSAdd OU* command. For a description of common parameters, please refer to the section "Parameters Common to All DSAdd Commands," earlier in this chapter.

DSAdd User

You use the *DSAdd User* command to add a new user object to Active Directory. The syntax of this command is:

```
DSAdd User UserDN [-samid SAMName] [-upn UPN] [-fn FirstName] [-mi Initial] [-ln
LastName] [-display DisplayName] [-empid EmployeeID] [-pwd {Password | *}] [-
desc Description] [-memberof Group ...] [-office Office] [-tel PhoneNumber] [-
email Email] [-hometel HomePhoneNumber] [-pager PagerNumber] [-mobile
CellPhoneNumber] [-fax FaxNumber] [-iptel IPPhoneNumber] [-webpg WebPage] [-
title Title] [-dept Department] [-company Company] [-mgr Manager] [-hmdir
HomeDirectory] [-hmdrv DriveLetter:][-profile ProfilePath] [-loscr ScriptPath] [-
mustchpwd {yes | no}] [-canchpwd {yes | no}] [-reversiblepwd {yes | no}] [-
pwdneverexpires {yes | no}] [-acctexpires NumberOfDays] [-disabled {yes | no}]
[{-s Server | -d Domain}] [-u UserName] [-p {Password | *}] [-q] [{-uc | -uco |
-uci}]
```

UserDN is a required parameter that specifies the DN of the user you want to create with the *DSAdd User* command. Table 10.8 explains the parameters that are specific to the *DSAdd User* command.

Table 10.8 Parameters of the *DSAdd User* Command

Parameter	Description
-samid SAMName	Specifies the user's SAM account name. If you omit this parameter, the command attempts to extract the SAM name from the UserDN parameter.
-upn UPN	Specifies the user's UPN—for example, GaryB@Books.Syngress.com.
-fn FirstName	Specifies the user's first name.
-mi MiddleName	Specifies the user's middle name.
-ln LastName	Specifies the user's last name.
-display DisplayName	Specifies the user's display name.
-empid EmployeeID	Specifies the user's employee ID.
-pwd {Password	*}	Specifies the user's password. If you use the * option, you are prompted for a password when the command is executed.
-memberof Group ...	Specifies the user's group membership. You can add the user to multiple groups by using spaces between names of the groups.
-office Office	Specifies the location of the user's office.
-tel PhoneNumber	Specifies the user's telephone number.
-email Email	Specifies the user's e-mail address.

Continued

Table 10.8 continued Parameters of the *DSAdd User* Command

Parameter	Description
-hometel HomePhoneNumber	Specifies the user's home telephone number.
-pager PagerNumber	Specifies the user's pager number.
-mobile CellPhoneNumber	Specifies the user's cell/mobile phone number.
-fax FaxNumber	Specifies the user's fax number.
-iptel IPPhoneNumber	Specifies the user's IP telephone number.
-webpg WebPage	Specifies the user's Web page.
-title Title	Specifies the user's title.
-dept Department	Specifies the user's department.
-company Company	Specifies the name of the company where the user works.
-mgr Manager	Specifies the name of the user's manager.
-hmdir HomeDirectory	Specifies the path of the home directory assigned to the user. If you use the universal naming convention for the *HomeDirectory* variable, you must specify the drive letter to be mapped to this path using the *–hmdrv* parameter.
-hmdrv HomeDrive	Specifies the drive letter for the home directory.
-profile ProfilePath	Specifies the path of the user's profile.
-loscr ScriptPath	Specifies the path to the user's logon script.
-mustchpwd {yes | no}	Specifies whether the user must change the password on next logon (*yes*) or not (*no*). By default, the user is not required to change the password on next logon.
-canchpwd {yes | no}	Specifies whether the user is allowed to change the password (*yes*) or not (*no*). If you choose *yes* for this parameter, the value of *–mustchangepwd* must be set to *yes*.
-reversiblepwd {yes | no}	Specifies whether the password will be stored using reversible encryption in Active Directory (*yes*) or not (*no*). By default, the user password is not stored using reversible encryption.
-pwdneverexpires {yes | no}	Specifies whether the password never expires (*yes*) or does expire (*no*). By default, the user password does expire.

Continued

Table 10.8 continued Parameters of the *DSAdd User* Command

Parameter	Description
-acctexpires NumberOfDays	Specifies the number of days from today after which the user account expires. If you specify a value of *0* for this parameter, the account expires by the end of today. You can set the value to *never* if you do not want the account to expire. A positive value sets the account to expire in the future and a negative value sets a back date for expiry.
*-disabled {yes	no}*	Specifies whether the new user account remains in a disabled state (*yes*) or in an enabled state (*no*).

For a description of common parameters, please refer to the section "Parameters Common to All DSAdd Commands," earlier in this chapter.

NOTE

You can use the *%UserName%* variable to replace the value of the user's SAM account name for the *–email, -hmdir, -profile*, and *–webpg* parameters. For example, if a user's SAM account name is *GaryB*, you would specify the *–hmdir* parameter as *-hmdir\Users\%USerName%\home*.

DSAdd Quota

You use the *DSAdd Quota* command to add quota entries (specifications) for the specified Active Directory partition. Setting a quota limit on a directory partition allows you to control the number of objects that a security principal (user, group, computer, or *InetOrgPerson*) can own in the specified directory partition. The syntax of this command is:

```
DSAdd Quota -part PartitionDN [-rdn RelativeDistinguishedName] -acct Name -
qlimit Value [-desc Description] [{-s Server | -d Domain}] [-u UserName] [-p
{Password | *}] [-q] [{-uc | -uco | -uci}]
```

Parameters specific to the *DSAdd Quota* command are as follows:

- **–part PartitionDN** A required parameter that specifies the DN of the Active Directory partition on which you want to create the quota specification.

- **–rdn RelativeDistinguishedName** Specifies the RDN of the quota specification you want to create. If you omit this parameter, the RDN is set to the

Domain_AccountName using the name of the domain and the security principal specified by the *–acct Name* parameter.

- **-acct Name** A required parameter that specifies the security principal (user, group, computer, or *InetOrgPerson*) to whom the quota specification applies.

- **-qlimit Value** A required parameter that specifies the number of objects that the security principal can own in the Active Directory partition. To set an unlimited quota for a security principal, you can use *-1* as the value of the *–qlimit* parameter.

For a description of common parameters, please refer to the section "Parameters Common to All DSAdd Commands," earlier in this chapter.

Displaying Object Properties with DSGet

You use the *DSGet* command to display the properties (attributes) of specified objects. These commands work with most of the Active Directory objects, including computers, contacts, users, groups, OUs, sites, subnets, quotas, and partitions. The object you want to modify with the *DSGet* command must exist in Active Directory. You can use the *DSQuery* command to get a list of existing objects in Active Directory and pipe the output to one of the *DSGet* commands. The following sections explain the *DSGet* commands and their syntax when used with different types of objects.

NOTE

It is important to understand the difference between the *DSQuery* and *DSGet* commands. You use the *DSQuery* command to search for all objects in the Active Directory database that match the specified search criteria. You use the *DSGet* command, on the other hand, to display the properties (or attributes) of a specified object. With the *DSQuery* command, you will need to specify one or more attributes of the Active Directory object(s) and with the *DSGet* command, you will have to specify the DN of a particular object.

Parameters Common to All DSGet Commands

All of the *DSGet* commands use a large number of parameters. When you look at the syntax of these commands, you will find that a number of parameters are common to all *DSGet* commands. We have sorted out these common parameters in this section. The parameters that are unique to each *DSGet* subcommand will be discussed in their respective sections.

- **ObjectDN** A required parameter that specifies the DN of the object for which you want to display properties. In the syntax of the *DSGet* commands, you will notice that this parameter is replaced by parameters such as *ComputerDN*, *ContactDN*, and *UserDN*, making it easy for you to understand the command syntax. If you omit this parameter, the command interpreter will attempt to obtain this parameter from STDIN. This standard input can be from the keyboard, redirected input from a file, or piped output from another command. If you decide to use the keyboard or a redirected file for the *ObjectDN* parameter, you can use the **Ctrl + Z** (**^Z**) key combination to mark the end of the input.

- **-Desc** Specifies that the description of the Active Directory object be displayed.

- **-q** Used to put the command interpreter in quiet mode so that no output is displayed when the command is executed.

- **{-uc | -uco | -uci}** Specifies that the command will use Unicode format for input or output. If the command input is taken from a pipe or the output is sent to a pipe, you use the *–uc* parameter. If only the output to a pipe or file is to use the Unicode format, you use the *–uco* parameter. If only the input from a pipe or file is to use the Unicode format, you use the *–uci* parameter.

In addition to the preceding parameters, you can use the following parameters when working on remote computers. If you omit the following parameters, the commands are executed on the local computer:

- **S Server | -d Domain** Specifies a remote server or a domain. You can use either the name of the server or the name of the domain, but not both. If you do not specify the domain name, the domain where you logged on is assumed by default.

- **-u UserName** Specifies the name of the user whose account permissions are to be used to execute the DS command on the remote server. If you omit this parameter, the account permissions of the currently logged-on user are used by default.

- **-p Password** Specifies the password for the user account. You can use an asterisk (*) as an argument for the *-p Password* parameter (*-p ***). When the command is executed you will be prompted to type the password. This option is good to use when you are concerned with Active Directory security.

You can specify the username in any of the following formats:

- **UserName** This is the simplest form of the username. We have been using this format with most of the commands discussed in previous chapters.

- **Domain\User** Using this format, you can specify a domain name along with the username. For example, you would specify a user named *GaryB* in the domain named *Syngress* as *Syngress\GaryB*.

- **UPN** The UPN name of a user includes the at sign (@) after the username. Examples of UPN names are *GaryB@Syngress.com* and *JohnS@Books.Syngress.com*.

The following sections discuss the purpose and command syntax of the *DSGet* commands.

DSGet Computer

You use the *DSGet Computer* command to obtain information about computers (desktops and member servers) that match the specified search criteria. This command has two variations. The first variation allows you to display the properties of multiple computers using a single command. The syntax of the first variation of the *DSGet Computer* command is:

```
DSGet Computer ComputerDN ...[-dn] [-samid] [-sid] [-desc] [-loc] [-disabled]
[{-sServer | -dDomain}] [-uUserName] [-p {Password | *}] [-c] [-q] [-l] [{-uc | -
uco | -uci}] [-partPartitionDN[-qlimit] [-qused]]
```

The second variation of this command allows you to search for membership information of a single computer. The syntax of this variation of the *DSGet Computer* command is:

```
DSGet Computer ComputerDN [-memberof [-expand]] [{-sServer | -dDomain}] [-
uUserName] [-p {Password | *}] [-c] [-q] [-l] [{-uc | -uco | -uci}]
```

Most of the parameters of the *DSGet Computer* command are similar to the ones we discussed earlier in this chapter; here we will explain the new parameters that are specific to these commands:

- **–ComputerDN ...** A required parameter that specifies the DKNY of the computer whose properties you want to display. If you omit this parameter, the command attempts to get this parameter from standard input.

- **–dn** Used to display the computer's DNs.

- **–samid** Used to display the specified computer's SAM IDs.

- **–desc** Used to display a description of the specified computer.

- **–loc** Used to display the computer's location.

- **–disabled** Used to display the status of the computer account. The command returns a value of *Yes* for disabled computer accounts and *No* for computers whose accounts are not disabled.

- **–part PartitionName** Used to connect to the directory partition specified by *PartitionName*.

- **–qlimit** Used to display the computer's effective quota limit.

- **-qused** Used to display the quota amount the computer used in the specified directory partition.

- **-ComputerDN** Used in the second variation of the *DSGet Computer* command and specifies the DN of the single computer whose properties you want to display.

- **-memberof** Used in the second variation of the command to display the immediate list of groups of which the computer is a member.

- **-expand** Used to display an extended list of all the groups of which the computer is a member.

For an explanation of the common parameters of this command, please refer to the section "Parameters Common to All DSGet Commands," earlier in this chapter.

DSGet Contact

You use the *DSGet Contact* command to display one or more properties of the specified contacts. The syntax of this command is:

```
DSGet Contact ContactDN ...[-dn] [-fn] [-mi] [-ln] [-display] [-desc] [-office]
[-tel][-email] [-hometel] [-pager] [-mobile] [-fax] [-iptel] [-title] [-dept] [-
company] [{-sServer | -dDomain}] [-uUserName] [-p {Password | *}] [-c] [-q] [-1]
[{-uc | -uco | -uci}]
```

In the preceding code, *ContactDN...* is a required parameter that specifies the DN of the contact whose properties you want to display. You can specify DNs for multiple contacts by using spaces between DNs. For an explanation of the common parameters of this command, please refer to the section "Parameters Common to All DSGet Commands," earlier in this chapter.

DSGet Group

You use the *DSGet Group* command to display properties of one or more groups. This command has two variations. The syntax of the first variation of the command is:

```
DSGet Group GroupDN ...[-dn] [-samid] [-sid] [-desc] [-secgrp] [-scope] [{-
sServer | -dDomain}] [-uUserName] [-p {Password | *}] [-c] [-q] [-1] [{-uc | -uco
| -uci}] [-partPartitionDN[-qlimit] [-qused]]
```

The syntax of the second variation of the command is:

```
DSGet Group GroupDN [{-memberof | -members}] [-expand] [{-sServer | -dDomain}][-
uUserName] [-p {Password | *}] [-c] [-q] [-1] [{-uc | -uco | -uci}]
```

You use the first variation of the *DSGet Group* command to display information about one or more groups specified by the list of groups given in the *GroupDN...* parameter. In the second variation of the *DSGet Group* command you can specify only the DN of a single group and display detailed information about its membership. This command is very useful for displaying information about nested groups in Active Directory.

For an explanation of the common parameters of this command, please refer to the section "Parameters Common to All DSGet Commands," earlier in this chapter.

DSGet OU

You use the *DSGet OU* command to display information about the specified OU. The syntax of this command is:

```
DSGet OU OrganizationalUnitDN ...[-dn] [-desc] [{-sServer | -dDomain}] [-
uUserName] [-p {Password | *}] [-c] [-q] [-l] [{-uc | -uco | -uci}]
```

OrganizationaUnitDN... is a required parameter that specifies the OU whose properties you want to display. You can specify DNs for multiple OUs by using spaces between DNs.

For an explanation of the common parameters of this command, please refer to the section "Parameters Common to All DSGet Commands," earlier in this chapter.

DSGet Server

You use the *DSGet Server* command to display properties of one or more server objects (domain controllers) in Active Directory. There are three variations of the *DSGet Server* command. You use the first variation to display general properties of one or more domain controllers. The syntax of the first variation of this command is:

```
DSGet Server ServerDN ...[-dn] [-desc] [-dnsname] [-site] [-isgc] [{-sServer | -
dDomain}] [-uUserName] [-p {Password | *}] [-c] [-q] [-l] [{-uc | -uco | -uci}]
```

ServerDN... is a required parameter that specifies the DN of the server object. You can specify DNs of multiple server objects by using spaces between DNs.

You use the second variation of the *DSGet Server* command to display the list of security principals that own the largest number of objects on a single domain controller specified by the *ServerDN* parameter. The syntax of this variation of the *DSGet Server* command is:

```
DSGet server ServerDN [{-sServer | -dDomain}] [-uUserName] [-p {Password | *}]
[-c] [-q] [-l] [{-uc | -uco | -uci}] [-topobjownerDisplay]
```

You use the third variation of the *DSGet Server* command to display the list of directory partitions on a single domain controller specified by the *ServerDN* parameter. The syntax of this variation of the *DSGet Server* command is:

```
DSGet Server ServerDN [{-sServer | -dDomain}] [-uUserName] [-p {Password | *}]
[-c] [-q] [-l] [{-uc | -uco | -uci}] [-partPartitionDN]
```

The parameters specific to the *DSGet Server* command are as follows:

- **–dn** Used to display the DN of the specified server object(s).

- **–dnsname** Used to display the DNS name of the specified server object(s).

- **-site** Used to display the names of the sites to which the specified domain controller(s) belong.

- **-isgc** Used to display whether the specified domain controller is a GC server. The command returns a value of *Yes* if the specified domain controller is a GC server and *No* if it is not.

- **-topobjectowner** Used with the second variation of the command to display a list of security principals that own the most objects on the specified domain controller.

- **-part PartitionDN** Used in the third variation of the command to display a list of directory partitions existing on the specified domain controller.

For an explanation of the common parameters of this command, please refer to the section "Parameters Common to All DSGet Commands," earlier in this chapter.

DSGet User

You use the *DSGet User* command to display properties of one or more user objects. This command has two variations. The first variation allows you to display the general properties of multiple users using a single command. The syntax of the first variation of the *DSGet User* command is:

```
DSGet User UserDN ...[-dn] [-samid] [-sid] [-upn] [-fn] [-mi] [-ln] [-display]
[-empid] [-desc] [-office] [-tel] [-email] [-hometel] [-pager] [-mobile] [-fax] [-
iptel] [-webpg] [-title] [-dept] [-company] [-mgr] [-hmdir] [-hmdrv] [-profile] [-
loscr] [-mustchpwd] [-canchpwd] [-pwdneverexpires] [-disabled] [-acctexpires] [-
reversiblepwd] [{-uc | -uco | -uci}] [-partPartitionDN [-qlimit] [-qused]]
```

The *UserDN* ... parameter allows you to specify DNs for multiple users by using a space between DNs. You use the second variation of the *DSGet User* command to display detailed information about group memberships of a single user specified by the *UserDN* parameter. The syntax of this variation of the *DSGet User* command is:

```
DSGet User UserDN [-memberof] [-expand] [{-uc | -uco | -uci}]
```

The *DSGet User* command uses the same parameters as *DSAdd User*. The only difference is that with *DSAdd User*, these parameters are used to configure the user properties, and with *DSGet User*, they are used to display one or more specified properties.

The parameters used with the second variation of the *DSGet User* command are as follows:

- **-memberof** Used to display an immediate list of group memberships of the user specified with the *UserDN* parameter.

- **-expand** Used to display an expanded list of all of the user's group memberships.

For an explanation of the common parameters of this command, please refer to the section "Parameters Common to All DSGet Commands," earlier in this chapter.

DSGet Subnet

You use the *DSGet Subnet* command to display the properties of one or more specified subnet objects. The syntax of this command is:

```
DSGet Subnet SubnetDN ...[-dn] [-desc] [-loc] [-site][{-sServer | -dDomain}][-
uUserName] [-p {Password | *}] [-c] [-q] [-1] [{-uc | -uco | -uci}]
```

The parameters specific to *DSGet Subnet* are as follows:

- **-dn** Used to display the DN of the specified subnet.
- **-loc** Used to display the locations of the subnet as defined in Active Directory.
- **-site** Used to display the names of the sites to which the specified subnet belongs.

For an explanation of the common parameters of this command, please refer to the section "Parameters Common to All DSGet Commands," earlier in this chapter.

DSGet Site

You use the *DSGet Site* command to display the properties of one or more specified site objects. The syntax of this command is:

```
DSGet Site SiteCN ...[-dn] [-desc] [-autotopology] [-cachegroups] [-prefGCsite]
[{-sServer | -dDomain}] [-uUserName] [-p {Password | *}] [-c] [-q] [-1] [{-uc | -
uco | -uci}]
```

SiteCN ... is a required parameter that specifies the CN of the site whose properties you want to display. You can specify CNs of multiple sites by using spaces between the CNs. If you do not specify the *SiteCN* parameter, the command attempts to get the site CN from standard input. Note that you must specify the CN of the site and not the DN.

The parameters specific to *DSGet Site* are as follows:

- **-dn** Used to display the DNs of site(s) specified by the *SiteCN* parameter.
- **-autotopology** Used to display information about autotopology configuration. The command returns a value of *Yes* if autotopology is enabled on the site and *No* if autotopology is disabled for the site.
- **-cachegroups** Used to display information about whether automatic caching of group memberships is enabled for the specified site. When automatic caching of group memberships is enabled for a site, users do not have to contact the GC server for logons. The command returns a value of *Yes* if caching is enabled and *No* if it is disabled.

■   **-prefGCsite** Used to display the name of the preferred GC site that enables the site to refresh its universal group membership caching.

> **NOTE**
>
> The *DSGet Site* command uses the CN to specify the site(s) for which you want to display properties. Thus, the parameter becomes *SiteCN*. In most of the other commands, the *ObjectDN* parameter is used to specify the object's DN.

For an explanation of the common parameters of this command, please refer to the section "Parameters Common to All DSGet Commands," earlier in this chapter.

DSGet Quota

You use the *DSGet Quota* command to display the properties of one or more quota objects (specifications) defined in Active Directory. The syntax of this command is:

```
DSGet Quota ObjectDN ... [-dn] [-acct] [-qlimit] [{-sServer | -dDomain}] [-uUserName] [-p {Password | *}] [-c] [-q] [-l] [{-uc | -uco | -uci}]
```

ObjectDN ... is a required parameter that specifies the DN of the quota whose specifications you want to display. You can specify multiple quotas by using spaces between the DNs of the quotas. The parameters specific to the *DSGet Quota* command are as follows:

■   **-dn** Used to display the DNs of quota specifications.

■   **-acct** Used to display the names of accounts to which the quota specifications have been assigned.

■   **-qlimit** Used to display the quota limits for the specified quotas. A value of *-1* means unlimited quota.

When none of the optional parameters is used with the command the command displays the DNs of the quota specifications, the names of the accounts to which quotas are assigned, and quota limits of each account.

For an explanation of the common parameters of this command, please refer to the section "Parameters Common to All DSGet Commands," earlier in this chapter.

DSGet Partition

You use the *DSGet Partition* command to display the properties of one or more Active Directory partition objects. The syntax of this command is:

```
DSGet Partition ObjectDN ... [-dn] [-qdefault] [-qtmbstnwt] [-
topobjownerDisplay] [{-sServer | -dDomain}][-uUserName] [-p {Password | *}] [-c]
[-q][-l] [{-uc | -uco | -uci}]
```

ObjectDN ... is a required parameter that specifies the DN of the partition whose properties you want to display. You can specify multiple partitions by using spaces between the DNs of partitions. The parameters specific to the *DSGet Partition* command are as follows:

- **-dn** Used to display the DNs of the directory partition objects.

- **-qdefault** Used to display the default quota limit for any security principal (user, group, computer, or *InetOrgPerson*) who creates objects in the specified partition. The default quota applies to any security principal for which the quota limit has not been defined. A value of *-1* means unlimited quota.

- **-qtmbstnwt** Used to display the percentage by which the tombstone object count is reduced to calculate the quota limit.

- **-topobjectownerDisplay** Used to display a sorted list of security principals that own the largest number of objects in the specified directory partition and the number of directory objects they own. The *Display* option specifies the number of accounts you want to display. To display all accounts (object owners) you can use a value of *0* for the *Display* option. If you do not use the *Display* option, the command displays 10 accounts by default.

When you use the *−topobjectowner* parameter, the *DSGet Partition* command ignores other parameters and displays only a list of top object owners for the specified directory partition. For an explanation of the common parameters of this command, please refer to the section "Parameters Common to All DSGet Commands," earlier in this chapter.

Modifying Objects with DSMod

You use the *DSMod* command to modify the properties (attributes) of a specified object in Active Directory. You can use this command with such objects as computers, contacts, groups, OUs, servers, users, quotas, and partitions. The object you want to modify with the *DSMod* command must exist in Active Directory. You can use the *DSQuery* command to get a list of existing objects in Active Directory and pipe the output to one of the *DSMod* commands. Different subcommands of the *DSMod* command use a syntax that is very similar to the *DSAdd* subcommands. In the following sections, we will summarize the *DSMod* subcommands and explain the parameters that have not been covered so far in this chapter.

With each of the *DSMod* subcommands the *ObjectDN* parameter is used to specify one or more objects in Active Directory. If you omit this parameter, the command attempts to obtain this parameter from standard input. The *ObjectDN* parameter is replaced by parameters such as *ComputerDN*, *ContactDN*, and *UserDN* in the *DSMod* subcommands.

When working on remote computers you can use the −*s Server, -d Domain, -u UserName*, and −*p Password* parameters to specify a remote server, domain, username, and password, respectively. For more information on running the DS commands on remote computers refer to the section "Working on Remote Computers," earlier in this chapter.

> **NOTE**
>
> The *DSMod* command does not allow you to add any security principal (user, group, computer, or *InetOrgPerson*) from one Active Directory forest to a group in another forest. This operation is not allowed even when the two forests are joined by a forest trust. To add security principals from one forest to groups in another trusted forest, you must use the Active Directory Users and Computers snap-in.

DSMod Computer

You use the *DSMod Computer* command to modify the properties of one or more existing computer objects (desktops and member servers) in the Active Directory database. The syntax of this command is:

```
DSMod Computer ComputerDN ... [-desc Description] [-loc Location] [-disabled
{yes | no}] [-reset] [{-s Server | -d Domain}] [-u UserName] [-p {Password | *}]
[-c] [-q] [{-uc | -uco | -uci}]
```

You can use the −*reset* parameter to reset the computer account in Active Directory. Most of the other parameters of this command are similar to the ones discussed earlier regarding the *DSAdd Computer* command. Remember that you can modify only a subset of the attributes of the computer object with this command.

DSMod Contact

You use the *DSMod Contact* command to modify the properties of one or more existing contacts in the Active Directory database. The syntax of this command is:

```
DSMod Contact ContactDN ... [-fn FirstName] [-mi Initial] [-ln LastName] [-
display DisplayName] [-desc Description] [-office Office] [-tel PhoneNumber] [-
email Email] [-hometel HomePhoneNumber] [-pager PagerNumber] [-mobile
CellPhoneNumber] [-fax FaxNumber] [-iptel IPPhoneNumber] [-title Title] [-dept
Department] [-company Company] [{-s Server | -d Domain}] [-u UserName] [-p
{Password | *}] [-c] [-q] [{-uc | -uco | -uci}]
```

The parameters used for this command are similar to the parameters used with the *DSAdd Contact* command.

DSMod Group

You use the *DSMod Group* command to modify the properties of one or more existing groups in the Active Directory database. The syntax of this command is:

```
DSMod Group GroupDN ... [-samid SAMName] [-desc Description] [-secgrp {yes |
no}] [-scope {l | g | u}] [{-addmbr | -rmmbr | -chmbr} MemberDN ...] [{-s Server
| -d Domain}] [-u UserName] [-p {Password | *}] [-c] [-q] [{-uc | -uco | -uci}]
```

The *DSMod Group* command allows you to add, remove, or replace members in specified group(s) by using one of the following parameters with the *MemberDN ...* parameter:

- **-addmbr** Used to add one or more members to the group specified by the *MemberDN* parameter.

- **-rmmbr** Used to remove one or more members from the group specified by the *MemberDN* parameter.

- **-chmbr** Used to replace members specified by the *MemberDN* parameter.

Remember that you can use only one of the parameters from *–addmbr, -rmmbr,* and *–chmbr* and the parameter must be followed by a list of members (*MemberDN ...*). This command uses several parameters that are similar to the parameters used with the *DSAdd Group* command.

> **NOTE**
>
> The *DSMod Group* command uses two parameters for which you can provide the input either from the command line or from standard input. These parameters are *GroupDN ...* and *MemberDN ....* The command allows you to omit only one of the parameters so that the value of the omitted parameter can be supplied from standard input. You cannot omit both the *GroupDN ...* and the *MemberDN ...* parameters. One of the parameters must be supplied from the command line.

DSMod OU

You use the *DSMod OU* command to modify the properties of one or more existing OUs in the Active Directory database. The syntax of this command is:

```
DSMod OU OrganizationalUnitDN ... [-desc Description] [{-s Server | -d Domain}]
[-u UserName] [-p {Password | *}] [-c] [-q] [{-uc | -uco | -uci}]
```

The parameters you use with this command are similar to the parameters you use with the *DSAdd OU* command.

www.syngress.com

DSMod Server

You use the *DSMod Server* command to modify the properties of one or more existing server objects (domain controllers) in the Active Directory database. The syntax of this command is:

```
DSMod Server ServerDN ... [-desc Description] [-isgc {yes | no}] [{-s Server | -
d Domain}] [-u UserName] [-p {Password | *}] [-c] [-q] [{-uc | -uco | -uci}]
```

The parameters you use for this command are similar to the parameters you use with the *DSAdd Server* command.

DSMod User

You use the *DSMod User* command to modify the properties of one or more existing user objects in the Active Directory database. The syntax of this command is:

```
DSMod User UserDN ... [-upn UPN] [-fn FirstName] [-mi Initial] [-ln LastName] [-
display DisplayName] [-empid EmployeeID] [-pwd (Password | *)] [-desc
Description] [-office Office] [-tel PhoneNumber] [-email E-mailAddress] [-hometel
HomePhoneNumber] [-pager PagerNumber] [-mobile CellPhoneNumber] [-fax FaxNumber]
[-iptel IPPhoneNumber] [-webpg WebPage] [-title Title] [-dept Department] [-
company Company] [-mgr Manager] [-hmdir HomeDirectory] [-hmdrv DriveLetter:] [-
profile ProfilePath] [-loscr ScriptPath] [-mustchpwd {yes | no}] [-canchpwd {yes |
no}] [-reversiblepwd {yes | no}] [-pwdneverexpires {yes | no}] [-acctexpires
NumberOfDays] [-disabled {yes | no}] [{-s Server | -d Domain}] [-u UserName] [-p
{Password | *}] [-c] [-q] [{-uc | -uco | -uci}]
```

The parameters you use for this command are similar to the parameters you use with the *DSAdd User* command. Remember that you can modify only a subset of the attributes of the user object with this command.

DSMod Quota

You use the *DSMod Quota* command to modify the properties of one or more existing quota objects in the Active Directory database. The syntax of this command is:

```
DSMod Quota QuotaDN ... [-qlimit Value] [-desc Description] [{-s Server | -d
Domain}] [-u UserName] [-p {Password | *}] [-c] [-q] [{-uc | -uco | -uci}]
```

You use the *–qlimit Value* parameter to change the quota limit specification to a number given as *Value* for the quota specification(s) identified by the *QuotaDN* parameter. The quota limit refers to the number of directory objects a security principal can own in a directory partition. You can specify *-1* for the *Value* argument to set an unlimited quota.

Remember that you can modify only a subset of the attributes of the specified quota object with this command.

DSMod Partition

You use the *DSMod Partition* command to modify the properties of one or more existing directory partitions in the Active Directory database. The syntax of this command is:

```
DSMod Partition PartitionDN ... [-qdefault Value] [-qtmbstnwt Percent] [{-s
Server | -d Domain}] [-u UserName] [-p {Password | *}] [-c] [-q] [{-uc | -uco |
-uci}]
```

The parameters specific to the *DSMod Partition* command are as follows:

- **-qdefault Value** Used to change the default quota for the directory partition to *Value*. The default quota applies to any security principal for whom the quota has not been set.

- **-qtmbstnwt Percent** Used to set the percentage by which the tombstone object count is reduced when the quota usage is calculated. The value of the *Percent* argument must be between *0* and *100*.

Remember that you can modify only a subset of the attributes of the specified partition object with this command.

Moving and Renaming Objects with DSMove

You use the *DSMove* command to move an Active Directory object from one container to another container within a domain. You can also use this command to rename an object by specifying the old name and the new name. You can rename an object without moving it within the directory tree in Active Directory. The syntax of this command is:

```
DSMove ObjectDN [-newname NewName] [-newparent ParentDN] [{-s Server | -d
Domain}] [-u UserName] [-p {Password | *}] [-q] [{-uc | -uco | -uci}]
```

The parameters specific to the *DSMove* command are as follows:

- **ObjectDN** A required parameter that specifies the DN of the object that you want to move or rename. If you omit this parameter, the command will attempt to get this parameter through standard input.

- **-newname NewName** Specifies the new RDN of the object.

- **-newparent NewParent** Specifies the DN of the new parent container within the Active Directory hierarchy.

It is also possible to combine the move and rename operations with a single command. The *—newname NewName* parameter allows you to specify a new DN for the object. The *DSMove* command allows you to rename an object after moving it. When you use the *—newparent ParentDN* parameter, you are actually moving the specified object to a new container in Active Directory.

> **NOTE**
>
> You can use the *DSMove* command only to move or rename objects with the current domain or the domain specified by the *—d Domain* parameter. You cannot use this command to move objects across domains. If you need to move objects from one domain to another domain, you must use the *MoveTree* command. The *MoveTree* command is available as part of the Windows Support Tools.

Deleting Directory Objects with DSRm

You use the *DSRm* command to remove (delete) a specified object from the Active Directory database. The specified object is permanently deleted from Active Directory and there is no way that you can recall it. The syntax of this command is:

```
DSRm ObjectDN ... [-subtree [-exclude]] [-noprompt] [{-s Server | -d Domain}] [-
u UserName] [-p {Password | *}][-c][-q][{-uc | -uco | -uci}]
```

The parameters specific to the *DSRm* command are as follows:

- **ObjectDN ...** A required parameter that specifies the DN of the object that you want to move or rename. If you omit this parameter, the command will attempt to get this parameter through standard input.

- **-subtree [-exclude]** Used to specify that the specified object and all objects under the subtree be deleted. The *—exclude* parameter specifies that the base object specified by the *—ObjectDN* parameter should not be deleted. You can use the *—exclude* parameter only when you use the *—subtree* parameter. For example, you can delete all objects under *OU Production* but leave *OU Production* intact; you can use the *—exclude* parameter along with the *—subtree* parameter.

- **-noprompt** Used to suppress the display of a message to confirm the deletion of the specified object. By default, you are prompted to confirm the delete operation.

WARNING

DSRm is the most powerful command of all the DS commands discussed in this chapter. If you delete an object by mistake, there is no way to recall it. So, be careful when using the *DSRm* command in a live production environment. If you want to experiment with *DSRm* or any of the DS commands, do so in a test environment.

Summary

In this chapter, we introduced you to the basic syntax of the DS commands for managing Active Directory objects. The object classes that you can use with DS commands include computers (desktops and member servers), contacts, users, groups, servers (domain controllers), OUs, sites, subnets, quotas, and directory partitions. We learned how to use the *DSQuery* command with different types of objects to search for objects in Active Directory. We also learned that you can use the *DSGet* command to display properties of specified objects; the *DSAdd* and *DSRm* commands to add objects to or remove objects from the directory database, respectively; the *DSMod* command to modify certain properties of specified objects; and the *DSMove* command to move objects from one container to another within the domain. In the next chapter, we will explore the DS commands further to see how to use them to manage directory objects such as users, groups, and computers.

Chapter 11

Managing Active Directory Users, Groups, and Computers

Topics in this chapter:

- Managing User Accounts
- Managing Group Accounts
- Managing Computer Accounts
- Managing Domain Controller Accounts

Introduction

In the preceding chapter, we took a tour of various DS commands included with the Windows Server 2003 operating system. The DS commands are a powerful set of command-line utilities that you can use to manage Active Directory objects such as users, groups, and computers. In this chapter, we will look at some common issues concerning Active Directory object management which you can resolve using the DS commands. We will look at some examples of DS commands in use, and discuss how to use them to query, add, modify, move, and remove Active Directory objects such as users, groups, and computers.

You can manage accounts in Active Directory from the command line in three ways:

1. Using the DS family of commands (*DSAdd, DSMod, DSRm, DSMove, DSQuery, DSGet*) for individual actions

2. Using *csvde* for creating individual or multiple new account objects from a Comma Separated Value (CSV) import file

3. Using *ldifde* for creating, modifying, or deleting individual or multiple new account objects from a Lightweight Data Interchange Format (LDIF) import file

This chapter will focus on the first method. Methods two and three are discussed in the sidebar titled "Master Craftsman: Using Import Files to Work on Multiple Objects."

Managing User Accounts

Users are the heart of any organization and managing their credentials in Active Directory will, in all likelihood, consume more time than any other activity. The ability to perform a complete range of administration activities on user accounts from the command line facilitates strict control and precision, as well as the ability to automate routine repetitive tasks through simple shell scripts. This section will describe how to perform the most common user account-related administrative tasks using a handful of commands; namely, *DSQuery, DSGet, DSAdd, DSMove, DSMod*, and *DSRm*.

The one piece of information that is required for every command in the DS family of commands is the Active Directory Object Distinguished Name, or *ObjectDN*. The ObjectDN consists of the object's account name and its precise location in the Active Directory domain structure. For example:

```
CN=Brian Barber,OU=Ottawa,DC=ad,DC=commandlinepros,DC=com
```

The preceding ObjectDN indicates that the common name (CN) is Brian Barber, and that the account is stored in the Ottawa organizational unit (OU) within the ad.commandlinepros.com domain (DC). The requirement to specify the exact object is critical for ensuring that other similarly named objects or objects located in close proximity are not accidentally added, modified, or, in the worst case, deleted.

Master Craftsman...

Using Import Files to Work on Multiple Objects

Sometimes the number of objects to be created or modified vastly outstrips the amount of time and number of people an organization can devote to performing these tasks individually. In these situations, you can "bulk import" objects from the command line using one of two utilities: *csvde* (CSV Directory Exchange) or *ldifde* (LDAP Data Interchange Format Directory Exchange).

The utility you choose depends on the task you need to complete. If you need to create objects, you can use either *csvde* or *ldifde*; if you need to change or delete objects, you must use *ldifde* because only *ldifde* allows you to modify existing objects. *csvde* uses files formatted in the Microsoft CSV format. The advantage of this format is that it is widely supported and easy to edit in any text editor or spreadsheet that can work with comma-delimited files. You can use *ldifde* to extend the Active Directory schema, export data from Active Directory in LDIF format (an Internet standard file format for performing batch import and export operations that conform to Lightweight Directory Access Protocol [LDAP] standards), or populate Active Directory.

You launch both utilities from the command line. You can use the following syntax to import with both *csvde* and *ldifde*:

```
csvde -or- ldifde [-i] [-f FileName] [-s ServerName] [-c String1 String2]
[-v] [-t PortNumber] [-k] [-a UserDistinguishedName Password] [-b
UserName Domain Password]
```

Table 11.1 describes the switches.

Table 11.1 csvde and ldifde Arguments

Switch	Description
–i	Indicates import mode (export mode is the default).
–f FileName	Identifies the file used for importing.
–s ServerName	Identifies the server that will process the import.
–c String1 String2	Specifies that all instances of *String1* will be replaced with *String2*.
–v	Specifies verbose output.
–t PortNumber	Specifies the port number on the server used for inbound connections: 389 for LDAP and 3268 for Global Catalog (GC) servers.

Continued

Table 11.1 continued csvde and ldifde Arguments	
Switch	Description
–k	Instructs the utility to ignore errors during the import process and continue processing.
–a UserDistinguishedName Password	Provides "run as" credentials for the import process.
–b UserName Domain Password	Provides "run as" credentials for the import process.

Many of the commands in this chapter are designed to be run on individual objects. However, you can "pipe" them together to permit manipulation of multiple objects. (Please refer to the sidebar "Swiss Army Knife: UNIX-Style 'Plumbing' with DSx Commands," for more information.) The creation, modification, or deletion of a large quantity of objects is a huge undertaking and one that you do not perform every day (or even every year); however, when you need to do it, *csvde* and *ldifde* come to the rescue. You must create the import files carefully and test them extensively to ensure accuracy. Once you do this, you can complete this cumbersome and potentially risky operation cleanly with a fraction of the resources usually required when manipulating each object individually.

Searching for Users in Active Directory

As we saw in the preceding chapter, you can use *DSQuery* to locate and retrieve information on any object in your Active Directory forest (or forests). Specifying the "user" object type after *DSQuery* focuses the search on user account objects, and will return information on user accounts located anywhere in your organization's implementation of Active Directory. For example, you can search for user accounts in the Winnipeg OU of the ad.commandlinepros. com domain that have been inactive for more than two weeks with the following command:

```
dsquery user OU=Winnipeg,DC=ad,DC=commandlinepros,DC=com -inactive 2
```

Although this is useful information on its own, the power of these command-line utilities is demonstrated when you use this *DSQuery* command to feed (or pipe) information into other commands for additional account management operations. (Please see the sidebar "Swiss Army Knife: UNIX-Style 'Plumbing' with DSx Commands" for additional details.)

As mentioned in the preceding chapter, the command syntax for *DSQuery User* is:

```
DSQuery User [{StartNode | forestroot | domainroot}] [-o {dn | rdn | upn |
samid}] [-scope {subtree | onelevel | base}] [-name Name] [-desc Description]
[-upn UPN] [-samid SAMName] [-inactive NumberOfWeeks] [-stalepwd NumberOfDays]
[-disabled] [{-s Server | -d Domain}] [-u UserName] [-p {Password | *}] [-q] [-r]
[-gc] [-limit NumberOfObjects] [{-s Server | -d Domain}] [-u UserName] [-p
{Password | *}] [-q] [{-uc | -uco | -uci}]
```

To search for all user accounts in your Active Directory forest, simply enter **dsquery user** at the command line, as shown in Figure 11.1. In the first example in the screenshot,

DSQuery User has returned all user accounts in all containers. The second execution of *DSQuery* has been augmented with a *StartNode* (*OU=Montreal,DC=ad,DC=commandlinepros,DC=com*) to search for and return all user accounts in the Montreal OU.

Figure 11.1 Searching for User Accounts

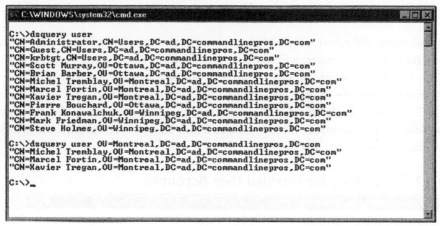

The *–name, –desc, –upn,* and *–samid* switches enable you to search for specific full names (such as Michel Tremblay), descriptions (such as Project Manager), User Principal Names (UPNs, entered as michel.tremblay@ad.commandlinepros.com), and user identifiers (a.k.a. login IDs, such as mtremblay), respectively. You can use shell wildcards (? and *) with the *DSQuery* command. In addition, to assist in administering the security of Active Directory, *–inactive* and *–stalepwd* will return accounts where the user has not logged on for a specified number of weeks and has not changed his or her password in a specified number of days. The user of the *–disabled* switch is described in the next section.

> **! WARNING**
>
> In the parlance of database queries, every switch you add to *DSQuery* is treated as a Boolean AND, which makes your query more restrictive. For example:
> > dsquery user OU=Montreal,DC=ad,DC=commandlinepros,DC=com –name Sally* –desc Accountant –stalepwd 60
>
> The preceding command will search for accounts that belong to someone named Sally who is an accountant in Montreal and has not changed her password in 60 days. Unless you are searching for a particular individual's account, this query will probably turn up few, if any, results. The general rule of thumb is to use the fewest switches possible in order to return the information you require. It is usually best to start with a broad query that returns many results and then to narrow it down from there.

Searching for Disabled User Accounts

The *–disabled* command-line switch permits searching for disabled user accounts. This switch is common to both user accounts and computer accounts. You use the following basic syntax to search for disabled user accounts:

dsquery user -disabled

This command will return all disabled accounts everywhere in your Active Directory implementation, as demonstrated with the first command in Figure 11.2. Because this returned a number of unwanted results, the search was narrowed to a particular OU—Montreal, in this example—by specifying a *StartNode* of *OU=Montreal,DC=ad,DC=commandlinepros,DC=com*. As a result, all disabled user accounts in Montreal are displayed. As stated earlier, you could pipe the results of this command into another command, such as *DSRm*, to remove the disabled user accounts.

Figure 11.2 Searching for Disabled User Accounts

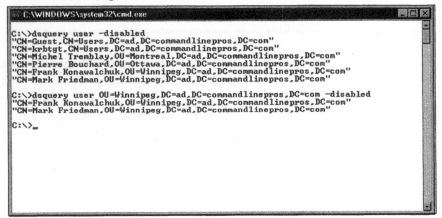

```
C:\>dsquery user -disabled
"CN=Guest,CN=Users,DC=ad,DC=commandlinepros,DC=com"
"CN=krbtgt,CN=Users,DC=ad,DC=commandlinepros,DC=com"
"CN=Michel Tremblay,OU=Montreal,DC=ad,DC=commandlinepros,DC=com"
"CN=Pierre Bouchard,OU=Ottawa,DC=ad,DC=commandlinepros,DC=com"
"CN=Frank Konawalchuk,OU=Winnipeg,DC=ad,DC=commandlinepros,DC=com"
"CN=Mark Friedman,OU=Winnipeg,DC=ad,DC=commandlinepros,DC=com"

C:\>dsquery user OU=Winnipeg,DC=ad,DC=commandlinepros,DC=com -disabled
"CN=Frank Konawalchuk,OU=Winnipeg,DC=ad,DC=commandlinepros,DC=com"
"CN=Mark Friedman,OU=Winnipeg,DC=ad,DC=commandlinepros,DC=com"

C:\>_
```

NOTE

If there are any blank spaces in your search criteria, you will need to enclose the search criteria in quotation marks. Using a slightly modified example from this section, if you wanted to search for disabled user accounts in the Montreal Finance OU, you would need to enter the following as your search criteria:
OU=Montreal Finance,DC=ad,DC=commandlinepros,DC=com
You do this to ensure that the command is properly parsed, and processed the way you intended it to be.

Determining Group Memberships of Users

Although *DSQuery* is useful for locating objects of a particular type that meet certain criteria, it will not return information on the objects' properties. This is a job for *DSGet*, which has two complementary purposes. The first purpose of the *DSGet* command is to display the specified properties (or attributes) of all manner of Active Directory objects. In this case, *DSGet* uses the following syntax:

```
dsget user UserDN [-dn] [-samid] [-sid] [-upn] [-fn] [-mi] [-ln] [-display]
[-empid] [-desc] [-office] [-tel] [-email] [-hometel] [-pager] [-mobile] [-fax]
[-iptel] [-webpg] [-title] [-dept] [-company] [-mgr] [-hmdir] [-hmdrv] [-profile]
[-loscr] [-mustchpwd] [-canchpwd] [-pwdneverexpires] [-disabled] [-acctexpires]
[-reversiblepwd] [-part PartitionDN [-qlimit] [-qused]] [{-s Server | -d Domain}]
[-u UserName] [-p {Password | *}] [-q] [{-uc | -uco | -uci}]
```

The second purpose, and the one we are interested in for this section, is to return the groups to which a particular user belongs. In this case, you would use the following syntax:

```
dsget user UserDN [-memberof] [b] [{-uc | -uco | -uci}]
```

In Figure 11.3, the first execution of *DSGet* displays group membership information for the user account Brian Barber. The second execution displays the group membership for the Administrator account. This command is useful for troubleshooting permissions issues, especially when a user reports that he or she cannot do something (or when the user is discovered to be doing something that he or she should not be doing).

Figure 11.3 Retrieving a User's Group Membership Information

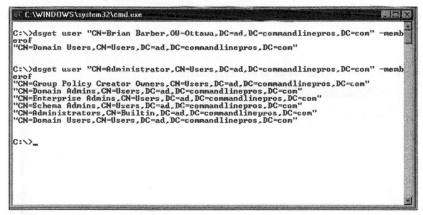

> **TIP**
>
> The flip side of *dsget user –memberof*, which displays the groups of which an individual user is a member, is *dsget group –members*, which displays the members of a particular group.

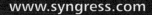

Creating New User Accounts

You can create user accounts from the command line using the *DSAdd* command. Here is the syntax to use to create a new account:

```
dsadd user UserDN [-samid SAMName] [-upn UPN] [-fn FirstName] [-mi Initial] [-ln
LastName] [-display DisplayName] [-empid EmployeeID] [-pwd {Password | *}] [-desc
Description] [-memberof Group] [-office Office] [-tel PhoneNumber] [-email E-mail]
[-hometel HomePhoneNumber] [-pager PagerNumber] [-mobile CellPhoneNumber] [-fax
FaxNumber] [-iptel IPPhoneNumber] [-webpg WebPage] [-title Title] [-dept
Department] [-company Company] [-mgr Manager] [-hmdir HomeDirectory] [-hmdrv
DriveLetter:] [-profile ProfilePath] [-loscr ScriptPath] [-mustchpwd {yes | no}]
[-canchpwd {yes | no}] [-reversiblepwd {yes | no}] [-pwdneverexpires {yes | no}]
[-acctexpires NumberOfDays] [-disabled {yes | no}] [{-s Server | -d Domain}] [-u
UserName] [-p {Password | *}] [-q] [{-uc | -uco | -uci}]
```

From the description of the modifier that follows each switch, you can probably discern the user account properties that you can add when creating a user account. Most of these properties are optional. The only required information is the User distinguished name (UserDN); therefore, the following is the most basic command syntax for creating a user:

dsadd user "CN=John Smith,OU=Ottawa,DC=ad,DC=commandlinepros,DC=com"

If you do not use the *–samid* switch, Active Directory will create a Security Account Manager (SAM) account name from the first 20 characters of the CN of the UserDN, including spaces, and the account will be disabled.

Figure 11.4 demonstrates using the *DSAdd* command to create a new user, John Smith, in the Ottawa OU using the following command:

dsadd user "CN=John Smith,OU=Ottawa,DC=ad,DC=commandlinepros,DC=com" –samid
jsmith –pwd Welcome!

Figure 11.4 Creating a New User Account

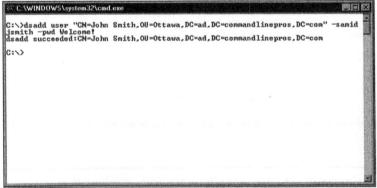

In this example, the *–pwd* modifier sets "Welcome!" as the initial account password. If you want the user to set the password the first time he or she logs on with the new account, you can use *–pwd* *) and the user will be prompted to enter the password. Furthermore, because the *–pwd* switch was used, the account will be enabled when created; if the *–pwd* switch is not used when the account is created, the account will be disabled until an administrator enables the account through Active Directory Users and Computers or using the command *dsmod user UserDN –disabled no*, described later in this chapter. If you want to ensure that the user changes the password the next time he or she logs on with the new account, you should append the command used in the example with the *–mustchpwd yes* switch.

Setting and Modifying User Account Properties

Now that you know how to create and locate user accounts, as well as display their properties, we can begin adding properties that were previously left unset and changing existing properties. For this, you can use a new command, *DSMod*. *DSMod* replaces the contents of an identified field with the new value specified with a particular switch. If the field is empty, the property is set; if the field is populated, the existing property is overwritten with the new property.

WARNING

Be very careful when using *DSMod* to modify an object's properties. It will not prompt you to confirm the change; it will simply overwrite the value, and the action is irreversible.

The number of options available for modifying user accounts with *DSMod* is the same as what is available when creating an account with *DSAdd*. The following is the syntax for *DSMod*:

```
dsmod user UserDN [-upn UPN] [-fn FirstName] [-mi Initial] [-ln LastName]
[-display DisplayName] [-empid EmployeeID] [-pwd (Password | *)] [-desc
Description] [-office Office] [-tel PhoneNumber] [-email E-mailAddress] [-hometel
HomePhoneNumber] [-pager PagerNumber] [-mobile CellPhoneNumber] [-fax FaxNumber]
[-iptel IPPhoneNumber] [-webpg WebPage] [-title Title] [-dept Department]
[-company Company] [-mgr Manager] [-hmdir HomeDirectory] [-hmdrv DriveLetter:]
[-profile ProfilePath] [-loscr ScriptPath] [-mustchpwd {yes | no}] [-canchpwd {yes
| no}] [-reversiblepwd {yes | no}] [-pwdneverexpires {yes | no}] [-acctexpires
NumberOfDays] [-disabled {yes | no}] [{-s Server | -d Domain}] [-u UserName] [-p
{Password | *}] [-c] [-q] [{-uc | -uco | -uci}]
```

Displayed in Figure 11.5, the command syntax for the example is:

```
dsmod user UserDN -office Office -tel PhoneNumber -fax FaxNumber
```

The preceding command translates to:

```
dsmod user "CN=John Smith,OU=Ottawa, DC=ad,DC=commandlinepros,DC=com"
-office "Cubicle 21b" -tel (555)321-4321 -fax (555)321-1234
```

Figure 11.5 Modifying a User's Contact Information

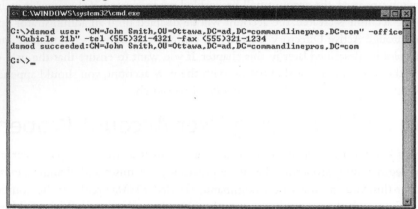

A quick check of the user account properties in Active Directory Users and Computers, shown in Figure 11.6, demonstrates that the contact information for our new user, John Smith, was added or modified using *DSMod*. You also can confirm this information using *DSGet* from the command line with the following syntax:

dsget user "CN=John Smith,OU=Ottawa, DC=ad,DC=commandlinepros,DC=com" -office -tel -fax

Figure 11.6 Confirming That the New Properties Have Been Set

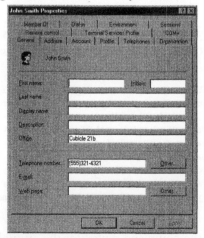

Moving and Renaming User Accounts

You use the *DSMove* command to move a single existing object in Active Directory within the same domain from one location to another. You also can use *DSMove* to rename an object. This command uses the following syntax:

```
dsmove ObjectDN [-newname NewName] [-newparent ParentDN] [{-s Server | -d
Domain}] [-u UserName] [-p {Password | *}] [-q] [{-uc | -uco | -uci}]
```

> **NOTE**
>
> Both the *DSMove* and *DSRm* commands do not require that you specify the object type. For these commands, all that is required immediately following the command is the Active Directory object's ObjectDN. All other commands in the DS family of commands require the object type and the ObjectDN.

In Figure 11.7, John Smith's user account is being moved from the Ottawa OU to the Montreal OU. For this operation, the command syntax is very straightforward:

```
dsmove UserDN -newparent ParentDN
```

In the example shown in Figure 11.7, the UserDN is enclosed in quotation marks because the account name, John Smith, has a space between the first and last names.

Figure 11.7 Moving a User Account to a New OU

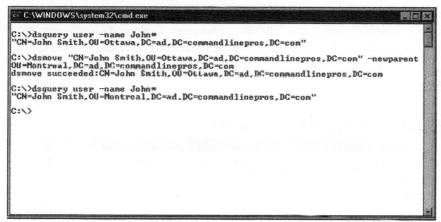

In Figure 11.8, John Smith's name has been misspelled and his user account is being renamed. To rename users (and all other Active Directory objects), the syntax for *DSMod* is slightly different from what you use to move objects:

```
dsmove UserDN -newname NewName
```

Note that the new name of the object is all that is required after the *–newname* switch. Specifying the ObjectDN will result in an error.

Figure 11.8 Renaming a User Account

Resetting User Passwords

One of the most common activities for a network administrator, if not the most common, is resetting user passwords. It's easy to reset a user's password from the command line using the *DSMod* command with the following syntax:

dsmod user *UserDN* **-pwd** *NewPassword* **-mustchpwd** {*yes|no*}.

Using the *–mustchpwd* switch produces the same result as checking the box for "User must change password at next logon" in Active Directory Users and Computers. Figure 11.9 demonstrates use of *DSMod* to reset John Smythe's password using the following command:

```
dsmod user "CN=John Smythe,CN=Users,DC=ad,DC=commandlinepros,DC=com" -pwd *
-mustchpwd yes
```

Figure 11.9 Resetting a User's Password

In this example, John Smythe's user account password was set to "ChangeYourPassword!" and he will be forced to enter a new password at his next successful logon.

WARNING

If you specify a new account password (as opposed to using *–pwd* *), the new password must conform to your domain's password policy requirements. Failure to do so will produce an error message.

Enabling and Disabling User Accounts

Another common use of *DSMod* is enabling and disabling computer and user accounts from the command line. Disabling user accounts is a good practice for preventing authentication by inactive users, such as a user who leaves an organization. For enabling and disabling user accounts, you can use the following syntax:

dsmod user *UserDN* **-disabled** {*yes|no*}

Figure 11.10 demonstrates the use of *DSMod* to disable Michel Tremblay's user account. In this situation, the command is:

dsmod user "CN=Michel
Tremblay,OU=Montreal,DC=ad,DC=commandlinepros,DC=com" –disabled yes

Again, the UserDN is in quotation marks because of the space in the account name. You use the technique for searching for disabled users, explained earlier, to confirm that the account was enabled prior to running the *DSMod* command and is disabled after running it.

Figure 11.10 Disabling a User Account

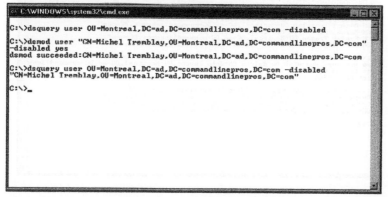

You can use the same command structure for disabling a user account to enable a disabled account, except that the modifier for the *–disabled* switch is changed from *yes* to *no*. Figure 11.11 shows how to enable a user account and confirm that it is enabled with *DSQuery*.

Figure 11.11 Enabling a Disabled User Account

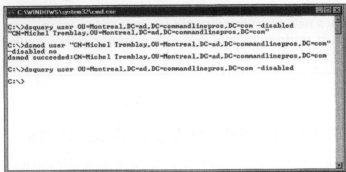

Deleting User Accounts

The final stage in the life cycle of a user account is its outright removal from Active Directory. You can delete any object from the command line using the *DSRm* command by entering **dsrm**, followed by the ObjectDN (*dsrm ObjectDN*). In Figure 11.12, the following command is used to delete John Smythe's user account:

```
dsrm "CN=John Smythe,OU=Montreal,DC=ad,DC=commandlinepros,DC=com"
```

With this command, you will be prompted to confirm deletion of the object. Quite intuitively, entering **y** (for "yes") will instruct *DSRm* to continue deleting the object, and **n** (for "no") will cancel the operation.

Figure 11.12 Deleting a User Account

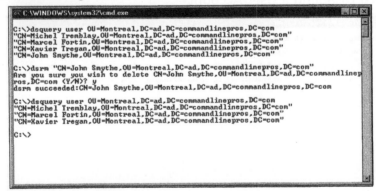

NOTE

In identical fashion to *DSMove*, the *DSRm* command does not require identification of the object type, such as "user", "computer", "server", or "group", among others. Specifying the object type when using *DSRm* will result in a syntax error.

Swiss Army Knife...

UNIX-Style "Plumbing" with DSx Commands

Throughout this chapter, we have been looking at *DSQuery*, *DSMod*, *DSGet*, *DSMove*, and *DSRm*, and how they work on their own for specific tasks. You can see the real power of these DS commands in Active Directory administration, however, when you combine their capabilities. You combine them using a pipe, or "|".

Anyone familiar with shell scripting in UNIX knows that you can pass data from one command to another command by "plumbing" the commands together in sequential order with a pipe or a tee. For example, in UNIX, if you want to find a filename in the present working directory that contains the string *"acct"*, you can enter **ls –al | grep "acct"**, and the directory listing will be piped into the *grep* command that will, in turn, filter out all filenames that do not contain the string *"acct"* and print the returned data to the screen.

Microsoft has provided this functionality for working with the DS commands. Specifically, *DSMod*, *DSGet*, *DSMove*, and *DSRm* support piping data from *DSQuery*. Normally, you use *DSMod*, *DSGet*, *DSMove*, and *DSRm* for operations on individual objects. In reality, network administrators are very busy and frequently need to work on multiple objects which, if performed repetitively on individual objects, wastes valuable time. For example, an administrator could run *"dsquery computer –inactive 8"* in order to find computer accounts that have been inactive for more than eight weeks, and then run *DSRm* and the Computer distinguished name (ComputerDN) for every computer account in the list produced by *DSQuery*. Or the administrator could run *"dsquery computer –inactive 8 | dsrm"* once and the operation would be complete. As a second example, if you needed to add the description "Accountant" to everyone in the Accounting group, you could run the following:

```
dsquery user –memberof Accounting | dsmod user –desc
Accountant
```

Normally, you can run *DSMod* only on individual objects; however, all of the user accounts returned by *DSQuery*, when piped into *DSMod*, can be modified at once. The combinations are virtually endless.

Managing Group Accounts

Groups greatly reduce the effort required to manage a number of users with similar access requirements. Instead of administering each user individually, you can assemble users into groups by role or function, and ascribe permissions to the groups. In this section, we will discuss a wide variety of group administration activities. In many respects, the management of groups mirrors that of users.

Searching for Group Accounts in Active Directory

With newer releases of Windows Server, the types of groups have been expanded. This increase in functionality comes with an increase in complexity. The ability to search for groups by their specific location in Active Directory, or by their name or description, makes group management much more straightforward. The following is the complete syntax for the *dsquery group* command:

```
dsquery group [{StartNode | forestroot | domainroot}] [-o {dn | rdn | samid}]
[-scope {subtree | onelevel | base}] [-name Filter] [-desc Description] [-samid
SAMName] [{-s Server | -d Domain}] [-u UserName] [-p {Password | *}] [-q] [-r]
[-gc] [-limit NumberOfObjects] [{-uc | -uco | -uci}]
```

Figure 11.13 demonstrates how to search for a group by name. If you do not specify a place to start searching, *dsquery group* will search the current forest. Using the example in Figure 11.13, groups of all types and scopes where the account name begins with "man" will be returned. You could narrow the search (and increase its speed) using the *–scope* switch.

Figure 11.13 Searching for Groups

> ⚠ **WARNING**
>
> There is no switch for querying by group type (security and distribution) or scope (universal, global, or local). All group types and scopes will be returned.

Creating New Group Accounts

You can create new groups from the command line using the *dsadd group* command. The syntax required to create a new group is:

```
dsadd group GroupDN [-secgrp {yes | no}] [-scope {l | g | u}] [-samid SAMName]
[-desc Description] [-memberof Group] [-members Member ...] [{-s Server | -d
Domain}] [-u UserName] [-p {Password | *}] [-q] [{-uc | -uco | -uci}]
```

The only required element for the *DSAdd* group is the Group distinguished name (GroupDN). In Figure 11.14, a global security group called Marketing is created at the root of the *ad.commandlinepros.com* domain with the description of "All Members of Local Marketing Teams." No members were added in this example. You can add members when a group is created by adding the *–members* switch and a list of UserDNs, separated by spaces.

Figure 11.14 Creating a New Group

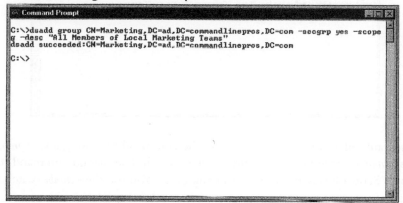

> **NOTE**
>
> Entering *dsadd group GroupDN* with any switches will create a global security group with a SAM account name that is the same as the CN and no members. You can add members later.

Managing Membership of Groups

A group is nothing without its members. You use the *dsmod group* command for setting and modifying the properties of groups. The focus of this section is on managing group memberships. The following is the complete syntax for *dsmod group*:

```
dsmod group GroupDN [-samid SAMName] [-desc Description] [-secgrp {yes | no}]
[-scope {l | g | u}] [{-addmbr | -rmmbr | -chmbr} MemberDN ...] [{-s Server | -d
Domain}] [-u UserName] [-p {Password | *}] [-c] [-q] [{-uc | -uco | -uci}]
```

The GroupDN is immutable; however, you can change the SAM account name as well as the group description, type, and scope. In the next section, we will use *dsmod group* to modify the properties of group accounts.

The exact syntax for adding a member to a group is *dsmod group GroupDN –addmbr MemberDN.* The first command issued in Figure 11.15 demonstrates this command by adding Scott Murray's user account to the Marketing group using the following command:

```
dsmod group "CN=Marketing,DC=ad,DC=commandlinepros,DC=com" -addmbr "CN=Scott
Murray,OU=Ottawa,DC=ad,DC=commandlinepros,DC=com"
```

Figure 11.15 Adding and Removing a Member from a Group

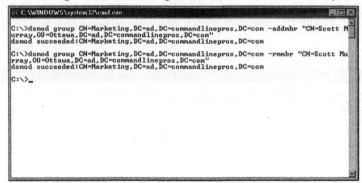

You also can remove group members from the command line using *dsmod group*, except you use the *–rmmbr* switch rather than the *–addmbr* switch. The second command in Figure 11.15 removes Scott Murray from the Marketing group. You use the *–chmbr* switch to replace the entire list of group members.

The example in Figure 11.15 demonstrates the addition and removal of a single group member. You can add or remove many members simultaneously by entering, after the appropriate switch, the UserDN of each desired member, separated by a space.

Modifying Group Account Properties

You also can use the *dsmod group* command to modify group properties from the command line. As mentioned earlier, *dsmod group* can set or modify the SAM account name, group description, type, and scope. To demonstrate this, we will modify the group type (security and distribution) and scope (local, global, and universal).

You modify the group type using the following syntax:

```
dsmod group GroupDN [-secgrp {yes | no}]
```

Because there are only two types of group, you use the *–secgrp* switch with a *yes* or *no* modifier. Entering *yes* changes a distribution group to a security group; *no* converts a security group to a distribution group. Figure 11.16 demonstrates the use of *dsmod group* to convert the Marketing security group to a distribution group.

Figure 11.16 Changing the Group Type

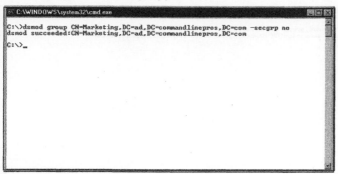

> **NOTE**
>
> You cannot change the group type if the domain functional level is Mixed Mode. The domain functional level must be Windows 2003 Native Mode.

You can change the group scope in a similar way. Use the following syntax:

dsmod group *GroupDN* **[-scope** {*l* | *g* | *u*}**]**

Because there are three possible scopes (local, global, and universal), you must specify the scope using the *–scope* switch with an *l* (local), *g* (global), or *u* (universal). The modifier will change the current group scope to the newly specified scope. Figure 11.17 demonstrates use of *dsmod group* to convert the Marketing global group to a universal group.

> **WARNING**
>
> Although the *dsget group* command will return the DN of the group and a description, it cannot return the group type (security or distribution) or scope (universal, global, or local). Active Directory Users and Computers can provide this information.

You must use Active Directory Users and Computers to confirm that the change in type or scope has been made. Navigate to the proper container and right-click on the appropriate group object; left-click on the **Properties** entry of the **Context menu**. The group type and scope are visible on the General tab.

Figure 11.17 Changing the Group Scope

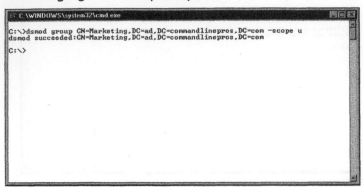

> **NOTE**
>
> The *dsmod group* command does not support changing from a domain local group to a global group.

Moving and Renaming Group Accounts

Similar to user accounts, you can use the *dsmove group* command to move and rename a single group account object in Active Directory within the same domain from one location to another. You use the same command syntax for all object types:

dsmove *GroupDN* [**-newname** *NewName*] [**-newparent** *ParentDN*] [{**-s** *Server* | **-d** *Domain*}] [**-u** *UserName*] [**-p** {*Password* | *****}] [**-q**] [{**-uc** | **-uco** | **-uci**}]

In Figure 11.18, the Sales group is renamed to Product Sales. If you needed to move the group, you would use the *–newparent* switch with the new Parent distinguished name (ParentDN).

Figure 11.18 Renaming a Group

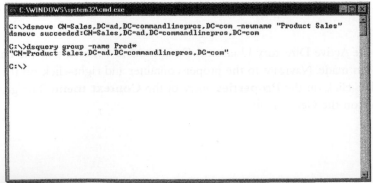

Deleting Group Accounts

Just as with user account objects (and all other objects in Active Directory), you delete a group from the command line using the *DSRm* command. The command syntax required for deleting a group is *dsrm GroupDN*. Figure 11.19 demonstrates deleting the Product Sales group using *dsrm "CN=Product Sales,DC=ad,DC=commandlinepros,DC=com."*

Figure 11.19 Deleting a Group

The GroupDN is in quotation marks because of the space in the Product Sales group name, and you must confirm the deletion by entering a **y** for "yes" when prompted in order for the operation to proceed to completion. Once the group is deleted, none of its former members will have access to network resources that the group permitted them to have. Any permissions that were granted to the former members through the group will need to be assigned through other means.

Managing Computer Accounts

So far in this chapter, we have focused on users—the actual user accounts and the groups to which they belong. We now turn our attention to computers and servers. In this section, we will examine and use *DSQuery, DSAdd, DSMod, DSMove,* and *DSRm* with the *computer* object type, to locate, add, modify, reset, move, rename, enable (and disable), and remove computer accounts.

Searching for Computer Accounts in Active Directory

Many of the search options that are available for locating users are also available for locating computers. The following is the complete command syntax for *dsquery computer:*

```
dsquery computer [{StartNode | forestroot | domainroot}] [-o {dn | rdn | samid}]
[-scope {subtree | onelevel | base}] [-name Name] [-desc Description] [-samid
SAMName] [-inactive NumberOfWeeks] [-stalepwd NumberOfDays] [-disabled] [{-s
```

```
Server | -d Domain}] [-u UserName] [-p {Password | *}] [-q] [-r] [-gc] [-limit
NumberOfObjects] [{-uc | -uco | -uci}]
```

Simply entering **dsquery computer** will return all computer accounts in the current forest. In Figure 11.20, *dsquery computer* is used with the *StartNode* of the Winnipeg OU. This returns the DNs for all of the computer accounts (ComputerDNs) in the container. You could refine the search by adding switches for searching in a defined scope within the forest or domain, or by computer account properties, such as account name (*–name*), description (*–desc*), or SAM account name (*–samid*), among others.

Figure 11.20 Searching for Computer Accounts

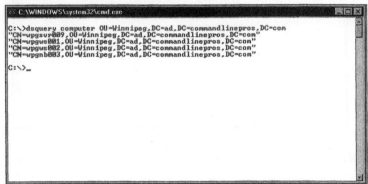

Creating New Computer Accounts

You can create computer accounts from the command line the same way you create user accounts. Without a computer account, a computer—a workstation or a member server—will not be able to participate in Active Directory. The following is the complete syntax for *dsadd computer*:

```
dsadd computer ComputerDN [-samid SAMName] [-desc Description] [-loc Location]
[-memberof GroupDN] [{-s Server | -d Domain}] [-u UserName] [-p {Password | *}]
[-q] [{-uc | -uco | -uci}]
```

The simplified command syntax is *dsadd computer ComputerDN*, which will add an account that is enabled with a SAM account name that matched the CN in the ComputerDN, yet is without a description or location. Figure 11.21 demonstrates the use of *dsadd computer* to create a computer account for a member server with an account name of "wpgsvr044," which also becomes the machine name, in the Winnipeg OU.

NOTE

In the context of Active Directory, computer accounts (the *Computer* object) are used for workstations and for member servers. Domain controllers are considered servers and use the *Server* object type. Despite the name, member servers do not use server accounts.

Figure 11.21 Creating a New Computer Account

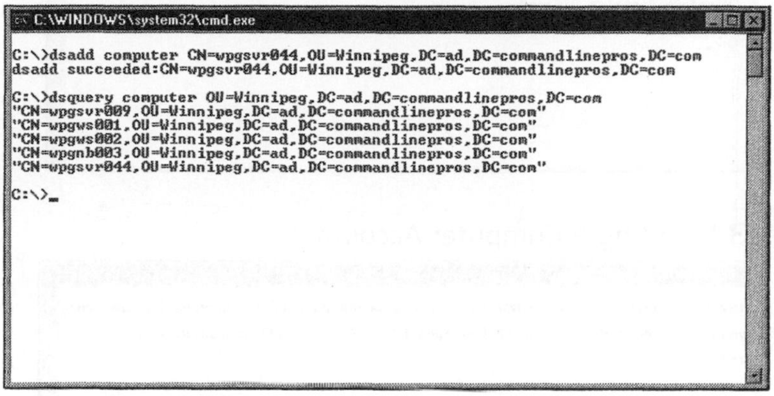

```
C:\WINDOWS\system32\cmd.exe

C:\>dsadd computer CN=wpgsvr044,OU=Winnipeg,DC=ad,DC=commandlinepros,DC=com
dsadd succeeded:CN=wpgsvr044,OU=Winnipeg,DC=ad,DC=commandlinepros,DC=com

C:\>dsquery computer OU=Winnipeg,DC=ad,DC=commandlinepros,DC=com
"CN=wpgsvr009,OU=Winnipeg,DC=ad,DC=commandlinepros,DC=com"
"CN=wpgws001,OU=Winnipeg,DC=ad,DC=commandlinepros,DC=com"
"CN=wpgws002,OU=Winnipeg,DC=ad,DC=commandlinepros,DC=com"
"CN=wpgnb003,OU=Winnipeg,DC=ad,DC=commandlinepros,DC=com"
"CN=wpgsvr044,OU=Winnipeg,DC=ad,DC=commandlinepros,DC=com"

C:\>_
```

Managing Properties of Computer Accounts

So far, we have managed user accounts and computer accounts from the command line in a similar fashion. One noticeable difference between the two, however, is the options available for *DSMod.* You can set or modify 30 user account properties with *dsmod user.* With *dsmod computer*, there are four properties, displayed in the following command syntax:

```
dsmod computer ComputerDN [-desc Description] [-loc Location] [-disabled {yes |
no}] [-reset] [{-s Server | -d Domain}] [-u UserName] [-p {Password | *}] [-c]
[-q] [{-uc | -uco | -uci}]
```

In Figure 11.22, the computer account for the member server that was added earlier is being modified. Because the location property was not set when the account was created, *dsmod computer* is used with the *–loc* switch to set the description as "Winnipeg District Office." You can use multiple switches to set the description (*–desc*) or to disable the account (*–disable yes*) until the server is ready to be connected to the domain.

Resetting Computer Accounts

Sometimes a computer account needs to be reset. For instance, you may need to reset the account if the Security Identifier (SID) changed when a computer account was disabled and then enabled again after a rebuild of Active Directory. Another example is if the computer account was removed from Active Directory offline. In any case, the command syntax for resetting the account is *dsmod computer ComputerDN –reset*, as depicted in Figure 11.23.

Figure 11.22 Modifying Computer Account Properties

Figure 11.23 Resetting a Computer Account

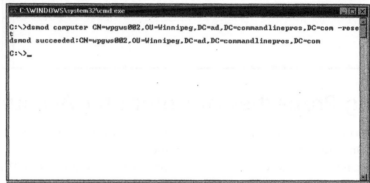

Moving and Renaming Computer Accounts

Just as you can for user and group accounts, you can use the *dsmove computer* command to move and rename a single group account object in Active Directory within the same domain from one location to another. You use the same command syntax for all object types:

dsmove *ComputerDN* [**-newname** *NewName*] [**-newparent** *ParentDN*] [{**-s** *Server* | **-d** *Domain*}] [**-u** *UserName*] [**-p** {*Password* | *****}] [**-q**] [{**-uc** | **-uco** | **-uci**}]

In Figure 11.24, the computer that needs to be moved to the Montreal OU is located in the Winnipeg OU using *dsquery computer*. Again, in the same manner as users and groups, the command is very straightforward: *dsmove ComputerDN –newparent ParentDN*. The network administrator does not need to confirm the move.

Once the computer is moved, it needs to be renamed in accordance with our fictitious organization's naming convention. The last command displayed in Figure 11.24 demonstrates the use of the *–newname* switch with *dsmove computer*. All you need for the modifier is the new name of the object. Executing *dsquery computer* for the Montreal OU confirms that the computer has been moved and renamed.

Figure 11.24 Moving and Renaming a Computer Account

```
C:\WINDOWS\system32\cmd.exe

C:\>dsquery computer OU=Winnipeg,DC=ad,DC=commandlinepros,DC=com
"CN=wpgsvr009,OU=Winnipeg,DC=ad,DC=commandlinepros,DC=com"
"CN=wpgws001,OU=Winnipeg,DC=ad,DC=commandlinepros,DC=com"
"CN=wpgws002,OU=Winnipeg,DC=ad,DC=commandlinepros,DC=com"
"CN=wpgnb003,OU=Winnipeg,DC=ad,DC=commandlinepros,DC=com"
"CN=wpgsvr044,OU=Winnipeg,DC=ad,DC=commandlinepros,DC=com"

C:\>dsmove CN=wpgsvr044,OU=Winnipeg,DC=ad,DC=commandlinepros,DC=com -newparent O
U=Montreal,DC=ad,DC=commandlinepros,DC=com
dsmove succeeded:CN=wpgsvr044,OU=Winnipeg,DC=ad,DC=commandlinepros,DC=com

C:\>dsquery computer OU=Montreal,DC=ad,DC=commandlinepros,DC=com
"CN=mtlnb001,OU=Montreal,DC=ad,DC=commandlinepros,DC=com"
"CN=mtlnb002,OU=Montreal,DC=ad,DC=commandlinepros,DC=com"
"CN=mtlws003,OU=Montreal,DC=ad,DC=commandlinepros,DC=com"
"CN=mtlsvr033,OU=Montreal,DC=ad,DC=commandlinepros,DC=com"
"CN=wpgsvr044,OU=Montreal,DC=ad,DC=commandlinepros,DC=com"

C:\>dsmove CN=wpgsvr044,OU=Montreal,DC=ad,DC=commandlinepros,DC=com -newname mtl
svr044
dsmove succeeded:CN=wpgsvr044,OU=Montreal,DC=ad,DC=commandlinepros,DC=com

C:\>dsquery computer OU=Montreal,DC=ad,DC=commandlinepros,DC=com
"CN=mtlnb001,OU=Montreal,DC=ad,DC=commandlinepros,DC=com"
"CN=mtlnb002,OU=Montreal,DC=ad,DC=commandlinepros,DC=com"
"CN=mtlws003,OU=Montreal,DC=ad,DC=commandlinepros,DC=com"
"CN=mtlsvr033,OU=Montreal,DC=ad,DC=commandlinepros,DC=com"
"CN=mtlsvr044,OU=Montreal,DC=ad,DC=commandlinepros,DC=com"

C:\>_
```

Enabling and Disabling Computer Accounts

As with user accounts, you use *DSMod* to enable and disable computer accounts. You use the following syntax to accomplish these tasks:

dsmod computer *ComputerDN* **-disabled** {*yes* | *no* }.

Figure 11.25 demonstrates use of *dsmod computer* to enable and disable a server in the Montreal OU. In this situation, the command is:

```
dsmod computer "CN=mtlsvr033,OU=Montreal,DC=ad,DC=commandlinepros,DC=com"
-disabled no
```

First, the disabled server's computer account is located using *dsquery computer* with the –*disabled* switch. The computer account is then enabled with *dsmod computer* and the –*disabled no* switch and modifier. The success message indicated that the account has been enabled and another execution of the same *dsquery computer* command confirms that there are no disabled computer accounts in the Montreal OU.

Figure 11.25 Enabling and Disabling a Computer Account

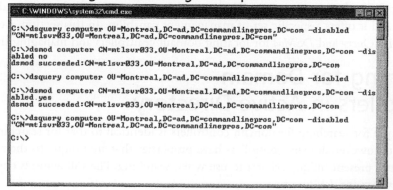

```
C:\WINDOWS\system32\cmd.exe

C:\>dsquery computer OU=Montreal,DC=ad,DC=commandlinepros,DC=com -disabled
"CN=mtlsvr033,OU=Montreal,DC=ad,DC=commandlinepros,DC=com"

C:\>dsmod computer CN=mtlsvr033,OU=Montreal,DC=ad,DC=commandlinepros,DC=com -dis
abled no
dsmod succeeded:CN=mtlsvr033,OU=Montreal,DC=ad,DC=commandlinepros,DC=com

C:\>dsquery computer OU=Montreal,DC=ad,DC=commandlinepros,DC=com -disabled

C:\>dsmod computer CN=mtlsvr033,OU=Montreal,DC=ad,DC=commandlinepros,DC=com -dis
abled yes
dsmod succeeded:CN=mtlsvr033,OU=Montreal,DC=ad,DC=commandlinepros,DC=com

C:\>dsquery computer OU=Montreal,DC=ad,DC=commandlinepros,DC=com -disabled
"CN=mtlsvr033,OU=Montreal,DC=ad,DC=commandlinepros,DC=com"

C:\>
```

You can disable the server's computer account using the same command you use to disable a computer account, except that the modifier for the *–disabled* switch is changed from *no* to *yes*. Figure 11.25 demonstrates how to disable the account and confirm that it is enabled with *DSQuery*.

Deleting Computer Accounts

You can delete a computer account from the command line using the *DSRm* command. The command syntax required for deleting a computer is ***dsrm** ComputerDN*. Figure 11.26 demonstrates deleting a member server in the Montreal OU using *dsrm "CN=mtlsvr033,OU=Montreal,DC=ad,DC=commandlinepros,DC=com."*

Figure 11.26 Deleting a Computer Account

```
C:\>dsrm CN=mtlsvr033,OU=Montreal,DC=ad,DC=commandlinepros,DC=com
Are you sure you wish to delete CN=mtlsvr033,OU=Montreal,DC=ad,DC=commandlinepro
s,DC=com (Y/N)? y
dsrm succeeded:CN=mtlsvr033,OU=Montreal,DC=ad,DC=commandlinepros,DC=com

C:\>
```

You must confirm the deletion by entering either a **y** or **yes** when prompted in order for the operation to proceed to completion. Once you have deleted the computer account, you cannot use the computer to authenticate to Active Directory.

Managing Domain Controller Accounts

By their very nature, domain controllers are special and are managed differently than member servers and other computers. The *server* object type refers exclusively to domain controllers, and it offers a specific set of management capability. In this section, we will discuss use of *DSQuery* and *DSMod* for locating domain controllers and managing their roles.

Searching for Domain Controllers in Active Directory

The technique for searching for domain controllers is identical to that for searching for any other object; however, domain controllers have properties that are unique to their object type and, thus, present unique criteria to use when searching. The following is complete command syntax for *dsquery server*:

```
dsquery server [-o {dn | rdn}] [-forest] [-domain DomainName] [-site SiteName]
[-name Name] [-desc Description] [-hasfsmo {schema | name | infr | pdc | rid}]
[-isgc] [{-s Server | -d Domain}] [-u UserName] [-p {Password | *}] [-q] [-r]
[-gc] [-limit NumberOfObjects] [{-uc | -uco | -uci}]
```

The *–forest*, *–domain*, and *–site* switches set the scope for searching to the current forest, and to the domain and site specified in the modifier. The *–name* and *–description* switches enable searching by the exact or partial name (using wildcards) and description. The *–hasfsmo* switch is described in detail in the next section. As seen in Figure 11.27, the command *dsquery server*, without switches and modifiers, returns a list of all domain controllers in the current forest.

Figure 11.27 Searching for Domain Controllers

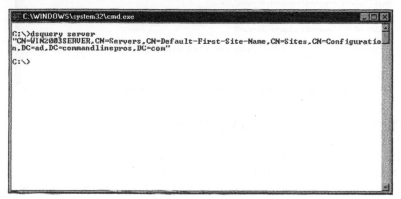

Searching for Domain Controllers with an Operations Master Roles

Managing a distributed, enterprise-class implementation of Active Directory requires that the location of certain domain controllers with special roles is known. These special roles are called Flexible Single-Master Operation (FSMO) roles, and their placement around the network is a key contributor to a network's performance and stability. There is a special switch for *dsquery server* for searching for domain controllers with FSMO roles:

```
dsquery server -hasfsmo {schema | name | infr | pdc | rid}
```

The following list provides the full name associated with the five modifiers for the *–hasfsmo* switch:

- **schema** Schema master.
- **name** Domain naming master.
- **infr** Infrastructure master.

- **pdc** Primary domain controller (PDC) emulator.
- **rid** Relative ID master.

In Figure 11.28, *dsquery server –hasfsmo* is executed with each modifier. In this situation, one domain controller is holding all FSMO roles.

Figure 11.28 Discovering Which Domain Controllers Have FSMO Roles

Searching for GC Servers

In an enterprise deployment of Active Directory, placement of the GC is critical for determining the performance of users' and computers' interaction on the network. In order to accelerate authentication and access to network resources, GC servers should be placed on domain controllers in close proximity to the users who need access to them. Before changing the locations of copies of GCs, you must locate the domain controllers that host the copies. The command syntax for locating these domain controllers uses the *–isgc* switch, as shown in Figure 11.29:

dsquery server -isgc

Figure 11.29 Searching for GC Servers

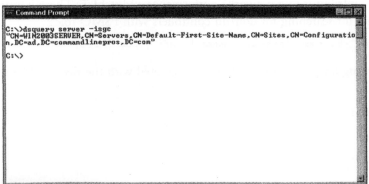

Managing Roles of GC Servers

As stated in the preceding section, you can determine the perceived and actual performance of your network by where you place the GC servers on domain controllers. The disadvantage to adding copies of the GCs around your network is that they need to replicate with each other, and increasing the number of GC servers may degrade performance, especially across slow network links. You can add or remove GCs from domain controllers from the command line.

The command for adding or removing a GC from an individual server is *dsmod server*. When using *DSMod* with other object types, the command permits you to set and modify myriad properties. With the server object type for domain controllers, it only permits you to set and modify the description and management of the GC role. The following is the full command syntax for *dsmod server*:

```
dsmod server ServerDN [-desc Description] [-isgc {yes | no}] [{-s Server | -d
Domain}] [-u UserName] [-p {Password | *}] [-c] [-q] [{-uc | -uco | -uci}]
```

To manage the GC role, however, the following command is required:

```
dsmod server ServerDN -isgc {yes | no}
```

Earlier in the chapter, we discussed the technique for locating domain controllers that host a copy of the GC. Figure 11.30 shows how to remove the GC from a server. Once the server is found, enter the following command:

```
dsmod server CN=WIN2003SERVER,CN=Servers,CD=Default-First-Site-
Name,CN=Sites,CN=Configuration,DC=ad,DC=commnadlinepros,DC=com -isgc no
```

No confirmation is required to complete performance of this task, and the success message is displayed when complete. Adding the GC involves entering the same command using a server that is not currently hosting a copy of the GC, and changing the modifier for *–isgc* from *no* to *yes*.

Figure 11.30 Managing GC Roles

Summary

In this chapter we took our knowledge of DS commands to the next level by providing you with detailed examples for some of the commands that are most commonly used for managing Active Directory objects. We discussed some common examples of DS commands and explained how to use them to query, add, modify, move, and remove Active Directory objects such as users, groups, and computers. Although some of the examples given in this chapter were taken from a particular working Active Directory domain, the same commands can be used in any domain with slight modifications. The purpose of this chapter was to learn the usage of DS commands for everyday administration of Active Directory objects. The DS command syntaxes look complex, but you learned that most of these arguments are optional and that you need to use only the required arguments. In the next chapter, we will move forward with some commonly used command-line utilities for managing computer networks.

Part V
Windows
Networking

Chapter 12

Basic TCP/IP Networking Commands

Topics in this chapter:

- Overview of the Net Commands
- Starting and Stopping TCP/IP Services
- Troubleshooting Commands for TCP/IP
- Commands for Remote Computers
- Commands for UNIX Printers

Introduction

In this chapter, we will explore how to perform rudimentary administrative tasks on a Windows computer using the available command-line utilities and commands. We will start with the powerful *Net* command that provides us with a wide selection of subcommands for performing network-specific tasks as well as general administrative tasks. We will continue with the various commands for troubleshooting potential problems with network settings and discuss how to perform diagnostic tasks. We will focus in particular on commands such as *Netstat* and *NBTStat*, and, of course, the ever-popular *Ping*. We will close the chapter with a discussion of the commands available for communicating with UNIX servers from a Windows computer, either by executing commands remotely or by printing on a UNIX box.

Overview of the Net Commands

The *Net* command provides an extremely versatile way to perform any number of tasks on a computer—from starting and stopping services, to managing access to shared resources, to sending messages to users on a domain. The syntax of the *Net* command is as follows:

```
Net [ Accounts | Computer | Config | Continue | File | Group | Help | Helpmsg |
Localgroup | Name | Pause | Print | Send | Session | Share | Start | Statistics |
Stop | Ttime | Use | User | View ]
```

The first parameter of this command is the subcommand that will dictate the type of function you want *Net* to perform. Table 12.1 provides brief descriptions of these subcommands.

Table 12.1 Subcommands of the Net Command

Subcommand	Description
net accounts [**/forcelogoff**:{*minutes* | *no*}] [**/minpwlen**:*length*] [**/maxpwage**:{*days* | **unlimited**}] [**/minpwage**:*days*] [**/uniquepw**:*number*] [**/domain**]	Updates user accounts, manages passwords, and modifies login requirements for all accounts.
net computer *ComputerName* {**/add** | **/del**}	Adds or deletes computers from the domain.
net config [{**server**|**workstation**}]	Displays and manages the configurable services that are running.
net file [*ID* [**/close**]]	Displays the names of all open shared files on a server and the number of file locks, if any, on each file. This command also closes individual shared files and removes file locks.

Continued

Table 12.1 continued Subcommands of the Net Command

Subcommand	Description
net group [*groupname* [**/comment:**"*text*"]] [**/domain**] **net group** [*groupname* {**/add** [**/comment:**"*text*"] | **/delete**} [**/domain**]] **net group** [*groupname username*[...] {**/add** | **/delete**} [**/domain**]]	Adds, displays, or modifies global groups in domains.
net helpmsg *message#*	Explains why an error occurred and gives troubleshooting information.
net localgroup [*GroupName* [**/comment:**"*text*"]] [**/domain**] **net localgroup** [*GroupName* {**/add** [**/comment:**"*text*"] | **/delete**} [**/domain**]] **net localgroup** [*GroupName name* [...] {**/add** | **/delete**} [**/domain**]]	Adds, displays, or modifies local groups.
net name [*name* {**/add**|**/delete**}]	Adds, deletes, or displays a messaging name.
net pause *service*	Pauses services that are currently running.
net send {*name* | * | **/domain**[:*name*] | **/users**} *message*	Sends messages to other users or computers.
net session [*ComputerName*] [**/delete**]	Manages server computer connections.
net share [*ShareName*] **net share** [*ShareName=Drive:Path* [{**/users:**number|**/unlimited**}] [**/remark:**"*text*"] [**/cache:** {**manual**|**automatic**|**no**}]] **net share** [*ShareName* [{**/users:**number|**unlimited**}] [**/remark:**"*text*"] [**/cache:** {**manual**|**automatic**|**no**}]] **net share** [{*ShareName*|*Drive:Path*} **/delete**]	Manages shared resources.
net start [*service*]	Starts a service.
net statistics [{**workstation** | **server**}]	Displays the statistics log for the local workstation or server service, or the running services for which statistics are available.
net stop *service*	Stops running a service.

Continued

Table 12.1 continued Subcommands of the Net Command

Subcommand	Description
net time [{*ComputerName* | **/domain**[:*DomainName*] | **/rtsdomain**[:*DomainName*]}] [**/set**] **net time** [*ComputerName*] [**/querysntp**] [**/setsntp**[:*NTPServerList*]]	Synchronizes the computer's clock with that of another computer or domain.
net use [{*DeviceName* | *****}] [*ComputerName**ShareName* [*volume*]] [{*Password* | *****}] [**/user:**[*DomainName**UserName*] [**/user:**[*DottedDomainName*\ *UserName*] [**/user:** [*UserName@DottedDomainName*] [**/savecred**] [**/smartcard**] [{**/delete** | **/persistent:**{**yes** | **no**}}] **net use** [*DeviceName* [**/home**[{*Password* | *****}] [**/delete:**{**yes** | **no**}]] net use [/persistent:{yes | no}]	Connects/disconnects a computer to/from a shared resource. Also displays information about computer connections.
net user [*UserName* [*Password* | *****] [*options*]] [**/domain**] **net user** [*UserName* {*Password* | *****} **/add** [*options*] [**/domain**]] net user [*UserName* [/delete] [/domain]]	Adds or modifies user accounts or displays user account information.
net view [*ComputerName*] [**/domain**[:*DomainName*]] net view /network:nw [*ComputerName*]	Displays a list of domains, computers, or resources that are being shared by the specified computer.

Starting and Stopping TCP/IP Services

Though we have seen other ways to start and stop services in this book, here we will examine how to use the *Net* command to control network-specific services. To start a service, you execute the command *net start <servicename>*. For example, in order to start the Dynamic Host Configuration Protocol (DHCP) service, use the following command:

```
C:\>net start dhcp
```

In the same fashion, to stop a service, you use the *net stop* command. For example, to stop the DHCP service we just started, use the following command:

```
C:\>net stop dhcp
```

When using this command, you must be careful to use the service name registered in the system, and not the name used in the service management console. For example, the service that is listed as "DHCP Client" is actually registered as simply "DHCP". Also note that when used in the command prompt, the service names are not case-sensitive.

Table 12.2 lists network-related services along with their actual service names and descriptions as they are registered in Windows.

Table 12.2 Network Services and Their Respective Names

Service Name	Long Name	Description
Alerter	Alerter	Broadcasts administrative alerts to select users and computers on a network.
Wuausrv	Automatic Updates	Checks and downloads updates for your Windows system.
Bits	Background Intelligent Transfer Service	Transfers data between clients and servers in the background.
Browser	Computer Browser	Maintains an updated list of computers on the network and supplies this list to computers designated as browsers.
Dhcp	DHCP Client	Manages network configuration by registering and updating Internet Protocol (IP) addresses and domain name system (DNS) names.
TrkWks	Distributed Link Tracking Client	Maintains links between New Technology File System (NTFS) files within a computer or across computers in a network domain.
DnsCache	DNS Client	Resolves and caches DNS names for this computer.
PolicyAgent	IPSEC Services	Manages IP security policy and starts the ISAKMP/Oakley (IKE) and IP security drivers.
Netman	Network Connections	Manages objects in the Network and Dial-Up Connections folder, in which you can view both local area network and remote connections.

Continued

Table 12.2 continued Network Services and Their Respective Names

Service Name	Long Name	Description
NetDDE	Network DDE	Provides network transport and security for Dynamic Data Exchange (DDE) for programs running on the same computer or different computers. If this service is stopped, DDE transport and security will be unavailable.
NetDDEdsdm	Network DDE DSDM	Manages DDE network shares.
Nla	Network Location Awareness	Collects and stores network configuration and location information, and notifies applications when this information changes.
Xmlprov	Network Provisioning Service	Manages XML configuration files on a domain basis for automatic network provisioning.
NtLmSsp	NTLM Security Support Provider	Provides security to Remote Procedure Call (RPC) programs that use transports other than named pipes.
Rsvp	QoS RSVP	Provides network signaling and local traffic control setup functionality for Quality of Service (QoS)-aware programs and control applets.
RasAuto	Remote Access Auto Connection Manager	Creates a connection to a remote network whenever a program references a remote DNS or NetBIOS name or address.
RasMan	Remote Access Connection Manager	Creates a network connection.
RdSessMgr	Remote Desktop Help Session Manager	Manages and controls Remote Assistance.
RpcSs	Remote Procedure Call (RPC)	Provides the endpoint mapper and other miscellaneous RPC services.
RpcLocator	Remote Procedure Call (RPC) Locator	Manages the RPC name service database.
RemoteRegistry	Remote Registry	Enables remote users to modify Registry settings on this computer.
RemoteAccess	Routing and Remote Access	Offers routing services to businesses in local area and wide area network environments.

Continued

Table 12.2 continued Network Services and Their Respective Names

Service Name	Long Name	Description
Lanmanserver	Server	Supports file, print, and named-pipe sharing over the network for this computer.
SMTPSVC	Simple Mail Transport Protocol (SMTP)	Transports electronic mail across the network.
SSDPSRV	SSDP Discovery Service	Enables discovery of UPnP devices on your home network.
LmHosts	TCP/IP NetBIOS Helper	Enables support for NetBIOS over TCP/IP (NetBT) services and NetBIOS name resolution.
TlntSvr	Telnet	Enables a remote user to log on to this computer and run programs, and supports various TCP/IP Telnet clients, including UNIX- and Windows-based computers.
TermService	Terminal Services	Allows multiple users to be connected interactively to a machine, and displays desktops and applications to remote computers. This is the underpinning of Remote Desktop (including RD for Administrators), Fast User Switching, Remote Assistance, and Terminal Server.
WebClient	WebClient	Enables Windows-based programs to create, access, and modify Internet-based files.
SharedAccess	Windows Firewall/ Internet Connection Sharing (ICS)	Provides network address translation, addressing, name resolution, and/or intrusion prevention services for a home or small office network.
W32Time	Windows Time	Maintains date and time synchronization on all clients and servers on the network.
WZCSVC	Wireless Zero Configuration	Provides automatic configuration for 802.11 adapters.
Lanmanworkstation	Workstation	Creates and maintains client network connections to remote servers.

Continued

www.syngress.com

Table 12.2 continued Network Services and Their Respective Names

Service Name	Long Name	Description
W3SVC	World Wide Web Publishing	Provides Web connectivity and administration through the Internet Information Server (IIS) snap-in.

NOTE

Service names are case-insensitive and never contain spaces. To view the actual service name for any given service, open the Services management console either via **Start | Programs | Administrative Tools | Services** or by clicking **Start | Run**, entering **services.msc**, and clicking **OK**. Then double-click on the service on which you want to work. You will notice that the registered name of the service is located next to the "Service Name" label, as shown in Figure 12.1.

Figure 12.1 Locating the Name of a Service in the Service Properties Dialog Box

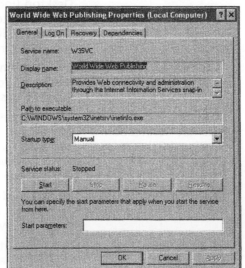

Troubleshooting Commands for TCP/IP

Beyond starting, stopping, and restarting network-related services using the *net start* and *net stop* commands, you will find that in some situations you will need to figure out exactly what is going wrong with your network connections. This diagnosis will require delving into some of the lower-level network maintenance commands available in Windows XP and Windows Server 2003. This section discusses some of the commonly used Transmission Control Protocol/Internet Protocol (TCP/IP) commands that you can use for troubleshooting network-related problems.

Arp

The *Arp* command manages the system's Address Resolution Protocol (ARP) cache, allowing an administrator to clear, modify, and list the entries therein. In a nutshell, the *Arp* command works by translating an IP address to the network adapter's physical Ethernet or Token Ring address. A table with these mappings is stored for each network interface card (NIC) in the system. The syntax of the *Arp* command is:

Arp -s inet_addr eth_addr [if_addr]

Arp -d inet_addr [if_addr]

Arp -a [inet_addr] [**-N** if_addr]

Table 12.3 lists the parameters of the *Arp* command.

Table 12.3 Parameters of the Arp Command

Parameter	Description
−a	Displays current ARP entries by interrogating the current protocol data. If *inet_addr* is specified, the IP and physical addresses for only the specified computer are displayed. If more than one network interface uses ARP, entries for each ARP table are displayed.
−g	Same as *−a*.
inet_addr	Specifies an IP address.
−N if_addr	Displays all entries in the ARP cache for the NIC specified by *if_addr*.
−d	Deletes the entry specified by *inet_addr*. If *inet_addr* is a wildcard, all entries are deleted.
−s	Adds an entry associating the IP address passed in the *inet_addr* parameter with the Media Access Control (MAC) address specified in *eth_addr*.
Eth_addr	Specifies a physical Ethernet address (MAC).

Continued

www.syngress.com

Table 12.3 continued Parameters of the Arp Command

Parameter	Description
If_addr	This parameter is optional. If it is passed, the modifications happen on this NIC. If it is not passed, the first available NIC is used.

In the following example, we start by listing the entries in the ARP cache, and then we add an entry that will associate an IP address to a specific MAC address. When this is done, we will relist the entries to verify that the command was executed successfully.

```
C:\>arp -a
```

The preceding command lists the entries in the ARP cache of the computer where the command is executed. If the ARP cache is empty, the following message is displayed:

```
No ARP Entries Found
```

We use the following command to make a static entry in the ARP cache:

```
C:\>arp -s 10.10.1.2 00-0D-65-CC-3E-C2
```

Assuming that the command executed successfully, we will relist the entries in the ARP cache to verify that our entry was successful. The output of the following command shows that the command executed successfully:

```
C:\>arp -a

Interface: 0.0.0.0 --- 0x10003
  Internet Address      Physical Address      Type
    10.10.1.2           00-0d-65-cc-3e-c2     static
```

You may notice from this listing that the *arp –s* command successfully made a static entry in the ARP cache.

IPConfig

The *IPConfig* command is arguably the most-used network-related administrative command on any Windows computer. At a minimum, it displays the basic IP settings for all active NICs on the system. For example:

```
C:\>ipconfig

Windows IP Configuration


Ethernet adapter Local Area Connection:
```

```
Connection-specific DNS Suffix  . : domain.com
IP Address. . . . . . . . . . . . : 192.168.0.100
Subnet Mask . . . . . . . . . . . : 255.255.255.0
Default Gateway . . . . . . . . . : 192.168.0.1
```

The syntax for this command is:

IPConfig [/**all**] [/**renew** [*Adapter*]] [/**release** [*Adapter*]] [/**flushdns**] [/**displaydns**]
[/**registerdns**] [/**showclassid** *Adapter*] [/**setclassid** *Adapter* [*ClassID*]]

Table 12.4 describes the parameters of the *IPConfig* command.

Table 12.4 Parameters of the IPConfig Command

Parameter	Description
/all	Displays all the TCP/IP configuration settings for all active NICs. This includes IP addresses, DNS settings, gateways, MAC addresses, and so on.
/renew [Adapter]	Renews the DHCP configuration for the specified adapter. If no adapter is given, all adapters are renewed. This command is applicable only when the adapter has been set to obtain the IP configuration automatically.
/release [Adapter]	Releases (clears) the DHCP configuration for the given adapter. If no adapter is specified, all adapters are released. This command is applicable on NICs that have been set to obtain their IP configuration automatically.
/flushdns	Clears and resets the contents of the DNS cache. This includes the entries loaded from the local HOSTS file as well as those resolved by the computer.
/displaydns	Lists the contents of the DNS resolver cache. The DNS client (*dnscache*) uses this information to resolved frequently queried names.
/registerdns	Starts the manual registration of entries into the DNS cache.
/showclassid Adapter	Displays the DHCP class ID for the given adapter. You can use an asterisk (*) to display all class IDs.
/setclassid Adapter [ClassID]	Sets the DHCP class ID for the given adapter. If a class ID is not provided, it is cleared. Using an asterisk (*) affects all adapters.

We saw the output of *IPConfig* without any arguments. Now we'll look at the results of the *IPConfig* command when used with the */all* parameter:

```
C:\>ipconfig /all
```

The output of this command is:

```
Windows IP Configuration


        Host Name . . . . . . . . . . . . : cmptr03
        Primary Dns Suffix  . . . . . . . :
        Node Type . . . . . . . . . . . . : Broadcast
        IP Routing Enabled. . . . . . . . : No
        WINS Proxy Enabled. . . . . . . . : No
        DNS Suffix Search List. . . . . . : domain.com


Ethernet adapter Local Area Connection:

        Connection-specific DNS Suffix  . : domain.com
        Description . . . . . . . . . . . : Broadcom 440x 10/100 Integrated Cont
roller
        Physical Address. . . . . . . . . : 00-0D-66-CD-3E-C2
        Dhcp Enabled. . . . . . . . . . . : Yes
        Autoconfiguration Enabled . . . . : Yes
        IP Address. . . . . . . . . . . . : 192.168.0.100
        Subnet Mask . . . . . . . . . . . : 255.255.255.0
        Default Gateway . . . . . . . . . : 192.168.0.1
        DHCP Server . . . . . . . . . . . : 192.168.0.1
        DNS Servers . . . . . . . . . . . : 192.168.0.1
        Lease Obtained. . . . . . . . . . : Saturday, August 26, 2006 09:58:07
        Lease Expires . . . . . . . . . . : Saturday, September 02, 2006 09:58:07
```

We see a lot more information now that can help us identify what is wrong (or right) with our connection. If *IPConfig* reports an IP address in the 169.*.*.* format, the computer does not have a valid IP address on the network and there is some issue with connectivity.

If the network adapter has been configured to use DHCP (obtain IP address and DNS information automatically) and there is an issue with connectivity, the first thing you should try is to refresh the DHCP settings. To do this, first release the DHCP settings and then renew them. Consider the following example:

```
C:\>ipconfig /release

Windows IP Configuration


Ethernet adapter Local Area Connection:

        Connection-specific DNS Suffix  . :
```

```
      IP Address. . . . . . . . . . . : 0.0.0.0
      Subnet Mask . . . . . . . . . . : 0.0.0.0
      Default Gateway . . . . . . . . :

C:\>ipconfig /renew

Windows IP Configuration


Ethernet adapter Local Area Connection:

      Connection-specific DNS Suffix  . :
      IP Address. . . . . . . . . . . : 192.168.0.101
      Subnet Mask . . . . . . . . . . : 255.255.255.0
      Default Gateway . . . . . . . . : 192.168.0.1
```

After obtaining a valid IP address, you can issue a *Ping* command against the given gateway (192.168.0.1 in the results shown in the preceding example) to make sure that IP packets can be transmitted.

Finger

The *Finger* command displays the information that a user has placed in his or her profile on a system. This is a leftover command from old UNIX systems where users used to write information about themselves in the .plan file in their $HOME directory. You also can use the *Finger* command to display a list of users logged in to a remote system. For this command to work, the remote host system must be running the finger service. If the remote system is a UNIX/Linux system, there is a good chance that the service is running, though more and more servers are disabling this service for security reasons, and it is almost unheard of to find this service running on a Windows system. The syntax of the command is:

Finger [-1] [user]@host [...]

Table 12.5 explains the parameters used with the *Finger* command.

Table 12.5 Parameters of the Finger Command

Argument	Description
–l	Displays information in long list format.
User	Specifies the user for which information is requested. If you omit this, information on all the users is displayed.
@host [...]	Specifies the remote host on which the users you are querying reside.

The following example illustrates use of the *Finger* command when used against a user on a remote host:

```
C:\>finger root@slackware.com
```

The output of this command is:

```
[slackware.com]
Login: root                              Name: (null)
Directory: /root                         Shell: /bin/bash
Last login Thu Mar  9 10:11 (PST) on pts/2
New mail received Fri Aug 25 16:02 2006 (PDT)
     Unread since Fri Aug 18 01:04 2006 (PDT)
No Plan.


C:\>
```

Getmac

You use the *Getmac* command to list all known MAC addresses in the system. These include the MAC addresses of the NICs installed on the system as well as the *eth_addr* entries stored in the ARP cache. The syntax of the *Getmac* command is:

```
Getmac [/S system [/U username [/P [password]]]] [/FO format] [/NH] [/V]
```

Table 12.6 explains the parameters of this command.

Table 12.6 Parameters of the Getmac Command

Parameter	Description
/S system	Specifies the remote system to which to connect.
/U [domain\]user	Specifies the user context under which the command should execute.
/P [password]	Specifies the password for the user specified with the /U switch. If *password* is not provided, the command prompts for it.
/FO format	Specifies the format in which the output should be displayed. The possible values are *TABLE*, *CSV*, and *LIST*.
/V	Requests verbose output.
/NH	Suppresses the printing of column headers; valid only with output in TABLE and CSV formats.

The following examples illustrate use of the *Getmac* command. You may notice that you can change the format of the command output using the */fo* parameter.

```
C:\>getmac

Physical Address      Transport Name
==================    ===================================
Disabled              Disconnected
00-0D-56-AB-E3-2C     Media disconnected
Disabled              Disconnected
Disabled              Disconnected

C:\>getmac /FO csv

"Physical Address","Transport Name"
"Disabled","Disconnected"
"00-0D-56-AB-E3-2C","Media disconnected"
"Disabled","Disconnected"
"Disabled","Disconnected"

C:\>getmac /FO list

Physical Address: Disabled
Transport Name:   Disconnected

Physical Address: 00-0D-56-AB-E3-2C
Transport Name:   Media disconnected

Physical Address: Disabled
Transport Name:   Disconnected

Physical Address: Disabled
Transport Name:   Disconnected
```

Hostname

Hostname is a simple command that you can use to display or print the name of the computer where the command is executed. This command does not take any parameters and its syntax is very simple:

Hostname

The hostname of a computer is the leftmost section of a fully qualified domain name (FQDN). For example, the hostname of the computer *ch012.books.syngress.com* is *ch012* and that is what *Hostname* will return.

Netstat

As the Microsoft Help says, the *Netstat* command displays the currently active Transmission Control Protocol (TCP) connections, the ports on which the computer is listening, Ethernet statistics, the IP routing table, IPv4 statistics (for IP, Internet Control Message Protocol [ICMP], TCP, and User Datagram Protocol [UDP]), and IPv6 statistics (for the IPv6, ICMPv6, TCP over IPv6, and UDP over IPv6 protocols). Used without parameters, *Netstat* only displays active TCP connections. The syntax of this command is:

```
Netstat [-a] [-b] [-e] [-n] [-o] [-p proto] [-r] [-s] [-v] [interval]
```

Table 12.7 explains the parameters of the *Netstat* command.

Table 12.7 Parameters of the Netstat Command

Argument	Description
–a	Displays all the active TCP connections as well as all the TCP and UDP ports on which the system is listening.
–b	Displays the ID and name of the process owning the connection. This switch works only if the user has the appropriate permissions. Also, because of the way this information is retrieved, it may be time consuming.
–e	Displays Ethernet statistics such as bytes and packets sent and received. You can combine this with the *–s* switch.
–n	Does not perform reverse DNS resolution of IP addresses. Returns only numeric IP addresses.
–o	Displays the process ID (PID) of the process that opened the connection or has the port bound. You can combine this with the arguments *–a*, *–n*, and *–p*.
–p Protocol	Shows connections only for the protocol specified. Valid values for *Protocol* are *tcp*, *udp*, *tcpv6*, and *udpv6*. If you combine it with *–s*, statistics are shown and the valid values are *tcp*, *udp*, *icmp*, *ip*, *tcpv6*, *udpv6*, *icmpv6*, and *ipv6*.
–s	Displays statistics by protocol. If you do not use the *–p Protocol* argument, *Netstat* will display statistics for TCP, UDP, ICMP, and IP. If the IPv6 protocol has been installed, statistics for the same protocols over IPv6 are displayed.
–r	Displays the contents of the routing table. It prints the same information as the *route print* command.
Interval	If specified, the same information is displayed every *Interval* seconds.

You can combine different parameters of the *Netstat* command without needing to separate them, as shown in the following example:

```
Netstat -a -n -b
```

```
Netstat -anb
```

When executed, these two commands return the same results.

Before examining typical tasks, let's identify the report columns and what they mean. Table 12.8 explains different report columns.

Table 12.8 Report Columns Used with the Netstat Command

Column Header	Description
Proto	The protocol whose statistics about which you are getting information.
Local Address	The local IP address or resolved name, along with the port number/service name that has the connection.
Foreign Address	Same as *Local Address* but for the remote computer.
State	The state of the connection. Possible values for this are (relevant to TCP only; refer to RFC 793): *CLOSE_WAIT* (the connection is waiting to close) *CLOSED* (the connection is closed) *ESTABLISHED* (the connection is live) *FIN_WAIT_1* (step 1 in closing a TCP connection; send out the request) *FIN_WAIT_2* (step 2 in closing a TCP connection) *LAST_ACK* (remote end closing connection) *LISTEN* (listening for connections) *SYN_RECEIVED* (inbound is half-open) *SYN_SEND* (outbound half-open connection) *TIME_WAIT* (waiting for connection to close)

In a typical troubleshooting scenario you may need to examine whether a process has actually bound to a TCP port and is listening for connections. In addition to this, you can use the *Netstat* command to look for network servers that are not known and could potentially be Trojans. Consider the following example:

```
C:\>netstat -anp tcp
```

When this command is executed, the output is displayed as follows:

```
Active Connections

  Proto  Local Address          Foreign Address        State
  TCP    0.0.0.0:135            0.0.0.0:0              LISTENING
  TCP    0.0.0.0:445            0.0.0.0:0              LISTENING
  TCP    0.0.0.0:3306           0.0.0.0:0              LISTENING
  TCP    127.0.0.1:1028         0.0.0.0:0              LISTENING
```

```
TCP     127.0.0.1:1031          0.0.0.0:0               LISTENING
TCP     127.0.0.1:1372          127.0.0.1:1373          ESTABLISHED
TCP     127.0.0.1:1373          127.0.0.1:1372          ESTABLISHED
```

You may notice that the output of the given command lists all TCP connections (listening and outbound) without performing reverse DNS lookups for the IP addresses found.

To continue our investigation, consider that you have identified a listening port that you do not recognize. In this situation, you might want to know which process is actually listening. You can do this by executing the *Netstat* command with the *–o* parameter. The following example illustrates use of the *Netstat* command for this purpose:

```
C:\>netstat -anop tcp
```

Here is the output of this command:

```
Active Connections
```

Proto	Local Address	Foreign Address	State	PID
TCP	0.0.0.0:135	0.0.0.0:0	LISTENING	1244
TCP	0.0.0.0:445	0.0.0.0:0	LISTENING	4
TCP	0.0.0.0:3306	0.0.0.0:0	LISTENING	1716
TCP	127.0.0.1:1028	0.0.0.0:0	LISTENING	772
TCP	127.0.0.1:1031	0.0.0.0:0	LISTENING	804
TCP	127.0.0.1:1372	127.0.0.1:1373	ESTABLISHED	3608
TCP	127.0.0.1:1373	127.0.0.1:1372	ESTABLISHED	3608

You can use the PID returned by this command to identify the offending process, or you can use the *–b* parameter that gives you detailed output, as shown in the following example:

```
C:\>netstat -anbp tcp
```

Now let's look at the output of this command:

```
Active Connections
```

Proto	Local Address	Foreign Address	State	PID
TCP	0.0.0.0:135	0.0.0.0:0	LISTENING	1244

```
c:\windows\system32\WS2_32.dll
C:\WINDOWS\system32\RPCRT4.dll
c:\windows\system32\rpcss.dll
C:\WINDOWS\system32\svchost.exe
C:\WINDOWS\system32\ADVAPI32.dll
[svchost.exe]
```

TCP	0.0.0.0:445	0.0.0.0:0	LISTENING	4

```
[System]
```

```
TCP     0.0.0.0:3306          0.0.0.0:0              LISTENING    1716
[mysqld-nt.exe]

TCP     127.0.0.1:1028        0.0.0.0:0              LISTENING    772
[alg.exe]

TCP     127.0.0.1:1031        0.0.0.0:0              LISTENING    804
[ccApp.exe]

TCP     127.0.0.1:1372        127.0.0.1:1373         ESTABLISHED  3608
[FIREFOX.EXE]

TCP     127.0.0.1:1373        127.0.0.1:1372         ESTABLISHED  3608
[FIREFOX.EXE]
```

The output of the command not only displays the executables that have open connections but also shows the associated modules (dynamic link libraries, or DLLs). This information can be very helpful when trying to identify problems on the system.

To check the statistics for the TCP connections, you can run the *netstat –snp tcp* command, as shown in the following example:

```
C:\>netstat -snp tcp
```

Here is the output of this command:

```
TCP Statistics for IPv4

    Active Opens                 = 338
    Passive Opens                = 2
    Failed Connection Attempts   = 3
    Reset Connections            = 20
    Current Connections          = 2
    Segments Received            = 13116
    Segments Sent                = 11868
    Segments Retransmitted       = 2

Active Connections

    Proto  Local Address        Foreign Address        State
    TCP    127.0.0.1:1372       127.0.0.1:1373         ESTABLISHED
    TCP    127.0.0.1:1373       127.0.0.1:1372         ESTABLISHED
```

NBTStat

The *NBTStat* command provides an easy way to get NetBT statistics and related information. It also gives us a way to refresh the NetBIOS name cache along with the names registered with the Windows Internet Name Service (WINS). The syntax of this command is:

```
NBTStat [-a RemoteName] [-A IPAddress] [-c] [-n] [-r] [-R] [-RR] [-s] [-S]
[Interval]
```

Table 12.9 explains parameters of the *NBTStat* command.

Table 12.9 Parameters of the NBTStat Command

Parameter	Description
–a RemoteName	Displays the NetBIOS name table of a remote computer. The table returned is a list of names that correspond to NetBIOS applications running on that computer.
–A IPAddress	Displays the NetBIOS name table of a remote computer (specified by the IP address). Returns the same results as the *–a* switch.
–c	Displays the contents of the NetBIOS name cache, the NetBIOS names, and their resolved IP addresses.
–n	Displays the NetBIOS name table of the local computer. A status of *Registered* indicates that the name is registered either by broadcast or with a WINS server.
–r	Displays NetBIOS name resolution statistics. On Windows XP, when using WINS, this returns the number of names that have been resolved and registered using broadcast and WINS.
–R	Purges the contents of the NetBIOS name cache and then reloads the *#PRE*-tagged entries from the LMHOSTS file.
–RR	Releases and then refreshes NetBIOS names for the local computer that is registered with WINS servers.
–s	Displays NetBIOS client and server sessions, attempting to convert the destination IP address to a name.
–S	Displays NetBIOS client and server sessions, listing the remote computers by destination IP address only.
Interval	Redisplays selected statistics, pausing for the number of seconds specified in *Interval* between each display. When you omit this parameter, the information requested is listed only once.

The following example illustrates how you can display the name table on the local computer:

```
C:\>nbtstat -n
```

```
Local Area Connection:
Node IpAddress: [192.168.0.100] Scope Id: []

            NetBIOS Local Name Table

     Name               Type          Status
-----------------------------------------------
   CMPTR03      <00>  UNIQUE       Registered
   WORKGROUP    <00>  GROUP        Registered
   CMPTR03      <20>  UNIQUE       Registered
```

Now, let's examine the column headers of the report we just saw (see Table 12.10).

Table 12.10 Columns Headers for the NBTStat Command Report

Column Header	Description
Input	The number of bytes received.
Output	The number of bytes sent.
In/Out	Whether the connection is outbound or inbound.
Life	The remaining time that the cache entry will live before being purged.
Local Name	The local NetBIOS name associated with the connection.
Remote Host	The name or IP address associated with the remote computer.
<??>	The last byte of a NetBIOS name converted to hex. This information is very important as you can use it to distinguish among multiple entries with the same name.
Type	The name can be a unique name or a group name.
Status	Whether the NetBIOS name on the remote computer is running (*Registered*) or a duplicate computer name has registered the same service (*Conflict*).
State	The state of NetBIOS connections. Possible values are: *Connected* (a session has been established) *Associated* (a connection endpoint has been created and associated with an IP address) *Listening* (the endpoint is waiting for connections) *Idle* (the endpoint is opened but cannot accept connections) *Connecting* (the session is trying to connect and the name to the IP address mapping is being resolved)

Continued

Table 12.10 continued Columns Headers for the NBTStat Command Report

Column Header	Description
	Accepting (an inbound connection has arrived and it is being accepted)
	Reconnecting (a session is trying to reconnect because it failed on its first attempt)
	Outbound (an outbound session is in the connecting phase and the TCP connection is currently being created)
	Inbound (an inbound connection is being created)
	Disconnecting (a session is in the process of disconnecting)
	Disconnected (the local computer has issued a disconnect and is waiting for the remote computer to acknowledge)

NSLookup

The *NSLookup* command performs commands against a DNS. This command is very commonly used to diagnose problems with DNS servers. The syntax of this command is:

```
NSLookup [-SubCommand ...] [{ComputerToFind| [-Server]}]
```

Before going into the details of the utility, let's examine the parameters of this command:

- **–SubCommand** Specifies one or more *NSLookup* subcommands to execute.

- **ComputerToFind** Specifies the computer name to find. You cannot use this parameter when you use the *–Server* parameter.

- **–Server** Specifies the DNS server to use for executing the commands. If you omit this parameter, the default primary DNS server is used.

You can use either the *ComputerToFind* parameter or the *–Server* parameter with the *NSLookup* command. A common task performed using the *NSLookup* command is to find the IP address of a given computer. That computer can reside on the local network or anywhere on the Internet. Consider the following example:

```
C:\>nslookup www.syngress.com
Server:  DNS
Address:  192.168.0.1

Non-authoritative answer:
Name:    www.syngress.com
Address:  155.212.56.73
```

From the output of this command, you can see that the IP address of the Syngress Web site, *www.syngress.com*, is 155.212.56.73.

When you run this command on your home network, you might get an error such as this:

```
*** Can't find server name for address 192.168.0.1: Server failed
*** Default servers are not available
```

Don't worry about this error as it does not affect the results of the DNS query.

Beyond the basic function of looking up an IP address for a given hostname, you can perform a whole slew of DNS queries by using the *NSLookup* subcommands. You can enter these subcommands via the command line, or you can use them when entering *NSLookup* in interactive mode.

In order to enter interactive mode, you can execute the *NSLookup* command without any arguments, as shown in the following example:

```
C:\>nslookup
*** Can't find server name for address 192.168.0.1: Server failed
*** Default servers are not available
Default Server:  UnKnown
Address:  192.168.0.1

>
```

NSLookup is a commonly used TCP/IP utility. It supports several subcommands when it is run in interactive mode. Table 12.11 lists all the subcommands that the *NSLookup* utility supports.

Table 12.11 Subcommands Available with the NSLookup Utility

Subcommand	Description
Exit	Exits from interactive mode.
finger [UserName] [{[>] FileName| [>>] FileName}]	Works exactly like the *Finger* command described earlier.
{help|?}	Displays a short list of subcommands.
ls [Option] DNSDomain [{[>] FileName|[>>] FileName}]	Lists information for a DNS.
lserver DNSDomain	Changes the default DNS to *DNSDomain*.
Root	Changes the default server to the root server for the DNS domain.
Server DNSDomain	Changes the default DNS to *DNSDomain*.

Continued

Table 12.11 continued Subcommands Available with the NSLookup Utility

Subcommand	Description
set KeyWord[=Value]	Sets a value for the specified keyword. Executes set all for a list of all values.
view FileName	Sorts and lists the output from the previous ls commands.

Another common task that you can perform using the *NSLookup* subcommands is to look up the name of the server that is handling mail for a given domain. The DNS record containing this information is called the *MX record*. Consider the following example:

```
> set type=MX
> syngress.com
Server:  UnKnown
Address:  192.168.0.1

Non-authoritative answer:
syngress.com    MX preference = 20, mail exchanger = spool.conversent.net
syngress.com    MX preference = 10, mail exchanger = mailhost.syngress.com
>
```

Pathping

The *Pathping* command provides information about network latency and network loss at intermediate hops between a source and a destination. *Pathping* identifies the hops between two endpoints, a function similar to the *Tracert* command, and then pings each of them. When the process is completed, *Pathping* displays the computed statistics. The syntax of this command is:

```
Pathping [-n] [-h MaximumHops] [-g HostList] [-p Period] [-q NumQueries [-w
Timeout] [-T] [-R] [TargetName]
```

Table 12.12 explains the different parameters of the *Pathping* command.

Table 12.12 Parameters of the Pathping Command

Parameter	Description
−n	Does not resolve hostnames; only displays IP addresses.
−h MaximumHops	Specifies the maximum number of hops to process.
−g HotList	Specifies that the Echo Request messages use the Loose Source Route option.
−p Period	Specifies the number of milliseconds to wait between pings.

Continued

Table 12.12 continued Parameters of the Pathping Command

Parameter	Description
–q NumQueries	Specifies the number of Echo Request queries to send to each hop. The default value is 100.
–w Timeout	Specifies the number of milliseconds to wait for each reply. The default is 3000.
–T	Attaches a layer-2 priority flag to each Echo Request sent out. This helps test for QoS connectivity.
–R	Used to determine whether each hop supports the RSVP protocol. Used to test for QoS connectivity.

To illustrate use of the *Pathping* command, we will execute it against the Syngress Web site, as shown in the following example. Note that your results may be different depending on the target Web site against which you execute this command:

```
C:\>pathping www.syngress.com
```

Now let's look at the output of this command. The following is a partial listing that shows how the command traces its route to the destination *www.syngress.com*:

```
Tracing route to www.syngress.com [155.212.56.73]
over a maximum of 30 hops:
  0  cmptr03.launchmodem.com [192.168.0.100]
  1  192.168.0.1
  2  launchmodem [192.168.1.254]
  3  65.41.225.92
  4  65.41.245.254
  5  205.152.145.217
  6  axr00mia-1-3-0.bellsouth.net [65.83.237.8]
  7  pxr00mia-0-0-0.bellsouth.net [65.83.236.16]
  8  0.so-1-0-0.GW8.MIA4.ALTER.NET [65.208.86.133]
  9  0.so-1-3-0.XL1.MIA4.ALTER.NET [152.63.84.54]
 10  0.so-3-0-0.XL1.NYC1.ALTER.NET [152.63.27.29]
 11  POS6-0.GW12.NYC1.ALTER.NET [152.63.29.193]
 12  65.200.139.145
 13  host116.209.113.217.oem.net [209.113.217.116]
 14  ma1-bb1-as0.conversent.net [209.113.217.229]
 15  host99.101.41.216.conversent.net [216.41.101.99]
 16  ma-brockton-s1-0.conversent.net [209.113.217.126]
 17  host65.155.212.56.conversent.net [155.212.56.65]
 18    *      *      *
Computing statistics for 450 seconds...
```

```
                  Source to Here    This Node/Link
       Hop  RTT   Lost/Sent = Pct   Lost/Sent = Pct   Address
        0                                              cmptr03.launchmodem.com
       [192.168.0.100]
                                    0/ 100 =  0%   |
        1   0ms   0/ 100 =  0%      0/ 100 =  0%   192.168.0.1
                                    0/ 100 =  0%   |
        2   1ms   0/ 100 =  0%      0/ 100 =  0%   launchmodem [192.168.1.254]
                                    0/ 100 =  0%   |
        3   9ms   0/ 100 =  0%      0/ 100 =  0%   65.41.225.92
                                    0/ 100 =  0%   |
       -- -- -- --
       18  ---    100/ 100 =100%    0/ 100 =  0%   kimon03 [0.0.0.0]


Trace complete.
```

Ping

You use the *Ping* command to verify IP connectivity to another computer. This command works by sending ICMP Echo Request messages. The replies are displayed along with the round-trip times. Typically you would use this command to check whether a remote computer is up and connected to the network or to check the local computer's connectivity. The syntax of the *Ping* command is:

```
Ping [-t] [-a] [-n Count] [-l Size] [-f] [-i TTL] [-v TOS] [-r Count] [-s Count]
[{-j HostList | -k HostList}] [-w Timeout] [TargetName]
```

Table 12.13 explains the parameters of the *Ping* command.

Table 12.13 Parameters of the Ping Command

Parameter	Description
–t	Continue pinging indefinitely until the user presses **Ctrl + C**.
–a	Perform reverse DNS lookup on the IP address.
–n Count	The number of requests to send out. The default is *4*.
–l Size	The size (in bytes) of the data to send out in the Echo Request. The default is *64*.
–f	Don't fragment the IP packet.
–i TTL	Specifies the Time to Live (TTL) for the Echo Request message.
–v TOS	Specifies the value for the Type of Service field. The default is *0*.

Continued

Table 12.13 continued Parameters of the Ping Command

Parameter	Description
−r Count	Specifies that the Record Route option in the IP header is used. When using this, specify a number greater than or equal to the number of hops. The range of values is 1 to 9.
−s Count	Specifies that the Internet Timestamp option is used. The range for this is 1 to 4.
−j HostList	Specifies that the Echo Request messages use the Strict Source Route option in the IP header with the set of intermediate destinations specified in HostList.
−w Timeout	Specifies the number of milliseconds to wait for a message to return.
TargetName	The name or IP address of the remote host to ping.

One of the first things an administrator does to test network connectivity is to *Ping* another IP address, as shown in the following example:

```
C:\>ping 192.168.0.1
```

When this command is executed the output is displayed as follows:

```
Pinging 192.168.0.1 with 32 bytes of data:

Reply from 192.168.0.1: bytes=32 time<1ms TTL=127
Reply from 192.168.0.1: bytes=32 time<1ms TTL=127
Reply from 192.168.0.1: bytes=32 time<1ms TTL=127
Reply from 192.168.0.1: bytes=32 time<1ms TTL=127

Ping statistics for 192.168.0.1:
    Packets: Sent = 4, Received = 4, Lost = 0 (0% loss),
Approximate round trip times in milli-seconds:
    Minimum = 0ms, Maximum = 0ms, Average = 0ms
```

NOTE

To better understand the information in this section, it may be helpful to review the Request for Comments (RFC) documents on the various protocols—TCP, UDP, ICMP, and so on. You can read the document on the Web site for the Internet Engineering Task Force (IETF) at *www.ietf.org*. Table 12.14 includes a list of protocols and RFC numbers.

Table 12.14 Protocols and RFC Numbers

Protocol	RFC Number
TCP	793
UDP	768
ICMP	792
IP	791
DNS	1034 and 1035

Commands for Remote Computers

Network administration is not only about figuring out what is wrong with your network connectivity; it is also about using commands to communicate with remote computers. Basic functions such as transferring files from one computer to another using the standard File Transfer Protocol (FTP), Trivial File Transfer Protocol (TFTP), and Remote Copy Protocol (RCP) are sometimes extremely important when trying to accomplish a task. More advanced functions, such as executing commands on remote computers, can be lifesavers when you need to perform simple tasks and creating a full remote session would be overkill.

FTP

The *FTP* utility provides client access to remote FTP servers to transfer files over FTP. Files can be transmitted or received in either text (ASCII) or binary mode. The syntax of this command is:

FTP [**-v**] [**-d**] [**-i**] [**-n**] [**-g**] [**-s:**FileName] [**-a**] [**-w:**WindowSize] [**-A**] [Host]

Table 12.15 lists the different parameters of the *FTP* command.

Table 12.15 Parameters of the FTP Command

Argument	Description
–v	Suppresses server responses.
–d	Enables debugging. Displays all messages sent between the server and client.
–i	Disables interactive prompting.
–n	Suppresses the ability to log on automatically when the initial connection is made.
–g	Disables file globbing. Glob permits the use of wildcards.

Continued

Table 12.15 continued Parameters of the FTP Command

Argument	Description
–s:FileName	FileName specifies a script file containing FTP commands to execute.
–a	Specifies that any local interface can be used.
–w:WindowSize	Specifies the size of the transfer buffer. The default size is 4096.
–A	Logs into the ftp server anonymously.
Host	The remote FTP server to which to connect.

When connecting to an FTP server, you will be prompted to authenticate before being granted access. Public FTP sites allow anonymous FTP access. To log on anonymously, you can specify the *–A* switch or you can log on as shown in the following example:

```
C:\>ftp ftp.slackware.com
```

When this command is executed, the output is displayed as follows:

```
Connected to ftp.slackware.com.
220 207.173.172.131 FTP server ready
User (ftp.slackware.com:(none)): anonymous
331 Anonymous login ok, send your complete email address as your password.
Password:
230-**********************************************************************
 Welcome to ftp.slackware.com,

You are user 65 of 96.

On This Site:
/pub/slackware/                Slackware Linux

If you experience any problems e-mail us:  volkerdi@slackware.com
********************************************************************

230 Anonymous access granted, restrictions apply.
ftp>
```

Once you're logged on, you can perform several functions, such as getting directory listings, navigating the directory tree, and of course, downloading and uploading files. Table 12.16 explains different FTP commands available in Microsoft's implementation in Windows XP and Windows Server 2003. It is important to note that different operating systems support different FTP commands, and the commands discussed in this section may not be available in some other operating systems.

Table 12.16 FTP Commands Available in Windows XP and Windows Server 2003

Command	Description
!	Repeats last command.
append LocalFile [RemoteFile]	Appends the local file to the file on the remote server.
Ascii	Sets the connection to transmit in ASCII format.
Bell	Sounds the computer tone when a file transfer is completed.
binary|bin	Sets the file transfer format to binary.
Bye	Disconnects from the server and exits FTP.
cd [Path]	Changes the directory to the given path. If executed without any parameters, prints the current working directory.
Close	Closes the connection but does not exit the FTP client.
Debug	Toggles the debug mode.
delete RemoteFile	Deletes the remote file.
Dir	Prints a directory listing of the current working directory.
Disconnect	Disconnects from the remote server.
get [FileName]	Starts downloading the given file.
Glob	Toggles globbing (the use of wildcards).
Hash	Prints a hash character (#) for every 1,024 bytes.
Help	Prints help.
Lcd	Changes the directory on the local computer.
literal Argument	Sends a literal (raw) command to the FTP server.
Ls	Performs a directory listing.
mdelete [Files]	Deletes multiple files as per the pattern or file list provided.
mget [Files]	Downloads multiple files as per the pattern or file list provided.
mkdir [Directory]	Creates a directory.
mput [Files]	Uploads multiple files as per the pattern or file list provided.
put [File]	Uploads the given file.
Quit	Disconnects and exits FTP.

TFTP

You use the *TFTP* command to transfer files to and from a remote computer that is running the TFTP service. The syntax of this command is:

```
TFTP [-i] [Host] [{get | put}] [Source] [Destination]
```

In principle, the *TFTP* command works in a similar way as the *FTP* command. Unlike the *FTP* command, however, the *TFTP* command does not support an extensive list of features; thus, the use of the word *Trivial* in its name. You can upload and download commands via the command line when executing this command. Table 12.17 lists different parameters that you can use with the *TFTP* command.

Table 12.17 Parameters of the TFTP Command

Parameter	Description
–i	Specifies binary image download mode. If you omit this parameter, the transfer occurs in ASCII mode.
Host	Specifies the remote computer to which to connect.
Get	Downloads the given file.
Put	Uploads the given file.
Source	Specifies the file to transfer.
Destination	Specifies the target location of the file transferred.

RCP

You use the *RCP* command to copy files between a client computer and a server computer running the Remote Shell Service (RSHD) or deamon. RSHD is not available on computers running Windows 2000 or Windows XP. The syntax of this command is:

```
RCP [{-a | -b}] [-h] [-r] [Host][.User:] [Source] [Host][.User:]
[Path\Destination]
```

Table 12.18 lists parameters of the *RCP* command.

Table 12.18 Parameters of the RCP Command

Parameter	Description
–a	Specifies ASCII transfer mode.
–b	Specifies binary transfer mode.
–h	Specifies that some or all of the source files have the hidden attribute set. If this is not specified, hidden files are skipped.
–r	Recursively copies files.
Host	Specifies the local and/or remote host computer.
User	Specifies the username. If not provided, the current user is used.

Continued

Table 12.18 continued Parameters of the RCP Command

Parameter	Description
Source	Specifies the files to copy.
Path\Destination	Specifies the path relative to the logon directory on the remote computer.

To understand use of the *RCP* command, consider that you need to copy a file named test.txt from the local Windows XP computer to a remote UNIX computer named *Unix Server* in the */Upload* directory. The syntax of that command would be:

```
RCP test.txt UnixServer:/Upload
```

RSH and REXEC

You use the *RSH* and *REXEC* commands to run commands on remote computers running the RSH (for the *RSH* command) or REXEC (for the *REXEC* command) service or daemon. These services are typically on UNIX/Linux computers and are not available on Windows 2000 or Windows XP. The syntax of these commands is:

```
RSH [Host] [-l UserName] [-n] [Command]
REXEC [Host] [-l UserName] [-n] [Command]
```

Both of these commands take similar command-line parameters, as listed in Table 12.19.

Table 12.19 Parameters of the RSH and REXEC Commands

Argument	Description
Host	Specifies the remote host on which to execute the command.
–l Username	Specifies the username to use on the remote computer. If omitted, the currently logged-on user is used.
–n	Redirects the *rsh* inputs to the *NUL* (nothing) device. In other words, ignores the results of the command executed.
Command	Specifies the command to execute on the remote computer.

To explain use of these commands, consider that you want to start the Web server on a remote computer named *UnixServer*. You would use the following command:

```
RSH UnixServer -l root httpd
REXEC UnixServer -l root httpd
```

LPR

You use the *LPR* command to send a file to a printer connected to a computer running the Line Printer Daemon (LPD) service. The syntax of this command is:

```
LPR [-S ServerID] -P PrinterName [-C BannerContent] [-J JobName] [{-o | -o 1}]
[-d] [-x] FileName
```

Table 12.20 lists the parameters of the *LPR* command.

Table 12.20 Parameters of the LPR Command

Parameter	Description
–S ServerID	Specifies the remote computer name or IP address that is running the LPD service.
–P PrinterName	Specifies the name of the printer on which to print.
–C BannerContent	Specifies the content of the banner that will be printed along with the file.
–J JobName	Specifies the *jobname* that will be printed on the banner.
*{–o	–o l}*	Uses *–o* to print a text file and *–o l* to print a binary file (such as a PostScript file).
–d	Specifies that the data file must be sent before the control file.
–x	Specifies that the *LPR* command must behave in a mode compatible with SunOS 4.1.4_ul.

LPQ

You use the *LPQ* command to display the status of a print queue on a computer running the LPD service. The syntax of this command is:

```
LPQ -S ServerName -P PrinterName [-1]
```

Table 12.21 explains the parameters used with this command.

Table 12.21 Parameters of the LPQ Command

Argument	Description
–S ServerName	Specifies by name the remote computer to query.
–P PrinterName	Specifies by name the printer on the computer to query.
–l	Specifies that status details are requested.

Summary

In this chapter, we examined how to perform basic diagnostic tasks and how to use the standard network tools available with Windows command-line utilities. We discussed use of the *Net* command and its associated subcommands. We learned which Windows services are network related and how to find their "real" name. We then went on to examine a number of other network administration tools, such as *Ping*, *IPConfig*, *Pathping*, *Finger*, and *ARP*. We spent extra time investigating how to use the more powerful *Netstat* and *NBTStat* commands and how to interpret the results of those commands. We even delved into the world of DNS by looking at the versatile DNS querying command-line tool, *NSLookup*. Finally, we looked at how to communicate with remote UNIX computers and the services they use which are not commonly, if at all, found on Windows computers. We introduced the *RSH* and *REXEC* commands, and then closed with a discussion on how to print on UNIX printers and how to monitor those print jobs.

Chapter 13

Administering
Network Services

Topics in this chapter:

- **Overview of the NETSH Commands**

- **NETSH Commands for Troubleshooting**

- **Managing Interfaces with NETSH**

- **Managing Automatic Addressing Using DHCP Services**

- **NETSH Commands for AAAA**

Introduction

Bypassing the network configuration graphical user interface (GUI), NETSH is a command-line scripting utility that you can use, locally or remotely, to display or modify the network configuration of a computer. NETSH interacts with other operating system components using helpers (dynamic link library [DLL] files), each providing an extensive set of features called a *context*, which is a group of commands specific to a networking component. You can direct the context commands you enter to the appropriate helper, and the helper will then carry out the commands. These contexts extend the functionality of NETSH by providing configuration and monitoring support for one or more services, or protocols. In addition, NETSH provides a scripting feature that allows you to run a group of commands in batch mode against a specified computer, and save those configuration scripts in a text file for future configuration of other computers.

Overview of the NETSH Commands

The NETSH commands run within the NETSH command interpreter. To use NETSH you need to start the NETSH command interpreter from within the command prompt window, as follows:

```
Start | Run | Cmd
```

Type **NETSH** at the prompt and press **Enter**. This will change the prompt to the *netsh>* context prompt. As with most Microsoft command-line utilities, typing a **?** at the prompt will provide you with a list of available commands.

Commands Available within the NETSH Prompt

The NETSH command interpreter provides several subcommands for managing network services in a Windows Server 2003 environment. First, let's look at some of the internal commands that you can use within the NETSH context. Most of these commands are similar to the traditional Windows command prompt and you can use them in a similar way. Table 13.1 provides a review of these commands.

Table 13.1 List of Internal NETSH Commands

Command	Function
..	Goes up one context level.
?	Displays a list of commands.
Abort	Discards changes made while in offline mode.
Add	Adds a configuration entry to a list of entries.
Alias	Adds an alias.

Continued

Table 13.1 continued List of Internal NETSH Commands

Command	Function
Bye	Exits the program.
Commit	Commits changes made while in offline mode.
Delete	Deletes a configuration entry from a list of entries.
Dump	Displays a configuration script.
Exec	Runs a script file.
Exit	Exits the program.
Help	Displays a list of commands.
Offline	Sets the current mode to offline.
Online	Sets the current mode to online.
Popd	Pops a context from the stack.
Pushd	Pushes the current context onto the stack.
Quit	Exits the program.
Set	Updates configuration settings.
Show	Displays information.
Unalias	Deletes an alias.

The following commands, when entered at the *NETSH>* prompt, will open a NETSH subcontext presenting you with a subcontext prompt, *NETSHsub-context>*.

List of Subcommands Available within the NETSH Prompt

The following is a list of the subcommands available within the NETSH prompt:

Bridge

Dhcp

Diag

Firewall

Interface

Ras

Routing

Wins

Winsock

Typing a **?** or **help** after any of the aforementioned commands will show the subcommands for each respective subcontext command.

Master Craftsman...

Show Helper

If you see the words *The following command was not found: "sub-context name"* after entering a subcontext command at the NETSH prompt, you probably do not have the necessary helper (DLL) installed (e.g., you need to have the Dynamic Host Configuration Protocol [DHCP] installed to utilize the DHCP subcontext). If you want to find which helpers you have installed, you can use the *show helper* command:

```
netsh>show helper
Helper GUID                              DLL Filename Command
---------------------------------------- ------------ -------
{00770721-44EA-11D5-93BA-00B0D022DD1F} HNETMON.DLL  bridge
{CC41B21B-8040-4BB0-AC2A-820623160940} DGNET.DLL    diag
{8B3A0D7F-1F30-4402-B753-C4B2C7607C97} FWCFG.DLL    firewall
{0705ECA1-7AAC-11D2-89DC-006008B0E5B9} IFMON.DLL    interface
{89D00931-1E00-11D3-8738-00600837C775} IFMON.DLL    ip
{05BB0FE9-8D89-48DE-B7BB-9F138B2E950C} IPV6MON.DLL  ipv6
{F1EFA7E5-7169-4EC0-A63A-9B22A743E19C} IPV6MON.DLL  6to4
{F1EFA7E5-7169-4EC0-A63A-9B22A743E19C} IPV6MON.DLL  isatap
{86A3A33F-4D51-47FF-B24C-8E9B13CEB3A2} IPV6MON.DLL  portproxy
{65EC23C0-D1B9-11D2-89E4-006008B0E5B9} IPMONTR.DLL  routing
{0705ECA0-7AAC-11D2-89DC-006008B0E5B9} IPMONTR.DLL  ip
{0705ECA3-7AAC-11D2-89DC-006008B0E5B9} IPPROMON.DLL autodhcp
{0705ECA3-7AAC-11D2-89DC-006008B0E5B9} IPPROMON.DLL dnsproxy
{0705ECA3-7AAC-11D2-89DC-006008B0E5B9} IPPROMON.DLL igmp
{0705ECA3-7AAC-11D2-89DC-006008B0E5B9} IPPROMON.DLL nat
{0705ECA3-7AAC-11D2-89DC-006008B0E5B9} IPPROMON.DLL ospf
{0705ECA3-7AAC-11D2-89DC-006008B0E5B9} IPPROMON.DLL relay
{0705ECA3-7AAC-11D2-89DC-006008B0E5B9} IPPROMON.DLL rip
{0705ECA3-7AAC-11D2-89DC-006008B0E5B9} IPPROMON.DLL routerdiscovery
{B1641451-84B8-11D2-B940-3078302C2030} IPXMONTR.DLL ipx
{D3FCBA3A-A4E9-11D2-B944-00C04FC2AB1C} IPXPROMN.DLL netbios
```

Continued

```
{D3FCBA3A-A4E9-11D2-B944-00C04FC2AB1C} IPXPROMN.DLL  rip
{D3FCBA3A-A4E9-11D2-B944-00C04FC2AB1C} IPXPROMN.DLL  sap
{BF563723-9065-11D2-BE87-00C04FC3357A} WINSMON.DL1   wins
{B2C0EEF4-CCE5-4F55-934E-ABF60F3DCF56} IFMON.DLL     winsock
```

Here we see that the preceding system does not have the RAS or DHCP subcontexts available.

NOTE

Because the NETSH commands are meant primarily for managing network services running on Windows Server 2003, you cannot run these NETSH commands locally on Windows XP Professional or Windows XP Home Edition. To run these NETSH commands on a remote Windows 2000 Server, you must first use a Remote Desktop Connection to connect to a Windows 2000 Server that is running Terminal Server.

Now we'll look at some of the things you can quickly view and/or change with NETSH.

NETSH Available Information

It's easy to obtain information about available interfaces, system configurations, and the operating system from the NETSH prompt.

For instance, to obtain information about our mail configuration (Internet proxy and news client), along with operating system, modem, and network interface information, you can use the *diag show all* command:

```
netsh>diag show all

Default Outlook Express Mail (pop.111.111 / smtp.111.111)

Default Outlook Express News (nntp.111.111)

Internet Explorer Web Proxy (127.0.0.1)

Loopback (127.0.0.1)

Computer System (YOUVEBEENHACKED)
```

```
Operating System (Microsoft Windows XP Professional)

Version (5.1.2600)

Modems (Conexant Modem)

Network Adapters
     1. [00000010] Gigabit Integrated Controller
     2. [00000011] Wireless

Network Clients
     1. Microsoft Terminal Services
     2. Microsoft Windows Network
     3. Web Client Network
```

The *interface show interface* command returns a list of available interfaces with their type and state:

```
netsh>interface show interface
```

Here is the output of the preceding command:

Admin State	State	Type	Interface Name
Enabled	Connected	Loopback	Loopback
Enabled	Connected	Internal	Internal
Enabled		Dedicated	Broadcom LAN
Enabled	Connected	Dedicated	Wireless
Enabled	Connected	Dedicated	Local Area Connection 4
Enabled	Connected	Dedicated	Wireless Network Connection 2
Enabled	Connected	Dedicated	Local Area Connection 3
Enabled	Connected	Dedicated	{B0208494-099C-4FE8-8B67-
5DCED3A6ED32}			
Enabled	Connected	Dedicated	1394 Connection 7
Enabled	Connected	Dedicated	1394 Connection 6
Enabled	Connected	Dedicated	1394 Connection 3
Enabled	Connected	Dedicated	Local Area Connection 2
Enabled	Connected	Dedicated	Local Area Connection

You can check the operational mode of the Windows firewall on each interface from the command line with NETSH:

```
netsh>firewall show opmode
```

The output of the preceding command is:

```
Domain profile configuration:
-----------------------------------------------------
Operational mode              = Enable
Exception mode         = Enable


Standard profile configuration (current):
-----------------------------------------------------
Operational mode              = Enable
Exception mode         = Enable


Gigabit LAN firewall configuration:
-----------------------------------------------------
Operational mode              = Enable


Wireless firewall configuration:
-----------------------------------------------------
Operational mode              = Enable


1394 Connection 5 firewall configuration:
-----------------------------------------------------
Operational mode              = Disable
```

Now that we have taken a quick look at the basics, let's start with some troubleshooting techniques using NETSH.

NETSH Commands for Troubleshooting

NETSH can be a handy tool for troubleshooting and diagnosing network service parameters such as connecting to mail and proxy servers, pinging interfaces, and showing OS and network information. You can do this by utilizing the *Diag* (short for diagnostic) subcontext. Let's look at the useful information we can retrieve with the NETSH *Diag* commands.

TIP

To see a list of the available *Diag* context commands, you simply type **diag ?** at the NETSH prompt:
    NETSH>diag ?

Using Ping to Verify Connectivity

If you were having an issue connecting to the Internet or an Internet-based server, such as a mail server, you would begin by checking basic connectivity with the *Ping* command. The NETSH *ping adapter* command offers quite a bit more than a standard ping. If left alone without any parameters, it will verify connectivity of all adapters and their respective gateways, domain name system (DNS) servers, and Internet Protocol (IP) addresses.

If you wanted to see the statistic for all adapters, you could use the following command:

```
NETSH>diag ping adapter
```

For a specific adapter, you could list part of the adapter name or the adapter number, as follows:

```
NETSH>diag ping adapter wlan*
NETSH>diag ping adapter 2
```

Here is the output of the preceding commands:

```
Network Adapters

    2. [00000011] ADAPTER NAME
       DefaultIPGateway = xxx.xxx.100.111 Same Subnet
               Pinging xxx.xxx.100.111 with 32 bytes of data:
               Reply from xxx.xxx.100.111: bytes=32 time=1ms TTL=1
               Reply from xxx.xxx.100.111: bytes=32 time=1ms TTL=1
               Reply from xxx.xxx.100.111: bytes=32 time=1ms TTL=1
               Reply from xxx.xxx.100.111: bytes=32 time=1ms TTL=1
               Ping statistics for xxx.xxx.100.111:
                   Packets: Sent = 4, Received = 4, Lost = 0 (0% loss)
               Approximate round trip times in milli-seconds:
                   Minimum = 1ms, Maximum = 1ms, Average = 1ms
       DNSServerSearchOrder = xxx.xxx.1.42
               Pinging xxx.xxx.1.42 with 32 bytes of data:
               Reply from xxx.xxx.1.42: bytes=32 time=10ms TTL=10
               Reply from xxx.xxx.1.42: bytes=32 time=11ms TTL=11
               Reply from xxx.xxx.1.42: bytes=32 time=11ms TTL=11
               Reply from xxx.xxx.1.42: bytes=32 time=13ms TTL=13
               Ping statistics for xxx.xxx.1.42:
                   Packets: Sent = 4, Received = 4, Lost = 0 (0% loss)
               Approximate round trip times in milli-seconds:
                   Minimum = 10ms, Maximum = 13ms, Average = 11ms
                           xxx.xxx.1.46
               Pinging xxx.xxx.1.46 with 32 bytes of data:
               Reply from xxx.xxx.1.46: bytes=32 time=11ms TTL=11
```

```
        Reply from xxx.xxx.1.46: bytes=32 time=11ms TTL=11
        Reply from xxx.xxx.1.46: bytes=32 time=10ms TTL=10
        Reply from xxx.xxx.1.46: bytes=32 time=11ms TTL=11
        Ping statistics for xxx.xxx.1.46:
            Packets: Sent = 4, Received = 4, Lost = 0 (0% loss)
        Approximate round trip times in milli-seconds:
            Minimum = 10ms, Maximum = 11ms, Average = 10ms
    IPAddress = xxx.xxx.100.112
        Pinging xxx.xxx.100.112 with 32 bytes of data:
        Reply from xxx.xxx.100.112: bytes=32 time<1ms TTL=0
        Reply from xxx.xxx.100.112: bytes=32 time<1ms TTL=0
        Reply from xxx.xxx.100.112: bytes=32 time<1ms TTL=0
        Reply from xxx.xxx.100.112: bytes=32 time<1ms TTL=0
        Ping statistics for xxx.xxx.100.112:
            Packets: Sent = 4, Received = 4, Lost = 0 (0% loss)
        Approximate round trip times in milli-seconds:
            Minimum = 0ms, Maximum = 0ms, Average = 0ms
```

You can see that you have connectivity to the gateway, DNS servers, and interface IP. You can further verify connectivity to the Internet Explorer proxy server, by utilizing the *diag ping ieproxy* command:

```
NETSH>diag ping ieproxy
```

The output of this command is:

```
Internet Explorer Web Proxy (127.0.0.1)
    IEProxy = 127.0.0.1
            Pinging 127.0.0.1 with 32 bytes of data:
            Reply from 127.0.0.1: bytes=32 time<1ms TTL=0
            Reply from 127.0.0.1: bytes=32 time<1ms TTL=0
            Reply from 127.0.0.1: bytes=32 time<1ms TTL=0
            Reply from 127.0.0.1: bytes=32 time<1ms TTL=0
            Ping statistics for 127.0.0.1:
                Packets: Sent = 4, Received = 4, Lost = 0 (0% loss)
            Approximate round trip times in milli-seconds:
                Minimum = 0ms, Maximum = 0ms, Average = 0ms
```

Now that you have verified the Web proxy server, you can verify connectivity to the mail server by utilizing the *diag ping mail* command:

```
NETSH>diag ping mail
```

The output of this command is:

```
Default Outlook Express Mail (xxx.xxx.254.254 / xxx.xxx.254.254)
    InBoundMailServer = xxx.xxx.254.254
```

```
Pinging xxx.xxx.254.254 with 32 bytes of data:
Request timed out.
Request timed out.
Request timed out.
Request timed out.
Ping statistics for xxx.xxx.254.254:
    Packets: Sent = 4, Received = 0, Lost = 4 (100% loss)
OutBoundMailServer = xxx.xxx.254.254
Pinging xxx.xxx.254.254 with 32 bytes of data:
Request timed out.
Request timed out.
Request timed out.
Request timed out.
Ping statistics for xxx.xxx.254.254:
    Packets: Sent = 4, Received = 0, Lost = 4 (100% loss)
```

With this, you can conclude that you do not have connectivity to your mail server and connectivity is a remote issue.

To wrap up this section on NETSH *Diag* we will utilize perhaps the most thorough and informative command: *show test*. For this command, we are going to exit out of the NETSH command prompt and issue the following command to write all of the data to a text file named testinfo.txt:

```
NETSH>exit

C:\>netsh diag show test /v > c:\testinfo.txt
```

TIP

You can utilize the /v or /p switch to allow (/v) or suppress (/p) fields with null values in the output from this command.

One of the nice features of this command is its capability to report not only all the network statistics and interface information, but operating system information as well. The following listing details the output of the NETSH *diag show test* command:

```
Loopback (127.0.0.1)
    Loopback = 127.0.0.1
            Pinging 127.0.0.1 with 32 bytes of data:
            Reply from 127.0.0.1: bytes=32 time<1ms TTL=0
            Reply from 127.0.0.1: bytes=32 time<1ms TTL=0
```

```
         Reply from 127.0.0.1: bytes=32 time<1ms TTL=0
         Reply from 127.0.0.1: bytes=32 time<1ms TTL=0
         Ping statistics for 127.0.0.1:
             Packets: Sent = 4, Received = 4, Lost = 0 (0% loss)
         Approximate round trip times in milli-seconds:
             Minimum = 0ms, Maximum = 0ms, Average = 0ms


Computer System (YOUVEBEENHACKED)
     AdminPasswordStatus = 3
     AutomaticResetBootOption = TRUE
     AutomaticResetCapability = TRUE
     BootOptionOnLimit = (empty)
     BootOptionOnWatchDog = (empty)
     BootROMSupported = TRUE
     BootupState = Normal boot
     Caption = YOUVEBEENHACKED
     ChassisBootupState = 3
     CreationClassName = Win32_ComputerSystem
     CurrentTimeZone = -240
     DaylightInEffect = TRUE
     Description = AT/AT COMPATIBLE
     Domain = HACKERS
     DomainRole = 0
     EnableDaylightSavingsTime = TRUE
     Manufacturer = XYZ
     Model = XYZ
     Name = YOUVEBEENHACKED
     NetworkServerModeEnabled = TRUE
     NumberOfProcessors = 1
     PartOfDomain = FALSE
     PrimaryOwnerName = My
     SystemStartupOptions = "Microsoft Windows XP Professional" /fastdetect /sos
/noguiboot
     SystemStartupSetting = 0
     SystemType = X86-based PC
     TotalPhysicalMemory = 1072930816
     UserName = YOUVEBEENHACKED\SuperHacker
Operating System (Microsoft Windows XP Professional)
     BootDevice = \Device\HarddiskVolume1
     BuildNumber = 2600
     BuildType = Uniprocessor Free
     Caption = Microsoft Windows XP Professional
```

```
    CodeSet = 1252
    CountryCode = 1
    CreationClassName = Win32_OperatingSystem
    CSCreationClassName = Win32_ComputerSystem
    CSDVersion = Service Pack 2
    CSName = YOUVEBEENHACKED
    CurrentTimeZone = -240
    ForegroundApplicationBoost = 2
    FreePhysicalMemory = 479472
    FreeSpaceInPagingFiles = 2075596
    FreeVirtualMemory = 2052124
    Manufacturer = Microsoft Corporation
    Name = Microsoft Windows XP
Professional|C:\WINDOWS|\Device\Harddisk0\Partition1
    Organization = Self
    OSLanguage = 1033
    OSProductSuite = (empty)
    OSType = 18
    Primary = TRUE
    ProductType = 1
    RegisteredUser = My
    SerialNumber = xxxxxxxxxxxxxxxx
    TotalVirtualMemorySize = 2097024
    TotalVisibleMemorySize = 1047784
    Version = 5.1.2600
    WindowsDirectory = C:\WINDOWS
Version (5.1.2600)
    Version = 5.1.2600
    BuildVersion = 2600.0000
```

Although the preceding code shows only partial information, you can still see that the command provides a wealth of information that you can use for diagnostic purposes.

Managing Interfaces with NETSH

Another useful aspect of the NETSH context commands is their capability to view and manage IP statistics and settings. You can accomplish everything, from viewing IP addresses to configuring interfaces, from the command line of the NETSH context commands.

Managing IP Addressing

Managing static IP addressing often requires reviewing and even saving current configurations before making changes. We will begin by checking our current settings and statistics and saving them before making changes to the adapters.

NETSH Interface IP Show Commands

To display the basic IP address information of your interfaces, you utilize the *ip show address* command. The syntax of this command is:

```
NETSH>interface ip show address
```

The output of this command is:

```
Configuration for interface "Wireless"
    DHCP enabled:               No
    IP Address:                 xxx.xxx.xxx.112
    SubnetMask:                 255.255.255.0
    Default Gateway:            xxx.xxx.xxx.111
    GatewayMetric:              0
    InterfaceMetric:            0
```

NETSH offers the ability to view Management Information Base (MIB) information for network management of Transmission Control Protocol/Internet Protocol (TCP/IP)-based networks: (MIB-II) Internet standard RFC 1213-compliant IP statistics for the interfaces. You utilize the *interface ip show ip address* command to retrieve this information, as follows:

```
NETSH>interface ip show ip address
```

Here is the output of this command:

```
MIB-II IP Statistics
--------------------------------------------------------------
Forwarding is:          Enabled
Default TTL:                    128
In Receives:                    1368603
In Header Errors:               0
In Address Errors:              1541
Datagrams Forwarded:    0
In Unknown Protocol:    0
In Discarded:                   195659
In Delivered:                   1172896
Out Requests:                   818500
Routing Discards:               0
Out Discards:                   132
Out No Routes:          0
Reassembly Timeouts:    60
Reassembly Required:    0
Reassembled Ok:         0
Reassembly Failures:    0
Fragments Ok:                   0
```

```
Fragments Failed:                         0
Fragments Created:                        0
```

Additionally, you can see the MIB-II Interface information by utilizing the *interface ip show interface* command, as shown here:

```
NETSH>interface ip show interface
```

Here is the output of the preceding command:

```
MIB-II Interface Information

---------------------------------------------------------

Index:                              65539
User-friendly Name:                 Wireless
GUID Name:                          {3829510E-B4C2-473A-A449-xxxxxxxxxxxxx}
Type:                               Ethernet
MTU:                                1500
Speed:                              54000000
Physical Address:                   00-xx-xx-xx-xx-xx
Admin Status:                       Up
Operational Status:                 Operational
Last Change:                        143616584
In Octets:                          27145664
In Unicast Packets:                 35639
In Non-unicast Packets:             2031
In Packets Discarded:         0
In Erroneous Packets:         0
In Unknown Protocol Packets:  0
Out Octets:                         33507292
Out Unicast Packets:          69333
Out Non-unicast Packets:            1325
Out Packets Discarded:        0
Out Erroneous Packets:        0
Output Queue Length:          0
Description:                        Wireless
```

You may find it useful to store interface information, especially if you need to make changes to an interface. If those changes cause problems, having the original configuration information stored can be quite handy. To do this, you exit the NETSH context command prompt by typing **Exit** at the *NETSH>* prompt.

To help automate this process, you can create a batch file named winterface.bat and enter the following four commands in the batch file:

```
netsh interface ip show address wireless > w-interface.txt
```

```
netsh interface ip show ip address wireless >> w-interface.txt
netsh interface ip show interface wireless >> w-interface.txt
netsh interface ip show config wireless >> w-interface.txt
```

For the command prompt, you run the winterface.bat file, which outputs the same information you reviewed previously, into a text file named winterface.txt, with the additional information from the *interface ip show config* command. You can run this command from the command prompt as shown here:

```
C:>winterface.bat
```

When you execute this command, the output is displayed as shown here:

```
Configuration for interface "wireless"
    DHCP enabled:                       No
    IP Address:             xxx.xxx.100.112
    SubnetMask:             255.255.255.0
    Default Gateway:        xxx.xxx.100.111
    GatewayMetric:                      0
    InterfaceMetric:        0
    Statically Configured
    DNS Servers:                        xxx.xxx.1.42
                                        xxx.xxx.1.46
    Statically Configured
    WINS Servers:                       None
    Register with which suffix:None
```

NETSH Interface IP Set Commands

Now that we have saved our interface configuration, let's discuss changing, adding, and deleting the interface information from the command line with NETSH. The following sections explain how you can use the NETSH Interface IP commands for these purposes.

NETSH *Interface IP Set Address*

You can set the IP address, gateway address, and metric on an interface with the *set address* command. You can use this command to switch the interfaces to receive dynamic or static addressing by specifying the DHCP or static switch. If the interface is configured statically, the DNS server address for the interface must also be configured statically, a process we will cover later in this chapter. If a default gateway is not specified, the current configuration is maintained.

We will begin by utilizing the following command to set our interface to receive a static address, and then we will switch to a dynamic address:

```
NETSH>interface ip set address name=" Gigabti lan " source=static
addr=192.168.111.112 mask=255.255.255.0 gateway=192.168.111.
111 gwmetric=1
```

When you execute this command, the command interpreter configures the interface and displays **OK** at the command prompt.

Master Craftsman...

Show Address

To verify that the configuration changes were made correctly, use the *show address* command:

```
netsh>interface ip show address "gigabit lan"
Configuration for interface "gigabit lan"
    DHCP enabled:              No
    IP Address:                192.168.111.112
    SubnetMask:                255.255.255.0
    Default Gateway:           192.168.111.111
    GatewayMetric:        1
    InterfaceMetric:           0
```

To switch the interface to accept dynamic IP information and to verify the configuration changes, use the following command:

```
NETSH>interface ip set address name="gigabit lan" source=dhcp
```

When you execute this command, the command interpreter displays **OK** at the prompt. You can view the new configuration of the interface by using the following command:

```
netsh>interface ip show address "gigabit lan"
```

When you execute this command, the information about the specified interface is displayed as follows:

```
Configuration for interface "gigabit lan"
    DHCP enabled:                    Yes
    InterfaceMetric:        0
```

NETSH Interface IP Add Address

Say you are required to add additional IP addresses and gateways to your interfaces. Under normal situations, you would use the Windows GUIs, but that can be time consuming. As an alternative, you can use the NETSH commands to accomplish the same task in much less time and with much less effort. Specifically, you can use the *NETSH interface ip add address* command to simplify this task. The following example explains the syntax and use of this command:

```
NETSH>interface ip add address name="gigabit lan" addr=192.168.121.122
mask=255.255.255.0 gateway=192.168.121.121 gwmetric=50
```

When you execute this command successfully, the command interpreter displays the **OK** message. Now let's look at the results of this command by viewing the IP address of the interface:

```
NET>interface ip show address "gigabit lan"

Configuration for interface "gigabit lan"
     DHCP enabled:                  No
     IP Address:           192.168.111.112
     SubnetMask:           255.255.255.0
     IP Address:           192.168.121.122
     SubnetMask:           255.255.255.0
     Default Gateway:      192.168.111.111
     GatewayMetric:                 1
     Default Gateway:      192.168.121.121
     GatewayMetric:                 50
     InterfaceMetric:      0
```

You can see that the interface now contains the IP addresses of both the *set* and *add* commands.

NETSH Interface IP Delete Address

Deleting an IP address from an interface is just as easy with NETSH. One additional function you have with the *delete* command is the ability to delete all active gateways on an interface. The following example shows the syntax and use of this command:

```
NETSH>interface ip delete address adress name="gigabit lan" addr=192.168.121.122
mask=255.255.255.0 gateway=192.168.121.121
```

You can simply change the gateway syntax to *all* by using the following command:

```
NETSH>interface ip delete address adress name="gigabit lan" addr=192.168.121.122
mask=255.255.255.0 gateway=all
```

www.syngress.com

Swiss Army Knife...

Add and Delete Commands

With the *add* and *delete* commands, you can use all or any part of the command syntax. If you just wanted to set the gateway on an interface, you would simply enter only that portion of the command:

```
netsh>interface ip set address name="gigabit lan" gateway=192.168.111.222
gwmetric=1
```

To delete all the gateways, use this command:

```
netsh>interface ip delete address name="gigabit lan" gateway=all
```

Managing the DNS Settings of an Interface

You are probably familiar with the DNS tab in the TCP/IP Properties GUI under Network Connections. You can utilize NETSH functionality to view and change the DNS settings on any interface from the command line. The following sections explain how you can use the NETSH commands to view or configure the DNS settings of a specified interface.

NETSH Interface IP Show DNS

Similar to the *show address* command, the *show dns* command provides information on current DNS settings. The basic syntax of this command is:

NETSH>interface ip show dns

When you run this command from within the NETSH prompt, output is displayed as follows:

```
Configuration for interface "Wireless"
    Statically Configured DNS Servers:        192.168.100.1
                                              192.168.100.2

    Register with which suffix:               None


Configuration for interface "Gigabit LAN"
    Statically Configured DNS Servers:        192.168.111.1
                                              192.168.121.1

    Register with which suffix:               None
```

NETSH Interface IP Set DNS

If you want to set the DNS address on a Gigabit LAN interface to have a static address and enable dynamic DNS registration to register under the primary DNS suffix as well as the connection-specific suffix, you would execute the following command at the NETSH prompt:

```
NETSH>interface ip set dns name="gigabit lan" source=static addr=10.0.0.1
register=both
```

To view and verify the configuration changes you made, you can use the *show* command as follows:

```
NETSH>interface ip show dns "gigabit lan"
```

When you execute this command at the NETSH prompt, the following output is displayed:

```
Configuration for interface "gigabit lan"

    Statically Configured DNS Servers: 10.0.0.1
    Register with which suffix:Both primary and connection-specific
```

NETSH Interface IP Add DNS

You can also add additional DNS servers to the current list of DNS servers for an interface and assign a preference to each of them. To accomplish this, you utilize the *add dns* command with the index parameter, as shown here:

```
NETSH>interface ip add dns name="gigabit lan" addr=10.0.0.2 index=3
```

```
NETSH>interface ip add dns name="gigabit lan" addr=10.0.0.3 index=3
```

NETSH Interface IP Delete DNS

If you need to remove any DNS servers from the configured DNS servers for an interface, you can use the following command:

```
NETSH>interface ip delete dns name="gigabit lan" addr=10.0.0.3
```

When you execute this command, the specified DNS server is deleted from the list of DNS servers assigned to the interface.

Master Craftsman...

The Set Command

Do you know that you can delete interface-specific information by using the *set* command you normally use for setting interface information? If you substitute the word *none* where you normally place information you want to set, you will delete the current entries. For example:

```
netsh>interface ip set dns name="gigabit lan" source=static addr=none
Ok.
netsh>interface ip show dns name="gigabit lan"
Configuration for interface "gigabit lan"
    Statically Configured DNS Servers:      None
    Register with which suffix:             None
```

Managing Interface IP WINS Settings

You can view and edit interface-specific Windows Internet Name Service (WINS) settings in the same way you can view and change interface-specific DNS settings from the command line with NETSH.

NETSH Interface IP Show WINS

To view the current WINS settings you can use the *show wins* command:

```
NETSH>interface ip show wins name="gigabit lan"
```

When you execute this command, the output is displayed as follows:

```
Configuration for interface "gigabit lan"
    Statically Configured WINS Servers:     192.168.111.222
```

You may notice from this output that only one WINS server is configured on the specified interface and it is statically configured.

NETSH Interface IP Set WINS

To set an interface-specific WINS setting you can use the *set wins* command:

```
NETSH>interface ip set wins name="gigabit lan" source=static addr=192.168.111.123
```

Master Craftsman...

NETSH Syntax

Do you know that you can limit the amount of information you have to enter with NETSH commands once you get used to the syntax? Instead of beginning the parameter data with the parameter name, you can leave that information off.

So this command:

```
netsh>interface ip set wins name="gigabit lan" source=static
addr=192.168.111.123
```

...becomes this command:

```
netsh>interface ip set wins "gigabit lan" static 192.168.111.123
```

NETSH Interface IP Add WINS

To add additional WINS server entries in the WINS list for an interface, you can use the *add wins* command. This command takes the index parameter to set the preference level for the newly added WINS server. The following example shows the syntax and use of this command:

```
NETSH>interface ip add wins "gigabit lan" 192.168.111.222 2
```

You can verify the configuration by using the *show* command:

```
NETSH>interface ip show wins "gigabit lan"
```

The following listing displays the WINS configuration of the interface. You may notice that the newly configured WINS server has been added to the list.

```
Configuration for interface "gigabit lan"
    Statically Configured WINS Servers:        192.168.111.123
                                               192.168.111.222
```

NETSH Interface IP Delete WINS

To delete one or all of the interface-specific WINS entries, you can use the *delete wins* command. The following example shows the syntax and use of this command:

```
NETSH>interface ip delete wins "gigabit lan" all
```

When you execute this command, all WINS servers configured on the specified interface are deleted.

Swiss Army Knife...

NETSH Context

Using the NETSH context command-line utility makes viewing and changing interface-specific information a breeze.

If you have a system you travel with that requires different settings in different environments, NETSH can really be a timesaver (and keep you from making "fat" finger mistakes). We will set up our system to be ready for different environments—"Home," "Work," and "Travel"—by creating three batch files with all the commands we need for these environments.

Requirements:

Home configuration Static

IP address 192.168.1.2

Subnet 255.255.255.0

Default Gateway 192.168.1.1

DNS Servers 192.168.1.100 and 192.168.1.150

Register DNS No

WINS Servers NONE

Work configuration Static

IP address-1 10.0.0.2

IP address-2 192.168.200.2

Subnet-1 255.0.0.0

Subnet-2 255.255.255.0

Default Gateway-1 10.0.0.1

Gateway-2 192.168.200.1

DNS Servers 10.0.0.100 and 192.168.200.100

Resister DNS Both

WINS Servers 10.0.0.150 and 192.168.200.150

Continued

Travel configuration DHCP

DNS DHCP

Register DNS No

WINS none

The HOME.bat file:

We begin with setting the address information:

```
netsh interface ip set address "gigabit lan" static 192.168.1.2
255.255.255.0 192.168.1.1 1
```

...followed by the DNS information:

```
netsh interface ip set dns "gigabit lan" static 192.168.1.100 none
```

Remember to use the *add* command and index parameters for the second DNS entry:

```
netsh interface ip add dns "gigabit lan" 192.168.1.150 2
```

It is important to remember to set *WINS* to *none* because there are no WINS servers at home. Alternatively, you could use the *delete* command to delete all the WINS information:

```
netsh interface ip set wins "gigabit lan" static none
```

The WORK.bat file:

We begin with the IP address information. Remember that there are two addresses, so we need to use the *add* command and set the gateway metric:

```
netsh interface ip set address "gigabit lan" static 10.0.0.2 255.0.0.0
10.0.0.1 1
```

```
netsh interface ip add address "gigabit lan" 192.168.200.2 255.255.255.0
192.168.200.1 20
```

...then the DNS:

```
netsh interface ip set dns "gigabit lan" static 10.0.0.100 both
```

```
netsh interface ip add dns "gigabit lan" 192.168.200.100 2
```

...then the WINS. Remember the index setting because there are two WINS servers:

```
netsh interface ip set wins "gigabit lan" static 10.0.0.150
```

```
netsh interface ip add wins "gigabit lan" 192.168.200.150 2
```

The TRAVEL.bat fie:

We will use the NETSH command to delete any unnecessary entries, and set the DNS and the address to use DHCP:

```
netsh interface ip set address "gigabit lan" dhcp
```

```
netsh interface ip set dns "gigabit lan" dhcp none
```

```
netsh interface ip delete wins "gigabit lan" all
```

Now we can run any of these batch files when necessary to give us the settings we need.

Managing Automatic Addressing Using DHCP Services

Administrators use DHCP in medium to large computer networks to manage automatic assignment of IP addresses to DHCP clients. It is easy to manage DHCP servers using the GUI when you have just a few DHCP servers in the organization. However, when you must manage multiple DHCP servers spread across different locations of the organization and connected by slow wide area network (WAN) links, you may find that NETSH is a better tool for managing DHCP services than the usual GUI.

The NETSH DHCP prompt is located within the NETSH environment. To access the DHCP prompt, just type **DHCP** at the *NETSH>* prompt and press **Enter**. The following prompt is displayed:

```
Dhcp>
```

Within the *DHCP>* prompt, several commands are available for managing DHCP servers. These are mainly categorized as follows:

- *NETSH DHCP*
- *NETSH DHCP SERVER*
- *NETSH DHCP SERVER SCOPE*
- *NETSH DHCP SERVER MSCOPE*

NETSH DHCP

The commands available from the *DHCP>* prompt are listed in the following sections.

Server

The *Server* command shifts the context of the *DHCP>* prompt to the specified DHCP server. The syntax of this command is:

```
Server [{\\ServerName | ServerIP}]
```

You may specify the DHCP server by its name or by its IP address. When you use the name of the DHCP server, you must precede the name with double backslashes (\\).

Show Server

You use the *Show Server* command to obtain a list of DHCP servers that are authorized in Active Directory. The syntax of this command is:

```
Show Server
```

There is no required parameter with this command.

Add Server

You use the *Add Server* command to add a new server to the list of authorized DHCP servers in Active Directory. The syntax of this command is:

```
Add Server ServerDNS ServerIP
```

The parameters of this command are:

- **ServerDNS** Specifies the DNS domain name of the DHCP server that you want to add to the list of authorized DHCP servers in Active Directory.

- **ServerIP** Specifies the IP address of the DHCP server that you want to add to the list of authorized DHCP servers in Active Directory.

The following example illustrates use of the *Add Server* command:

```
Add Server DHCPServ1.books.syngress.com 192.168.0.10
```

This command adds a DHCP server named *DHCPServ1.books.syngress.com* with an IP address of *192.168.0.10* as an authorized server in Active Directory.

Delete Server

You use the *Delete Server* command to delete a DHCP server from the list of authorized servers in Active Directory. The syntax of this command is:

```
Add Server ServerDNS ServerIP
```

The parameters of the *Delete Server* command are similar to those of the *Add Server* command. The following example illustrates use of the *Delete Server* command:

```
Delete Server DHCPServ1.books.syngress.com 192.168.0.10
```

This command removes (deletes) a DHCP server named *DHCPServ1.books.syngress.com* with an IP address of *192.168.0.10* from the list of authorized servers in Active Directory.

Dump

The *Dump* command dumps the configuration of a specified DHCP server to the command prompt window or to a specified file. If you do not use any parameters with this command, the configuration of the DHCP server that is currently in focus is displayed in the command prompt window. The syntax of this command is:

```
[{\\ServerName | IPAddress}] Dump > [FileName]
```

Here are the parameters of this command:

- **\\ServerName** Specifies the name of a remote DHCP server. You must precede the name with double backslashes (\\).

- **IPAddress** Specifies the remote DHCP server by its IP address.
- **Filename** Specifies the name of the file where you want to direct the output of the command. The configuration of the specified DHCP server is saved in this file.

It is important to note that you can use either the name or the IP address of the remote DHCP server. You need not use both of these parameters.

Master Craftsman...

DHCP Servers

Saving the configuration of a DHCP server is useful when you need to diagnose problems with any DHCP servers in the network. Microsoft recommends that you reconcile all scopes on the specified DHCP server. This will ensure that if there are any inconsistencies with the scopes, they are removed. When the DHCP configuration is saved in a text file, the same file can be copied to another DHCP server to configure it. This not only saves you time in configuring a new DHCP server from scratch, but it also ensures that the configuration is correct and accurate.

For example, the following command dumps the configuration of a DHCP server to a text file named DHCPConf.dmp:

```
Dump> DHCPConf.dmp
```

When you execute this command, you can copy the file to another DHCP server and use the *EXEC* command to copy this configuration to the destination DHCP server. You must not open the DHCP console before using the *EXEC* command. You must also delete all default server options, scope options, and any defined user or vendor classes. You use the *EXEC* command as follows on the DHCP server:

```
NETSH EXEC DHCPConf.dmp
```

Once you execute this command, you can start the DHCP services on the destination server using the following command:

```
NET START DHCPSERVER
```

The changes in the configuration of the destination DHCP server take place after the DHCP service starts.

NETSH DHCP SERVER

You can narrow down the NETSH DHCP prompt to a single DHCP server by typing **SERVER** at the *DHCP>* prompt. The prompt changes as follows:

```
DHCP SERVER>
```

Within the DHCP SERVER prompt, there are several different subcommands that you can use to manage a single DHCP server. You can use these commands to view, configure, add, delete, import, or export the DHCP settings. The following sections discuss these commands.

Viewing Configuration Settings

The following commands are available for viewing DHCP server settings. Most of these commands are self-explanatory.

```
Show All
Show Auditlogging
Show Bindings
Show Class
Show Detectconflictretry
Show Dnsconfig
Show Mibiinfo
Show Mscope
Show Optiondef
Show Optionvalue
Show Scope
Show Server
Show Dbproperties
Show Serverstatus
Show Userclass
Show Venderclass
Show Version
```

It is interesting to note that most of these commands do not require any parameters.

Configuring the DHCP Server

The following subcommands are available for configuring the DHCP server:

```
Scope
Mscope
Add Class
Add Scope
Add Mscope
```

```
Delete Class
Delete Scope
Delete Mscope
Delete Superscope
Set Server
Set USerclass
Set Vendorclass
Set Auditlog
Set Dnsconfig
Set Optionvalue
Set Databasename
Set Databasepath
Set Databasebackupinterval
Set Databasebackuppath
Set Databasecleanupinterval
Set Databaseloggingflag
Set Databaserestoreflag
Set Detectconflictretry
```

Besides the preceding commands, you can authorize a DHCP server in Active Directory by using the following command:

```
Initiate Auth
```

This command initiates the process pf authorizing the current DHCP server in Active Directory.

NETSH DHCP SERVER SCOPE

You can narrow down the NETSH DHCP SERVER prompt to a single DHCP scope by typing **SCOPE** at the *DHCP SERVER>* prompt. The prompt changes as follows:

```
DHCP SERVER SCOPE>
```

Within the DHCP SERVER SCOPE prompt, there are several different subcommands that you can use to manage a single DHCP server scope. These commands are discussed in the following sections.

Viewing the Scope Configuration

The following subcommands are available for viewing the current configuration of a DHCP server's scopes:

```
Show Scope
Show State
Show Clients
```

```
Show Clientsv5
Show Iprange
Show Excluderange
Show Reservedip
Show Optionvalue
Show Reservedoptionvalue
```

It is interesting to note that most of these commands do not require any parameters.

Configuring a Scope

The following subcommands are available for configuring DHCP server scopes:

```
Add Iprange
Add Excluderange
Add Reservedip
Delete Iprange
Delete Reservedip
Delete Optionvalue
Delete Reservedoptionvalue
Set Name
Set Comment
Set Scope
Set Superscope
Set State
```

You can initiate the process of reconciling a DHCP server scope by using the following command:

```
Initiate Reconcile
```

When you execute this command, the DHCP server starts reconciling the configured scopes.

NETSH Commands for AAAA

You use the NETSH AAAA command set to view, save, and configure authentication, authorization, accounting, and auditing (the four A's) of the Internet Authentication Service (IAS) and the Routing and Remote Access Service (RRAS). You primarily use NETSH AAAA to export the database of one IAS server and import it to another IAS server. The IAS database is stored as IAS.MDB on the IAS server. To get the AAAA prompt within the NETSH command prompt, you must first type **AAAA** and press **Enter**. The prompt then changes as follows:

```
NETSH AAAA>
```

When this prompt is displayed, you can use other commands in the AAAA context to manage IAS database files.

Master Craftsman...

Using the NETSH AAAA Commands

As we discussed earlier, you cannot run the NETSH commands locally on computers running Windows XP Professional or Windows XP Home Edition. To run these NETSH commands on a remote Windows 2000 Server system, you must first use Remote Desktop Connection to connect to a Windows 2000 Server that is running Terminal Server. You can run these commands from the Windows 2000 command prompt or from the command prompt for the NETSH AAAA context. For these commands to work at the Windows 2000 command prompt, you must type **NETSH AAAA** before typing commands and parameters as they appear in the syntax in the remaining sections of this chapter. There might be functional differences between NETSH context commands on Windows 2000 and Windows XP.

The following sections discuss different subcommands available with the AAAA context.

Show Version

This is the simplest of all NETSH AAAA commands and you use it to view the version of the IAS database on the IAS server where the command is executed. The syntax of the command is:

Show Version

This command does not require any parameters.

Show Config

You use the *Show Config* command to view configuration information of the IAS server where the command is executed. The command displays the NETSH AAAA command script that you can use to duplicate the configuration of a server running IAS or RRAS. The configuration information (IAS.mdb) is stored as a large data block in a compressed text file format. The syntax of this command is:

Show Config

This command does not require any parameters and is equivalent to the *Dump* command, discussed shortly. You can redirect the output of this command to a text file by using the following command:

```
Show Config >Path\FileName.Txt
```

The configuration information is stored in the specified file as compression text data. You can use this configuration to configure another IAS server by using the *NETSH EXEC* command. You may also use this text file to configure the same IAS server in case its current database becomes corrupt.

Set Config

You use the *Set Config* command to configure an IAS server by using the data saved from another IAS server using the *Show Config* or *Dump* command. The syntax of this command is:

```
Set Config [blob=] DataBlock
```

…where *Set Config [blob=]* is a required parameter used to specify the configuration of the IAS database saved in a compressed text format using the *Show Config* or *Dump* command.

NOTE

You must make sure that the versions of the IAS database used to save the configuration matches the destination IAS server where the configuration is restored using the *Set Config* command. You can use the *Show Version* command on both IAS servers to view version numbers. It is also important to note that you should not use the *Set Config* command manually at the command prompt. It is recommended that you use this command within a NETSH AAAA command script or batch file.

Dump

The *Dump* command is similar to the *Show Config* command that you use to display the NETSH AAAA command script that you can use to duplicate the configuration of a server running IAS or RRAS. The configuration information (IAS.MDB) is stored as a large data block in a compressed text file format.

Summary

In this chapter, we discussed the NETSH commands for viewing the settings and configuring networking components in a Windows Server 2003 or Windows XP environment. NETSH runs as a separate command interpreter within the Windows command shell and has a bundle of subcommands associated with it. Although it is not possible to discuss every command or subcommand within the scope of this book, we have tried to explain the most commonly used commands in this chapter. Most experienced system administrators depend on preconfigured batch files or scripts to manage networking services. A search on the Web can be very helpful for you to find ready-made scripts. However, you must try these freely available scripts on a test server before using them on any production server.

Appendix A

MS-DOS Commands Not Supported in Windows XP and Windows 2003

Topics in this chapter:

- **MS-DOS Commands Not Supported in Windows XP/2003 32-Bit Operating Systems**

- **MS-DOS Commands Not Supported in Windows XP/2003 64-Bit Operating Systems**

Introduction

The command shell in Windows XP/2003 uses a command-line interpreter program called cmd.exe. This interpreter provides a command-line environment to execute DOS commands, in a way similar to MS-DOS's command.com. cmd.exe is a 32-bit application, whereas command.com is a 16-bit application. In addition, cmd.exe offers many advantages over command.com, one of which is support for long filenames.

In this appendix, we will discuss the commands that were discontinued in Windows XP/2003 because either they were replaced with a better command or program or they are incompatible with the Windows XP/2003 operating system architecture.

MS-DOS Commands Not Supported in Windows XP/2003 32-Bit Operating Systems

In this section, we will discuss the MS-DOS commands that are not supported in Windows XP/2003 32-bit operating systems.

assign

The *assign* command redirects disk-drive requests to any other specified drive. Executing the command without any parameters makes all the drive assignments reset to normal.

Syntax

```
assign x=y[…] /sta
```

Table A.1 lists the switches that are available in the *assign* command.

Table A.1 Switches Available in the *assign* Command

Switch	Description
x=y	*x* and *y* specify the drive letters of the original and redirected disk drives, respectively.
/sta	Displays the status of disk assignments.

Example

You can use the following command to redirect requests from the B: drive to the A: drive:

```
assign b=a
```

backup

backup is an external MS-DOS command that you can use to make backups of file(s).

Syntax

```
backup [Source:\Path\Filename] [Target:] [/S] [/M] [/A] [/D:date] [/T:time] [/F:size]
[/L:LogDrive:\Path\Log]
```

Table A.2 lists switches that are available in the *backup* command.

Table A.2 Switches Available in the *backup* Command

Switch	Description
Source:\Path\Filename	Specifies the path and name of the file which is to be backed up.
Target:	Specifies the drive letter of the target drive where the backup is created.
/S	Makes a backup of all directories, subdirectories, and files in the specified source location.
/M	Makes the utility back up only files which changed since the last backup.
/A	Creates new backup files instead of overwriting already existing backups.
/D:Date	Backs up only files which are created or modified on the specified date.
/T:Time	Backs up only files which are created or modified at the specified time.
/F:size	Creates backup files of the specified size so that they can be stored on removable media such as floppy disks.
/L:LogDrive:\Path\Log	Specifies the drive, path, and name of the log file which logs all the backup operations carried out.

Example

You can use the following command to back up all the files and subdirectories in the Windows System32 directory:

```
backup C:\Windows\System32\*.* d: /S
```

choice

The *choice* command is useful only in batch file programming. By using this command, you can specify a batch file or script to wait for the user to choose an option from a set of choices.

Syntax

```
choice [/C[:]choices] [/N] [/S] [/T[:]c,nn] [text]
```

Table A.3 lists switches that are available in the *choice* command.

Table A.3 Switches Available in the *choice* Command

Switch	Description
/C[:]choices	Specifies allowable keys, with *Y/N* as the default.
/N	Does not display choices and *?* at the end of a prompt string.
/S	Treats the choice keys as case-sensitive.
/T[:]c,nn	The default choice to choice *c* after *nn* seconds.
Text	The prompt string to display.

Example

In a batch file, if you want to prompt the user to select either Yes or No, the command would be:

```
choice /c:yn
```

In addition, upon execution of the batch file, the user would see the following text at the command prompt:

```
[Y,N]?
```

ctty

You use the *ctty* command to change the standard I/O device to an auxiliary device.

Syntax

```
ctty <device name>
```

Table A.4 lists the valid device names that you can use in the *ctty* command.

Table A.4 Valid Device Names Available in the *ctty* Command

Switch	Description
AUX	Auxiliary port
LPT1	Line printer terminal 1
LPT2	Line printer terminal 2
LPT3	Line printer terminal 3
COM1	Communication port 1
COM2	Communication port 2
COM3	Communication port 3
COM4	Communication port 4
CON	Console

Example

By using the following command, you can redirect the I/O to a remote terminal connected to the auxiliary port:

```
ctty aux
```

Similarly, you can redirect the I/O back to the main terminal by using this command:

```
ctty con
```

deltree

You use the *deltree* command to delete a directory along with all the subdirectories and files in it. In Windows XP/2003, you can obtain this functionality by using the */s* switch for the *rmdir* command.

Syntax

```
deltree [/Y] [drive:]path
```

Table A.5 lists the switches that are available in the *deltree* command.

Table A.5 Switches Available in the *deltree* Command

Switch	Description
/Y	Suppresses the prompt which confirms subdirectory deletion.
[drive:]path	The path and name of the directory you want to delete.

Example

If a nonempty directory named Test situated in the C:\ drive is to be deleted, you would use this command:

```
deltree /y C:\Test
```

emm386

You use the *emm386* command to enable/disable extended memory support for computers running on Intel 80386 and higher processors. *emm* stands for Extended Memory Manager and you use it to access memory greater than 640KB. The function to access higher memory is now coherent in Windows XP/2003 operating systems.

Syntax

```
emm386 [ON | OFF | AUTO] [W=ON | W=OFF]
```

Table A.6 lists the switches available in the *emm386* command.

Table A.6 Switches Available in the *emm386* Command

Switch	Description
ON | OFF | AUTO	Activates or suspends the emm386.exe device driver. If AUTO is chosen, the driver is placed in auto mode.
W=ON | OFF	Turns on or off Weitek coprocessor support.

Example

To enable extended memory support, use the following command:

```
emm386 ON
```

fdisk

fdisk is one of the most powerful and frequently used commands in the MS-DOS and Windows 9X/ME operating systems. *fdisk* allows you to create and/or delete partitions on a hard disk. By simply typing **fdisk** at the command prompt and pressing the **Enter** key, you can invoke the *fdisk* option screen, from where the partitions can be created or deleted.

In Windows XP/2003, you can achieve similar functionality by using the *DiskPart* command.

Syntax

fdisk [/STATUS] /X

Table A.7 lists the switches that are available in the *fdisk* command.

Table A.7 Switches Available in the *fdisk* Command

Switch	Description
/STATUS	Displays partition information.
/X	Ignores support for access of large disk drives.

Example

To get the partition layout of a system the command would be:

fdisk /status

mscdex

You use the *mscdex* command to provide access to CD-ROM drives in MS-DOS subsystems. In Windows XP/2003, this command is uncalled for, as Windows provides CD-ROM drive access for the MS-DOS subsystem.

Syntax

mscdex.exe /D:driver /M:n /E /V /L:x /S /K

Table A.8 lists the switches that are available in the *mscdex* command.

Table A.8 Switches Available in the *mscdex* Command

Switch	Description
/D:driver	Specifies the driver signature of the first CD-ROM device driver.
/M:n	The *n* parameter specifies the number of sector buffers to be used as a cache for the CD-ROM.
/E	Enables extended memory support for the device.
/V	Shows system memory information during system boot up.
/L:x	The *x* parameter specifies the drive letter that is to be assigned to the CD-ROM drive.
/S	Enables the CD-ROM drives to be shared on Windows Workgroup servers.
/K	Makes MS-DOS recognize Japanese disks by enabling the *Kanji* file structure.

Example

You can access a CD-ROM drive from the MS-DOS environment by using the following command:

mscdex.exe /D:MSCD001

Here, *MSCD001* is the driver signature of the CD-ROM drive. If there were two CD-ROM drives in the computer, the command would be:

```
mscdex.exe /d:MSCD001 /d:MSCD002
```

scandisk

You use the *scandisk* command to check the integrity of a computer's hard-disk drive. *scandisk* checks for errors such as bad clusters, lost file fragments, and truncated files. In Windows XP/2003, the *scandisk* command is replaced by *chkdsk*.

Syntax

scandisk [drive: | /all] [/checkonly | /autofix [/nosave] | /custom] [/fragment] [/surface] [/mono] [/nosave] [/nosummary]

Table A.9 lists the switches that are available in the *scandisk* command.

Table A.9 Switches Available in the *scandisk* Command

Switch	Description
drive:	*scandisk* checks the specified drive only.
/all	*scandisk* checks and repairs all local disk drives.
/checkonly	*scandisk* checks the drives for errors but will not repair them.
/autofix	Automatically fixes errors. You cannot use this switch with /*checkonly* or /*custom.*
/custom	*scandisk* runs according to the settings defined in the *[custom]* section of the scandisk.ini file.
/surface	Automatically checks the disk surface without prompting the user.
/fragment	*scandisk* checks a specified file for fragmentation. You cannot use this switch with any other switches.
/mono	Uses a monochrome display.
/nosave	Deletes all the detected lost file fragments and clusters.
/nosummary	Suppresses the full-screen summary that is displayed after the scanning of each drive.

Example

You can use the following command to check all drives for errors:

```
scandisk.exe /all
```

Similarly, if the errors were to be repaired automatically, the command would take the form:

```
scandisk.exe /all /autofix
```

Smartdrv

Smartdrv, which stands for *Smart Drive*, is an external MS-DOS command. You use it to create a disk cache in the extended memory area. *Smartdrv* significantly speeds up MS-DOS disk operations by minimizing disk accesses, as it caches the system files in RAM.

Syntax

Smartdrv [/X] [[drive[+|-]]...] [/U] [/C | /R] [/F | /N] [/L] [/V | /Q | /S] [InitCacheSize [WinCacheSize]] [/E:ElementSize] [/B:BufferSize]

Table A.10 lists the switches that are available in the *smartdrv* command.

Table A.10 Switches Available in the *smartdrv* Command

Switch	Description
/X	Disables write-behind caching for all drives.
Drive	Specifies the drive(s) to which the caching options are to be applied.
+ (or -)	Enables (or disables) write-behind caching for the specified drive(s).
/U	Prevents *smartdrv* from loading the CD-ROM caching module.
/C	Makes *smartdrv* write all the cache information to the hard disk.
/R	Restarts the Smart Drive.
/F	Makes *smartdrv* write the cached data before the command prompt is returned to the user.
/N	Makes *smartdrv* not write the cached data before the command prompt is returned to the user.
/L	Makes *smartdrv* load in the lower memory area.
/V	Displays a Smart Drive status message when loading.
/Q	Disables the Smart Drive status message.
/S	Displays additional Smart Drive status information.
InitCacheSize	Specifies the eXtended Memory Specification (XMS) memory size for the cache, in KB.
WinCacheSize	Specifies the XMS memory size for Windows, in KB.
/E:*ElementSize*	Specifies the number of bytes of data to be moved at once.
/B:*BufferSize*	Specifies the size of the read-ahead buffer.

Example

You would use the following to disable write-behind caching for all drives using the *smartdrv* command:

```
smartdrv /x
```

sys

You use the *sys* command to create a bootable disk, by copying the system files from one drive to the target drive.

Syntax

```
sys [drive1:] [path] drive2:
```

Table A.11 lists the switches that are available in the *sys* command.

Table A.11 Switches Available in the *sys* Command

Switch	Description
[drive1:][path]	Path to the location of the system files.
drive2:	Drive letter of the drive to which the system files are to be copied.

Example

To create a bootable floppy disk using *sys*, the command would be:

```
sys C:\Windows A:
```

MS-DOS Commands Not Supported in Windows XP/2003 64-Bit Operating Systems

In this section, we will discuss commands not supported in Windows XP/2003 64-bit operating systems.

debug

debug is a utility for editing and testing programs. *debug* allows hardware-level access to a programmer.

Syntax

```
debug [[drive:] [path]filename [parameters]]
```

Table A.12 lists the switches that are available in the *debug* command.

Table A.12 Switches Available in the *debug* Command

Switch	Description
[drive:][path]filename	Name and path of the program that is to be tested.
Parameters	Specifies the command-line parameters of the program that is to be tested.

To obtain a list of supported commands in *debug*, type **?** and press the **Enter** key.

Example

To edit a program—say, calc.exe-using *debug*—use the following command:
```
debug C:\windows\calc.exe
```

Once the aforementioned command is run, the assembly language instructions of the program *calc.exe* can be viewed by typing **U** and the **Enter** key.

edit

edit is an MS-DOS-based, full-screen text editor you can use to create or edit ASCII-encoded text files.

Syntax

```
edit [/B] [/H] [/R] [/S] [/<nnn>] [/?] [file(s)]
```

Table A.13 lists the switches that are available in the *edit* command.

Table A.13 Switches Available in the *edit* Command

Switch	Description
/B	Starts the edit in monochrome mode.
/H	Displays as many lines as possible on-screen, depending on the hardware.
/R	Opens the files in read-only mode.
/<nnn>	Specifies character wrapping when opening binary files.
/?	Displays the *edit* command's help.
file(s)	List of the files to load initially when the edit starts.

Example

To edit the autoexec.bat file from the command prompt, you can use the following command:
```
edit c:\autoexec.bat
```

edlin

edlin is a line-based text editor and is a predecessor of the Edit text editor. *edlin* provides a rudimentary command-driven environment for editing and creating text files.

Syntax

```
edlin [drive:] [path] [filename]
```

Table A.14 lists the switch available in the *edlin* command.

Table A.14 Switch Available in the *edlin* Command

Switch	Description
[drive:][path][filename]	Specifies the path and name of the file that is to be opened by *edlin*.

Example

To edit a text file—say, autoexec.bat—using *edlin* the command would be:

```
edlin C:\autoexec.bat
```

exe2bin

exe2bin is a utility for converting EXE files to binary files. The binary files will have a BIN extension.

Syntax

```
exe2bin [drive:] [path]exe_filename [drive:] [path]bin_filename
```

Table A.15 lists the switches that are available in the *exe2bin* command.

Table A.15 Switches Available in the *exe2bin* Command

Switch	Description
[drive:][path]exe_filename	Name of the EXE file that is to be converted to binary.
[drive:][path]bin_filename	Name of the binary file that is going to be created.

Example

To convert an EXE file—say, test.exe—to binary you can use the following command:

```
exe2bin test.exe test.bin
```

expand

You use the *expand* command to expand compressed files from installation media or distribution disks. You can expand CAB, EX_, and DL_ files.

Syntax

```
expand [-R] source destination
expand -D source.cab [-F:files]
expand source -F:files destination
```

Table A.16 lists the switches that are available in the *expand* command.

Table A.16 Switches Available in the *expand* Command

Switch	Description
-R	Automatically renames the expanded files.
Source	Name of the compressed file.
Destination	Name and path of the destination file. If the –R switch is not used, the destination should be a directory.
-D	Displays all the files present in the source (compressed) file. For example, CAB files have multiple files inside them.
-F:files	Specifies the file(s) in the CAB source file that is to be expanded.

Example

To expand the hal.dll file from the installation media to its location on disk, you can use the following command:

```
expand X:\i386\hal.dl_ C:\windows\system32\hal1.dll
```

Here, the drive letter X signifies the installation media.

fasthelp

The *fasthelp* command displays a brief explanation of the specified MS-DOS command. In Windows XP/2003, this command is replaced by the *Help* command.

Syntax

fasthelp [command]

Table A.17 lists the switch available in the *fasthelp* command.

Table A.17 Switch Available in the *fasthelp* Command

Switch	Description
Command	Name of the MS-DOS command on which help is required.

Example

To obtain help about the *delete* command, you can use the following:

```
fasthelp delete
```

fastopen

fastopen improves the performance of a system by keeping track of frequently used files and directories. After *fastopen* is run whenever a file or directory is accessed, MS-DOS first searches in the frequently used location.

Syntax

fastopen drive:[[=]n] [/X]

Table A.18 lists the switches that are available in the *fastopen* command.

Table A.18 Switches Available in the *fastopen* Command

Switch	Description
drive:	Specifies the drive letter of the drive for which *fastopen* has to track the frequently used files.

Continued

Table A.18 continued Switches Available in the *fastopen* Command

Switch	Description
n	Specifies the number of files that *fastopen* can cache. *n* can range from 10 to 999; the default is 48.
/X	Creates the frequently used files in the expanded memory area rather than in the conventional memory area.

Example

To cache 100 frequently accessed files of C: drive in the expanded memory area, you can use the following command:

```
fastopen C: =100 /X
```

forcedos

forcedos is an external MS-DOS command and you use it to load a specified program in the MS-DOS environment.

Syntax

```
forcedos [/d directory] filename [parameters]
```

Table A.19 lists the switches that are available in the *forcedos* command.

Table A.19 Switches Available in the *forcedos* Command

Switch	Description
/d directory	Specifies the current directory for the specified program to use.
Filename	The name of the program that is to be started in MS-DOS mode.
Parameters	Specifies the command-line parameters to be passed to the program.

Example

You can use the following command to start a program named DosProg.exe in the MS-DOS environment:

```
forcedos C:\PathToProg\DosProg.exe
```

graphics

The external MS-DOS command, *graphics*, provides a way to print displayed contents on the screen. After executing this command, pressing **Shift + Print Screen** will print the on-screen contents.

Syntax

```
graphics [printer type] [profile] [/B] [/R] [/LCD] [/PB:(id)] [/C] [/F] [/P(port)]
```

Table A.20 lists the switches that are available in the *graphics* command.

Table A.20 Switches Available in the *graphics* Command

Switch	Description
printer type	Specifies the type of the printer.
Profile	Specifies the name of the file that gives information about the printer.
/B	Prints the background in color.
/R	Reverses the print layout—i.e., prints white on black.

Continued

Table A.20 continued Switches Available in the *graphics* Command

Switch	Description
ILCD	Prints from an LCD type of screen.
IPB:(id)	Specifies the size and shape of the image (STD or LCD).
IC	Prints the image aligning it, centered on the paper, with an image resolution of 640 x 200.
IF	Prints an image of the resolution 320 x 200 by rotating it 90 degrees.
P=port	Sets the printer port. The default port is Port #1.

Example

To print the contents of the screen using an IBM PC-compatible color printer as *printer type* in 640 x 200 resolution, you can use the following command:

```
graphics /COLOR1 /C
```

After you execute this command, whenever the **Shift** and **Print Screen** key combination is pressed, the onscreen display is printed according to the settings provided in the *graphics* command.

loadfix

loadfix is an internal MS-DOS command which ensures that a specified program is loaded above the first 64KB of conventional memory.

Syntax

```
loadfix [drive:][path]filename [parameters]
```

Table A.21 lists the switches that are available in the *loadfix* command.

Table A.21 Switches Available in the *loadfix* Command

Switch	Description
[drive:][path]filename	Specifies the name and path of the program that is to be loaded in the memory area above the first 64KB.
Parameters	Specifies any command-line parameters that are to be passed to the program.

Example

To load a command-line program—say, Test.exe—to a memory location higher than 64KB using *loadfix*, the command would be:

```
loadfix C:\Test.exe
```

loadhigh

loadhigh is an internal MS-DOS command used to load a specified program into the upper memory area (UMA). Loading a program into UMA leaves more room for other programs in the lower memory area.

Syntax

```
loadhigh [drive:][path]filename [parameters]
```

Table A.22 lists the switches that are available in the *loadhigh* command.

Table A.22 Switches Available in the *loadhigh* Command

Switch	Description
[drive:][path]filename	Specifies the name and path of the program that is to be loaded in the UMA.
Parameters	Specifies any command-line parameters that are to be passed to the program.

Example

To load the MS-DOS-based text editor, Edit, to UMA using *loadhigh*, the command would be:

```
loadhigh edit
```

mem

mem is an external MS-DOS command that displays the total and available memory.

Syntax

```
mem [/program|/debug|/classify|/free|/module(name)] [/page]
```

Table A.23 lists the switches that are available in the *mem* command.

Table A.23 Switches Available in the *mem* Command

Switch	Description
/program	Specifies the name and path of the program for which the memory information is to be displayed.
/debug	Gives additional information about the programs in memory.
/classify	Displays the programs that are in the conventional and upper memory areas.
/free	Displays the free areas in the conventional and upper memory areas.
/module(name)	Shows memory usage information for a specified program module.
/page	Pauses after each screen of output.

Example

The following command displays the free areas in the conventional and upper memory areas:

```
mem /free
```

nlsfunc

You use the external MS-DOS command, *nlsfunc*, to load information specific to a country or region. The country-specific information should be contained in the Config.sys file. If there's no country-specific information in Config.sys, MS-DOS looks for a file named Country.sys in the root directory.

Syntax

```
nlsfunc [[drive:][path]filename]
```

Table A.24 lists the switch available in the *nlsfunc* command.

Table A.24 Switch Available in the *nlsfunc* Command

Switch	Description
[drive:][path]filename	Specifies the name and path of the file which contains country-specific information.

Example

To utilize the country-specific information found in the Config.sys or Country.sys file, you would use the following command:

```
nlsfunc
```

setver

setver, the external MS-DOS command, sets the version of MS-DOS that the system reports, to an application.

Syntax

```
setver [[drive:][path]filename (number)] [/delete] [/quiet]
```

Table A.25 lists the switches that are available in the *setver* command.

Table A.25 Switches Available in the *setver* Command

Switch	Description
[drive:][path]filename	Specifies the name and path of the program for which the MS-DOS version is to be set.
Number	Specifies the MS-DOS version to be set.
/delete	Deletes a file from the MS-DOS version table.
/quiet	Suppresses the messages displayed by the command.

Example

The following command lists the MS-DOS version table for the programs present in the root drive:

```
setver
```

share

share is an external MS-DOS command which is used to activate file sharing and locking over a network.

Syntax

```
share [/F:(space)] [/L:(locks)]
```

Table A.26 lists the switches that are available in the *share* command.

Table A.26 Switches Available in the *share* Command

Switch	Description
/F:(space)	Specifies the size (in bytes) of the memory in which MS-DOS will record sharing information.
/L:locks	Specifies the number of locks to allow.

Example

The following command enables file sharing with default values for */F* and */L*:

```
share
```

Index

Printed and bound by CPI Group (UK) Ltd, Croydon, CR0 4YY

03/10/2024

01040343-0020